ISBN 978-0-282-58160-2
PIBN 10857781

1 MONTH OF
FREE
READING

at

www.ForgottenBooks.com

By purchasing this book you are eligible for one month membership to ForgottenBooks.com, giving you unlimited access to our entire collection of over 1,000,000 titles via our web site and mobile apps.

To claim your free month visit:

www.forgottenbooks.com/free857781

English
Français
Deutsche
Italiano
Español
Português

www.forgottenbooks.com

Mythology Photography **Fiction**
Fishing Christianity **Art** Cooking
Essays Buddhism Freemasonry
Medicine **Biology** Music **Ancient
Egypt** Evolution Carpentry Physics
Dance Geology **Mathematics** Fitness
Shakespeare **Folklore** Yoga Marketing
Confidence Immortality Biographies
Poetry **Psychology** Witchcraft
Electronics Chemistry History **Law**
Accounting **Philosophy** Anthropology
Alchemy Drama Quantum Mechanics
Atheism Sexual Health **Ancient History**
Entrepreneurship Languages Sport
Paleontology Needlework Islam
Metaphysics Investment Archaeology
Parenting Statistics Criminology
Motivational

Date due

83 02 26			
91 02 05			
91 01 07			

A *CAILLEACH* SPINNING

Wanderings in the Western Highlands and Islands

Recounting Highland & Clan History, Traditions,
Ecclesiology, Archæology, Romance, Literature,
Humour, Folk-Lore, etc.

BY

M. E. M. DONALDSON

AUTHOR OF
"ISLESMEN OF BRIDE," "THE ISLES OF FLAME," "TONAL MACTONAL," ETC.

*Sometime Exhibitor at the Scottish Photographic Salon
and The Royal Photographic Society's Exhibitions.*

Illustrated by 42 of the Author's Photographs;
A Special Map, Line Drawings, Original Plans,
and Cover Design by ISABEL BONUS

"Theid Duthchas an aghaidh nan Creag"

SECOND EDITION (REVISED)

PAISLEY: ALEXANDER GARDNER, LIMITED
1923

LONDON
SIMPKIN, MARSHALL, HAMILTON, KENT & CO., LTD.

Printed in Great Britain by Alexander Gardner, Ltd., Paisley.

Dedicated

TO

ALL THOSE FRIENDS

WHO AT DIFFERENT TIMES HAVE SHARED WITH ME
IN
THE JOYS OF THE HIGHLANDS,
FROM THE MOUNTAINS TO THE MIDGES,

AND

ESPECIALLY TO THOSE TWO,

I. M. AND I. B.,

TO WHOSE ART IN DIFFERENT SPHERES
THE BOOK OWES MUCH

PREFACE TO FIRST EDITION

To the Gael, the love of his country is in the nature of a personal friendship which can only be cultivated through a sympathetic and understanding intimacy of years. To him, whether at home or in exile, the Highlands call with many voices, and with none more insistently perhaps than that of which Ossian, true Scotland's national poet, speaks — :

> " It is the voice of the years that are gone—
> They roll before me with all their deeds."

It is these deeds of the years that are gone and the famous doers of them that dictated the wanderings which these pages chronicle. In the great majority of cases my purpose, during the past 15 years, was to strengthen an intimacy with some of the most fascinating of characters and of events in Scottish history by becoming familiar with scenes from which their memory is inseparable. And the aim of this book is identical: to invite the reader to accompany me: to introduce him to Highland friends: to recreate the Highland atmosphere and, if possible, to impart to him those Celtic and Jacobite sympathies which are indispensable for a complete appreciation of the West Highlands.

Destruction, however, must precede construction in making this attempt, for the Sasunnach mind has to be disabused of many erroneous ideas commonly entertained, which are usually traceable to the initial error of identifying the Highlands with the rest of Scotland. It is all too general for the Southerner, however well educated, to think and speak of the Highlands in Lowland terms, and to accredit to the Highlander *a' Bheurla leathann,* " the broad English," as the Gaelic speaker calls the Lowland dialect of English—as different from the English the Gael really uses as is Cockney.

The same disposition has not only been fostered by the fictitious writing of novelists, who have not considered a sublime ignorance of the Highlands any obstacle to adopting them and their people as the subject of a " romance," but unfortunately, also, by famous Jacobite songs, incongruously written in the Lowland dialect, while purporting to emanate from the Gaels. It is grievous to have to include in the list of the legion of those who have put different brands of the Lowland dialect into the mouths of their " Highlanders," Sir Walter Scott, R. L. Stevenson, and Jeffrey Farnol.

Infinitely more to be deplored, however, than the rubbish that Sasunnachs write about the Highlands and Saxon burlesques on the stage, is the dominion that too many strangers, distinguished only by wealth, have acquired by purchase in a country where they must for ever remain aliens. To the conservative mind of the true Celt, it is grievous that in so many parts of the Highlands alien plutocrats should have supplanted clan chiefs. The dominating idea of the monied and sometimes titled nobodies from England or America, seems to be to advertise their sovereign power, and their money-archy has had the most disastrous effects upon the Gael. Naturally of spontaneously generous instincts, the only material benefit that the Highlander has received from aliens seeking advertisement for themselves, their trade or their business, is the lesson of appraising every service in terms of money. That a local Press, mesmerised by the display of so much wealth, should show itself obsequious in all its references to these plutocrats, is not the least deplorable feature in the situation.

" The King may make a Duke, but God alone can make a Highland Chief," declared an old Gael, raising his bonnet reverently. This is a truth of which foreigners who buy Highland estates need to be kept in mind. Though money, alas, can buy the lands, it can never, thank Heaven, buy papers of naturalisation for the Sasunnach. For whatever may be said in favour of individual Saxon landlords, millions cannot purchase what birth has denied them, and, as aliens in race, without the capacity to grasp the Gael's mentality, it is impossible for them to acquire those attributes upon which the ideal relationship of a chief to his clan is based. In this intimate relationship—that of a father to his family (Gaelic *clann*)—understanding and sympathy are alike vital elements. The English or American proprietor only benefits his acquired Highland dependents materially to their moral deterioration. From their rightful chief the clansmen derive psychical advantage.

I can easily both anticipate and answer every objection to the war-cry of " The Highlands for Highlanders! " but the space allocated to the preface forbids.

I also anticipate another objection—to the pronounced colourings of this book. I own to an innate inability to see anything in neutral tints. I must also plead that, without pronounced views, this book never would, and never could, have been written, for the ineradicable defects of enthusiasm, of passionate attachments and strong convictions supplied all the motive power in these " Wanderings." I can only claim to have the courage of my convictions. Is there anyone who really likes a colourless person or who admires a bleaching-out process? Where, to some, therefore, the hues in which I have painted certain subjects may seem too vivid, I can at least demonstrate that I have not falsified facts. If I may justly be accused of, *e.g.*, laying on colour too heavily, no one can deny that, at least, the colour *was* red, and could not with any regard for a truthful rendering be represented, let us say, in blue. Let me assure those readers who paint in clashing shades or wear opposing tartans, especially Sasunnachs and members of the Campbell clan, that no personal animus has dictated my writing. On the contrary, all the Campbells I have met have invariably been delightful enough to be Macdonalds. I like to think that they were all descendants either of the three Campbells who fought for the Prince at Culloden (as indeed two actually were), or of that Donald Campbell who was one of the devoted rowers who brought the Prince from Uist to Skye. As for Sasunnachs, amongst them I number my best friends, all great souls generous in appreciating Celtic fervours.

While a book purporting to give a full and faithful picture of the Highlands cannot possibly ignore the influence of religion and religious questions which are as the warp and woof of Highland texture, controversy on such topics is undesirable. But in the interests of historical truth, justice, and right, popular myths, especially in the sphere of religion, must be shattered. Scotsmen, generally, have been persistently accused of being so prejudiced ecclesiastically that they not only refuse to face distasteful facts, but will not tolerate a case presented as they do not like it to be presented. Let this book put the truth of the accusation to the test. I have simply stated incontrovertible facts and represent the situation in the light of those facts, not ascertained without long and careful study. All views, whether in this or in any other sphere, are simply honest expressions of opinion, not formed without knowledge. I trust they may, at least, be exempt from the elementary mistake of the small-minded critic, of being construed into any personal issues. If thus my friends treated me, I, whose wealth of them is greater than I deserve, and few of whom share all my views, should be left without one—even amongst my fellow-clansmen.

With the exceptions of the Islands of Skye and Iona, the places with which the chapters of this book deal have only been treated of discursively, or partially, in one or two rare volumes—Eigg and Appin not at all, outside stray articles. Both Canon MacCulloch's *Misty Isle of Skye,* and Father Trenholme's *Story of Iona,* are ideal volumes, with which my chapters on these respective islands do not pretend to compete.

I have not attempted a bibliography, because a complete one would attain an inordinate length. I shall be glad to hear of any book, of whatever calibre, bearing on any subject appertaining to the Western Highlands, which, during the twenty years I have been studying the subject, I have not read. I can claim also to have studied recognised authorities on various more general subjects, such as church history, heraldry, arms and armour, and various ecclesiastical lores, and to a much lesser extent, botany and ornithology, all as having some bearing on the matter in hand.

It is my greatest regret, that owing to the prohibitive cost of reproductions in colour, it has been impossible to illustrate the book with the exquisite water-colour pictures of my friend, Miss Isabel Bonus, with whose rare talent, readers of my previous books, and other people's, are familiar. Hence the inadequate, because far less vivid photographs, the selection of which from the 900 odd negatives I have taken during my wanderings, has been no easy task. As pictorial and technical qualities have permitted, considerations of fast disappearing aspects of life and of interesting subjects not usually photographed, rather than of familiar scenes, have dictated my choice.

As regards the spelling of the place-names and other Gaelic words, it is impossible for any one, who is not a Gaelic scholar, to pronounce as to the correct rendering, especially where many variants are found. The best that it has been possible to do is to accept reliable guidance, where it may be had, and where none has been available, to accept the more usual rendering.

For the rest, it is hoped that nothing of interest, whether concerning history, tradition, folk-lore, Gaelic nomenclature, archæology, ecclesiology and cognate subjects,

natural history or scenery, has been passed over, and that
the manner or relation will appeal to all classes interested
in the Highlands, whatever their stage of knowledge.
Despite the many difficulties of obtaining information, no
pains have been spared to be as accurate as possible, so
that every statement of fact may be accepted as, at least,
well authenticated.

M. E. M. DONALDSON.

DUROR OF APPIN,
May, 1920.

———

NOTE that here and throughout the book the terms "alien" and
"foreigner" are used, in accordance with Highland use, for any one who
is not a Gael, *i.e.*, a Highlander.

Regarding the alien in architecture, I desire earnestly to commend to
all readers a perfectly admirable pamphlet entitled *Housing in the Highlands,* with a preface by Dr. Neil Munro, published by An Comunn
Gaedhealach, 108 Hope Street, Glasgow.

THE AUTHOR

PREFACE TO REVISED EDITION

IT has been a matter of very great gratification to me that in spite of—sometimes because of—its prejudices, this book has won so much appreciation from different parts of the world, as well as from every class of people. This has been evidenced by the very many kind letters I have received from strangers in addition to those from friends and acquaintances. Of the only two censorious communications addressed to me, one imputation was withdrawn at once when the writer found her accusation was quite undeserved: to the other I will revert later.

Since the original Preface was written, many of its remarks have been stressed by recent happenings. First amongst these are those on the offence of the sway of vulgarian Sasunnachs in Gaeldom, emphasised by a singularly gross example—Mr. Lloyd George's parting legacy to the new nobility of this country. Is there anything to be said for a man whose wealth alone enables him to usurp, and whose obstinate self-conceit insists on retaining, a style from the assumption of which his alien blood initially debars him, and who thus consciously outrages the susceptibilities of Scots, engenders the bitterest feelings amongst them against him, and makes all right-minded English people ashamed to own such a fellow-countryman? If such an one would set himself to learn from those native to that Gaeldom which now he would patronise, the qualities of character that make a gentleman, would study to understand his humble superiors, he would see his conduct in its true light; but persistence in it only places him permanently without the pale. As well might a crofter having bought a tablet of Sunlight Soap term himself " of Port Sunlight," as the chairman of a company having bought *one* out of over 500 islands of the Hebrides style himself " of the Western Isles." It is indeed extraordinary that many Englishmen are apparently so ashamed of their own country that they must needs ape Scotsmen, who, far from being flattered, only regard the ridiculous assumption as they do all other shams.

The latest testimony to the baleful influence of alien domination in Scottish Gaeldom, and its deteriorating effect upon the character of the Gael, has been forcibly borne by Dr. Ernest Baker in the introductory chapter of his *The Highlands with Rope and Rucksack*. This witness is all the more arresting as coming from an Englishman who effectively exposes the callous selfishness of " sportsmen " of the type of the American millionaire Willans and kindred plutocrats, who prefer the needs (?) of deer to those of the native people. Dr. Baker instances a case where children must perforce make do with tinned milk in order that the deer may enjoy undisturbed the pastures from which the cows have been driven.

Another point bearing on some remarks in the original Preface has reference to Presbyterian intolerance. To the various adverse comments on the admitted prejudices of the book, I, of course take no exception, for they are perfectly legitimate. But I am frankly contemptuous of the inconsistency in the attitude of those who, whilst they applaud the indiscriminate glorification of their own predilections, as, *e.g.*, in favour of the Covenanters when some Covenanting part of Scotland is being described, yet take exception to the presentation of the case of the persecuted native Scottish Episcopal Church when the country of the Scottish Episcopalians is under survey. This one-sided attitude simply brands those who adopt it as intolerant of unpalatable truths, and, alas, justifies that accusation against the generality of Scotsmen spoken of in the first Preface. These objectors, as I have already told them, have but to produce authentic evidence to refute my statements, and these, in that case, would be at once withdrawn. Lacking, however, any such refutation, which, let it be noted, has never even been attempted, no considerations whatsoever will induce me to suppress the truth, which thus must continue to " spoil " this book. As evidence of the desire by which I am actuated—to write the truth, and not what I would like to be the truth— whereas in the first edition I definitely asserted Flora Macdonald to be an Episcopalian, I have now modified that statement. As there is only influence from vague statements and other equally inconclusive evidence to go upon, it seems impossible to determine whether she was actually an Episcopalian or a Presbyterian. Reconsideration of the slight authentic material available on this point seems to tell as much the one way as the other.

Most of the reviews, though laudatory, were not helpful, for the reason that the majority of their writers had evidently no first-hand knowledge of the subject under review. Perhaps the most inept of all appeared in the most unexpected quarter—the *Scottish Historical Review*. Entirely ignoring the historical side of the book, the " review " comprised a list of the photographs and plans, a few criticisms of trivialities, a phase taken from its context, and so misapplied—this and nothing more! Surely authors who have devoted years of study to their subject have just cause of complaint when editors subject their serious work to such " reviewers " with manifestly no sort of equipment for their task.

So far from resenting criticism, however, I welcome it —from recognised authorities, or those whose competency qualifies them to give it. Hence, though Professor Watson has, to my sorrow, detected many faults, specially in the Gaelic, I owe him an increased debt of gratitude for going all through the book prior to this revision. I am also much

indebted to the great authority on Clan Donald—and many
other Highland genealogical matters—for his help.
Though suffering from many disabilities at the time,
A. R. Macdonald, Esq., of Waternish, in his passion for
accuracy and statements authenticated by documentary
evidence, spared no pains to put me right on several
obscure points.   To my own extended enquiry, however,
and further reading I owe perhaps the greater part of the
corrections made in this new edition.

That the charge of being merely a " paste and scissors "
author might not be laid at my door, I was originally
careful to check all my reading as far as possible by
making enquiries on the spot of those accredited locally as
authorities.   Thus I hoped to ensure accuracy in my
information, but, alas, in two outstanding instances, I was
woefully misinformed, in one case actually by a relative
of the family concerned.   In the latter instance, arrangements (prior to the publication of this book) for a meeting
between us having twice fallen through, I was dismayed
myself to discover that I had been made to libel
Lt.-Col. A. K. Stewart of Achnacon on p. 311 of this
volume as originally published.   I now tender him publicly
the apologies I at once spontaneously offered him by letter
and subsequently in person, instantly to receive his understanding forgiveness.   I have not only to thank him for
this generosity, but for the correction of other unwitting
errors in the chapter on the Country of the Stewarts,
concerning whom he is the greatest living authority.

I also apologise for assertions which originally appeared
on pp. 43, 44, and 61, respectively, since these gave offence
to relatives and friends of the gentleman mentioned.   Had
I not received these statements in all good faith on native
authority, they would, of course, never have appeared, and
I regretted very much to hear from the lady most
concerned that I had recorded misstatements of fact.

While I have striven after accuracy, I have never
claimed immunity from error, and thus I trust that those

who are likewise subject to this human infirmity, if such be amongst my critics, will not condemn an honest admission of mistakes.   In one case, however, a correspondent in the *Oban Times,* criticising my chapter on Eigg, held me up to contempt because, after my wont, I frankly admitted a point on which I had been wrong, and retracted a negligible opinion I had, since writing it, had cause to change.   If such charges are to constitute my only condemnation, I shall indeed be proud to be convicted of the offence.

M. E. M. DONALDSON.

AN AROCH,
    ARDNAMURCHAN,
        June, 1923.

CONTENTS

CHAPTER   PAGE

I.—IN THE LAND OF PRINCE CHARLIE, ... 17

II.—THE ISLE OF MIST, ... 99

III.—FROM THE CASTLE OF EILEAN DONNAN TO THE BROCHS OF GLENELG, ... 191

IV.—THE ISLAND OF EIGG, ... 222

V.—THROUGH LOCHABER TO THE COUNTRY OF THE MACDONALDS, ... 262

VI.—THE COUNTRY OF THE STEWARTS, ... 308

VII.—THE HOME OF S. COLUMBA AND THE ISLAND OF STAFFA, ... 336

VIII.—THE ATTRACTIONS OF ARDNAMURCHAN, ... 395

IX.—PLACES OF UNIQUE INTEREST OUT OF THE BEATEN TRACK, ... 436

MEANINGS OF PLACE-NAMES, ... 489

INDEX, ... 499

MAP.

LIST OF ILLUSTRATIONS

A *Cailleach* Spinning, ... *Frontispiece*

The Author, ... *Facing page* 6

Castle Tirrim from the North-East, ... ,, 32

Rough Plan of Castle Tioram, ... ,, 34

" Prince Charlie's Beach " and Loch nan
Uamh, ... ,, 46

Platform of Logs on Island in Loch nan Eala, ,, 62
(By kind permission of the Society of Antiquaries
of Scotland)

Church of Kilmory of Arisaig from South-
East, ... ,, 74

Plan of Kilmory Church, Arisaig, ... ,, 76

Mosaic at Kilmory of Arisaig, ... ,, 82

A Cottage that was at Morar, ... ,, 90

Cutting Peats, ... ,, 94

Sunset at Armadale, Skye, ... ,, 104

Blaven and Clach Glas from Torran, Skye, ..., 120

The Hamlet of Luib, the Red Coolin behind, ,, 128

John Mackenzie, Sligachan—Chief of Mountain Guides, ... ,, 132

Using the *Cas chrom,* ... ... ,, 136

In Glen Sligachan, shewing in distance situation of Harta Corrie, ... ,, 142

Below the " Bad Step," Loch Scavaig, ... ,, 144

Plans of Dunvegan Castle, ..., 156
(By permission from MacGibbon & Ross' *Castellated
and Domestic Architecture of Scotland,* with
several names inserted by M. E. M. D.)

The Dunvegan Mail Coach,... ... ... *Facing page* 164

Duntulm Castle, Skye, ... ,, 174

Eilean Donnan Castle—as it was, ... ,, 196

Entrance to the Broch at Totaig, ... ,, 200

Plan of Broch of Dun Telve, Glenelg, ... ,, 214
(By kind permission of the Society of Antiquaries
of Scotland)

The Broch of Dun Troddan from the Back—
before excavation, ... ,, 216

Sandstone Formations, Laig Bay, Isle of Eigg, ,, 230

A Little West Highlander, ... ,, 234

Taking the Peats home on the Isle of Eigg, ,, 242

A Miniature Pass on the Heights of Eigg, ... ,, 248

The Sgurr, from Gruline, Isle of Eigg, ... ,, 252

Sunset over the Isle of Rum from Laig Bay,
Isle of Eigg, ... ,, 258

Rough Plan of Inverlochy Castle, ... ,, 266

Clach-a-Charra, Onich, ... ,, 270

Image of Oak from Ballachulish Peat Moss,
4-ft. 6-in. high, ... ,, 272
(By kind permission of the Society of Antiquaries
of Scotland)

Evening on Loch Leven, shewing Ballachulish
Ferry, ... ,, 274

Eilean Munde from Tayfuirst, Ballachulish, ,, 282

The Ruined Church on Eilean Munde, ... ,, 286

Site of Massacre at Inveriggan, Glencoe, ... ,, 302

Castle Stalcaire and Loch Laich, Appin, ... ,, 312

Sunset on Cuil Bay, Duror, ... ,, 320

Looking Out from " Ardsheal's Cave," Lag-
na-ha, shewing Waterfall on right, ... ,, 324

Sunset on Loch Leven, ... ,, 334

Port a' Churaich, Iona, from the Hills, ... ,, 342

Surmised Site of S. Columba's Monastery,
Iona, ... *Facing page* 350

Rough Plan of Mediæval Monastery of Iona,   ,,   374

Sacristy Door, Abbey Church, Iona,   ...   ,,   376·

Plan of the Nunnery, Iona, ...   ,,   382
(By permission from MacGibbon & Ross' *Ecclesiastical Architecture of Scotland,* with several
names inserted by M. E. M. D.)

The Herdsman, Staffa, ...   ,,   388

The Shelter on Staffa, ...   ,,   392

Greideal Fhinn, looking over to Mull,   ...   ,,   400

Sculptured Monolith at *Cladh Chiarain,*   ...   ,,   414

Mingary Castle, Ardnamurchan, from North-
East, ...   ,,   424

At Kilmory of Ardnamurchan, Rum and Eigg
in distance, ...   ,,   432

Rough Plan of Approximate Positions of
Monastery Buildings on na h-Eileacha
Naomha, ...   ,,   448

The Church on na h-Eileacha Naomha from
the East, ...   ,,   450

Central Chamber of Burial Cairn, Nether
Largie, ...   ,,   462

Unique Cross Shaft at Kilmartin, ...   ,,   464

Plan of Fort of Dunadd, by Thos. Ross,
Architect, ...   ,,   468
(By kind permission of the Society of Antiquaries
of Scotland)

The Natural Entrance to Dunadd, looking
out, ...   ,,   470

Portrait of " Green Maria," with Author, ...   ,,   474

Cross Slab at Kilmory Oib, ...   ,,   476

South Entrance to Fort on Druim an Dun,
shewing Doorway into Guard Chamber,   ,,   478

CHAPTER I

IN THE LAND OF PRINCE CHARLIE

" We call up each inspiring scene
In history's brightest last romance,
Wherein he fills the hero part
Whose bearing shewed the heart within,
Whose tender, generous, gallant heart
So passionate a love could win."

PART I

THE RAISING OF THE STANDARD

" Sound the pibroch loud on high
From John o' Groat's to Isle of Skye,
Let all the clans their slogan cry
And rise and follow Charlie!"

IN response to the call of the pibroch which had for many years resounded in my ears, unchained at last we were able " to rise," but it was only through the unromantic medium of the railway, and in peaceful fashion, with camera instead of claymore, that we were enabled to " follow Charlie." As we ran through the last tunnel before entering the Clanranald country, the slogan of the Macdonalds at least was not lacking to greet the Prince upon the first glimpse of him on his monument beneath us at the head of Loch Shiel.

If it is good to be a clanswoman, it is better to be entering upon your own clan territory, for then, however landless you may be in reality, you feel fastening upon you a pride of possession such as is unknown to the pedigreeless proprietor who is landed only by purchase. But best of

17

all it is to realise the pride of kinship with the greatest of all the clans, the Macdonalds,[1] " son of the world ruler," as the Gaelic surname means: warriors equally renowned *per mare et per terras,* as their motto has it.   If they can no longer boast the proud title " Lord of the Isles," alleged to have been forfeited in 1493, it is at least a consolation to know that after being annexed by the Crown in 1540, it is still borne by no less a person than the heir to the British throne.   Recently, however, a lesser being, English born and bred, has thought fit to challenge comparison with this ancient Celtic style.   By the power that wealth confers, he has made himself supremely ridiculous by assuming the title " of the Western Isles " on the strength of his chairmanship of a company owning one only out of the five hundred islands in question!   Since the Scottish heraldic authority was entirely ignored, the affair is in every way an indefensible act of aggression by an ahen.

On entering the district of Moidart, you come into the inheritance of the Clanranalds, which, being interpreted, is the family of Reginald, one of the many septs or branches of the great clan, or confederacy of clans, Donald.

Indeed, there is no part of the Highlands which is not the country of one of the clans, a territory where the old clan name still predominates.   Every clan was constituted upon the same lines, each with its family in which the right of succession to the chiefship was hereditary.   This right, however, did not descend from father to son, but was elective by the family, whose aim was to select the fittest.   This they generally deemed the senior male member, so that brother succeeded brother, and nephew uncle, and this principle of chiefship—hereditary as regards

---

[1] In the reign of James I. of Scotland, a Spaniard visited Edinburgh. and on his return to Spain stated that what had impressed him more than anything else in Scotland was " a grand man called Macdonald. with a great train of men after him, and that he was called neither Duke nor Marquis."

family, but elective as regards individual—is the law of tanistry.

The chief was the leader of the clan in battle and the law-giver in time of peace, the divider also of the clan territory amongst the whole clan, so that even the meanest member had his own portion of land.   After the chief came the tanist, elected in the lifetime of the chief as his successor; and next in importance were the chieftains, the *ceann tigh,* or " heads of the houses " into which the clan was divided.   The oldest cadet of these was known as the *toiseach* (one who takes precedence) or leader, who, after the chief, enjoyed the highest dignity in the clan.   He, as his name implies, occupied the post of honour in war time, marching in the forefront of the clan and supporting the chief on the right of the line, or, in his absence, leading the clan, when his title was that of its Captain.   Often tanist and *toiseach* were the same individual.

After the clansmen came the *daoine uaisle,* or gentlemen, and besides the ordinary clansmen might be included men of " broken " clans, and others who had detached themselves for various reasons from the clans to which they belonged by birth.

There were many confederacies of several clans, such as the Clan Donald, already mentioned, the famous Clan Chattan, Siol Alpin (the seed of King Alpin), etc.   Each clan had its own tartan, distinguishing badge of some native tree or plant, worn in the bonnet of every clansman, and to this all Jacobites added a white cockade.   A chief is distinguished by wearing in addition three pinion feathers of an eagle, a chieftain by two, and a gentleman one.   Every clan, too, had its own gathering place, where all the clansmen assembled at the call of the fiery cross: its own slogan or battle-call, and distinctive pipe music— salute, gathering, march, or lament, as different occasions required.

The genesis of tartan, or *breacan,* is wrapped in that obscurity which shrouds most Highland origins.   In the first instance, however, it would seem that the number of colours composing the *breacan* (literally striped or chequered material) was regulated by the position of the wearer, the *ard righ,* "high king," or supreme chief, attaining to seven, eight being reserved for use in the Eucharistic vestments and the veils of the altar vessels. Thus in the earlier periods the ordinary clansman, irrespective of clan, wore a kilt of brown. But latterly tartans were evolved on the protective principle that the observant eye of the Highlander had noted in nature, where wild life adapted its coloration to its surroundings; and thus the *breacan* became of the nature of *camouflage.* I have often proved for myself, for instance, the invisibility which, in the Macdonald country, the Macdonald tartan confers upon its wearers. Such tartans, however, were initially associated not with a clan but with a territory, which might comprise several clan countries having natural characteristics in common. But latterly tartans came to be assigned to different clans, and the great confederacies often shew a ground-work common to many of the tartans of the clans comprised within them. Taking Clan Donald, for example, the red tartan of the Isles provides the theme upon which those of Staffa, MacDougal, and Macalister alike are based, the fundamental red and green checks being preserved through all of them. So in Clan Chattan, the Mackintosh tartan remains the base, of which the Macpherson, Macgillivray, and Macbean are variants: in Siol Alpin, the chief clan of MacGregor provides the simple tartan on which that of MacKinnon, MacQuarrie, and MacPhie are based; and the groundwork of the Connacher trio, Mackay, Urquhart, and Forbes, is the same.

Where in the general clan tartan red predominates, as in the Stewart, there is usually a hunting tartan, where green or darker colours prevail, to serve on occasions when *camouflage* is desirable. Some clans have in addition a tartan whose wear is restricted to the chief: others mourning, and many have dress tartans.

The weaving of the tartan web is not the haphazard proceeding one would judge it to be from the variants of each alleged clan tartan produced by Sasunnach commercial enterprise whenever " plaids " are ruled to be " in fashion."   Correctness in every detail is of the essence of every tartan.   In each case the Highland weaver follows as strictly the size of the sett (or pattern) with its precise ordering of the lines of colour, as does a herald the rules of blazonry in marshalling a coat-of-arms.   A notched stick, shewing the exact width of every line, stripe, and square, and their correct colourings, was handed down from generation to generation in each clan.   It was owing to the loss of these measuring sticks during the years of proscription and persecution that is due any present disputes regarding many of the clan tartans and their rightful owners.

The Clanranald tartan differs only from the general Macdonald tartan in having two white stripes introduced, thicker than those which distinguish the Glengarry sett: it has the same badge as the rest of the clan in the common heath, and its war-cry is " Gainsay who dare ! "   It is this sept which now bears as its motto the words addressed by Robert the Bruce to the Macdonald chief, Angus Oig, at the Battle of Bannockburn.   So great was the reliance that the Bruce placed upon Macdonald support that, allocating to them the place of honour upon the right, and addressing young Angus, he said: " My hope is constant in thee."   It is in consequence of this incident that ever after it has always been the acknowledged right of the Macdonalds to form the right flank of the Highland army in battle.   *Mac-'ic-Ailein* is the hereditary style of the Chief and Captain of Clanranald, the second term being derived from the translation of " chief " by " capitanus " in a Crown Charter which thus referred to the eighth chief at whose instance the document was formulated.

A very great chief indeed was Clanranald, and very proud of him were his clansmen.   The old folk loved to relate how he would keep an imposing array of casks of the wine of Spain in his stable, and, if any stranger chanced to remark upon so curious a wine-cellar, he would be asked, " And where, then, should Clanranald keep the drink of his horses?" Or did he visit London, Clanranald would take with him his horse shod with one golden shoe, fastened with one nail only, so that when the shoe was cast, the Londoners, marking it lying in their street, would exclaim: " The great Chief of Clanranald honours our town! See, his horse has cast one of its shoes! "

It has been for many years a matter of hot dispute between the Chief and Captain of Clanranald, M'Donell of Glengarry, and Macdonald of Sleat as to which of the three were best entitled to claim the supreme chiefship of the whole Clan Donald, and the use of the proud style " of the Isles " (*nan Eilean*). Owing to the practice of " handfasting," to the lack of authentic records, and the conflicting evidence of others, Highland genealogies are above all other the most perplexing. To any one who has sought to follow through the bewildering maze of the Macdonald complications, the matter in dispute becomes the inevitable consequence. The conflicting claims (whose origin will be indicated briefly later) were happily and gracefully adjusted by a compact of the three Chiefs, addressed to the " Whole Kin and Name of Clan Donald," in 1911. It was then agreed that, while each retained his respective claim to the supreme chiefship, these should no longer be actively asserted: that, on any occasion when more than one of the three were present, the question of precedency should be determined, for that occasion only, by lot, and without prejudice to the permanent claims of each; and that no objection should be raised to the Chief of Sleat designating himself " of the Isles," not because the right was conceded, but because custom had generally associated the style with the House of Sleat.

The Clanranald territory in its varied natural features always seems to typify the characteristics of the race-rugged strength and forceful domination.   Under any circumstances of weather, it is a superb run that, after you have emerged from the tunnel, brings you with a fine sweep to the Prince's feet.   In the summer, when the sun is smiling, this is the impression you gain of Glenfinnan from the station: slopes richly wooded with larches, in startling contrast to the bare crags which crown them: a silver gleam of water, and golden masses of broom filling the foreground.   But perhaps the scenery at this particular point makes the greatest appeal when it is seen in wet weather, with the mist skulking over the hills and the rain scourging their unflinching sides, when the burns [2] coursing them are no longer thin lines of sparkling silver, but brown torrents lashed into creaming foam, dashing down with dull thundering.   Here you have a picture of the fine fury which has inflamed many a Macdonald on the field of battle to superhuman feats of valour, and has made his onslaught upon the foe a terror only to be met by flight.

But possibly the attraction of this aspect of Glenfinnan can only be felt by the real Jacobite.   One of the commoner make-believe variety is not likely to remember that it was in just such weather that royal Charlie arrived at the head of Loch Shiel, much less to find in the rain yet another link strengthening one's sympathy with the historic event.   Unless real Jacobite enthusiasms are yours to lift you above morasses, you would probably only be conscious of the squelching of the bog under your feet, as you pull them out laboriously after every step you take on the way to the monument of ugliness which disfigures the scene of the event it commemorates.

I have heard a charming tale of Queen Victoria, that when she was shewn this monument by someone who rashly referred to the Prince as " the Pretender," with great spirit she made instant and indignant response, " Sir, he was *no* Pretender!"

[2] *Bùrn* is one of the words meaning "water" in the Gaelic—the unsuspected origin of many another word acclimatised in Lowland usage.

If you care to imagine what the hideous structure is like, think of a fifth-rate lighthouse surmounted by an insignificant figure of the Prince and surrounded by a wall whose ugliness is in no way inferior to that of the column itself. Three iron panels set in the wall bear three inscriptions, of which the Latin is a translation of the noble one in Gaelic. The very different composition in English is as distinctly unhappy on such a monument as is the monument itself in such a landscape. Indeed, it is a case of where every prospect pleases and only man's work (which includes the viaduct as well as the monument) is vile. Happily, however, it is possible to turn your back on the monument if not upon the viaduct, and, having done so, I could exult without alloy in the glories amongst which, on August 19, 1745, the *bratach bhan* (white banner) was raised.

Mountains, of course, are everywhere; and southward between them flows the narrow fiord-like stretch of Loch Shiel, up which the Prince with a small company of Macdonalds came sailing on the eventful day. To summon the clansmen to rally round their Prince on the great occasion of the raising of the standard, the fiery cross had been sped. The preparation of this symbol, the usual method of assembling the clansmen, involved a strange ritual. A goat was killed, and in its blood were quenched the burning ends of the horizontal piece of two strips of yew bound together crosswise. Then to one of the burnt ends was fastened a rag dipped in the blood, the whole process symbolising the punishment by fire and sword which would overtake any clansman (between the ages of sixteen and sixty) failing instantly to obey this summons to betake himself, fully armed, to the gathering place. Two men bearing this emblem were dispatched in opposite directions, shouting the rallying cry and the place of gathering. The cross was delivered to the chief of each hamlet reached, and this recipient was bound, without loss of time, to dispatch it by a swift messenger upon its next

stage.   In this manner the whole of even an extensive
clan territory could be covered in an incredibly short time.

But at Glenfinnan downpour and disappointment went
hand in hand, for, instead of being greeted by the expected
gathering of the clans, Charles' landing was witnessed only
by a few ragged children.   Two dismal hours passed before
the welcome sound of the pipes on the hillside announced
the coming of some six hundred Camerons under the
gallant Lochiel.

> " And, see, a small devoted band
> By dark Loch Shiel have ta'en their stand,
> And proudly vow with heart and hand
> To fight for Royal Charlie!"

If you wish to obtain an accurate picture of the
clansmen, you must not suppose them to have been clad
in the " Highland costume " which is more or less familiar
to you.   The present " little kilt " (*féileadh-beag*) with
the shoulder-plaid worn separately is a modern adaptation
of the original " belted plaid."   This covered the whole
body, and consisted of from six to twelve yards of material,
two yards wide, part being pleated and confined round
the waist by a belt (whence its name) to form the kilt
proper, and the rest being brought over the back and
caught up by a brooch fastening it on the left shoulder.
This did not hamper the sword arm, and in inclement
weather the upper half could be wrapped round the
shoulders, or, unfastened, could protect the head as well,
in which fashion it was used when the wearer slept.   If,
then, you substitute this belted plaid with a *sporan* (purse)
of goat or other skin for the present-day kilt and sporan;
the round blue bonnet (where any head covering was worn)
for the modern Glengarry or Balmoral cap; *brògan* of
undressed deer hide, fastened with leather thongs and
worn hair side outwards, or footless hose, or nothing at all,
in place of modern shoes and stockings; and equip the
company with flint-lock muskets and pistols, the basket-
hilted sword (wrongly called the claymore), and the

Highland targe, you will have a very good idea of the appearance of the men who "rose and followed Charlie."

As soon as the Camerons were assembled, the Prince ordered that the banner should be unfurled. Though it was called the "white banner," neither of the conflicting accounts of it describe it as being white. One authority states that it was of large size, of red and white silk, another that it was of red with a white standard in the middle and the motto "*Tandem bona causa triumphans.*" Whatever it was like, however, it was first solemnly blessed by the Roman Catholic Bishop, Hugh Macdonald, son of the neighbouring laird of Morar, and then unfurled by the aged Marquis of Tullibardine, supported by two attendants. This nobleman had been present at the raising of the standard in 1715, and, in consequence of the share he had taken in that rising, had forfeited the dukedom of Atholl to which he was heir. But since James had conferred upon him the title anew, in Jacobite writings he is generally termed the Duke of Atholl, though a younger brother had succeeded as Duke *de facto*. Allowing for a Jacobite's heated imagination, which transforms hundreds into thousands, and a poetic licence which, amongst other things, substitutes the Scottish Standard for the *bratach bhan*, Aytoun's stirring lines certainly convey the true spirit of the scene:

> "When, in deep Glenfinnan's valley,
>   Thousands, on their bended knees,
> Saw once more that stately ensign
>   Waving in the northern breeze:
> When the noble Tullibardine
>   Stood beneath its weltering fold,
> With the Ruddy Lion ramping
>   In the field of tressured gold!
> When the mighty heart of Scotland,
>   All too big to slumber more,
> Burst in wrath and exaltation,
>   Like a huge volcano's roar!"

You can fancy that once more the hills re-echo the rousing cheers: that the air is black with bonnets enthusiastically tossed: that you can hear the tremulous tones of the old Marquis reading James' manifesto to his subjects.   Then the gallant young Chevalier, dressed simply as a private gentleman, in " a dun-coloured coat, scarlet-laced vest, and knee-breeches, with a yellow bob at his hat," steps forward to address his followers as their Prince Regent, and his spirit captivates you as surely as he himself captivated everyone with whom he came in contact in those wonderful days.   His magnificent audacity, his high courage, his patriotic spirit had those kindling qualities without which, for the purpose of raising a formidable following, they are valueless.   Could ever the Highland spirit resist the appeal made by the exaltation of Scotland over every other country: the reliance placed upon their renowned bravery, loyalty, and devotion?   But Charles shewed the master touch when, as a climax, he turned to an English officer whom Lochiel had brought as a prisoner, and, addressing him, said: " Go, sir, to your General!   Say what you have seen; and add that I am coming to give him battle!"

This was indeed the sweetest of music to Highland ears: music to which even to-day Highland blood responds; and " Hurrah for Royal Charlie!" was on our lips as well as in our hearts as we left the head of Loch Shiel and in imagination passed through the ranks of the Stewarts of Appin and Ardsheal, the Macdonalds of Glencoe and of Keppoch, who, before evening, had joined the other clansmen in Glenfinnan, making a total of some twelve thousand men.

> ' From every hill and every glen
> Are gathering fast the loyal men,
> They raise their dirks and shout again—
> ' Hurrah for Royal Charlie!' "

On the way back to the Hotel you pass the beautiful little church of S. Mary and S. Finan.   We, however, did not pass it, but went in at the gate, and were very interested in the big bell quaintly hung by the pathway at less than six feet from the ground, and very fittingly inscribed, " *Benedicite montes et colles Domino laudate et superexaltate eum in saecula.*"   Obviously the small bell-cote of the church would not carry so heavy a bell, but we could not think that, hung so low, its voice would carry far.

Those people—not a few—who think of Scotland and Presbyterianism as interchangeable terms, would be surprised to hear not only that it was a Roman Catholic church that we entered, but that any variety of Presbyterianism is a novel importation that has entered in the wake of Presbyterians whom the line has permanently introduced into a large tract of country which the Reformation never reached.   In these Highlands, indeed, may be seen the Roman Church at her very best—alike in her charming and tolerant priests, mostly drawn from old Highland families; in the courteous and altogether delightful natives; and in the simple dignity of her buildings, scrupulously clean, and utterly devoid of the tawdry trappings which one sees so plentifully even in England.

This little church, from a niche on whose exterior the Archangel Michael looks down protectingly, is peculiarly attractive, with its polished marble pillars and its wide flung door framing a wonderful view of the loch and mountainside.   As we stood silently in the brooding calm of the sanctuary, it seemed as though that open door were inviting all the works of the Lord without to praise and magnify through their angels His Presence enshrined on the altar, that, fortified by the act of adoration, they might the more effectually fulfil their purpose in creation.

———

P.S —

At the end of 1922, a brass was put up in this church: " In Loving Memory: Prince Charles Edward Stuart (*Bonnie Prince Charlie*). Glenfinnan, A.D. 1745. R.I.P." —a memorial most appropriate in such a setting.

PART II

THE OLD SEAT OF CLANRANALD

HAVING by some display of Jacobite sentiments at Glen-finnan so thoroughly entered into the spirit of the Clanranald country, we were eager to go a step farther and to enter into the Chief's ancient stronghold, hoping there to become acquainted with its spirit, or spirits, if it retained any.   The step took us on board the little boat *Clanranald II.*—the name a blissful relief from the *Mabels* and *Ethels* so atrociously out of place on some outraged Highland waters—and then we were generally " taken down."   Torrents of rain and driving wind took us down into the tiny cabin, whilst the boat itself took us down to the end of Loch Shiel.   Feeling our prompt descent required some excuse, we both agreed it was merely aggravating to attempt to follow the incidents of the Prince's voyage in their reverse order as we had been trying to do.   But the experience convinced us that it was nobler actively to resist being blown overboard than passively to submit to suffocation, so we speedily returned on deck.

Despite the obliterating rain, we did manage to distinguish the tiny island of S. Finan, which serves as the place of burial for the district, a usual choice in the Highlands, where, as some say, the superstition obtained that evil spirits could not cross water, and presumably were an unknown quantity on islands.   It is much more probable, however, that the desire to secure graves against the ravages of wild beasts dictated in the first instance the choice of island burial places.

The saint after whom the island itself is named is one of many Finans, seemingly S. Finan, " the Leper," to whom is attributed the evangelisation of part of Argyllshire. He died about 575.   He is said to have come to Moidart from Kilchoan, Ardnamurchan, and his island sanctuary on Loch Shiel became one of the most famous

in the Highlands, pilgrimages there often being enjoined
as penances. The later church on Eilean Finan is attributed to Ailein nan Creach (of whom more later), who is
reputed never to have roofed this or any of the other
churches with the building of which he is credited.
Eilean Finan in Loch Shiel cannot boast of much present
interest, since the remains of its church, two small chapels,
and stones around are apparently unremarkable. But
upon a stone slab, probably originally the top of the altar,
stands, seven inches high, one of the seven extant
quadrangular Scoto-Celtic bells.

Only twice, so it is alleged, has the bell been removed
from the island, and on the first occasion disaster overtook
the thief. In the eighteenth century some English soldiers
passing from Castle Tirrim to Fort William stole the bell,
but they were pursued by the incensed natives, who,
overtaking them at Glenfinnan, soundly thrashed the
ringleader. A Macdonald of Kinlochmoidart put the
present tongue in the recovered bell, to replace that which
had been wrenched out by the robbers. A local priest who
told us this was ignorant that the bell had been removed a
second time, and only became aware of the fact when he
suggested taking us to see it. Then I had to tell him that
in order to do so we should have to go, not down to Loch
Shiel, but to Glasgow, where it was then on loan in the
Scottish Exhibition. Our kind friend was considerably
disturbed at the information, saying he hoped the people
would not get to hear of the bell's temporary abstraction,
since the older inhabitants would consider its absence
presaged disaster, and to this would also attribute any
untoward event which might befall them.

To the district under the protection of S. Finan a
characteristic anecdote relates. One of its priests told a
parishioner that a Campbell had been made priest of ——.
Looking at him in consternation, the man questioned in-
credulously: " Wass you telling me that ta bishop would
pe making a Campbell ta priest?"

It is a common pronunciation of the name that gave rise to the following misapprehension of a certain passage in the Gospels. A Macdonald, returning from church, called in to see a fellow clansman who was laid up. The visitor had obviously been impressed with the sermon, for he remarked to his friend: " I wass never noticing pefore how terrible strong ta Holy Scriptures wass against ta Cam'lls. Ta priest he wass telling us what they wass saying apout a rich man that would pe going easier through ta eye of a needle than ta Cam'll would pe entering ta Kingdom of Heaven."

The scenery of Loch Shiel steadily decreases in impressiveness until at its end at Acharacle, " Torquil's ford," it is actually flat and uninteresting. It was on the occasions of sailing to Moidart that the Macdonalds would sing the beautiful " Dawn Prayer of Clanranald ":

" *Fragrant maiden of the sea,*
   Thou art full of the graces,
   And the Great White King is with thee,
   Blessed art thou, blessed art thou,
   Blessed art thou among women;
   Thy breath steering my prayer,
   It will reach the Haven White;
   Let me beseech thy gentle Son
   To Whom thou gavest knee and suck
           To be with us,
           To be on watch,
           To be awake;
   To spread over us His Sacred Cowl
   From ray-light to ray-light,
   To the new-born white ray of dawn,
   And through the dark and dangerous night
           To succour us,
           To guide us,
           To shine on us

With the guidance and glory of the nine rays
*   of the Sun,*
Through seas and straits and narrows
Until we come to Moidart,
And the good Clanranald,
O until we come to Moidart,
And the good Clanranald."

It was to Moidart, so says a legend, that in pity for its paganism, the blessed Columba sent two monks to redeem its people from the keeping of Beltane and the worship of serpents.   But the people would have none of the monks, so that the younger exclaimed: " Let us return to Iona. The seven curses of the Church be on Moidart!"   So in the evening both monks went down on the shore, and were preparing to leave Moidart when the younger exclaimed that he heard the dipping of oars, and, going round the point of land whence the sound proceeded, they saw a coracle sailing out into the night, and, lying on the shore, a lady clothed in white, with a babe at her breast that was cold.   Bending over the mother, the elder monk began to chant the death croon, but he had not finished it before the babe looked up into his face and said: " She is not dead, but she ever loses life and milk alike when the monks of Iona lose their love for the people."   Thus rebuked by the little Christ-Child, the monks stove in the bottom of their coracle and returned to their labours.

There was nothing to detain us at Acharacle, so we lost no time in making for the variously spelt Castle Tirrim. As you approach the castle from along by the seashore, you are at first sight captivated by the ancient stronghold. High up against the tree-clad " heights of the sea spray," built on a tongue of land thrust out into the sea, a stern forceful building dominates the scene, even as its chiefs in the past dominated both land and sea, as other clans knew to their cost.   Beyond a small island, practically blocking the narrowest arm of Loch Moidart, which lies

CASTLE TIRRIM FROM THE NORTH-EAST

behind the castle is Eilean Shona, entirely obscuring Castle Tirrim's view of the open sea (into which the north and south channels on either side of the land-locked island lead). With such splendid cover on all sides for any enemy approaching by sea, to keep watch must have been a most distracting duty; for the sentry, if he were single-handed, would have had to be a veritable Janus or Mr. Facing-all-ways-at-once. Even then he would have wanted eyes with the qualities of radium or röntgen rays to see through land and round corners. It says much for the Clanranald sentries that never was the castle taken except on one occasion when its defenders had temporarily vacated it. And it is an unpleasant reflection that even such a trumpery triumph should have been secured by the Earl of Argyll, chief of the Campbell clan, the hereditary foes of all who bear the Macdonald name.

It has been asserted that originally Campbell was *De Campo Bello* (of the beautiful field), and that the first of the name came over with the Conqueror. But alas for the fantastic etymology which brings forward an Italian appellation to prove a Norman origin: amongst the Conqueror's followers there is no trace of any such name as that of the ancient and most bitter enemy of the Macdonald race, as of most of the clans. The name is really derived from the Gaelic for " crooked mouth " (as Cameron means " crooked nose "), and in more than Macdonald estimation the crooked mouth, which is very apparent in the portrait of the most odious of all the Campbells, the first Marquis, is the least crooked character-istic of a wily and crafty clan.

The occasion when Castle Tirrim was temporarily seized by the Earl of Argyll was due to a congenial commission given him by the Government to attack Clanranald in his stronghold. So closely was Argyll able to approach the castle, that his galleys anchored right under its walls, and a strong force of men was landed to cut off all communica-tion with the mainland. After making an ineffective

attack, the Campbells resorted to a siege, which was much
more within their capacity, but when, after five weeks,
Clanranald still held out stoutly, the enemy gave up the
effort in despair, sailing out of Loch Moidart, and making
for Ardnamurchan Point.   Tired of the long enforced confinement, Clanranald, leaving only a small garrison behind,
speedily left Castle Tirrim for the freedom of the mainland.
Anticipating this move, Argyll had only sailed a few miles,
and, returning under cover of darkness, he re-entered Loch
Moidart, and, as it was within the compass of a large
company of the Campbells to surprise a handful of men
and put them to the sword, the castle was soon in the
enemy's occupation.   But this news was not long in
reaching the ears of Clanranald, who soon made short
work of the invaders.   In a hand-to-hand fight which the
Macdonalds waged with great fury, those Campbells who
failed to gain their ships when, in characteristic fashion,
they tried to slink away, were cut down to a man in the
castle courtyard.   After all, then, the Campbell triumph
at Castle Tirrim was not a very notable one!

The tide being out, we were able to approach the old
fortress by crossing the sands, and, as you survey the castle,
you remark how, with the usual ingenuity of Scots builders
in adapting their architecture to the natural advantages
of a selected site, this fortress is of pentangular shape to
fit its base, and that, wherever possible, the building is
incorporated with the solid rock itself.   We could
fortunately walk right round the seaward sides of the
castle, where the walls are all windowless, which fact,
doubtless, accounted for the Campbell galleys not being
sunk when they came so near to the castle on the occasion
of its siege.   Even safeguards have their drawbacks at
times, when, as in a case like this, defiance would have been
far more congenial than the tame defence that, imposed by
unfortunate conditions, was all that could be offered.

The castle was built before 1350 by Amie MacRuari,
the first wife of John of Isla, first Lord of the Isles,

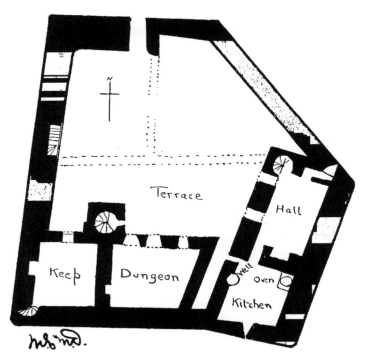

ROUGH PLAN OF CASTLE TIORAM

who, by reason of his many gifts to the Church, was called " Good John." It was from Ranald, the second son of " Good John " by Amie, that the Clanranald branch of the Macdonalds sprang, and it is from the rival claims of the respective descendants of Amie, and of her successor, the Lady Margaret Stewart, that the subsequent disputes as to the supreme Chiefship of the Clan Donald, and the claim to the title " of the Isles " arose.

In view of the fact that Castle Tirrim was fired by a follower acting under secret instructions from the chief, Allan Dearg (Red Allan), immediately after his departure to fight in the rising of '15, it is remarkable that there should still remain so much to be seen within. We climbed up to the only entrance of the castle, a small gateway at the extreme end of the landward wall, which opens on to a very small courtyard, as the plan will shew. Above the courtyard is an irregular terrace, some five feet higher, mostly of rock, to which some rude steps lead. As you look round about from the gateway, the general impression you obtain of the interior is one of general crampedness. All the buildings appear to be squashed up into corners, or jammed against the walls; and there is, as might be expected in such a situation, an eerie sense of loneliness and of oppressive desertion.

The first doorway inviting attention was the entrance, gained from the terrace, into the dungeon which, for a dungeon in such a castle, was disappointingly unthrilling. You feel that compromise was entirely out of place in any clan stronghold, yet here was a sad concession of first principles, for instead of being deep underground, as all respectable dungeons ought to be, this one was only half below the level of the ground. Certainly, with water oozing from the floor, which is on an inclined plane, and both the vaulted roof and the walls exuding moisture, the cellar was damp and clammy enough, but, apart from this, it must have been, in comparison with others, quite a desirable dungeon, since it is roomy and has a nice slit in the wall to admit light.   Men of Moidart say that, in consequence of a peculiarly atrocious murder committed in the dungeon, the stain of the victim's blood is still to be seen on the floor.   They point to some patches of rusty red, certainly of a very suggestive and realistic hue, and assert that it is useless to scrape them away, because the stains invariably reappear.   Of course the phenomenon, which need not be scouted, is easily capable of a perfectly natural explanation, since the damp obviously sets up in some mineral in the subsoil a chemical action which in time becomes visible on the surface.   I have not been able to discover any particulars of the alleged fearsome crime, and the only names associated with the dungeon appear to be those of three chiefs, of Mackintosh, Mackenzie, and Mackay, respectively, who were all confined there at the same time.

But, doubtless, in the same place would also have been imprisoned the three far more unlucky wretches who were treated as guilty of a theft which could not be brought home to anyone.   About the end of the seventeenth century, the chief, Black Donald, missed a sum of money from Castle Tirrim, and, suspecting his valet, another man, and a girl known as " James' daughter," he dealt summarily with them, merely on the strength of his suspicions.   The two miserable men were hanged on *Tom a' Chrochaidh*—the hill of hanging—a low eminence within sight of the castle, but for some inscrutable reason a more brutal fate was reserved for the poor girl.   Right in front of Invermoidart House on Eilean Shona, some 200 yards from the castle, and only visible at low tide, is a still called " *Sgeir nighinn-t-Sheumais* " (the rock of James' daughter).   To this rock the unhappy girl, bound hand and foot, was taken and left to perish by the rising tide.   The sequel to this story did not appear till the end of the last century, when the present proprietor, Lord Howard of Glossop, was engaged in making a path along the cliffs north of Dorlin House, just opposite Castle

Tirrim.   At a point almost midway between the castle and the rock where the girl perished, the workmen came across a loose heap of stones, and underneath they discovered over 150 Elizabethan coins.

Black Donald of Clanranald certainly earned his epithet if half the tales told of him be true.   He had a favourite gun, called " the cuckoo," with which he would sit on the battlements of Castle Tirrim to shoot whatever took his fancy, and if he shot, as he did, a harmless man by mistake, so much the worse for the victim.   A huge black toad was Donald's familiar, and no matter what precautions were taken to secure it in Castle Tirrim, the reptile was always found wherever the chief went.   It is said that a lion given by the Earl of Argyll ultimately swallowed the toad, and this is alleged as the reason why a lion appears as a charge on the Clanranald coat-of-arms!   Black Donald, having been prevented by Raonull Mac Ailein Oig, the famous composer of pipe music, from killing himself on Canna, died in 1686.

Beside the dungeon, there are one or two features of the building not without interest.   Various indications prove that the ceilings generally must have been remarkably low—in no case higher than eight feet; and in an apartment, obviously a kitchen, besides an oven, there is a well cut out of the solid rock to an unknown depth. It must have been this apartment with which is associated the quaint incident from which one of the chiefs obtained his second nickname.   The clan had killed its sixth chief and elected his uncle in his place.   Ranald, son of Allan Mac-Ruari, had in infancy been taken to live among his mother's people, the Frasers; and when at last young Clanranald claimed the chieftainship, he, as one brought up in an alien clan, was called Ronald *Gallda, i.e.,* foreigner.[3]   On

[3] Still Highlanders coming from another clan country are considered " foreigners."   Once having received some local history from a certain man, I subsequently found his authority scorned on the ground that he was " a stranger in these parts."   Inquiry elicited the fact that he had only lived thirty years in the district!

the occasion of his installation at Castle Tirrim, there was an inaugural banquet, and, noting the number of oxen that was being roasted, the young chief observed that a few hens would have served just as well. As Ronald the Stranger, he was not at all popular with his clansmen, but as Ronald of the Hens (*Raonull nan Cearc*) he became intolerable. Such an exhibition of parsimony proved him to be no fitting chieftain for Clanranald, and, being conducted to the bounds of the country, Ronald *Gallda* was given to understand he was expected to continue a stranger to it to the end of his days.

After this kitchen reminiscence, we climbed, not without risk to our limbs if not to our lives, a very ricketty wooden ladder in the last stages of decay, and gained a narrow walk along the seaward wall, in which look-out holes are pierced at regular intervals. It was a glorious view we obtained from this point of vantage—the only outlook obtainable from within the castle, and, looking out over the sea, and thinking of the days that were past, I recalled an incident, not without some grim humour, that is told in connection with a fifteenth century chief. Allan MacRuari (son of the red king) was renowned for his plundering exploits, from which the Macleans [4] of Duart had suffered considerably. Having one day rashly put out from Castle Tirrim without escort, Allan was consequently alarmed to find that his galley was running into a strong fleet of the Macleans. Realising that in strategy lay his only chance of escape, he ordered his men to lay him out as dead, and then to continue unconcernedly on their course. When the inevitable challenge came from Maclean, the chief was delighted to hear in response that the body of his formidable foe was being taken to Iona for burial; and, under these pleasant circumstances, the galley was allowed to proceed on its voyage. No sooner were the Maclean ships out of sight, however, than Allan

[4] Son of the servant of S. John.

speedily came to life again, and, realising his unique
opportunity for plunder, lost no time in heading for the
Maclean country.   As he anticipated, he found it un-
protected, so that he could burn and harry to his heart's
content without let or hindrance.   In due course the
Macleans returned home, only to find their lands desolated
and many of their families slain; whilst Allan MacRuari,
not in a shroud under the sacred soil of Iona, but in a
coat of mail within Castle Tirrim, was feasting on the
spoils of his latest raid.

Now, alas, the Chief and Captain of Clanranald no
longer reigns in his own country, which, parcelled out into
different estates, has fallen a prey to various aliens, whose
modern " mansion houses " are generally architectural
abominations having but one point in their favour—that
they serve to advertise by a foreign style the foreign
domination.   Hence now the sad Gaelic saying, " To whom
can I make my complaint and no Clanranald in Moidart?"

—————

PART III

LOCH NAN UAMH AND BORRODALE HOUSE

A GEOGRAPHICAL advance in our wanderings having
involved a historical retrospect, with a return to the head
of Loch Shiel, our thoughts returned to Prince Charles
Edward.   For, by beginning at Glenfinnan with the raising
of the Standard, I have anticipated by about a month the
royal youth's landing on the shores of Loch nan Uamh,
the " lake of caves."   And it was a companioning of the
Prince in his many adventurings around this superb arm
of the sea that we were now contemplating, intending to
walk there from Kinlochailort.

In the journey to the starting-point we traversed the
Macdonald territory which, lying between Loch Sunart and

Loch Hourn, is called *Garbh Chriochan* ("rough bounds"), and we realised the fitness of its Gaelic naming, for its roughness does indeed exceed ordinary bounds. So, too, we were able to appreciate the ingenuity which prompted a chief of Glengarry, when travelling with his family through this district, to pack his younger children into peat creels on either side of a pony, adjusting the balance by a few stones. As an instance, thoroughly characteristic of the delightfully casual ways which still obtain in the " Rough Bounds," the following incident may be mentioned before leaving them.

We were spending an afternoon with some friends, staying at a nice little hotel in the district, and were hearing of the inn's various quaint distinctions. The recital received amusing illustration by the entry of our friends' two children, fresh from a successful hunt for hens' eggs. We could not understand why so tame a pursuit provided so much excitement until we realised that the hens had the run of the house, and were apparently free to lay where they liked. On this occasion, eggs had been found in one nest under the housemaid's bed and another on top of the clean linen in the linen cupboard, both situations being accepted as nothing out of the ordinary !

As far as a fairly extensive acquaintance with Highland scenery goes, whilst it is possible to recall wilder and possibly more impressive landscapes, yet I do not believe that there is in all Scotland any other road which, for sheer beauty and ever-changing charm, can outrival the ten and a half miles between Kinlochailort and Arisaig. You begin the walk by the shores of Loch Ailort, which, with its glories of sea and mountain, is so enchanting that you feel you owe it an apology for having the heartlessness to turn your back upon it. This, however, is a feeling experienced increasingly at every turn of the fascinating stretch of road. The climb of a mile brings you to the summit of the hill above Loch Ailort, where by the wayside a plain little Roman Catholic chapel hallows the

scene; and, as it sheds its benediction over the loch, you
feel that, if its lost dedication is not, after the Roman
fashion, to " Our Lady Star of the Sea," it might well
be, especially when one of the Gaelic names for the sea
is *Cuilidh Mhoire,* " the treasury of Mary." When this
chapel is left behind, you have a first experience of the
glorious woodland scenery which enriches the road.
Beneath birches and rowan trees grow ferns and thick
moss, and a deer, red or fallow, may often be surprised
drinking at some burn, but never a one that reciprocates
your desire to make his better acquaintance. Startled by
your approach, he will instantly bound up the hillside and
be speedily lost to sight, leaving you with the sobering
reflection that if a deer be indeed the king here, you must
be considerably beneath a cat in the social scale.

If the wind is in the wrong quarter, and you do not see
any of the beautiful creatures, you may yet with good luck
on occasion come across a cast antler intact. It is more
usual, however, to pick up a horn that looks as if it had
rotted away at the tines owing to a prolonged exposure
on wet ground. When a stag does not hide the antler
that he casts, he eats it, and this fact, incredible as it may
seem in view of the hardness of the horn, is well attested
by keepers and others who have witnessed the proceeding
through their glasses. Thus, antlers which are picked up
more or less seemingly decayed at the points are simply
an evidence of a meal disturbed and abandoned by some
stag which has cast them. More rarely, beneath a rock
or in some secluded spot, you may chance upon the remains
of a stag which has sought retirement to die, or, being the
leader of the herd, has been killed by his fellows, having
outlived his capacity for leadership.

At intervals all along the roadside are funeral cairns,
which mark the places where the bearers have rested their
still burden on its last journey. Though the distance to
be traversed to the burial place is often very considerable,
the body is invariably borne on foot, and it is the custom

4

for each mourner to contribute a stone to the cairn, hence the beautiful Gaelic parting benediction, "Peace to thy soul and a stone to thy cairn." Sometimes, instead of a funeral party being content to add to a common cairn, each will make its own, so that in some roads there are little groups of these "resting" cairns at each halting place.

With the descent to Loch nan Uamh, the scenery ascends to the summit of beauty from which, however, the ugly concrete viaduct does its best to detract, happily with small success. Now there comes a succession of scenes which make you sigh for the skill of an artist in colour as being a medium better suited to attempt transcription than the dull medium of pen and ink or the inadequacy of the camera. There are the wooded hills, crag-frontiered, on either side of you, and right in front the rugged shores of Loch nan Uamh, strewn with rocky islets. To see this picture on a summer evening, when over the emerald of the water, purple shadowed, and the purple of the distant islands, the soft glow of the sinking sun casts a halo, many hued as the rainbow, is to have seen one of the most wonderful colour effects on a coast world-famous for its sunsets. Nor when you gain the shore itself does the scene lose its attractiveness: it is merely the exchange of distant for nearer charms: the wealth of flowering plants, notably yellow flags, growing right up to high tide mark. Leaving the sea behind, you climb inland up through Glen Beasdale, whose beautiful woods so often sheltered Prince Charlie during his wanderings when he was thought to be unsafe under the roof of Borrodale House.

If what I have already written has failed to convey some idea of the main characteristics of this road, no further description will achieve the impossible, so you shall be spared any more attempts, and be deposited forthwith at the white gate through which the Prince's Beach may be gained. The path from the gate runs right in front of Borrodale House, which lies across the grass and at no great distance from the gate, and, judging from the appearance of the long but extremely unpretentious-looking building of whitewashed roughcast, you would never imagine yourself to be looking upon what might be called the Holyrood of the Highlands. Yet this little dwelling in the hollow holds the eye where, on the height, the aggressive modern "mansion house" of nondescript architecture, as foreign to the country as its owners, and lacking in any sort of interest, fails to attract more than a passing glance of annoyance from those who consider that good taste is violated by incongruity, be the architect never so eminent. Only those, however, who by a parity of reasoning, would see nothing amiss in, *e.g.*, a Moorish house in the New Forest, can consider this building a thing of beauty.

But as nothing would succeed in investing a *parvenu* with interest, so nothing could detract from the romance of Borrodale House, for here, in the humble farmhouse of Angus Macdonald, Prince Charles Edward, with a hundred gentlemen of Clanranald for his guard of honour, held his court from August 4-11, 1745. A large room on the extreme left is shewn as that which became the centre of attraction to which, day after day, flocked the clansmen, high and low, comparatively rich and very poor, vying one with another in devotion, to pay their homage to the " lad with the yellow hair." Even at this distance of time, it is perfectly easy to realise, and for a Highlander even personally to experience, the spell which Charles cast upon all who saw him. His handsome and fascinating personality, his youth and gallant bearing, allied to the subtle Stewart charm, proved irresistible, quite apart from the tact and good taste that, right from the first, he displayed in making his own, as far as he could, all things distinctively Highland. On the occasion of his first dinner at Borrodale, for instance, he gave the Grace toast in English. A little later when *Deoch slainte an Righ* was called for and given amidst thunderous applause, the

Prince asked for the interpretation of this toast.   Being told it meant " Drink health to the King!" he persisted in repeating the Gaelic until he had mastered the phrase, which he then rose to propose—an effort acclaimed with tumultuous enthusiasm.   When subsequently he adopted the Highland dress, he riveted yet more firmly the tie which bound him deathlessly to the clansmen.

The original building had to pay by fire for its loyalty, and the fame unalienably attached to its rebuilding suffered no subsequent diminution.   For here, in the last century, were born two brothers Macdonald of the Glenaladale family, as illustrious for their piety as for the high position they both attained in the hierarchy of the Roman Catholic Church.   Yet, despite the rebuilding, Borrodale House substantially represents the same building that sheltered Charles on his first visit.   For, though it is now divided into two dwellings, it is said that the house was rebuilt with the same old stones, presumably on the old plan, for not only, as previously mentioned, is the room (or its site) where the Prince held court still pointed out, but also his bedroom.

Since I first visited Borrodale House, however, some late audacious tenant—needless to say, *not* a native—had attempted, Yankee fashion, to improve on tradition and to test the credulity of strangers by her inventive genius. Reckless of anachronisms, this lady would point to an isolated square of hideous but well-preserved wall paper as a portion of that with which the walls were papered in 1745, and would tell a story of the number of papers deep at which the Prince's paper had been found, though, apparently she forgot to mention how the paper pro-claimed itself to be the Prince's.   After this daring flight of invention, it was a small matter to associate the Prince with the bedroom immediately overhead.   According to native tradition, however, it is a small upstairs window, almost obscured by two tall elms on the extreme right of the house front, where the royal bedchamber really was.

Inside, there is still to be seen a stone staircase, which was said to lead up to the Prince's bedroom, and outside, at the back of the house, a small circular building in the wall shews its location. It is also a reliable tradition that identifies the bank just within the white gate as the site of the bothy where Macdonald of Borrodale received Charles after the house was burnt.

It is interesting to find that there are still living in Borrodale various families of MacEacherns, variously spelt, even as there were in 1745. They, " sons of the horse lord," are a sept of the Clanranald Macdonalds, and one, Angus MacEachine, a surgeon to Glengarry's regiment, was Borrodale's son-in-law, and a good friend to the Prince. Another, Neil MacEachainn, was one of his most faithful companions in his wanderings after Culloden.

After our halt in front of this house of departed glory, crossing a little bridge, we turned down a beaten track following the course of the Borrodale burn. Then, after traversing a meadow of tall grasses starred by huge ox-eye daisies, we reached the historic scene of the landing and, alas, also of the departure of Prince Charles Edward Stewart. To your right, beyond the clumps of coarse grass studded with sea pinks, and on the far side of the burn, lies the glittering expanse of silver shingle known as Prince Charlie's Beach—one of the many " raised " beaches in which the loch abounds. Here in the bay, *La Doutelle,* the variously-spelt barque which had brought the Prince from France, anchored, after having first landed him upon the tiny island of Eriskay. If only the royal youth saw this anchorage in sunshine as we have so often seen it, he would need nothing else to make him realise that Scotland was the one kingdom in all the world worth winning, for there is that subtle quality in the scenery of Loch nan Uamh which not only grips you at first sight but holds you for ever.

But if every view of the " loch of caves " is glorious,

there is one that is sublime.   Crossing the grass and
passing through bracken and heather, you gain the summit
of scoriated rocks rising sheer from the sea, which breaks
below with many a hollow rumbling in countless chasms
along the shore.   Amongst the wash of golden and brown
sea wrack, the legion of huge jellyfish do not enamour
you of a backboneless career.   But at your feet you will
find some attraction in many a shell of the little purple-
tipped sea urchin, often indeed broken, or with its spines
worn off, but rarely intact.   Pass onward and climb the
highest point on your right, easily identified by its solitary
storm-tossed tree.   This height is Rudh Ard Ghamhsgail,
to be identified, apparently, with " Arka Unskel," as the
name is phonetically rendered in Sasunnach archæological
writings, and it is easiest gained by a slope on the north
side.   When you have reached the summit, about 110 feet
above the sea level, the panorama spread before you
rewards you a thousandfold for the climb.   Overhead
various seabirds are on the wing.   Crying harshly, low
over the water, generally in pairs, with characteristically
short flight, speed the red-billed, orange-legged, black and
white oystercatchers.   High in the sky swerves the graceful
tern or sea-swallow.   Suddenly he darts with amazing
swiftness perpendicularly through the air, diving with a
splash into the sea after the fish that his keen eye has
sighted.   Gulls are everywhere on the rocks and on the
wing; and on the surface of the sea, rising and falling
with its swell as though part of it, a mother eider duck,
the bird of S. Cuthbert, with her brood of little ones floats
contentedly.   In front are the hills of Roshven, far to the
left stretch the dazzling waters to the head of the loch,
where, mercifully subdued by the distance, you can just
distinguish the viaduct against a background of craggy
mountains.   It is a scene arresting in every feature, and
is never two days alike.

In addition to these natural attractions, Rudh Ard
Ghamhsgail possesses what may be called an artificial one,

"PRINCE CHARLIE'S BEACH" AND LOCH NAN UAMH

in that it is the site of a vitrified fort. From the summit
of the eminence, you recognise what a point of vantage you
occupy, and you are not surprised to discover that it was
one of which the prehistoric people, probably of the Iron
Age, took advantage for the defence of their country
against the enemy. Not only does the height offer natural
advantages lending themselves to fortification, but its
elevation suggests it as a site suited for the beacon fires
which flashed from height to height as danger signals when
invasion threatened. Examination of such portions of the
vallum as have been in recent years denuded of their grass
overgrowth, as well as the hollowed top of Ard Ghamhsgail
itself, at first suggest volcanic origin. But since all Arisaig
was most intensely glaciated during the Ice Age, and no
trace of post-Glacial volcanoes has ever been found in
Britain, the prevailing fusing of stones constituting these
ramparts is clearly due to artificial means. Such vitrified
forts present one of the many baffling problems in which
Scottish archæology abounds, since it is not possible conclusively to determine if the vitrifaction were accidentally
accomplished or done intentionally. Quite probably, in
the first instance, vitrifaction was the undesigned result
of kindling fire against fuseable stones, the process afterwards being deliberately adopted with the purpose of
fusing in one compact mass the component stones of the
walls of a fort.

In the case of Ard Ghamhsgail, it seems to me that the
extremely interesting investigations and experiments conducted on the spot by Colonel M'Hardy have proved his
conclusions, with regard to this particular fort, to be
irrefragable. Before giving these, however, it will be well
to examine the fort itself, which has its foundation on
rocks of metamorphic gneiss, with indications of trap, the
whole covered with grass and bracken. Only on the
south-east does the " promontory of the height " (thus
Rhu Ard) go sheer down to the sea. At its base on the
west, approached through a gap in the rocks, there is a

tumble of large stones huddled together, which look to me as if they had once constituted an outwork guarding the main structure at the top. This is roughly of an oval shape, some 132 feet in diametei, and the fort itself, together with its better known fellow on Eilean nan Gobhar in Loch Ailort, is unique by reason of its double form; for the lower spur of the summit is fortified as well as the upper main depression. Apparently the fort has never been thoroughly excavated, investigation having gone no further than laying bare portions of the walls that their structure might be examined. In view of the finds for which the spade has been responsible in other similar forts, it is safe to conjecture that here in the hollow is an untapped source of archæological treasure.

There are still visible several vitrified portions of the wall, which is now highest at the widest part of the fort at its south-west end, and three feet thicker than it is high. Vitrified walls in two places supplement natural ramparts on the seaward side, or rather close up gaps between the cliffs which rise on a level between the sea and the top of the fort proper. These walls are in appearance of the most casual and haphazard construction, looking like promiscuous piling-up—after the nature of rubble work—of small pieces of felspar, gleaming beautifully with gold, silver, or copper sheen, and the pouring over them of some molten substance which has penetrated the crevices, cementing the whole together more or less successfully. The resultant slag is very suggestive of lava, and it was in order to discover how the vitrifaction had been produced that Colonel M'Hardy conducted his experiments on the shore below. His initial attempts, wherein he enclosed stones within a built-up wall, piling peat, brushwood, grass, and seaweed upon them for fuel, and keeping the resultant fire alight for thirty-nine hours, did nothing but fracture the stones. Ultimately he discovered the secret of vitrifaction lay in a very low combustion, generating an intense heat.   This he secured by piling brushwood over the stones and, when the fuel was alight, covering it· with more stones, adding a little wood when that below seemed nearly exhausted.   This sandwiching process was continued until the pile, six feet in diameter, had risen to a height of four feet, and had been burning for eighteen hours.   Then in the centre, and eighteen inches from the top of the heap, a portion of the stones, weighing about eight lbs., was found to be vitrified.   Now, since water-worn boulders, without a sign of having been touched by fire, form the base of such portions of the wall as were vitrified, Colonel M'Hardy came to the very commonsense conclusion that had vitrifaction been expressly adopted by the builders for the consolidation of their wall, they would obviously never have left unfused the foundation stones.   His opinion, therefore, is that, in this case certainly, vitrifaction was the unpremeditated result of keeping a fire continually smouldering that it might be stirred up into flame at a moment's notice, probably also being used for cooking purposes.

Col. M'Hardy supports this opinion by the result of his investigations round about, finding it justified by the discovery of traces of vitrified remains on Eilean na Ghoil in Loch nan Uamh, as well as on Eilean Port nam Murrach just round the corner.   These vantage points, together with the well-known fort on Eilean nan Gobhar (referred to previously), form a triangle, from the apex of which, Eilean Port nam Murrach, an extensive view of the open sea from Ardnamurchan Point to the Sound of Sleat, is obtainable.   Obviously, then, with this last fort serving to link up the other islands with the open sea, the case for these particular forts being primarily used for beacon fires seems fairly conclusive.   In the specific case of Ard Ghamhsgail, additional force is given to this theory by the fact that the entrance on the land side, which has the appearance of being by far the weakest point of the fort,

shews scarcely a trace of vitrifaction in the portion of wall
that here guards it.

Descending on this side, the shore for ever associated
with both the landing and the leaving of Prince Charles
Edward is soon gained.

PART IV

THE LANDING, HIDING, AND DEPARTURE OF THE PRINCE

IT was on July 25, 1745, that the French privateer brought
the Prince from the bleakness of Eriskay to the beauty of
Loch nan Uamh. Is it realised that the young Chevalier
was only twenty-five years of age when, practically un-
supported, and without either arms or money, he landed
to face the stupendous task of creating and inspiring an
army to lead against the organised might of Britain? Yet
such was the enthusiasm he was capable, not only of
arousing and sustaining but of transmitting, even to the
present generation, that he succeeded where, with all the
circumstances in their favour, others would have failed,
and accomplished that which had been declared to be
impossible of accomplishment. The burning verse of a
famous contemporary poet, born in Moidart, Alexander
Macdonald (*MacMhaighstir Alasdair*) (of whom more
anon) well expresses the fierce devotion which took
possession of the clansmen:

> "Let them tear our bleeding bosoms,
> Let them drain our latest veins,
> In our hearts is Charlie, Charlie,
> While a spark of life remains."

This verse is a translation from the Gaelic, and you
will remark its dissimilarity from the uncouth dialect with
which the beautiful Jacobite songs of the Baroness Nairne,
James Hogg the Ettrick Shepherd, Burns, and others have

to some extent familiarised most Sasunnachs.   These are popularly supposed to be written in the " Scotch " language, to employ the atrocious adjective in all too common use which a Scots purist will only tolerate in reference to whisky.'   Although the Doric successfully masquerades as the real Scots tongue, it is in reality nothing more than an alien dialect of Old English which has impudently ousted the Gaelic from its historical and rightful   position.   Was   not   the   Gaelic,   indeed,   the language spoken in the Garden of Eden?   At least a Celtic poet declares :

> " By Adam it was spoken,
> In Eden, I believe,
> And sweetly flowed the Gaelic
> From the lovely lips of Eve."

In the fifteenth century the Gaelic was still called the Scots language by contemporary writers, and it was not until 1520 that Lowlanders who had already supplanted   true   Scots   in   the   Lowlands—witness   the universal prevalence of Gaelic place-names—proceeded to usurp the title of Scots for their Teutonic tongue.   But for centuries afterwards the Highlanders persisted in maintaining their exclusive right to be called Scots; and still to a Highlander, a Lowlander and an Englishman are alike Sasunnachs—aliens   from   them   in   speech,   race,   and customs.   The language of the Highlander was first called Albanic (and still to the Gael, Scotland is *Alba*), then Scots; whilst the tongue of the Lowlander is by native writers prior to the sixteenth century called usually Inglis; in Gaelic *Beurla Shasunnach* or *a' Bheurla leathann,* as the Highlander always calls the "broad English" of the Lowlander, and his country *a' Ghalldachd,* the "home of the stranger," *i.e.,* the Lowlands.

True as is the sentiment of the familiar Jacobite songs, there is nothing even remotely Highland in any feature of their composition.   As, except in the case of the verb *to be,* there is no present tense in the Gaelic, this peculiarity naturally comes out in the English of Gaelic speakers. Therefore, to those who are accustomed to Highland English, it is simply ludicrous to associate with the Highlands either the dialect, style, or mode of expression of such as the following typical verse:

> " The news frae Moidart cam' yestreen,
>   Will soon gar mony ferlie;
> For ships o' war had just come in
>   And landed Royal Charlie!
> Come thro' the heather, around him gather,
>   Ye're a' the welcomer early;
> Around him cling wi' a' your kin,
>   For wha'll be king but Charlie?
> Come thro' the heather, around him gather;
> Come Ronald, come Donald, come all thegether
> And crown your rightfu'. lawfu' king,
>   For wha'll be king but Charlie?"

Where the melody, as in every instance of these songs, originates in an old Highland air, and where the sentiment of the song itself rings so true, one's regret is all the keener that the rest is so utterly alien to Highland characteristics. Less open to this objection is " Maclean's Welcome," which indeed Hogg claimed to be derived from the Gaelic:

> " Come o'er the stream, Charlie. dear Charlie, brave Charlie,
> Come o'er the stream, Charlie, and dine with Maclean,
> And though you be weary, we'll make your heart cheery,
> And welcome our Charlie and his royal train."

Contrast with this a genuine translation from the Gaelic of *Alasdair MacMhaighstir Alasdair,* the Clanranald Bard of the '45:

> " Hark the summons! Charlie's coming—
>   Heir of Scotland's rightful king!
> Gather, loyal clansmen, gather,
>   Broadsword gird and target sling.
> Hurrah, hurrah! Charlie's coming,
>   Royal Charlie, long away!
> Draw the broadsword, don the tartan;
>   Clansmen, rouse ye for the fray!"

Much as the genuinely Highland air of " Bonnie Prince Charlie " naturally appeals, again the incongruity of the dialect put into the mouth of a Highlander makes one rebel at singing:

> " Follow thee. follow thee, vha wadna follow thee?
> Lang hast thou lo'ed and trusted us fairly.
> Charlie, Charlie. wha wadna follow thee?
> King o' the Highland hearts, bonnie Prince Charlie!"

Though the verse is scarcely suggestive of Charles' initial difficulty in securing followers, at least it brings us back to the subject from which I have strayed; so let us imagine ourselves back on July 26, 1745, at Loch nan Uamh.

" A tall youth of most agreeable appearance," dressed as an English clergyman, was at first introduced as such to the chieftains who had obeyed the summons to come on board *La Doutelle*. But to two of them, Clanranald and Macdonald of Kinlochmoidart, he at once declared himself, urging them to rally round him that their lawful King might come to his own again. They, however, sensible of the hopelessness of the enterprise, and foreseeing its fatal results, returned cold arguments to the Prince's burning entreaty.

You can picture the scene as they paced the deck: the eloquent " priest " pleading with the two unresponsive chieftains. And then your eye is caught by a third Highlander standing apart from the group. He has evidently heard all that has passed on both sides, and, to judge from his heightened colour and flashing eye, has obviously been stirred to his depths. Charles, too, notices this young clansman, and, with his usual discernment, recognises and seizes the psychological moment. The challenge rings out as swiftly the Prince turns upon him:

" Will not *you* assist me?"

And instantly comes the response: " I will follow you to death were there none other to draw a sword in your cause!"

The spirited answer of Ronald Macdonald the younger of Kinlochmoidart shamed the two chieftains into yielding without further argument to the appeal of the Prince, who thus gained the nucleus of the following that all but overthrew the Hanoverian dynasty.

It was not till August 4 that the Prince actually landed to take up his quarters in Borrodale House, and it was here and then that Donald Cameron, the " gentle Lochiel," though warned by his brother of Fassifern not to risk the danger of an interview, came and met his fate. Lochiel was the chief who more than any other swayed the Highlands, and his purpose was to dissuade Charles from his project. But he might as well have attempted to dissuade fire from burning. Charles was not to be deflected, and won the day by his spirited and famous thrust: " Lochiel can stay at home and read in the newspapers of the doings of his Prince."

To which Lochiel replied: " No, I will share the fate of my Prince, and so shall every man over whom nature or fortune has given me any power."

After he had thus made conquest of the clansmen who came to pay their loyal homage, Charles left on Sunday, August 11, by sea across Loch nan Uamh and the entrance of Loch Ailort, landing in passing at Glen Uig Bay, on his journey to Caolas on Loch Moidart, for the seat of Macdonald of Kinlochmoidart, on his way to Glenfinnan.

When on April 20, 1746, he first returned to the farmhouse, it was at night as the hunted fugitive after the blasting of his hopes at Culloden. During his stay of six days on this occasion, Charles wrote farewell to his followers at Ruthven, and then, feeling that a French vessel might gain him with less risk amongst the islands than on the mainland, he secured the services of one Donald Macleod of Gaultergill to convey him to the Hebrides. This staunch old Jacobite procured an eight-oared fishing boat from Macdonald of Borrodale, manned her with seven Highlanders, and with himself as pilot took

the Prince and four of his followers on board.   The night
of April 26 was chosen for the departure, but, as the
weather was most threatening, Macleod urged delay.
Charles, however, would not listen to the suggestion, and,
seated between the knees of the pilot, began his hazardous
passage.   How dangerous it must have been you need only
visualise Loch nan Uamh to understand, since one of
its most distinctive features are the many rocky crags
which, breaking the surface of the waters, must endanger
boating, especially at night.   Soon the storm burst full
upon the fugitives.   Rain deluged: thunder crashed and
reverberated from the hills; and the thick darkness was
only relieved by flashes of blinding lightning.   So furious
was the sea that the Prince would have returned to the
mainland had not Macleod declared this impossible.
Ultimately the boat was swept on to Benbecula but without
the accomplishment of the Prince's purpose, for, after
protracted wanderings, on July 10, Charles once more
returned from Skye via Morar to Borrodale, to find,
however, that the farmhouse had been burnt down by
Captain Ferguson, a Hanoverian officer, whose brutalities
should have entitled him to high rank in an army as
distinguished as the German for barbarity.   The faithful
Angus Macdonald was living in a miserable hut near the
ruins of his house, but as the Hanoverian soldiery searching
for Charles infested the neighbourhood, the hut was
considered no safe place for the Prince.   Consequently,
for three days he lay in hiding in a cave, and this cave
I was, of course, keen to discover.

It seemed natural to look for this hiding place amongst
the rocks on the shore of the " loch of caves," but I had
been told that it lay inland, and, moreover, that the beaten
track to it was easily discoverable.   So I took the un-
mistakeable track, and began the search for the elusive
hiding place.   Through a thick screen of trees the path
led up a steep incline of fallen rocks, amongst which I
failed at first to discover any symptom of a cave.   Thinking

I must be on the wrong track, I searched in other directions, equally in vain, ultimately returning to have another hunt amongst the boulders under the trees. Then at last I literally stumbled into the cunning and very effective hiding place. This was a small triangular opening between the boulders, on the level of the ground, and into this I dropped, to find myself in a small damp hole, out of which a larger, damper, and darker hole opened, at a level of some three feet lower. Instead of the more or less pleasant and roomy cavern-by-the-sea of my imaginings, I found myself cramped and stifled in a veritable " little ease," best described literally as a dirty hole.

Such is the cave which you are told locally was the Prince's hiding place for the three days, and which even such a careful compilation as Norie's *Life and Adventures of Prince Charles Edward Stewart* accepts without question as being what it purports to be. Unfortunately, this traditional cave could not have satisfied in 1746, any more than it does to-day, some of the conditions of its location as described in the contemporary narrative of John Macdonald, Borrodale's son, whose account is known as the Dalilea MS. Young Borrodale describes the hiding place as a cave or cleft between two precipitous rocks on the foreshore in front of the house. This vague description does not help in the least to locate the cave, and would certainly lead anyone who did not know Borrodale to suppose the house was immediately on the shore, instead of being three-quarters of a mile distant at its nearest point. And since all the shore is in front of the house, it will be realised how very inadequately the situation is indicated. The first point in young Borrodale's narrative in which this traditional cave fails to answer to the conditions of the specific cave he is describing is the statement that from the entrance the Prince was able to watch the English warships as they sailed in and out of the loch. First, there is the objection that the wood, which in the

present July so effectually blocks out all view of the loch
a quarter of a mile distant, made probably as thick a screen
in July, 1746.   But, assuming that the trees then were not
sufficiently grown to obscure the view so thoroughly, at
such a distance it would be impossible for any one to
watch anything from an entrance which is practically a
hole in the ground, leaving altogether out of account
the risk that would be incurred by thus exposing to view
at least the royal head and shoulders.

There is indeed this same objection to another cave of
precisely the same character which I was told was to be
found off what is known as the " Duke's Walk."   I discovered this cave without any difficulty above the fallen
rocks lying between the two white marble boulders which
form so conspicuous a landmark on the shore.   The cave
lies in an angle at the base of what, I suppose, might be
called a precipitous rock, and its entrance is identical with
that of the other.   But since the loch runs parallel to, and
just below the cave, the entrance affords more possibilities
of a view of the shipping than that of the other, though one
would say the risk of discovery was greater.   But it is
not easy to understand how, in the case of either of these
caves there could have been any scope for the addition
of a roof of turf, which from the loch looked like a grassy
bank, and made the place fairly weatherproof, as related
by the Dalilea MS.   One would say nothing of such a
nature could add to the natural weatherproofness of either
cave, though, indeed, above the traditional one there is an
opening into the entrance passage.   A stone, however,
would be the simplest and most obvious method of
providing this with a roof; but however covered in, the
opening could no longer have served its traditional use
as the means of secretly lowering provisions into the cave:
nor, since a rock in front obscures approach to it from
view, could its roofing by any possibility have been seen
from the loch.   I can only conjecture that conceivably
the other cave still retains its artificial roof of turf some-

where on the rocks above it, and that in the lapse of time it has become indistinguishable amongst the growth of vegetation.   Whichever of the caves it may have been that sheltered the Prince for the three days, he was advised to seek yet more secure hiding-place when his safety was threatened by the activities of his enemies in the very near neighbourhood.   So on July 13 he removed to a still more inaccessible cave which young Borrodale's narrative is alone in naming.   He says that " M'Leod Cove " was upon a high precipice in the woods of Borrodale, and to this description the cave off the " Duke's Walk " may answer. But Clanranald states that this second cave in which the Prince took cover was four miles eastward of Borrodale, which certainly suggests a greater inaccessibility than that of a cave on the shore—a suggestion borne out by the fact that at the present day this cave is quite unknown, and indeed even in 1746 it was known to very few people.

It was of such days as these that the poet writes, picturing the surroundings of the hunted fugitive:

> " Lone places of the deer,
>   Corrie and loch and ben,
>   Fount that wells in the cave,
>   Voice of the burn and wave.
>   Softly you sing and clear
>   Of Charlie and his men!

> " Here has he lurked, and here
>   The heather has been his bed;
>   The wastes of the islands knew,
>   And the Highland hearts were true
>   To the bonny, the brave, the dear,
>   The royal, the hunted head."

Quite in keeping with the cave at Loch nan Uamh must have been Charles' costume, which at this time consisted of a coarse dark cloth coat, a shabby tartan waistcoat, belted plaid, and tartan hose, with Highland brogues so worn that the thongs could scarcely bind them to his feet. His solitary shirt was saffron-hued from wear, and under his bonnet he wore (for some inexplicable reason) a wretched yellow wig.

There is no subject which gives a Highlander more legitimate cause for pride than the reflection that even in their dire poverty the reward of £30,000 offered for the Prince's apprehension could not bribe the clansmen into betraying Charles.[5] On the contrary, chieftains and outlaws alike, scorning this bait, over and over again risked their lives in order to shield the Prince from his enemies.

Once again, but for the last time, on September 19, the Prince returned to Loch nan Uamh. Two French frigates had managed to elude the watch of the English warships, and had gained the loch in order to take on board Charles and some Highland chieftains who had elected to follow him into exile. It was the ironically named *L'Heureux* which, shortly after midnight on Saturday, September 20, 1746, bore away the Prince from Scotland and happiness into an eternal night. To the Highlander who has stood upon the field of Culloden and there re-created the scene of battle: whose Jacobite blood has surged wildly in response to the call of the fight: whose every sympathy has leapt out to those who fought with such desperate gallantry for the Prince—to such a one, standing solitary upon the Prince's Strand of Loch nan Uamh, tears are not far off. Had the Prince only fallen among the clansmen in the lost battle: did he but lie with them under the blood-stained heather of the lonely moorland—his monument, as theirs, a rough headstone— how infinitely more glorious a grave he would have filled than he does in all the hollow grandeur of S. Peter's, Rome. Often must similar repinings have filled the heart of the royal exile himself: often with a longing for their return must he have bewailed, even as Aytoun makes him

---

[5] There is an old change house in the neighbourhood of Kinlocheil where the Prince retaliated by offering first £30, then the same sum as offered for himself, for the person of German George.

do, the days that were past, crying, in the bitterness of his heart at Versailles,

> " Backwards—backwards let me wander
>   To the noble northern land:
> Let me feel the breezes blowing
>   Fresh along the mountain side;
> Let me see the purple heather.
>   Let me hear the thundering tide.
> Be it hoarse as Corrievreckan
>   Spouting when the storm is high—
> Give me but one hour of Scotland—
>   Let me see it ere I die!"

As you bid farewell to the shores of Loch nan Uamh, there rises a picture of the last scene of Scotland's dearest romance.   Upon the shore stand a few broken clansmen—broken in every single sense of the word—and out to sea sails the French frigate bearing—nay, rather tearing—away from them the Prince who was to them the soul of their most ardent longings.   And alien though the words be to the Highlands, so true is the sentiment of the Lowland song, so infinite the pathos of its melody, that its appealing strains seem to carry far over the water into that mysterious beyond whence the Highland heart is convinced Prince Charlie will surely one day return to his kingdom:

> " Bonnie Charlie's noo awa',
>   Safely o'er the angry main;
> Mony a heart will break in twa
>   Should he no' come back again.
> Will ye no' come back again? Will ye no' come back again?
> Better lo'ed ye canna be—Will ye no' come back again?"

PART V

THE ATTRACTIONS OF ARISAIG, AND OF SAILING THERE IN PARTICULAR

"Nowhere beats the heart so kindly
As beneath the tartan plaid."

FROM Borrodale there is a choice of routes to Arisaig. A walk along the road where, in the summer, the lingering scent of honeysuckle succeeds to the breath of pine trees, brings one, after a last glimpse of Loch nan Uamh, to a big iron gate on the left. Breaking off here from the main road to Arisaig, a bye-way through the " Glen " is entered. Passing a lochan whose still, dark waters mirror the surrounding birches, beyond where, under the leafy arches of woodland glades, tumbles the creaming waters of a burn, an uninteresting white-washed cottage comes into view on the left. This marks the site, but apparently does not incorporate any part, of that old house [6] which so unworthily succeeded Castle Tirrim as the seat of the Chief and Captain of Clanranald, and about half a mile distant is an enclosed orchard, still known as " Clanranald's Old Garden." Within living memory, the waters of Loch nan Eala, of which only a very small area now remains, came up to the present roadway, but the cutting of a canal drained the greater part of the water into the sea.

It was during the process of drainage that a *crannog* was brought to light. A *crannog* is a lake-dwelling constructed as a place of safety on an artificial island made by the inhabitants of Romano-British times. In order to make these *crannogs,* a large raft of floating material was launched upon the water and paddled out to a suitable distance, where piles were driven in at the corners to secure

[6] Built in the nineteenth century merely as a temporary residence pending the erection of a more suitable house.

it in position. Upon this foundation were laid loads of turf and stones, transverse sections of trees, etc., until there was built up a thoroughly solid base upon which fortified dwellings might be constructed. Where the loch on which the *crannog* was built was sufficiently shallow to allow of access by wading across from the land, a stone causeway was often laid down under the water, but taking an unexpected course. By this means, only those in the secret could thus gain the island, whilst enemies attempting a crossing and soon losing their footing would only flounder in the mud, and might in consequence be drowned. When Loch nan Eala was drained, the removal of sod and rushes exposed the remains of a *crannog* some fifty feet square, the upper layer being of oak trunks laid transversely upon rows of birch, and so on in repetition to a considerable depth. Having found the old man who had originally laid bare the *crannog,* I persuaded him to take me to it. But, unfortunately, a season of heavy rain had inundated the *crannog,* rendering the site unapproachable, so that all I saw was chiefly due to imagination exercised in an adjacent swamp.

By whichever path " the Glen " is left, one emerges at some point on the rough road that winds round for the greater part by the sea to the old pier and Rudh (promontory) of Arisaig. Again there are tracts of beautiful woodland, but the chief charm of this road lies in the rugged beauty of the wild and broken moorland, the shore where the waves come tumbling over rocks covered with golden sea-wrack, and beyond these the wonderful view of the jagged peaks of Skye and the islands of Eigg and Rum—

> " Ever floating, ever floating,
>   Ever floating round thee
> Lie white clouds of incense,
>   Altar Isle of the sea!
> Like incense of love
>   Rising out of the gloom
> Are the mist wreaths that float
>   Round thy blue peaks, O Rum!"

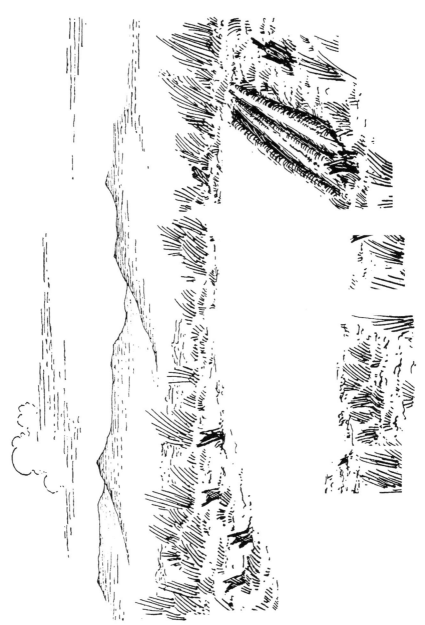

PLATFORM OF LOGS ON ISLAND OF LOCH NAN EALA
(By kind permission of the Society of Antiquaries of Scotland)

Then there are the birds. There is a heronry on a loch
of water-lilies near by, and from here the herons, with
dignified, if heavy, flight of slowly flapping wings, gain
the shore to stand, sentinels of the sea, as they patiently
watch for a fish. Seagulls, scarts (or cormorants) are
everywhere, on the wing screaming harshly, or out at sea
seated on rocks near which seals may appear. But it is
the lone cry of the curlew that gives best expression to
the spirit of the road, for it is the call of the spirit, and it
is to the spirit that this road makes its greatest appeal.
So many are its allurements, indeed, that it is always hard
to leave its seductions for the village of Arisaig itself.

If Arisaig means " the house on the bay," it probably
originally had reference to the chief house of the district
as its outstanding feature, but for me " the house on the
bay " will ever be the gaunt and ugly cottage which is the
first you pass on the shore of Loch nan Cilltean (loch of
the churches) on the road to Rudh' Arisaig, the " point of
Arisaig." There it stands on the marshy shore, studded
with sea pinks, just where the loch takes a curve inland,
so that on two sides the building is flanked by the sea.
This was the home of a decidedly picturesque personality
who displayed at their best the light-hearted characteristics
of the true Highlander unspoilt by the alien taint of a
devastating Calvinism. Donald Macallister [7] the boatman
was the first friend I ever made in the Highlands, and,
naturally therefore, though he has long since embarked
upon his last voyage, the sight of his cottage invariably
recalls many delightful memories of its old tenant.

When out with my camera early one morning I met him
first, strolling in front of his cottage with the air of a
perfectly contented man who has not a care in life and
knows nothing of time—a general feature of Highland
character, which, however, I have often had cause to
deplore. Tall and well set up, with the high cheek bones

---

[7] " Son of Alexander," a small clan subsequently merged again in the
Macdonalds, from whom they originated.

of the Celt; keen, kindly eyes deep set in a weather-beaten
face, and with a fine full beard, he looked, in his blue
jersey and peaked sea cap, an attractive figure, promising
well as a companionable and competent boatman.
Salutations were breezily exchanged, and soon we were
on excellent terms with each other, thanks in some measure
to that marvellous system of wireless telegraphy that in
these Highlands is an old institution, whereby at least your
name and where you are staying are flashed throughout
the district before ever you yourself appear on the scene.
Unlike the Lowlander or the Lowlandised Highlander who
thinks he gives evidence of his independence by rudeness
and a general lack of manners, Macallister's charm lay
in his genial friendliness — easy, certainly, but never
offensively familiar—and in his delightful sense of humour.
But he was a born flatterer—at least, like most Highlanders, where any of his own clan were concerned—and,
as belonging to the clan from which his own sprang,
I, in consequence, suffered heavily from his compliments.
With regard to the weather, Macallister, again true to type,
was always very optimistic.   No matter *how* hopeless the
downpour at the time of speaking, he would always assure
me in tones of earnest conviction that we were in for a
beautiful day.   If, exasperated by a long run of consistently
false prophecies, I gently hinted that his forecasts scarcely
inspired confidence, his reproachful look would suggest
that only the callous would add to the pain he already
felt at the weather's bad faith with him, and to give
expression to his hurt he would take a strictly non-
committal line of prophecy.

There is a great fascination in listening to the soft drawl
of a Highlander's English, and equal charm in the quaint
English itself as in the Highland construction of sentences.
A specimen of Macallister's conversation may give some
idea of this as well as a glimpse of the man himself: it
will at least prove how far removed is the Highlander's
English from the harsh and ugly dialect of the Lowlander

which is generally foisted upon the innocent Highlander in Sasunnach fiction. We would greet each other with a hearty handshake, and then, while I manipulated the camera, Macallister would begin:

" So you wass out sketching again? Uch, but you wass ta fine one to pe out at this time of ta morning! And it wass not nothing that you would pe doing neither. Chove, but you wass ta lifely one! And you would pe plaming me for ta weather? (after my contrasting yesterday morning's forecast of a " fery fine tay " with the actual one—a heavy and steady downpour lasting for twenty-four hours.) Uch, well, it wass not that wet but it might have been more wet, but I wass not understanding how it could pe wet at aall inteed. It wass fery strange it wass raining after what I did say to you. I'll not pe saying that this wass chust ta tay to-tay for sailing over to Eigg; no, no, ta wind she wass not in ta right quarter for Eigg and you would not pe wanting to pe aalways tacking—no, no. But aall ta same, if it wass keeping fine, it will pe ta peautiful tay. Wass it ta sketch of me that you wass wanting to pe making? No, no, I wass that ugly I would pe cracking ta glass. Uch, well, who would pe refusing you that wass a Mactonald, and a Macallister ta same clan whatefer? It will pe ta funny sketch you will pe getting of me. Would I pe helping you to put up ta sticks?"

As the camera was being packed up, Macallister, leaning up against his door, his legs crossed, his hands in his pockets and a twinkle in his eye, would begin again:

" Chove, but it's you that iss ta sturdy little wan to pe carrying aall that on your back! It's a fine time we'll pe having ta tay you and ta other ladies sail over with me to Eigg."

In this case he was a true prophet. We *did* have a " fine tay," though not exactly of the character he had led us to anticipate. One glorious morning Macallister said we should have the very day for our sail, and that if we started at ten o'clock we should just catch the wind to take us out of the loch on a straight tack, and so be able to cover the twelve miles in about an hour and a half. It happened that it was most important that we should meet a train at six o'clock that evening, but, trusting to Macallister's assurances that we should be back in good time, we agreed to set sail. To begin with, we sat on the rocks for fully an hour awaiting the unpunctual boatman, but on his belated appearance he apologised so contritely for being " a few minutes late, indeed," that we could not maintain our annoyance with him. And it must be charged to our credit that we retained the same forgiving spirit throughout the expedition, which turned out to be a very exasperating one. The Highlands, however, are the Highlands, and Macallister was Macallister, and they easily covered any number of annoyances. Besides any Highland grievance has wings: other grievances have weights, although this day's grievance was rather heavy in the wing. The breeze which was to have taken us easily and gaily over to Eigg seemed too light and skittish to undertake its duty. Macallister assuring us, however that there would be the good stiff wind at the mouth of the bay, we tacked hopefully out to meet it, and had quite an energetic time dodging the flapping sails as the boat was continually put about. At the mouth of the bay the faint wind had fainted away altogether, and so hot and powerful had the sun become that some of my friends in the boat felt inclined to follow suit. The ever-hopeful Macallister taking out the oars, we gave chase slowly and painfully to every little wandering breath of wind which might aid us on the way.

When at last, after a crossing four and a half hours long instead of the predicted one and a half hour, the shores of lovely Eigg were reached, my friends were too grilled by the heat to have eyes for anything but a corner under the shade of a big rock. We had barely time on shore for a very late lunch and a hurried expedition to the Macdonald cave, to be described in a later chapter, when we had to return to the boat and set off for the mainland again. Macallister's faith had not been strong enough to evoke the wind promised for our return journey, and the hour of our train's arrival found us still many miles out on a dead calm sea.

All the while Macallister's optimistic hopefulness never deserted him. It was strange, of course, that he who was on such intimate terms with the weather should have been deceived by the wind, but he and his son would get the oars out and pull until the breeze picked up again. I volunteered to take an oar, and plied it to the accompaniment of a running comment from the wily Macallister:

" Chove, but it's you that has ta strong arm! Ta way you wass pulling wass ass peautiful ass efer I did see before anywhere whatefer! Uch, but we'll pe there in no time now. My word, but it wass ta little wans that will pe having ta strength!" etc., etc.

To cut a long voyage short, so far from getting back by 6.30 P.M., we actually did not land until 11 P.M., after six and a half hours under " wooden topsails."

In spite of the lovely scenery and cooler air, this sail back would have grown very tedious had it not been that the sun, having made such a brilliant display all day, bethought himself of a masterpiece in the evening. Then everything was transfigured, and the wonderful panorama, which grew in ever-increasing splendour under the glowing touch of the sun, held our eyes in willing captivity. Eigg and Rum, always beautiful of contour, were crowned by haloes of tender colours, gradually passing into pale gold. Then the Isle of Skye, flooded at first with a gentle glow of gold, flamed at last into livid fire. Though it is years ago since I saw the actual scene, so vividly is this particular picture impressed upon my mental vision that it springs again into being as I write amidst far different surroundings. Skye is always strikingly handsome, with her bold outline of jagged peaks, whether they be a-glitter in the midday sun, or misty with the clouds softly curling round their crests.   But I have never seen her so awful in her beauty as on this occasion.   It was as though we beheld some vast fortress aflame " from turret to foundation stone," and from one end to another.   This illusion was heightened by a curious natural phenomenon of moving black shadows behind the island—shadows which seemed to ascend as the smoke of the burning from that stupendous conflagration.   Quivering through every shade of orange and red, the fire raged, flinging its ruddy glow far across the sea until our boat, too, was caught up in it and bathed in the spreading flood of molten gold.

Entranced by the awe-inspiring spectacle, we had become unconscious of the flight of time, which had previously seemed so leaden-footed, and the voice of the ever-cheerful Macallister seemed to summon us back to another world.   We were just at the entrance of Loch nan Cilltean, and, if we wanted to be home before midnight, we should take to the small boat and let Archie pull us ashore.   So, leaving Macallister senior to bring the big boat at his leisure by himself as a suitable punishment for inveigling us into a " sail " on a dead calm day, we entrusted ourselves to his son's pilotage, and gained our port at last.

Such was the attraction of Macallister, however, that even this experience did not deter us from sailing again with him.   Coming home on one of these occasions from Luinga Mhor, a small island just outside Loch nan Cilltean, we had rather a novel experience which it may be interesting to detail.   We were late (needless to say when out with Macallister), but cutting along under a fine breeze, when one of my friends called our attention to something on the left of us, and considerably out of our course.   It was a huddled group of some moving objects—too far off for us to distinguish—which seemed to be stranded on the summit of a rock on which the tide was visibly gaining fast.   Naturally, we were very much concerned at the discovery, and tried to make out these objects in distress, whom at first our heightened imaginations took to be human beings.   But as our boat was headed for the rapidly submerging rock, at closer quarters we discovered it was some sheep that were in imminent danger of drowning. They had obviously been put out to pasture on a small island a good distance behind their present position, and at low tide they must have crossed some strand, submerged at other times, and thus gained the small reef of rocks, also covered at high water.   So rapidly was the tide gaining upon the rock that we realised it was a question if we should be in time to effect a rescue of the five sheep and a lamb which we were now able to distinguish quite clearly.   Their bleating carried piteously across the water, and yet when at last we drew alongside the rock, over which the sea was by then lapping, the stupid animals actually resisted rescue.   Whilst I held on to the rock with the boat hook, Macallister and his son, each with one leg up to the knee in water, tried to get the sheep into the boat.   At the first attempt, however, the lamb's mother made a dive into the sea in the direction of the island pasture, but, ignoring her for the time being, we devoted our attention to the remaining sheep.   Each one that we got on board had, literally, to be sat upon to keep them from jumping into the water, and, fortunately, the four of us were equal to the task, so that both men were free to attend to the boat.   The five animals being all aboard and under control, we now gave chase to the ewe who, seemingly indifferent to the pitiful cries of her deserted lamb, continued her frantic efforts to escape us.   But when we got alongside her, Macallister soon hauled her on board, and, our rescue complete, we put about, and wet, dishevelled, and later than ever for dinner, soon triumphantly landed with our cargo, which curiously enough, belonged to the hotel where we were staying.

The Christmas of that same year there arrived for me one of the most thoroughly disreputable parcels that can ever have passed through the post.   The yellow covering

paper torn in all directions, with green leaves protruding
from every tear, yards of string hanging all tangled about
it, the address scrawled in the most primitive of hand-
writing over one side, the big ungainly parcel suggested
a practical joke. But when the wrapping was taken off
a fine branch of holly, heavily berried, appeared to view,
and a note intimating that it came as a kindly offering
with Christmas greetings from Macallister. This is the
last memory of the genial boatman whom we were never
to see again, for before another summer he had made the
Eternal Port—peace be to his soul!

Macallister's body rests amongst others of the greatest
of all clans in the little churchyard of Kilmory (*Cill
Ma'ru*), on a slope of the hillside overlooking Loch nan
Cilltean.

PART VI

KILMORY OF ARISAIG

THE beautiful bay on which Arisaig is situated is Loch
nan Cilltean, and near Keppoch, where the rocks abounded
with seals, a shameful tragedy occurred. Allan Maclain,
the ninth chief of Clanranald, with his second wife and his
sons, used to spend the summer here, the sons amusing
themselves by seal-shooting. In this pursuit the step-
mother, jealous of the secondary place occupied by her
own sons, saw her chance of getting rid of Allan Og, the
eldest son and heir. Beginning by inspiring his step-
brothers with the same hatred with which she was
animated, she was able to consummate her evil desire.
One day, as Allan Og was aiming at a seal, his brothers
simultaneously loosed their bows upon him, and so
unerring was their aim that their arrows pierced him, with
the result that the heir died from his wounds.

It was in Loch nan Cilltean, too, and not, as is usually
asserted, in Loch nan Uamh, that, just after Culloden, the

fight took place between three English frigates under Capt.
Howe and two French ships laden with arms and 35,000
louis d'or.   This was the unlucky treasure which, hastily
landed at Borrodale before the action took place, went
through such remarkable vicissitudes, the bulk of it being
ultimately buried in the adjacent Cameron country, whence
it has possibly never yet all been recovered.   For still
there is a Gaelic saying current in the locality " *Sporain
ghobhlach de òr a' Phrionnsa* " (forked purses of the
Prince's gold) applied to persons whose sudden acquisition
of wealth can only be explained by the suggestion that
they have chanced upon some of the buried treasure.

From the sea, the tower of the modern Roman parish
church is a landmark of distinction, but it is a pity that
its dedication to the Mother of God should tend to
stereotype a confusion of name with that of its predecessor,
the old church of Kilmory.   This, as is proved by
its traditional pronunciation, is one of the numerous
corruptions which the name of S. Maelrubha has undergone; and it has often been wrongly identified with *Moire,*
the Gaelic rendering of Mary used exclusively for the
Blessed Virgin, whereas *Mairi* is otherwise employed.
Strangely enough, ancient dedications to our Lady are
somewhat rare in the Highlands, those to S. Columba
being most frequent, and after him S. Maelrubha takes
precedence, even before S. Bride and S. Donnan, who
probably rank next in favour.   Certainly no other name
has suffered more corruptions than that of S. Maelrubha,
the variety of forms in which it appears affording an
interesting study in philology.   Best known in association
with the island on Loch Maree, which bears his name,
S. Maelrubha, an Irishman, educated at Bangor, founded
a monastery at Applecross in Ross-shire, accomplishing,
according to tradition, considerable missionary work
before, in A.D. 722, he rested from his labours.

A feature that you remark as soon as the graveyard
of Kilmory comes in sight is the somewhat unusual type

of its modern gravestones. The prevailing style is that of an ordinary upright plain slab surmounted by a free-standing cross, floriated or plain. Amongst those said to be buried here is the most celebrated of all the Highland poets, the Clanranald Bard, Alexander Macdonald, more familiarly known in the Gaelic as " Alexander the Son of Master Alexander," from some of whose poems quotations have been made in the previous part of this chapter. He was to have been buried on S. Finnan's Isle in Loch Shiel, but a great storm prevented the funeral taking place there. His body was said to have been transferred subsequently to the island, but, though the site of the grave in Kilmory churchyard is unknown, that the removal ever did take place is doubtful. Such is the information I received from the present parish priest, my good friend, Canon Chisholm.

It will be news to Sasunnachs to hear of the existence of any Highland poets, amongst whom, it may be mentioned, members of Clann Donuill overwhelmingly predominate. Indeed, outside the circle of Gaelic speakers, the poems of the Highland bards are practically an unknown quantity. This is neither surprising nor blame-worthy, however, for where all translations are more or less unsatisfactory, those from the Gaelic into English must be more inadequate than most to express the qualities of the original. Certainly Gaelic scholars are agreed in lamenting the impossibility of conveying in English any-thing of the beauty and melody of the original Gaelic to which they would fain introduce the Saxon—if only to disabuse him of the delusion that the Highlands have no native literature, or that it is represented by the Jacobite songs of the Lowlands. But whereas these Lowland songs were not written till long after the '45, contemporary Highland bards, fiery Jacobites, had poured out their souls in praise of Prince Charlie and his cause whilst he was yet amongst them. And the first and chief amongst these, warlike and fierce in his call to the clans, was *Alasdair Mac Mhaighstir Alasdair,* born in Moidart, and buried in

Arisaig.   His   father, "Master   Alexander,"   was   the
priest   of   the   Scottish   Episcopalian   congregation   in
Ardnamurchan.   The bard, however, after some terms at
Glasgow University, in the course of a chequered career
begun as a schoolmaster, passed through Presbyterianism
to the Church of Rome, which he joined previous to serving
as a captain in the army of the Prince.   It is said that on
the historic raising of the banner at Glenfinnan, the bard
had the honour of an interview with the Prince, and then
recited a song in his praise.   Tradition further asserts that
Allan Macdonald of Kinlochmoidart set the Prince upon
the knee of the poet who, in the exaltation born of this
great   privilege,   forthwith   extemporised   his   spirited
Tearlach Mac Sheumais (Charles the son of James).
After Culloden the bard and his brother took refuge (like
the Royal Fugitive himself) in the caves of Loch nan Uamh
above Borrodale, where they, and especially the poet,
suffered great privations.   Afterwards Alasdair's generous
chief, the Captain of Clanranald, recompensed him with
the gift both of office in his service and of lands.

Not only to *Alasdair Mac Mhaighstir Alasdair* belongs
the honour of being the first Gaelic author to publish
an original work, but a volume of his poems, entitled
Ais-eiridh na Sean Chanain (*The Resurrection of the Old
Language of Alba*), daringly published in Edinburgh in
1751, had the distinction of being burnt the next year by
the common hangman because of the passionate loyalty
it breathed to the exiled House of Stewart.   His poems
may be classed as love songs, descriptive, patriotic, and
Jacobite lyrics, the " Birlinn (barge) of Clanranald " being
considered by competent critics his masterpiece, though
since no English version is capable of doing it justice a
translation does not allow its merits to be appreciated.

Of all the genuine Highland Jacobite songs the most
famous is the Clanranald bard's *Morag,* in praise of the
Prince, who is cryptically represented as a maiden with
flowing yellow hair, wooed by the Highlanders. ' " She "

is implored to return with other " Maidens " to dress the
red cloth, under which simile the thrashing of English red
coats is to be understood.   This song is still commonly
used in the Outer Hebrides as a " Waulking Song " by
the women when engaged in the " fulling " or cleansing
and thickening of home-spun tweeds.   The following
extracts from Morag may convey some idea of contemporary Highland devotion to the Prince:

" *Morag of the flowing hair,*
It is of thy love my thoughts are full.
If over seas thou hast gone from us,
May it be soon thou wilt return.

                    *   *   *   *

I would follow thee through the world
If thou should'st but ask it of me.

                    *   *   *   *

Who would not go with sword and shield
Boldly to the cannon's mouth?

                    *   *   *   *

There is would rise with thee
Thy own Captain [8] *Mac ic Ailein,*
He drew near to thee before the rest,
And again would he do it did'st thou return;
Every man that is in Moidart and in Uist,
And in dark blue Arisaig of the birches,
In Canna and Eigg and Morar,
Foremost ever were the men of Ailein's race,
Spectres of terror to the Southron
In the days of Montrose and Alasdair. [9] "

Turning from the graves of Kilmory to the ruin which,
as you face the loch, stands on the extreme left of the
church, at the first glance you are disposed to dismiss it

[8] The Gaelic designation of the Chief of Clanranald.

[9] Alasdair Macdonald, " young Colkitto " (*Coll ciotach,* left-handed Coll),
a chief of great courage, who served with Montrose.

CHURCH OF KILMORY OF ARISAIG FROM SOUTH-EAST

as merely an uninteresting shell.   Examination, however,
will prove it to possess a great many interesting and some
unique features.   Throughout the Western Highlands, one
of the commonest sights you come across is the four
roofless walls of the old churches which, for the most part,
are practically identical in form and structure, *i.e.*, they are
generally simple parallelograms without any suggestion,
either inside or out, of a ritual division: of roughest
masonry and most primitive construction.   There is seldom
anything of architectural interest in the building, which,
in the absence of records and often even of local tradition,
it is generally impossible to date.

It is the same regarding the sculptured slabs which are
often found within and around these old churches.   Very
few indeed have any inscription upon them, and rarely is
there any tradition as to whom they commemorate, the only
local information you receive with regard to them being
the invariable story that such and such a stone was
" brought " from Iona.   In all these tales the underlying
suggestion is that a certain hallowing of the graveyard
accrues from the possession of a stone stolen from the
sacred isle, but were all the stories true in the sense
implied, it would be impossible to account for any
monumental stones at all being left by now in Iona.   But
in another sense tradition, which is seldom baseless, may
be right in ascribing the origin of so many stones to Iona
—not, however, stolen from its graves, but sculptured in a
Celtic school of art which it is thought, not without
probability, once flourished there.   Certainly as you go
from one churchyard to another you find, as might be
expected, stones of varying merit, and some whose
sculpturing has more distinction and is better executed
than that of others.   It is these stones of superior design
and workmanship which possibly have emanated from
some mediæval school of Celtic craftmanship.

If it is difficult in all but a few cases to surmise the
age of these monumental stones, in the absence of all

information, it is next to impossible to determine the date of the buildings in which they are found; for so primitive is their structure that it suggests a greater antiquity than in most cases could possibly be claimed for them, more especially as the same type of building has persisted down to quite recent times.

I have been unable to obtain any clue as to the date of the old church of Kilmory of Arisaig further than an allegation of origin common in other districts—that it was one of seven churches built by some notorious chief to atone for his evil deeds.   In this case it is *Ailein nan Creach* (Allan of the forays) who gets the credit of being the benefactor.   This twelfth chief of Clan Cameron lived in the reign of James III., and, resorting to witchcraft —of all things—to determine a penance proper to atone for his evil life, was ordered to build seven churches, one for each of his forays.

This building is probably of no later date than the sixteenth century, and might well be earlier; but although it exhibits points of interest which are lacking in other similar buildings which yet have found chroniclers, this has lacked the recognition it deserves.   There seems to be no more than one extensive notice of Kilmory of Arisaig, and that an obvious and unilluminative article in a fairly recent volume of the *Proceedings of the Society of Antiquaries of Scotland*.   Therefore it will be instructive to go over the building carefully, noting not only its unique features but its general characteristics, since from these will be gained a very good idea of the style that is typical of the old churches throughout the Western Highlands and Islands.

The dimensions of the main building, built north-east and south-west instead of due east and west, are $51\frac{1}{2}$ feet by $24\frac{1}{2}$ feet,[10] the thickness of the walls averaging 3 feet, their height 10 feet $2\frac{1}{2}$ inches, while the eke, or small

---

[10] One wall, however, is nearly 2 feet longer than the other!

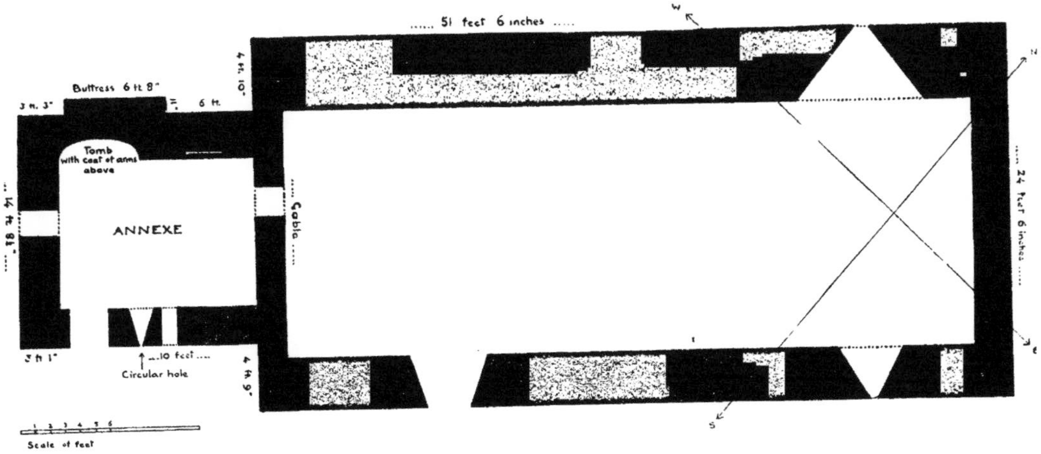

PLAN OF KILMORY CHURCH, ARISAIG.   by Isabel Bonus

24 feet 6 inches

51 feet 6 inches

Gable

4 ft. 10"

6 ft.

Buttress 6 ft 8"

3 ft. 3"

Tomb with Coat of arms above

ANNEXE

14 ft 8½"

4 ft. 9"

10 feet

Circular hole

3 ft. 1"

Scale of feet

separate compartment on the south-west, measures 14 feet
8½ inches by 16 feet.   With the exception of the north-east
—the ritual east wall—which is very badly broken down,
the other walls of the building are intact; and a gable
(on the eke side of which traces of a slate roof may yet
be seen) tops the wall which entirely separates the small
chamber from the church proper.   The impression given
by an inspection of the structure is that it was cleverly
contrived by some very ingenious amateur so restricted
both in regard to tools and materials that he had to use
just the stones that came to hand, undressed and unshaped
as he found them.   Examine in detail the wall through
which the eke is entered.   The largest stones, quite
irrespective of shape or bulk, have been used to rear the
corners of the building, and between them have been fitted
in, without any regularity but with extraordinary skill, the
most remarkable collection of odd stones of all shapes and
sizes as well as pieces of slate.   A rough mortar, containing
curious ingredients, has been generally employed, but in
some places pieces of slate and thin flakes of stone have
been used to fill up interstices; and here no mortar
appears.   I was told by a West Highland friend, a native
of another district, that these old masons used to boil their
lime in sea-water, and that this accounted for the enduring
qualities of the mortar made with it, but whether this is
likely to be true I have not the technical knowledge to say.
Examination of the eke in more detail only increases
admiration for the mason's ingenuity.   Look at the door,
2 feet 7½ inches wide and barely 4 feet high, though doubtless when it was constructed the ground was at a lower
level and consequently the entrance would have been
higher.   Two lengths of stone have been laid side by side
on top of the door-posts to make the lintel, above which is
a simple tympanum—an architectural feature which I think
is unique in the Western Highlands.   It is quite unadorned
by sculpture, and is surmounted by an erratic-looking arch,
constructed haphazard of roughly round and roughly

oblong small stones.   To the right of the door as you
stand outside, just above the level of the tympanum is a
window having the same unconventional characteristics as
the rest of the architecture, for it is made crookedly
through the thickness of the wall by four uneven blocks
of stone.   Below, set in the wall, just a few inches above
the present outside level of the ground is the most curious
and unique feature of the whole building.   This is a large
round stone, intact save at one side where a small piece
has been cleanly broken off, and having a circular hole
5 inches in diameter and 6 inches deep piercing the centre,
the whole suggestive of a quernstone.[11]

But before passing in to investigate this curious feature
on the other side, you remark the growth of ivy-leaved
toadflax and many varieties of tiny fern in crevices all over
the walls, whereby their picturesque and venerable appearance is greatly enhanced.

The annexe may be contemporary with the church
proper, but that it was the original building, in the nature
of a solitary's cell, on to which the larger structure was
afterwards built, seems precluded by the advance in
architecture which is certainly suggested by the tympanum
of the cell doorway—in contrast to the very primitive
entrance into the church.   And that the cell was an after-
thought rather than contemporary with the main building,
is suggested by the fact that it is without a door leading
into the church proper, as you at once notice when you go
within.   But, six feet above the present grass-grown level,
a window pierces this inner wall, so much out of the centre
of the gable—no unusual feature in Scotland—that there
is barely 2 feet of wall on one side of it.   Opposite, a third
window conforms to convention, and occupies the centre
of the wall.

Coming again to the most interesting feature of the eke,
when you look at the inside of the round pierced stone,

---

[11] I have seen these elsewhere incorporated in buildings, but never
associated with any such special feature as is seen here.

you find behind it an ordinary window opening, splayed to 2 feet 5 inches, having, 3 inches below the hole in the centre and 8 inches above the present ground level, a sill extending through the whole depth of the wall. Is this, then, a unique and original West Highland version of that old friend, the " low side " window, with its attendant unsolved problems? In the course of my West Highland wanderings, I have only come across one other chapel— that of S. Charmaig on Eilean Mor—where there has been any suggestion of a lychnoscope. But, with some differences, there are certain points of similarity in the two cases which, therefore, may help to elucidate the present problem. In the island chapel, the " low side " window is in its more usual position in the chancel, but in the north wall instead of (as more commonly) in that opposite, as here, where it is in the ritual south side. But both lychnoscopes are alike in one respect—they look in this case directly on to a tomb within, as well as on the graveyard without—in the case of S. Charmaig's, on to the reputed tomb of the founder : here on to that of one, if not more of a sept of Macdonalds— that of Morar.

Eliminating from all the theories regarding the purpose of the " low side " window those which the situation of this small circular opening rule out as obviously impossible, even allowing for an original lower level of ground, one conjecture only seems to find any support—a conjecture which is strengthened by the conjunction above noted as common both to Kilmory of Arisaig and Eilean Mor. Surely the only possible purpose this unique contrivance can have served is in the capacity of a lantern having some association with the dead who lie buried on either side of it? There are instances in some English parishes of such lanterns whose purpose, as some say, was to symbolise by their continual burning the Church's prayer that " light perpetual " might shine upon the Faithful Departed, or, as others suppose, to keep evil spirits away from the churchyard.   In the absence of any other evidence in this case, with with some knowledge of the Western Highlands, I am inclined to adopt the second as the more probable interpretation.   This theory would fit in equally well if the eke were proved originally to have been either a cell built as a convenient lodging for the priest or the equivalent of a chantry chapel, where, indeed, quite possibly the priest who served it might also have lived. Against the chantry supposition the fact that above the altar tomb a monumental slab records a date—1641— obviously later than can attach to the building itself, in no wise militates; for it by no means follows that there was no tomb below the slab prior to 1641.   If any one is inclined to demur " But why use a quernstone for the construction of a lantern?" I suggest that it is simply a further example of the builder's ingenuity of making use of a quernstone at hand to secure, by its small circular hole, the maximum of protection for a naked light where glazed windows were unknown.   It is impossible to verify this theory, however, by searching for traces of smoke, because the original ceiling of stone has been plastered over.

Above the altar (?) tomb (on to which the lychnoscope looks), the curious pyramidical slab, with a parallelogram on its flattened apex, deserves attention by reason of its curious heraldry.   This tomb, recessed into the wall under a circular arch, belongs to the Macdonalds of Morar, whose matriculated coat-of-arms is sculptured on a red sandstone slab, dated 1843, above the arch.   Somewhat of a puzzle is presented by the fact that this tomb has an exact counterpart in that of the prince of pipers, Raonall Mac Ailein Oig, in the ruined church of Kildonan on Eigg, for both have the same date, 1641.   But the identity of the person buried here appears to be unknown, nor is any altogether satisfactory interpretation forthcoming of the curious cypher below the date here.   The letters, most of which are intertwined, appear to be MAIRG (or C) ML, but I have failed in every attempt to decipher the designation thus cryptically conveyed.

Between the matriculated coats-of-arms of the Clan-ranald and Morar families there is but a slight difference, the " dexter arm in armour embowed grasping a sword " on the Clanranald crest being absent from that of Morar. This coat-of-arms also shews the oak-tree in the fourth quarter with the " eagle displayed " surmounting it, as appears on the Clanranald shield. The curious old coat-of-arms on the Kilmory tomb is, like its twin of Kildonan, Eigg, innocent both of any attempt at quarterings— properly so called—or of any indication of tinctures. The marshalling of the charges, however, so suggestive of a promiscuous peppering, finds a parallel in the earliest engraved shield of the Clanranald arms. It is interesting to note that in these earliest examples the charges occupy different quarters—just as they do on this tomb—to those in which they are now found; and thus the engravings help in the elucidation of the very unconventionally executed charges of this sculpture.

In the first quarter there is a sinister hand grasping a cross unknown to heraldry, but of a type very common in West Highland sculpture. In the second quarter, the quaint-looking, man-faced animal, with a foliated tail, obviously does duty for the lion rampant. Between these two comparatively conventional quarterings on the Kilmory slab, there are two stray " charges," suggestive of free attempts fitted in to fill up an odd space. The topmost is a bird—more like the head of a mediæval lectern than anything else—but it is probably the forerunner of the eagle subsequently displayed both in the Clanranald and Morar arms. The lower looks like a big thistle-head, but, taken in conjunction with the bird above, it may be the sculptor's substitute, in the licence he allowed himself, for the oak-tree which should be shewn. The tree, springing from the base and reaching to the top of the shield, and a bird on its highest branches, on the early engraved shields above-mentioned, are probably the charges of which these two fanciful renderings are the equivalent.

The salmon of the Macdonald arms is, however, altogether omitted from this spirited native conception of the Morar coat-of-arms, but the castle, which has now disappeared from the field of the matriculated shield to surmount it as the crest, is here, more in the likeness of a chess pawn, found in the fourth quarter.

Since there is nothing further of general interest to be remarked either within or without the eke, except a small stone basin, probably for holy water, the church proper now claims attention.   As regards the structure itself, there is little to be noticed.   The door occupies the position usual in West Highland churches, *i.e.*, in the ritual south wall near the west end.   There are only two windows, and they are opposite each other—as close up against the east wall as they could be.   This was obviously to give as much light as possible to the sanctuary as the only part of the church where books would be used.   The outside openings average from six feet to eight feet across, but inside both are splayed to a width of five feet and nine feet respectively.   On the sill of the north window rests the stone basin, the font, which is of oval instead of the usual round shape.

Before detailing any of the gravestones which pave the ground, a few general remarks are necessary.   The reason why so many throughout the Western Highlands are found mutilated is that they have come to be appropriated by natives, whose practice seems to be to use one stone, transferring it if necessary to a fresh grave, for all the family burials consecutively.   Thus it is quite common to hear the people refer to one particular sculptured slab as, let us say, " Sandy M'Nab's stone."

One fragment of slate at Kilmory of Arisaig possessed such unique features that, in consequence of these having been impressed upon its well-intentioned custodian, he put in hand its " restoration."   When I first saw this slab, it was propped up against the wall: the second time it was prone on the ground, a prey to anyone's feet.   Then

MOSAIC AT KILMORY OF ARISAIG

the worst fate of all befell the stone, for, with the intention of securing its preservation, the luckless fragment was given over into a mason's hands. He prepared a concrete bed for it, and then, evidently wishing to make a complete job of it, he gathered together sundry other fragments of stones, and, wholly indifferent to the fact that they belonged to other slabs, pieced them in to make complete his parallelogram. In consequence, the " restoration " looks like a mixture of jig-saw puzzles of which no two pieces belong to the same set. Of this painful medley, it is the upper half and major portion in which are to be found the most interesting features. Under two foliated canopies are represented, on one side the Crucifixion, and, divided from it by an uncommon sword, a vested priest, and then a second sword like the first. The hilts of these weapons terminate in the crocketings of the canopies, and the guards are so short as to suggest the Roman rather than any other type of sword.

There is no tradition whatever regarding the identity of the ecclesiastic represented by this stone, and I have tried in vain to discover if he be bishop or priest, abbat or prior. In the absence of any old monastic foundations near, presumably one of the secular clergy is thus commemorated. If, as I think improbable, the two vestments shewing beneath the chasuble be intended for a dalmatic and tunicle, a bishop would be indicated; but if the representation is of an albe—abnormally short—over a cassock, the figure is that of a priest. But, in either case, as is not uncommon in the Western Highlands, where details of dress are often lacking on sculptured stones, the representation of Eucharistic vestments is incomplete, neither maniple or stole being shewn. I have sometimes wondered as I have looked on these representations if they may not, after all, depict local actuality instead of — as is generally assumed — unintentional omissions due to the sculptor's carelessness. So ingrained are the casual habits of the natives that it is not at all unlikely that they may even have affected usual ecclesiastical use and wont.

In this representation, the priest is holding the chalice instead of the wafer more usually found on English monumental brasses, but it is his extraordinary head-dress that is the absolutely unique feature of the whole representation. Indeed, the problem of what it is intended to represent is so baffling that it only confirms my conjecture that the West Highlands had sometimes in fact, if never in print, a " Use " of their own. The head-dress resembles nothing so much as a modern City of London policeman's helmet worn sideways on. It can scarcely by any conceivable distortion be a local variant of a mitre or ecclesiastical cap, and I can only hazard, on the " West Highland Use " theory, that, just as one has seen eccentric Anglican clergy of a certain school appear at outdoor functions vested in a surplice and top hat or wide-awake, so here a priest has been wont incongruously to don with the sacred vestments a layman's hat of the period. That, in keeping with the sword on either side of the figure, it might be a helmet is improbable, not from any antecedent objection, but simply because there is no affinity that I can trace to any helmets found on the many sculptured stones of warriors, since these helmets are invariably brimless. It has, however, something in common with the copotain hat which, in endless varieties, was in vogue from 1558 for over a century; and since the slab may well belong to the early part of this period, this appears to be the least unsatisfactory of any conjecture as to the nature of this curiously unpriestly head-dress.

It is not usual in these sculptures for the Crucified to be shewn hanging on a plain Latin cross as in this case, and some features of the fragment which have been so absurdly made into a mosaic are quite as unusual. One shews the arm of a warrior drawing a bow, and if, as seems apparent from what remains, he is represented in a kilt, this is almost, if not quite, unique on these monuments. There is documentary evidence for the curious fact that with the Highlanders the use of the bow and *dorlach* (quiver) as a weapon of warfare continued as late as 1688, when bows and arrows were used in the last clan battle fought at Mulroy. It is interesting to note in connection with archery that, whereas the Saxon drew the bow to his ear, the Celt drew it only to the breast, as appears on these stones. On the same fragment of slate, there is a cadaver, or corpse, also unique, probably introduced as an emblem of mortality; while below is a common representation of a hound chasing a hind.

With regard to the frequent occurrence on these West Highland stones of hunting scenes, it has been conjectured that they were intended to convey a symbolical meaning. The conversion of sinners being the pursuit proper to a Christian, "we pursue them with dogs when we arouse their fears by the preaching of the Word," says the *Hortus Deliciarum*—a twelfth century MS. But I am quite persuaded that the Celtic artists, even if they had ever heard of such a treatise, simply intended to convey that the man whose tombstone they were sculpturing was "a mighty hunter" by surrounding him with spirited representations of the chase, a familiar scene with which he would be most naturally associated.

There is a great similarity between the subject of the fragment already described and that of the only other stone that claims attention. On this stone, also three parts gone, the drawing of the dogs (one of which is most curiously confined by a leash) and of the stag is peculiarly graceful, which is more than can be said of the flat-capped head of the archer beside them. There is no more than the top of his bow left, and, below, the faint indication of the pommel and a quillon of a large sword running down the centre of the stone.

Of the one complete sculptured stone, the design is so weathered that it is seen much clearer in a rubbing than in actuality. It has a foliated square cross design at the head, a long sword running down the centre, and round about a beautiful foliated design springing from the tail of a beast on the left side of the hilt. Than swords, no design is more universal on these stones, and it is thought that their variety of details may be accounted for by the supposition that in every case the weapon shewn was an actual representation of the sword used by the person commemorated.

The swords shewn on the monuments are apparently the simple *claidheamh lann,* or *cliaranach* of the Highlander— perhaps in some cases the *claidheamh caol,* the small, narrow, or slender sword, in contradistinction to the *claidheamh mor,* the great double-handed sword. This, the true claymore, is peculiar to Scotland, and, coming into use about the close of the fifteenth century, seems to have been last used at the battle of Killiecrankie in 1689, when it was wielded with fearful effect. So big was the claymore, that it was carried slung over the back, the hilt rising above the shoulder, whence it could be readily grasped and drawn by both hands. A broken slab on Iona is the only one I have come across which thus represents the claymore. Their general characteristics were the depressed guard, as usually seen on the single-handed swords of the monuments, and quillons having quatrefoil ringed terminals.

What is now incorrectly called the claymore is really the basket-hilted sword—quite a distinct and a much later variety. The special distinctions of the sword shewn on the monuments, besides their guards depressed to an acute angle, is their five or seven lobed pommel, their quillons terminating sometimes like those found on the claymore, sometimes in knobs or bulbs.

Leaving Kilmory and passing out through the church-yard, the road on the left leads over the swelling moorland to Morar, but I will not here attempt any description such as can be given of a walk which has few equals and no rivals—none certainly on evenings of sunset which recall

the words of Ewan MacLachlan in his " Mavis of the
Clan ":

" The sun is on his flashing march. his golden hair abroad,
    It seems as on the mountain side of beams, a furnace glowed."

PART VII

MEMORIES OF MORAR

CRAGGY mountains, magnificent in naked strength;
between them the unquiet waters of a great loch, island
studded; wild moorland tracks climbing up by the lochside past rude crofting hamlets; a short length of swiftly-
flowing river flinging itself over falls where salmon leap;
lower again, other falls plunging heavily with foam and
roar into the sea; sands of silver; heather-clad headlands
and hillsides, all fragrant with bog-myrtle; and out at sea
the islands, Eigg, Rum, and Skye: such is Morar in barest
outline. Of the colour and beauty with which she is
clothed, of the soul that is enshrined in her, of the voice
with which she speaks, nothing can be said. Her voice
must be heard, she herself must be seen, and the faculty of
the inner sight be exercised to gain any adequate picture of
Morar.

Morar's loch, eleven and three-quarters miles long, and
the deepest in Great Britain, is said to be inhabited by a
monster called *Morag* which only makes an appearance to
foretell the death of a Macdonald or a Gillies. The loch,
too, is not without historical interest. In 1707, the Roman
Catholic Bishop Gordon established his headquarters here
during his visitation of the Arisaig district, when he confirmed nearly 3,000 people. When, as a result of his
report, the district was made a separate vicariate in 1731,
Hugh Macdonald (of the Morar family), as its first bishop,
continued to reside on one of the islands. The crafty
traitor, Simon Fraser of Lovat, at the age of eighty, in

June, 1746, sought refuge here, a victim of gout and asthma as well as—at last—his many coat-turnings. He thought himself secure from capture on the island since the bishop owned the only boat on the loch. But reckoning with his host on this occasion did not serve him, for he failed to reckon with his hunters—resourceful sailors, who, from their man-of-war out at sea, easily towed a boat over to the loch. Lovat managed to escape from the island, but not from the sailors, who captured him further up the loch side.[12] The bishop's house on the island was burnt to the ground by the sailors, but in 1768 the Roman Catholic authorities readjusted matters by building a college at Buorblach, at the mouth of the Morar river. Here many a " heather priest " was trained until, in 1778, the college was transferred to Samalaman in Moidart. From these priestly traditions, and from the fact that no Protestant preacher had ever thrown the apple of discord within its bounds, this district used to rejoice in the name of *Mòrair bheannaichte*, " blessed Morar," but it can no longer do so now.

Morar is also associated with the wanderings of the Royal Fugitive. It was on the night of July 8th, 1746, that Charles, accompanied by John Mackinnon, walked from Mallaig to Macdonald of Morar's house at Glen-na-cross, shewn on the map by the side of the line about half a mile after it ceases to run parallel with the road to Arisaig. Shortly before dawn the fugitives came in sight of the bothy in which Morar and his family had taken refuge after the burning of their house by the Hunnish Captain Ferguson. So touched was Morar's wife at the pitiful spectacle presented by the Prince whom, despite his unkempt and dishevelled appearance, she at once recognized, that she burst into tears. No trace of the bothy remains, and, despite several attempts, in each case defeated by

[12] It is a somewhat curious comment on this incident that the ownership of Morar should be now claimed by the present chief of Clan Fraser— Lord Lovat—of whom all Highlanders are justly proud.

atrocious weather and worse bogs, I have never yet succeeded in gaining the cave at Scamadale on Loch Morar
side, where, after partaking of the best meal Morar was
able to offer, Charles, for greater security, went to rest for
a while.   According to the map, the cave must have been
about two miles distant from the bothy, and is said to be
situate in the face of a cliff twenty-five feet high, having a
white beach to the west of it.   The refuge itself is described
as being small but deep, and well suited to concealment.
According to a photograph, alleged to be of this cave, a
dip into the ground beneath a small ledge of shelving rock,
with high heather in the foreground, is suggested.   It
was from this cave that Charles, accompanied by John
Mackinnon and a local guide, went on the same day to
Borrodale, travelling across the Mointeach Mhor.

These few details exhaust its historical associations, but
more than any other place in the Highlands, Morar is
associated in my mind with happy intercourse with the
incomparable gentlefolk of nature, whom the tourist
invasion, with its materialistic appraisement of everything
in terms of money, is doing its best irretrievably to ruin.
Some fifteen years ago, when I first knew it, Morar was
unknown to the tourist and the ordinary holiday-maker,
i.e., the person to whom any " holiday place " is no more
than a change of scene and air.   It is thanks to this genus
that the modern Highlander has gained a reputation for
grasping greed, since with the tourist's insistence upon the
valuation of any courtesy as well as every service—however
freely rendered—in terms of tips, the Highlander has
literally thrust upon him a character utterly alien, for all
his poverty, to his essentially generous nature.   The advent
of the railway has also been responsible for other modern
advances.   While it cannot be denied that improvements in
housing were a crying need, yet one must deplore the
passing of the picturesque primitive cottages of the natives,
notably of the thatch, in favour of corrugated or tarpaulin
roofs, and other equally hideous features.   Certainly, as

far as I have seen in the Highlands, housing improvements are synonymous with irredeemable ugliness—surely a wholly unnecessary alliance. At Morar, in the little hamlets up the loch-side, and indeed quite near the hotel, there are still some of the primitive drystone cottages to be seen, with their rudely turfed and thatched roofs.[13] Beside each one grows an elder or rowan tree, to keep off the evil eye, for throughout the Highlands the natives, wholly irrespective of the religion they profess, are not without relics of pagan superstition, being careful, for instance, to go *deiseil,* or sunwise, in leaving the house or in walking round anything. In this practice can be traced remains of sun-worship.

No cottage was more characteristic of the Western Highlands or more perfectly epitomized its domestic habits than that whose ruined walls may still be seen in a glorious woodland setting on the Arisaig road, about half a mile beyond the lower falls of the Morar river. Looking across the white sands to the rugged mountains, it stood on the roadside by a little burn, cheerfully dancing down to the sea between clusters of tall ferns and yellow water flags. A window on either side of the only door gave the cottage its sole light. These, indeed, and the old bottomless herring-barrel, set askew, for a chimney on the top of the withy thatch, were the only points distinguishing this and other cottages outwardly from the bothy where the cattle are housed. Crossing the burn by a plank, an irregular pathway led up to a rude pavement of stones before the door, where a large family of ducks and hens were invariably gathered in the old days. These fowls were often companioned by a lamb, a cat, and a smooth-haired collie, as well as by some members of the fisherman's family. Here the mother would set her washing-tub,

---

[13] Dr. Ross, the architect-author and authority, has recorded that, as recently as 1888, he had seen such roofs taken off in the morning to have their peat-begrimmed interior washed by the rain and replaced the same evening. Presumably the uncovered interior was washed at the same time!

A COTTAGE THAT WAS AT MORAR

boiling the water for it in a big three-legged pot placed over the fire on a bank of a burn. The peat used as fuel for the household was stacked by the side of the cottage under such shelter as the eaves afforded.

Under the beneficent shade of the elder tree before the cottage, the grandmother would sit busily employed trans-forming fleece—washed, dried, and teased out—into hanks of woollen yarn. For all our conversation was necessarily very restricted, since she had no English whatever, I have seldom met a more interesting Highland woman than this good-looking *cailleach* (old woman), whose pleasant in-telligent face and smooth grey hair, neatly parted in the centre, was always becomingly framed in a close-fitting, frilled, white cap. The first time I. saw her she was calling " *Pic, pic,*" for the hens to come and be fed—birds which used to be considered unclean by the Highlanders. She was scattering pieces to them outside the hen-house—a low, ramshackle, thatched shanty, which, judging from the many protruding garments, seemed to serve as a wardrobe as well. A more usual construction for fowls is made of turf walls covered by a disused inverted boat.

As the *cailleach* sat there out in the sunshine, I have watched her at every process concerned with the production of the dyed yarn, which is comprised in the Gaelic word *calanas*. First of all, she would do the carding, using two squares of wood studded with small iron teeth, between which small quantities of the wool, after it has been sorted and washed, are placed, and combed out by drawing the carders by their handles in opposite directions. Then would come the spinning, and it was fascinating to watch the wooden wheel as it went whirling round with the action of the *cailleach's* foot on the treadle. Next the yarn so produced was wound into hanks by hand on the *crois iarna,* the yarn-hanker, or cross, two pieces of wood roughly fashioned in cross shape.

In this stage the *cailleach* would dye the yarn, obtaining the colours from native vegetable sources, supplemented chiefly by chemicals, such as alum, to fix the dyes, though the fir club moss often served this purpose. Bog myrtle yields a beautiful yellow; heather, gathered just before it comes into flower, a dark green; whilst the elder, in combination with alum, gives a rich blue. Different varieties of lichen (*crotal*) produce fine shades of brown and reds, and it is such ancient native dyes which produce the correct colourings for the various clan tartans. The yarn would be left to steep for varying periods in pots of different dyes, many of which had to be kept air-tight, and afterwards the hanks were hung up to dry on the nearest tree.[14]

If the *cailleach* wanted to use any of the wool for knitting, she employed the *crois thachrais,* a very quaint but cunning wooden device of revolving cross laths set on a pedestal having a three-legged base. Rude pegs stuck out at an acute angle about a foot from the end of each of the four cross pieces, and over these the hank of yarn was placed, so that when the bars were set revolving, the wool was very quickly wound into a ball.

The cottage, for all the considerable family it accommodated, like the generality of its class, had only two rooms, one on either side of the door, with a bed in each. In one of these the father and two boys slept; the kitchen bed the mother, grandmother, and three girls, subsequently augmented by a baby, occupied. The floor, generally of hard, beaten earth, was in this case of paving stones, quite bare—unlike the walls which, in the kitchen, were papered with newspapers. Over the open fire, round which a supply of stacked peats served as a replenishable fender, hung at the end of a chain the *slabhruidh,* the big hook from which the kettle or pot, as occasion required, was suspended; and round the hearth the chirping of crickets made ceaseless music. After a short time has been spent inside such a

---

[14] In other districts, the dyeing takes place immediately after the washing of the wool. This is placed in a pot alternately with layers of the dye— *e g.*, *crotal*—and after boiling water is poured upon the sandwich thus produced, the whole is kept on the boil till the colour desired results.

room, where the open rafters are black with the smoke of years, and peat reek is the constant atmosphere, one no longer marvels at the sere and wrinkled faces of even young men and women, though a great addiction to the drinking of tea, kept on the hob continuously stewing in its leaves, is no doubt a contributory cause.

In older days the crofters had but two meals a day: in the morning barley or oaten bread, milk and cheese, and in the evening mutton, beef, or venison, bread and fish. Before the time of whisky, their beverage was *blannd*— whey kept maturing for several years—or birch cordial.

The master of the household, a fisher, was a fine stalwart man, and I never saw him without regretting that he did not wear the national dress. The main cause of the kilt being so very rarely seen now amongst the humbler Highlanders is its present price, wholly prohibitive to the poor, though its disuse was in the first place due to the cruelly repressive Lowland legislation that followed the '45. For thirty-five years, the wearing of the kilt or of any part of the Highland dress, or of tartan, or the playing of the pipes, was made a penal offence, punishable in some cases by transportation. It was after the repeal of the Act of Proscription that the Highland dress, as described in a previous part of this chapter, suffered its present mutilation, both in itself and its various accompaniments— a mutilation due largely to ignorance.

The fisherman was a Macdonald—one of the numerous families of the clan, which happily is still largely repre-sented in its old territory. Indeed, so many Macdonalds are there, that to distinguish one from another is not always an easy matter, and, in order to avoid mistakes of identity, it is quite common for individuals to be known by nick-names descriptive of some characteristic or peculiarity. Thus, here an elderly man of the Macdonalds who, in his youth was remarkable for his black hair, is still universally known as " Black John " for all his hair is now grey. His wife used to be our laundry woman, and, in the cottage adjoining hers, there lived another Mrs. Macdonald, who also took in washing.   Since our custom was to leave our bundle to be called for by Black John or his wife at a meeting place common to these two Macdonald families, we had to take precautions that our washing did not stray into the wrong hands.   Consequently one day, seeing no one about when I went to deliver over the bundle, I left it carefully addressed to " Mrs. Black John."   The next day I met Black John in a greatly agitated state, fingering the paper on which I had written his wife's name.   Perfectly politely he questioned me as to how I came to address his wife as " Mrs. Black John," a style, he protested, she had never received in her life before.   With every apology, seeing I had unwittingly given great offence by extending his own nickname to his wife, I gave Black John the obvious reason for so doing.   " Uch, I wass Black John right enough; but my wife, she wass Mistress Mactonald. Ta other wan, she wass only ta weedy (widow) Mactonald —not Mistress Mactonald at aall."

Angus, our landlord, was another characteristic Highland type—a good-natured and easy-going fellow, with a very hazy grasp of English.   On one occasion he confided to me that he had never worn either " niggers " or the kilt; and, after he had announced triumphantly the purchase of a mare, and I had asked what he called her, he, misunderstanding the question, informed me that a mare " wass chust a she-horse."   Then again, when I asked him if there was any thatching in progress in the district, since I would like to see the work being done, he looked puzzled; so I said, " Is there any cottage about here being thatched at present?"   At once his face cleared, and he was quick to apologise: " Uch, you must excuse me.   I wass not understanding what you wass asking.   I did think it wass *thatching eggs* you wass meaning!"

It was Angus who took me out to the peat-hag and shewed me how the native fuel was cut.   In May the people begin the work that is to provide them with firing through-

CUTTING PEATS

out the year, and the payment of 2s. 6d. secures to each crofter the allotment of a piece of ground, from which he may dig all the peat he requires. If there is a coarse overgrowth of vegetation, such as sturdy heather or bog-myrtle, this is burnt previous to peeling the peats, *i.e.,* removing the turf from the surface. For this purpose a two-handled implement, called a flauchter spade, is used. This is a turf-cutter having a big heart-shaped iron blade, and at the other extremity a cross-bar about half the length of the long shaft. After the peat has been laid bare by the turf-spade, the *tarraisgein,* or peat-cutting spade, comes into use. This implement has a wooden shank, slightly curved at the end to form a handle, and the cutter itself consists of two long and narrow iron blades, one shorter than the other, set at right angles. The spade is forced by the foot downwards into the peat, of which it cuts an oblong piece about a foot long. The peats, thus cast, are thrown to right and left of the trenches from which they are cut, being afterwards set up end to end in small piles, often turned, to dry. They are then built up into the rectangular stacks with the rounded tops which are such a feature of the Highland landscape in the summer.

From the stack on the peat-hag to the peat store under the lee of the cottage, the peats are carried in large creels borne on the back, generally by women, many of the elder of whom still wear the *brèid.* This, the old badge of the married woman, is a white square handkerchief of linen, worn three-cornerwise over the head, with the ends to the back. Unfortunately, the picturesque *stim,* or snood, the fillet binding the hair round the forehead to indicate a maiden, seems to have fallen into disuse as entirely as the old female garment, the *arisaid,* which—less ample but worn much in the same fashion as the belted plaid—was equally as picturesque and as serviceable in all kinds of weather.

As the original occupants of the first modern cottage built in Morar, we enjoyed all the primitive experiences of

life that the Highlands can offer.   Not so much as a loaf of
bread was obtainable in Morar itself, and we therefore were
dependent for supplies upon Mallaig, two and three-quarter
miles distant.   It was more the novelty of bestriding such
a steed as Katie than any delusion that the journey would
thereby be expedited, that I decided to ride the " She-
horse " into Mallaig for shopping one morning.   Since she
had spent thirteen and a half years carrying wood up to
the observatory on Ben Nevis, and was cow-like in girth as
well as in progress, you can judge of her desirability as a
steed.   And before saddling her with a harness in which
there was more rope than leather, it was a case of searching
the hills to find her.   Once mounted, I soon found that
ambling was all that might be expected of Katie, and that
apparently her previous owner had been accustomed to call
a halt, presumably for conversation, whenever he met
anyone on the road.   We soon encountered a few children
on their way to school, and at once Katie drew up, nor
could I get her to move on for quite a few minutes.   It
was the same when the train passed, and, indeed, on every
subsequent occasion when we met anyone on the road.
As I had several purchases to make, I had slung over my
back a leather satchel into which I packed various
groceries, including a goodly supply both of candles and
butter.   On the way home Katie, unhorselike, ambled more
leisurely than ever, but, as it was a very hot day, sitting
thus exposed to the blazing sun was to me some compensation for the dawdling journey.   The cottage was
reached long after the time it would have taken me to walk
there, and, after dismounting, I unslung my satchel and
handed it to one of my waiting friends.   As she unfastened
it, I heard sundry exclamations beginning, " What on
earth—— " and, turning to discover if I could answer, I
beheld, to my dismay, a greasy conglomeration of grocery
packages, mixed up in a mass of invertebrate candles.
Then my arm was seized, and my back examined, with the
result that it was discovered that what butter had not

been absorbed by the satchel itself and its contents, had spread itself over my clothing.

Another characteristic incident. I occupied a small bedroom on the ground floor, and one night I was roused from very sound slumber by a great noise of snorting, which seemed to emanate from my very bedside. Starting up, I found myself face to face with a long dark head looking through the open window. It was the " She-horse," who, having no restrictions imposed upon her wanderings, had upon this occasion elected to patrol our isolated cottage. Aroused by the noise she made on the pebbles, the others were in some alarm, thinking we had been invaded by gipsies—never welcome visitors in the Highlands.

While we generally procured fish from Macdonald the fisherman at Morar, when he could not give us any, we used to try to obtain a supply from Mallaig; and the following is a letter we received on one such occasion. I give it verbatim as a specimen of English as she is written by a real Highlander:

" *Dear friend you was wanting up the AC for the fish which I sent you I may tell you that you got 1/- and too sixpence that is 2/- altogether and you was telling me of not keeping my promise but I may tell you when it is as storm weather you will not get fish wherever you are I am your truell, Mr G. D——, Mallaig.*"

The maiden who was supposed to be our " attendance " made up in natural charm, both of appearance and manner, what she lacked in memory and domestic capability—practically everything. Her idea of cooking extended to everything eatable; for when we offered her a share in some strawberries we had sent us, she asked if they should be fried or stewed. But forgetfulness was her chief distinction. One morning she was reproached because the boots, left outside the door for cleaning, had never been

touched.   With the smile that was so disarming, she
answered, " Uch, well, Mem, it would pe chust ta same
if it wass your purse you wass leaving apout.   No wan
here would pe touching her."

The short length of road from Morar to Mallaig gives
glorious views of the stretch of the Skye hills, but Mallaig
itself no longer merits any attention.   *Ichabod* is written
all over it, for its interests lie all in the past.   For, about
4 A.M. on Saturday, July 5th, 1746, Prince Charlie landed
from Elgol in Skye, with the faithful chief of Mackinnon,
just a very short distance from the harbour that now com-
petes for first place amongst the monstrosities which have
successfully combined to ruin the once picturesque old
fishing village.   Modern aggressive buildings, hideously
incongruous in their setting, are an affront to the natural
beauties of " the bay of the agreement."   Indeed, so
contemptuous have those responsible for " opening up "
Mallaig shewn themselves for the place itself that the
builders have never even troubled to do any clearing up
after their work.   So littered up is the poor little hamlet
with all sorts of rubbish imported in the wake of modern
progress, that a dirtier or more untidy place can hardly be
found in the Highlands.   In fact, one only goes to Mallaig
in order to leave it for some place freer from the incursions
of excursionists and all that they bring in their train.

P.S. on some Highland weapons—

The points requisite for the best archer's outfit were:
" A bow of yew from Easragan; a shaft of French yew,
feathered from an eagle of Loch Treig, and with a head
made by the smith Mac Caillirin."   Highland smiths produced splendidly tempered blades without the aid of fire.
These were known as *claidheamhan fuar-iarunn, i.e.*, cold
iron swords, beaten into shape by a succession of rapid
blows from the hammer instead of being forged in the
ordinary way. .

CHAPTER II

THE ISLE OF MIST

" My heart is yearning to thee, O Skye,
Dearest of islands!"

———

PART I

ARMADALE AND AROUND

IN the Ossianic rendering of its name, the Isle of Skye is *Eilean a' Cheo,* the " Isle of Mist," and who that has watched the mists slowly veiling the crests of the Coolin, or bathed in the glow of sunset, swathing the hills about, does not appreciate its aptness and beauty? But the word Skye comes from the Gaelic *sgiath,* a wing, and has reference to the shape of the island, which puts out " wings " in all directions, so much so that there is no point more than four miles distant from the sea. The island is the largest of the Inner Hebrides—a word, as in so many cases, due to a misreading, in this instance of the classical *Hebudes.* To the Celts they were the *Innsegall,* or the " islands of the foreigners," because in the Norse occupation. They were known to the Norsemen as the Sodreys (hence Sodor) or South Isles, to distinguish them from the Orkneys or Nordereys.

Skye is divided longitudinally, broadly speaking, into three clan territories, mainly between the Macdonald and the Macleod, with Strath on the east coast from Portree to Lochalsh that is the country of the Mackinnons, *i.e.,* " sons of the fair born." For all they are one of the Clan Alpin federation, as hereditary marshals of the Lords of the

Isles and custodians of the standards of weights and measures, the Mackinnons were thus vassals of the Lords of the Isles, and as such held the town of Duisdalebeg, near Isle Ornsay.   Royalist and Jacobite to the core, their devoted services, as in the case of many another loyal clan, cost them their country; and since 1765, Strath has become largely Macdonald territory owing to the poverty of the Mackinnons.   Chiefs of Macdonald and Macleod still hold sway in Skye, though in the case of the Chief of Sleat, it is little more than a foothold, the fourth Lord Macdonald having sold large portions of the family inheritance to satisfy his creditors.   The Macalisters, a small clan, and the first to branch from the Macdonalds, used to own a small part of Strathaird, but it seems that this is usually accounted as practically belonging to the Mackinnon territory.

Many are the times, and often long has been the time that a friend and myself have waited upon the pier at Mallaig for the boat to bear us over the sea to Skye.   Prior to our first stay at Armadale, the first port of call on Skye, we were at Glenfinnan, and wired from there to enquire if the Hotel could take us in.   We could not understand why we had to wait so long—a matter of four hours in pre-war days—for an answer, Armadale being only five miles across from Mallaig, and Mallaig only an hour's run in the train from Glenfinnan.   But we had forgotten the complex telegraphic touring system thought good enough for the Highlands by the dictating Lowland postal authorities. Upon enquiry, we found that our wire had been transmitted in the usual course back to Fort William, from there to Glasgow, then to Inverness, and finally to Kyle of Lochalsh before it could cross the water to Armadale.

Ardvasar, still retained for the postal address, is a Celtic name, and the contiguous Armadale is Norse.   These names aptly serve to illustrate the history of the island, where Norse and Celtic characteristics are still found alike in the people and in the place names.   The racial difference is traceable yet in the tall, fair-haired, blue-eyed Skyemen and in the short, dark islander with high cheek bones and large mouth.

It was at Armadale where, after parting from the Prince, and on a visit to her mother, that Flora Macdonald was arrested and taken on board the *Furnace* without being allowed to take farewell of Mrs. Macdonald till three weeks later, when the ship was cruising off Sleat. Then Flora was allowed to land under escort with the proviso that she should not speak Gaelic.

The impression you get as you sail towards or along the shores of Sleat is one strikingly different from that of the greater part of Skye. The gently undulating slopes are bright in vivid green and yellow, suggesting a rich fertility of cultivation, and round Armadale Bay itself are beautiful woodlands, a rare and remarkable feature in Skye. Indeed, it is only when you walk southward from Ardvasar toward the Aird of Sleat that you gain any impression of that wild and rugged splendour which is generally and properly associated with Skye, for in this direction savage moorland soon replaces sylvan shades.

Set in the background of the woods, Armadale Castle, the seat of Lord Macdonald, looks more imposing from the sea than it does closer at hand, for it is a modern building in poor imitation of the Gothic, built in 1815 by the second Lord Macdonald, and lacks all interest except that which inalienably attaches to the family. From the stained glass of the hall window looks down an anachronistic representation of Somerled,[1] commonly accepted as the founder of Clan Donald, since he was the first Lord of the Isles, though the seannachies, or clan historians, trace its descent back to one *Conn Ceud Chatach,* or Conn of the Hundred Fights. Somerled, however, it is who is the clan hero,

[1] It seems more reasonable to identify the Celtic leader's name with the Gaelic *Somerhairle* (Samuel) than to derive it from that of his enemies the Vikings, who were known as Sumarlidi, or summer warriors, from the fact that their invasions were practically confined to the summer months.

for, despite much legend attaching to his name, he stands out clearly in history as a mighty warrior who laid the foundation of the clan's future greatness.

Skye tradition has it that Somerled, the youngest of four sons of Gillebride, cared only for the peaceful pursuits of the chase. One day, when he was fishing, there came to him the islanders seeking his leadership to deliver them from the Norsemen. His answer was, that only if he landed the salmon he was then after would he consent. Succeeding with great skill in his attempt, Somerled was enthusiastically acclaimed chief, and thus it is that a salmon finds a place in the Macdonald coat-of-arms, while the tree borne on the Clanranald shield may represent the sapling that Somerled is said to have plucked up by the roots on the same occasion.[2] It is not, however, Lord Macdonald, but Sir Alexander Wentworth Macdonald Bosville Macdonald, of the Isles, fourteenth Baronet of Sleat, the premier Baronet of Scotland, who is twenty-first Chief of the Macdonalds of Sleat, with his seat at Duntulm in the north of Skye. This came about in 1910, as the natural and inevitable sequence of the decision of the Court of Session in a curious question of legitimation, which had the effect of dispossessing Lord Macdonald of the chiefship and baronetcy. Since the honours in dispute centred round a peculiarity of Scots law, it may be interesting briefly to summarize the case.

In 1799, Godfrey Macdonald, second son of the late peer, first Lord Macdonald of Slate,[3] eloped in England

[2] The galley common to all the Macdonald arms is said to represent the vessel in which the three Princes Colla (thence Clan Colla for the Macdonald federation of clans), sixth in descent from Conn, sailed from Ireland to Scotland. Likewise the cross crosslet fitchy, originally carried in the hands of pilgrims and stuck in the ground before them when they, as devout worshippers, rested, is said to be conferred on the Macdonalds by S. Columba in recognition of their help to him in his mission work.

[3] Although this peer took as the *caput* for the new barony the family designation of Sleat, this had to be fictitiously described as being in Antrim, the peerage being an Irish one.

with Louisa Mary, daughter of H.R.H. the Duke of Gloucester. According to Scots law, which then deemed mutual consent, or even the fact of two persons living openly. together as man and wife, to constitute valid matrimony, Godfrey married her. As his wife, she went with him to Ireland in the course of his military duties, and there a son was born to them. Some time after their return to England, however, on the ground of his prolonged residence in Ireland and England, doubt was cast upon the question of Godfrey's domicile which, according to Scots law, alone could render valid his marriage by mutual consent. In order, therefore, to regularize their marriage in the eyes of everyone, the religious ceremony, according to the rites of the English Church, took place at Norwich in 1803. Previously to the religious ceremony, however, three children had been born, and it was with reference to the position of these in relation to the ten born after the celebration of the marriage rites that the dispute over the baronetcy and chiefship arose. For Godfrey had succeeded as third Baron to his unmarried brother, the second Lord Macdonald. The succession to the Irish barony was never in dispute, for it was on quite another footing. The law of Ireland, like that of England, did not recognize as marriage that which the Scots law accepted as constituting such, and, therefore, only the children born after the marriage rites could succeed to an Irish peerage. But as Godfrey was by the Edinburgh Court of Session held to be of Scots domicile, all his children were accordingly pronounced legitimate in the estimate of the law of Scotland; wherefore to the eldest, hitherto treated as illegitimate, and to his heirs were awarded the succession to the Scottish honours and estates. It was left to the present Chief of Sleat and his wife thus to vindicate by legal pronouncement the wrong done to the first born of the eleventh Baronet and his heirs.

It was the Macdonalds of Sleat who, taking neither reward nor fee, touched with the right hand, while repeating a *duan,* or ode, for *glacach,* a swelling of the hand. This complaint was in consequence known as " the Macdonald's disease," and the charm from which the power is alleged to have emanated is said to have been given by some foreigner to the Lords of the Isles. Various other qualities attributed to the Macdonalds generally are found in Gaelic proverbs. There is none more complimentary in Nicholson's lengthy list than that which estimates the quality of their energy, asserting " The Macdonalds are best at the end of the day," and amongst three proverbial rarities is " a Macdonald without cleverness."

The coat-of-arms of the chief of Sleat, like that of many another, has undergone considerable changes from time to time. In his " In Praise of Sir Alexander Macdonald of Sleat," the bard Iain Lom writes thus :

> " Thy well-known and beloved cognisance
> Was the graceful galley, the lion, and the salmon,
> All on a field of laughing ocean waves!
> With the unblemished wild fig tree
> That never failed in fruit of large-heartedness and generosity!
> And the Red Hand of the race that never blenched in combat."

Now both the " wild fig tree " and the " red hand " (still found on the Glengarry shield) have disappeared from that of Sleat.

The sunsets, looking over to the broken, rocky fore-ground of the shore at Armadale and the mountains of the mainland, are amongst the finest to be seen in the western Highlands. Then, as you walk northwards, by an instantaneous transition you are straightway trans-ported, as it seems, from Skye to the quiet beauty of an English countryside, for you find yourself walking amidst a profusion of stately foxgloves, the like of which either for quantity or quality I have never seen elsewhere. Ferns follow you all the way as you pass onwards through the policies of the castle, and a flight of heron may help you to locate the heronry in the tops of a cluster of dead fir trees on the shore side of the road. Continuing in this

SUNSET AT ARMADALE, SKYE

direction, you may make a circular tour of twenty-one miles over the peninsula of Sleat and round by Ord on the further coast and back again, in which case you follow a most magnificent route, yet probably the least known in Skye. A little over a mile from the castle, you see a road that strikes inland, and you begin a climb which makes you sigh for eyes behind as well as in front of you.

The day on which I took the tramp was singularly beautiful even for Skye, where sunshine seems to have a unique value in transforming scenery, always remarkable, into something quite unearthly. But the large sheep-fank which on the left is a prominent feature of the landscape presented quite a mundane if homely scene, for the crofters were busy sheep-dipping, and the plaintive cries of the animals mingled with the forceful Gaelic of their shepherds. The first revelation of the natural magnificence of the road, however, comes when its summit is gained, for thence the broken crests of the Coolin are first visible. " Cuchullin Hills " is a name, like many another, invented by guide books for a range which is *not* called after the Celtic hero, but is possibly derived from the Gaelic *a' chuilionn,* that is " holly." And as you are arrested by the sight of their jagged peaks, you agree that their resemblance to a holly leaf set on edge may have been the reason for their naming.

The legend associating the Coolin with Cuchullainn carries its own refutation on the surface. It relates that the chief was sent to Skye to complete his training. To give evidence of his capabilities, he was required to walk across the island's " bridge of cliffs, as narrow as the hair of one's head, as slippery as the eel of the river, and as steep and high as the mast of a ship." This feat Cuchullainn accomplished at his first attempt. When evidence of the existence of such a bridge of cliffs in Skye (or, for the matter of that, anywhere else) is forthcoming, then we may believe it was called after the super-Blondin who so successfully negotiated it!

9

Standing by the shores of little Loch Dhughaill, the rugged splendour of Skye, as seen from this viewpoint, fills alike both eye and spirit. In the foreground, through the rough grass of the heather-decked moorland, countless boulders, thrusting through the ground, assert themselves: in the middle distance, too, they strew the landscape. But it is the distance that grips you—where, above the narrow line of emerald sea, rise the mountains, aloof and mysterious in their dim, shimmering outline. You may stand here for hours on such a day, and the silence will remain unbroken until you move to descend through a glen of birch trees, when the roar of the Gillean Burn— so suggestive of a noisy lad or *gille*—strikes upon your ear.

Soon the little crofting hamlet of Tarskavaig, on Loch Eishort, is spread out before you, and, as you stand feasting your eyes on the scene, you become conscious of a startling contrast between the near and the distant landscape. At your feet the green fields, gemmed with the gold of wild flowers; here and there white-coifed women work amongst them, their homes the old-world thatched cottages from which the blue peat reek lazily curls—it is a scene that leaves upon the memory a lasting impression of peace and aloofness from the tumult of the world. Beyond the dividing line of a calm sea, however, for all the sunshine of the day, in the underlying grimness of the distant mountains, there is the suggestion of latent force but lightly curbed and ready to break forth without warning—a force terrible in resistless fury. It is the eternal contrast between the elemental instincts of a barbaric age and the softening influence of a beneficent civilization, and it is a scene rather suggestive of a peaceful community living at the base of an unextinct volcano.

Passing over the green plain stretching inland from Tarskavaig, you come down on to the rough, wild, rock-strewn shore of Ganscavaig Bay. Here was built

Dunscaith Castle, the ancient stronghold of the Macdonalds of Sleat.

> " The blue firth stretched in front without a sail,
>   Huge boulders on the shore lay wrecked and strewn;
>   Behind arose, storm-bleached and lichen-pale,
>   Buttress and wall of stone."

The ruins, the walls of which are now reduced to a height of fifteen feet, rise gaunt, grim, and awe-inspiring on the summit of a menacing rock which, on three sides, springs sheer from the sea to a height of some eighty or ninety feet. On the fourth side a deep gully (or fissure) cuts the crag off from the land, and still there remain the side walls bridging the gap for the support of a roadway, which was probably thrown across as a drawbridge. These walls, unless of late origin, surely constituted a dangerous feature where the security of the fortress was concerned, for, discounting the advantage of a drawbridge, they would offer a permanent means of approach of great value to an enemy. Beyond the gully the short road rises abruptly to the castle, which must have been very strongly fortified, judging from the remains; and if you climb within, you can still discover traces of the dungeon and draw-well.

The naturally frowning aspect of the castle, heightened by the sternness of its setting against the Coolin, was emphasized when I saw it. It was low tide, and the grim skeleton of a ship, evidently driven to destruction on the rocks, lay at the foot of the stronghold, like prey at the feet of a lion. Indeed, Dunscaith is in every way a fitting scene for tragedies such as that which occurred in 1506 when the chief of the Macdonalds of Sleat (or *Clann Uisdean,* the family of Hugh) was Donald Galldach (*i.e.,* " the stranger," so called because he was born and bred in Caithness). This Donald was visited at Dunscaith by his illegitimate brother, Archibald Dubh, whom the chief greeted very courteously, shewing him every hospitality. After dinner, the host took his guest to see a new galley he had on the stocks, and Archibald, examining it, pretended to detect a faulty plank in the keel.   When the chief in concern bent down to look for himself, his treacherous brother drew his dagger and stabbed him fatally.

Then there is the tale of another visit, resulting in a wanton tragedy in the sixteenth century, when Donald Galldach had been succeeded by the powerful Donald Gruamach, or the Grim.   A cousin of his, Ranald Herrach (of Harris), came as a guest to Dunscaith when his hostess was entertaining twelve of her kinsmen of Clanranald.   For some reason which does not appear, Ranald rose early one morning and killed all the twelve men of Clanranald, brutally stringing up the corpses on a wall facing the window of his hostess.   Then he went to Donald Gruamach and announced his immediate departure. Courteously pressed by the Gruamach to stay on at least until his wife could bid him farewell, Ronald replied, " No, I must go, for she will not thank me for my morning's work when she looks out of her bedroom window."   So thankless did she prove indeed, that her steward, by her orders, succeeded in assassinating the callous abuser of her hospitality.   In 1515, during the rebellion of Sir Donald of Lochalsh, Macleod of Harris, with the aid of Maclean of Duart, had seized Dunscaith Castle on behalf of the Gruamach, and this tragedy is alleged to have followed upon this event.

On a small rocky islet near the fortress is the remains of a vitrified fort—possibly the original castle, said to have been built in a single night—where Cuchulainn left his wife, Bragela, the " lonely sunbeam of Dunscaith," when he voyaged to Ireland.   " Spread now thy white sails for the Isle of Mist and see Bragela leaning on her rock. Her tender eye is in tears, and the wind lifts her long hair from her heaving breast.   She listens to the voice of thy rowers; to hear the song of the sea and the sound of thy distant harp.   And long shall she listen in vain.

Cuchulainn will never return." This is how Macpherson in *his* Ossian sings in his " Fingal."

A stone near by Dunscaith Castle is that to which Cuchulainn, when he returned from the chase, is said to have tethered his hound Luath.

Leaving Dunscaith reluctantly, you pass through Tokavaig to Ord, where you feel you are doing the Coolin a discourtesy to turn your back on them to climb inland. It was at Ord that Alexander Smith, the author of *A Summer in Skye,* stayed during his three summers spent on the island. Here the outlook over the sea to the splintered crests of the Coolin is such that you would feel delighted to find yourself literally rooted to the spot, and it is with more than the usual regret that you are *not* Argus-eyed that you force yourself to turn inland. Climbing up along the valley of the Ord river, the outcrop of white marble on the hills is a somewhat remarkable feature of the landscape, but in comparison with both prospect and retrospect when the summit of the road is gained, nothing either to right or left of you is at all noteworthy. The view of the mainland mountains—soft in the waning sunlight and with light clouds hovering over their heads—is only less arresting than that of the Coolin in the rear.

When you find yourself again upon the eastern coast of Sleat, you are soon in sight of another ruined castle, perched, like Dunscaith, on a crag jutting out to sea, and, like Dunscaith, too, another Macdonald fortress. But there the likeness ends. There is nothing fearsome in either the ruins or the situation of Knock Castle, or Castle Camus, as it is indifferently called. Perhaps its covering of ivy helps to soften its aspect: certainly its more serene background of the calm Sound of Sleat and the milder mountains of the mainland beyond tend to do so. And instead of a rock-strewn shore at its base, there is a sandy inlet, so that *camus,* a creek, and *cnoc,* a hill, are equally descriptive of the situation of the castle, where it is said a *glaistig,* to whom libations of milk were poured out, used to appear.

The folk lore of the *glaistig,* the fairy woman who haunts castles and folds of cattle, is inextricably confused with that of the *gruagach,* the " fair haired," originally the ancient Celtic sun-god, and later the kindly brownie who helped invisibly in the work of the people.   The castle-haunting *glaistig* is also called *maighdean sheomair, i.e.,* chambermaid, because she confines herself to housework. The true *glaistig* is a woman of mortal origin placed under enchantment, and endowed with a fairy nature.   She has long yellow hair reaching to her heels, and, like all fairies, wears a green dress.   Her face is wan and grey, hence her name *glais, stig* meaning a sneaking or crouching object, probably here having allusion to smallness of size or invisibility.

Knock Castle was besieged about the end of the fifteenth century by the Macleods.   One, " Mary of the Castle "— evidently an Amazon in the succession of Black Agnes of Dunbar—put up a brave defence, and, encouraged by her inspiriting leadership, the garrison defeated their rival clan.   In 1617 the famous chief of Clan Donald, Donald Gorm (of whom elsewhere much remains to be related), was bound by the Crown to have Castle Camus always ready for the reception of the King or his lieutenant.

The first occasion of our landing at Armadale was quite unpremeditated, for we were destined for Broadford.   By some mischance, however, we missed the only boat in the day, though our luggage, labelled for Broadford, had been duly hurled on board.   This fact, supported by our natural inclination, settled our determination not to waste twenty-four hours at Mallaig waiting for the next steamer; so, after sundry enquiries, we got hold of a fisherman who, for a consideration, agreed to take us across to Armadale in his motor fishing boat.   Once there, we were quite disposed to take our chance of finding some means to convey us the seventeen miles over the moors to Broadford.   But when we reached the Inn, we heard to our dismay that both the " machines," which were all the village could provide, were already in use, and the suggestion, therefore, was that we should telegraph to our hotel for its motor to fetch us. However, on the way to the Post Office, I noticed a venerable wagonette in the village, and, tactfully questioning the driver as to his destination, I was told he was in the employ of a traveller bound for Broadford. When the traveller himself emerged from the local general store, and I approached him, he made not the slightest objection to including us amongst his samples, so for the first time in our lives we found ourselves travelling for a firm of bootmakers in Glasgow.

Just opposite where the road strikes inland over to Ord, we passed the waterlily-fringed Loch nan Dubhrachan, held in direst dread by the natives, who believe it to be haunted by a water-horse, or kelpie. Belief in these and similar evil beings still persists in the Highlands, and endless are the lochs which are the reputed haunts of these monsters. The water-horse, water-bull, or kelpie, is a terrifying monster which causes the water to rise in order to drown some helpless victim; or else rises out of the water and seizes its prey—preferably a beautiful maiden—whom it devours beneath the waves. These kelpies have the power to assume human shape the more easily to snare their victims, and it is only when they have lured their prey to their watery haunts that the kelpies resume their true form—all too late for their dupes to escape their clutches. Different localities endue these kelpies with other features—such as that of assuming the shape of a beautiful horse as a lure—all as varied as the districts themselves. Persistence throughout the Highlands in the belief in kelpies is one of the many relics of primitive nature worship, when water and trees especially were considered to be endued with the power to exercise various influences—generally baleful. Let it not be thought that it is Roman Catholics who cling most tenaciously to these pagan beliefs. It is the " Wee Free " Presbyterians who are the most devoted adherents—at least in the Isle of Skye, where there are now practically no Papists.

I was told a most amusing story of the water-horse of Loch nan Dubhrachan by an old man who, as a boy fifty years ago, was present at an organized attempt to catch it. He told me that this water-horse was " more like a cow with a long mane," and that it left footmarks like the imprint of the foot of a wine bottle! The occasion of which the old man spoke was made a regular holiday in the district, even the children being freed from school, and people in carts and traps came from far and wide to take part in the proceedings. My informant told me that a great supply of provisions was taken, and that there was more whisky drunk there than at a funeral! Two boats had been brought, and when these were launched out on to the loch, a net was stretched out between them. In the course of the dragging proceedings that followed, the net caught in a snag, and the majority of the spectators, thinking that the water-horse was indeed enmeshed, in terror rushed for their horses and carts or fled precipitately from the scene. Beside the snag, all that was caught on this occasion was two pike, so that the fisherman who aspires to a catch out of the common still has his chance of the water-horse.

PART II

BROADFORD AND BEYOND

OUR drive over to Broadford was uneventful, and the road calls but for one remark, and that of an association rather than of scenery, since it traverses moorlands the like of which are found all over the island. The valley is a gloomy one, abounding in marshes and lochans, and it is, therefore, appropriately haunted by a peculiar spirit, a sort of Highland " Will o' the Wisp," robbed of his lamp and armed with hard fists. This goblin is called *Luideag,* possibly because he lives amongst the " little pools " of the marshlands, and, though he has two arms, he has but one leg, which shews the cloven hoof. This unique spirit may be seen when night falls, or when the mist fills the hollows, hopping about amongst the bogs. Woe betide the traveller whom he encounters, for the goblin will certainly beat him about the face, or knock him over into a pool!

Approaching Broadford from Kyleakin, you pass, a little beyond Lusa, an ancient burial ground called *Aiseig Ma-ruibhe,* which has many interesting associations. Tradition says that here, at this " Ferry of S. Maelrubha," the saint for whose name Dr. Watson gives no translation, was wont to cross from his monastery of Applecross on the mainland opposite. Standing within the churchyard, you can see across the river *Creag an Leabhair,* the " rock of the book," that S. Maelrubha is said to have used as his pulpit. Here at Ashaig was built the first church in Strath, and it became a sanctuary. There is a legend that beside it grew a tree on which S. Maelrubha's bell was hung, and that it rang of its own accord every Sunday until, when the church at Ashaig fell into ruins, the bell was moved to the succeeding church at Kilchrist. Then it ceased to ring, nor did it resume the habit when restored to its old tree at Ashaig. *Tobar Ma-ruibhe,* covered by a low building of large stones on the shore, is a well attributed to the saint. One day in old age, it is said, he was seated here, and, in order to raise himself up, he laid hold of a tree to aid him. In doing so, he pulled it up by the roots, and from the hole thus made a spring issued. August 27th used to be kept at Broadford as *Là Ma-ruibhe,* S. Maelrubha's Day, the date of old Scottish observance of his festival.

Continuing the read to Broadford, as soon as the sea is regained, you realize the magnificent sweep of its " broad bay " or " fiord," and, if the straggling, forlorn-looking buildings passed are superior in comfort to the older type of Skye cottage, they are severely ugly in outward aspect, and do not improve as they might the bare, bleak moorland. The newer road to the newer pier runs through the district known as Liveras, and passes, at Cairn Cottage, the remains of a great cairn which was opened in 1832, when skulls, ashes, flint weapons, and some of the stone wrist-guards worn by prehistoric archers, were found. Unfortunately afterwards the burial chamber was broken up and filled in with earth, and a similar vandal fate befell an earth house which was discovered in the field called the church park.

Not far from the pier, built right down on the rocks of the shore itself, is a small cottage, very like that at Morar already described. Over its thatch is spread a fishing-net weighted down with stones hanging just below the eaves— a very common west coast expedient to keep on the roof. A special feature of its chimney is its lengthening by the addition of two old bottomless pails set askew one over the other—crowning the original pot. A peculiarly fine elder tree blossoms at the door, but the greatest attraction was the *cailleach* who lives there.

Having been told that Seonaid was a very interesting character, well versed in the history and lore of the island, I went to call on her. She received me with characteristic Highland courtesy, and we sat down side by side on the bench outside her cottage. It was not long before the subject of our conversation shewed her capacity for that enthusiasm which is a distinguishing feature of the true Highlander. She had begun talking about the Macdonalds of Armadale Castle which she had sometimes visited, and, herself a member of a Jacobite clan always friendly to the Macdonalds, as she informed me, she sang without stint the praises of the family at Armadale. They it is who now own most of the country about Broadford, originally the possession of the Mackinnons. In her animation,

Seonaid seized my hand, then, something causing her to look down at it, she exclaimed, " Uch, it wass ta ploody hand, too, you hev got ! "

Naturally, I thought I had fallen in with one gifted with the second-sight, and, recalling some of the murderous exploits of clan ancestors, I wondered if she had traced in my unfortunate hand latent tendencies in the same direction. But her response to an agitated request for enlightenment was reassuring. I was wearing a signet ring with the family crest of the hand holding a dagger, and it was this to which Seonaid's startling announcement had reference. I give the rest of her conversation in her own words—her version of a story which is, I believe, not only substantially the same as that told of the Red Hand of Ulster, but, with variations, is similar to that recorded as happening off Kerrera, the island opposite Oban, to account for the Macdonald crest.

" Wass you inteed not knowing ta story of ta ploody hand, mem? Uch, well, it wass chust this way. There wass ta creat chief Tonal, he wass in wan sheep (ship), and there wass wan other chief that would pe in wan other sheep, and they wass racing to pe seeing who it wass would pe ta first that wass landing in Skye. For there wass ta profeesigh that ta clan whose flesh and whose plood they wass ta first to pe landing on Skye, they would pe heving ta island. And Tonal, he wass seeing ta other sheep that she wass getting on pefore him, and what should he do put pe taking out his *sgiandubh* to cut off his hand with her, and ta hand he did fling her on to ta land. And so it wass ta flesh and ta plood of ta Mactonal that did first land on *Eilean a' Cheo*. And it wass ta creat pig pit of ta island that wass pelonging to ta Mactonal to this fery tay moreofer. And it iss you that wass wearing ta fery hand that wass cut off, holding ta fery same *sgian dubh* that tid make ta cut whatefer—yess, yess ! "

Seonaid, after this recital, began spontaneously to lament the passing of the old days of Prince Charlie.

" *Ochain,* and if *Prionnsa Tearlach* chust wass lifing now! It wass he that was ta peautiful lad of ta yellow locks that wass aalways in ta Highland heart! There wass no tays like when he wass in ta Highlands, but it iss pack again he will pe coming to ta land he wass aalways loving. Yess, yess, he will pe coming pack, and it iss ta Highlanders that will pe rising again to pe giving him ta welcome of ta heart!" Indeed it is true to say of Seonaid:

> " She had many a plaintive rhyme
> Of Royal Charlie and his men;
> For her there was no later time—
> All histories had ended then."

The general impression you get of Broadford is of an open, sweeping bay, circled by bleak moorlands, and flanked in the distance on one side by Ben na Greine, the " mountain of the sun," and on the other by Ben na Cailleach. It is this peak of the Red Coolin, as distinguished from the other Ben na Cailleach behind Kyleakin, that is associated in tradition with some unknown Norwegian princess. She desired, so it is said, to be buried in the track of the wind blowing over to Norway, and thus she found a last resting-place on the cairn-topped summit of this mountain. Beneath its shadow is the scattered heap of stones which now represents all that remains of Coire-Chatachan, the old mansion house of the " Man (*i.e.,* tacksman) of Corrie," as the name indicates, the home where, in 1773, Dr. Johnson and his faithful biographer tasted of overflowing Highland hospitality.

About a mile up, there is a track, not easily discoverable, on the right, leading to the site of the old house as you take the road through Strath over to Elgol, the " place of the stranger." Beside this track there is a *sithean* (fairy hill) where the little people dance in the moonlight to fairy pipes, and tend the fairy breed of cattle. Skyemen believe devoutly in the *sithe,* and, fearful of their powers for ill, think to appease them by referring to them only indirectly as *daoine sith,* or *mnathan shith,* the men, or women, of peace.

Elsewhere in the Highlands fairy hills are generally smooth, green mounds: in Skye they appear to be more commonly identified with ancient cairns, as in this case, where there is the unusual feature of the remains of a stone circle near the top, as distinct from the usual situation round the base. Tradition says that the large stones of this *sithean* were carried thither in her apron by a woman of the big race which succeeded to the Picts. At the top of the hill, too, are some stunted storm-beaten trees of great age.

A mile or so further along the road, in a beautiful situation by the shores of Loch Cill Chriosd, where the curlew ceaselessly calls, are the ivy-covered walls and gable ends of the ruin of Kilchrist, in the burying ground of the Mackinnons of Strath. After the Norse conquered, both the churches of Kilmaree and Kilbride in Strath, beside that of Ashaig, fell into ruins, and were abandoned in favour of a successor built at Kilchrist. The fact that the rising ground between the present ruin and the loch is called *Cnoc na h-Aireinn,* the " hill of the Mass," suggests that service was held there before the church was built. Close by is *tir cheiridh,* and if this, as suggested, means the " land of wax," it probably yielded a tax applied to procure candles for altar use. It is in the records of 1505 that Strath reappears as the parish of Kilchrist " in Askibmiruby," but that the present ruin cannot be that of the original building is shewn both by its architecture and its lack of every feature indicative of Catholic worship. It is interesting to note that the first Reformed minister found in Skye was an Episcopalian, Neil Mackinnon the elder. He came in 1627, and was wont to preach in Kilchrist church, wearing not only the kilt, but armour as well, an item which quite probably commended him to his parishioners. Indeed, as late as 1773, so it is recorded of Strath, "the leading families," like many others throughout the Highlands, " leaned to Episcopacy."

Searching through the graveyard of Kilchrist, I came across one fragment of a sculptured stone and disinterred two other pieces which had all obviously formed part of one monument, which, from the outline of one fragment, I thought might have been a cross. I subsequently saw it conjectured that these were the remains of the gravestone of Sir Lachlan Mor Mackinnon, the third great chief of Skye in the days of Donald Gorm and Rory Mor. Certainly on one of the fragments there is faintly discern-ible the representation of a tower similar to that borne at the present day as a charge upon the shield of Mackinnon, and beside it, in a separate compartment, is an animal which apparently represents a cow. This, however, does not appear anywhere in the modern coat-of-arms. On the curiously-shaped fragment, which I take to have formed one arm of a cross, two indeterminate animals, rampant and respectant, can be distinguished under an ornamental heading. The third fragment has one end rounded, and shews nothing but a few scattered pittings in the stone on its surface.

Opposite Kilchrist are modern buildings connected with the abandoned marble quarries. From this source came the white marble from which the high altar of the Abbey Church of Iona was made—an altar whose last fragment is embedded in the centre of the altar of S. Andrew's Episcopal Church, Glasgow.

It is at Kilchrist that the road first begins to yield a promise of splendour, with the sight of Blaven and Clach Ghlas rising before the lovely, reed-fringed shores of Loch Cill Chriosd, which in the spring shews an abundance of the beautiful bog bean in blossom. Within a mile of the end of the loch, you enter a gate on the left, opening on a road through a field, in which was the site of the ancient church of S. Bride, of which, however, no trace now remains. But near its supposed site is a standing stone seven and a

half feet high, having at its base a flat stone with a round
hole, associated with the performance of penances.   This
monolith,Clach na h-Annait, fell down several years ago, and
beneath it were found a bell and a holy water stoup.   The
stone is also known as that "of reluctance," *na h-aindeon,*
because of an incident associated with it.   A pirate of the
Orkneys was converted to Christianity, and, before he died,
he made his crew promise they would bear his body to
Iona for burial.   In the course of fulfilling their promise,
the crew tried three times unavailingly to pass Strathaird
Point, but a violent storm always beat them back.   Then,
accepting this as a divine token that the body was too
wicked to be buried in the sacred soil of Iona, the crew
landed it at Camus Mallaig, the bay below Kilbride, and
buried the body at the foot of Clach na h-Annait.

At no distance from this stone, at the head of a trickle
through a swamp, is *Tobar na h-Annait,* probably originally
a sacred well in view of its name, which at least marks
both it and the standing stone as of Christian association.
Annait is a word which indicates that the place with which
it is associated was either where the patron saint was
educated, or that it was where his relics were deposited.
This well, built in and quaintly covered with a millstone
some generations back, was said to have been the home
of a little fish which was immortal.

You can regain the main road without retracing your
steps by taking a track which, climbing up the hillside,
cuts across into it.   On the way, and onwards through the
little township of Torran, you cannot fail to be struck by
the many associations of stones, presumably of natural
formation, yet suggesting both stone circles and cairns
made by human agency.   Indeed, the many " little hills,"
visible everywhere, evidently account for the name of
Torran, the approach to which in the late springtime glows
with the rich gold of gorse growing in magnificent
profusion.   Torran itself happily appears to be still a
flourishing,   well-inhabited   township   of   many   crofts,

picturesque with thatched cottages and shaggy Highland cattle.

At the foot of the steep descent through the township, you gain the shores of Loch Slapin, where, in its immensity towers Blaven, most beautiful of all the Coolin. If Blaven be not a hybrid word meaning " blue ben," then it is the " mountain of bloom " (*blath*). A Skyeman of whom I once enquired the meaning of the name, replied: " Uch, Blaven would chust pe meaning ta good-looking mountain," and, though he was quite wrong in his translation, he perfectly described this fascinating peak. And it is never more good-looking than when wisps of mist slowly climb its sides, and snow crowns its crest; or when the sun catches some wet patch upon its granite face, making it aglitter as though it were decked with a string of diamonds. If anything were needed to supply further charm to the scene, it is found in the sea-birds which, with mournful cries, so suited to the loneliness of the place, wheel and circle about the loch.

When, however, you have walked round the head of the inlet, and the road begins to climb the hillside, the scenery declines in distinction, and indeed does not recover its interest until you reach Elgol. But just before Kilmaree, that is, *Cille Maolruaidhe,* the site of another church of S. Maelrubha, about five miles short of Elgol, far off the road, and all solitary on the shore of Loch Slapin, are the undistinguished remains of the chief of the two castles of the Mackinnon. This is Dunringil, occupied in the tenth century by the first of the Mackinnons, who was established here by the Bruce.

When you reach the end of your journey, you will agree that Elgol is a hamlet worth gaining. Perched high on the cliffs, cottages are scattered, many of them in the last stages of dilapidation, but picturesque in the extreme, both in their setting and in their flower-grown thatching. A beaten track, twisting and twining through fields studded with wild flowers, leads you to them, and in the back-

BLAVEN AND CLACH GLAS FROM TORRAN, SKYE

ground is the whole range of the Coolin. You descend by the steep, broken path to the rugged shore, where great rocks and boulders are strewn about on end, like disordered monoliths. This is perhaps the supreme viewpoint from the seaward approach of the Coolin, with Loch Scavaig in the foreground.

It was from Elgol that I sailed into Loch Scavaig for the first time. The day was superb; the water was of the clearest and most vivid emerald, and, as the tide was low, you could look right down to the bottom of silver sand, out of which grew great plants of sea-wrack, waving slowly to and fro, just under the surface of the water, like the tentacles of some sentient creature.

> "Good is the smell of the brine that laves
>   Black rock and skerry,
> Where the great palm-leaved tangle waves
>   Down in the green depths,
> And round the craggy bluff, pierced with caves,
>   Seagulls are screaming."
>   Seagulls are screaming."

Above the storm-scarred rocks, upstanding sheer from the sea, rose Sgurr Dubh, thrown well back into the distance by the heat haze, and agleam, as it seemed, with dancing diamonds.

But this is a digression, for there is more to be said of Elgol itself. It was here that Prince Charlie, tramping from Portree over a long and rough track through the wilds of the mountains, arrived early on the morning of July 4, 1746. The Prince, for his greater safety, travelled as the servant of his faithful follower, Captain Malcolm Macleod, whose sister was married to John Mackinnon, late a captain in the Mackinnon regiment of the Prince's army, and his home was at Elgol. Charles took the name of "Lewie Caw," and, at the earnest request of his "master," attempted a disguise by replacing his periwig by a dirty white napkin tied low over his head and covered by his bonnet. But the disguise proved ineffectual, like his every previous attempt to disguise what could not be

hidden or dissipated—the innate distinction and arresting
personality of the Prince.   Two of Mackinnon's men, old
followers of the Prince, who encountered the wanderers
on the road at Kilmaree, instantly recognized him, and, in
pity at his sad plight—for he, like his companion, had
fallen into a bog—threw up their hands and wept.
Macleod severely reprimanded them for allowing their
emotions to betray a recognition that it behoved loyal men
to dissemble, and demanded of them a solemn promise of
silence regarding the encounter.   Drawing their dirks,
they swore upon them an oath of secrecy, kissing the naked
blade after the Highland fashion, and faithfully kept the
pledge thus given.[4]   Then, leaving the Prince by the
roadside, Macleod made for his brother-in-law's house, of
which the foundations still remain.   Presently he returned,
and, having ascertained that the neighbourhood was free
from soldiery, he informed the Prince that he would be
quite safe to shelter there.

So in the character of Lewie Caw, a servant and a hunted
Jacobite fugitive, Charles shouldered such poor baggage
as they had, and followed Macleod into John Mackinnon's
house.   Mrs. Mackinnon looked at the Prince very
critically, and, after remarking to her brother in an aside
that "there was something about the lad she liked unco'
well," she bade them both sit down to the table.   Lewie
Caw hesitated at the suggestion that he should take food
with his "master," but ultimately allowed himself to be
persuaded.   After the much needed meal, Macleod asked
the maid to wash his legs and feet, as he was too exhausted
to do so for himself.   On his further request that the maid
should perform the like offices for his poor companion,
Highland pride, ever easily roused by, and scornful
of, the Sasunnach, was at once in arms.   "No such thing!
Although I wash the master's feet, I am not obliged to

---

[4] The oath thus sworn was a most awful one, by which the taker renounced
his hope of Heaven and gave himself over to the devil if he broke it.

wash the servant's! What! He's but a low country-
woman's son: I will not wash his feet indeed!" When at
last, however, she was coaxed into doing so, she used the
poor Prince so roughly that he had to cry for mercy!

Afterwards, Charles, persuaded to take a few hours'
sleep while Mrs. Mackinnon and Macleod kept watch,
threw himself down on a bed without undressing. Mrs.
Mackinnon, who was stationed outside the house, seeing
her husband approaching, came to warn her brother, who
thereupon went out to meet Mackinnon and told him the
news, beseeching him not to shew that he recognized the
Prince. But when Mackinnon entered the house to find
his royal master bandaged and in soiled and tattered
clothing, nursing his little son Neil, and crooning to him,
the sight overcame the loyal Highlander, and he burst
into tears. Charles, however, preserved his usual
heroically cheerful attitude, and soon they began talking
about the possibility of getting a boat, under the pretext
that it was Macleod who wanted to cross to the mainland.
To arrange for this boat Mackinnon went out, pledged to
say nothing about the presence of the Prince to anyone;
but so full was he of the all-absorbing subject that, meeting
the old Chief Mackinnon, Iain Dubh, he at once told him
everything. Old man as he was, so devoted and spirited
a Jacobite was Iain Dubh, that he insisted upon taking
all arrangements, as of prescriptive right, into his own
hands, and procured the necessary boat. Local tradition
has it that, waiting for the vessel, the Prince sheltered in a
cave still known as *Uaimh a' Phrionnsa,* on the shore round
the point at Elgol; and that, after a dinner of bread, meat,
and wine, from here he set off at eight o'clock on the night
of July 4th, in a boat manned by four men, besides the
Mackinnon and Captain John Mackinnon.

The first time I was at Elgol, I had had no opportunity
of getting to the Prince's cave, and, therefore, I looked
forward to returning to Elgol to visit it. When the chance
came, the day looked doubtful, but, as it was the last

available day, my friend and I agreed to take the risk of the weather. No sooner had we started out than we were no longer left in doubt as to its intentions, and by the time we reached Elgol we were literally wet to the skin. But we knew, to the partial mitigation of our disgust, that there was a possibility of seeing the cave if the tide were low and we could therefore gain it by land. We were told by the courteous Mackinnon, to whom we were fittingly referred, that the tide *was* low, but he cautioned us that the tramp to the cave would be both wet and rough. As we could not possibly get any wetter, and thought nothing of rough going, we eagerly availed ourselves of his proffered guidance.

We had about a mile to tramp over the desolate moor-land, but, as the wet had penetrated even our boots, we did not have to trouble about picking our way, but plunged indifferently into pools and across burns, and squelched in and out of bogs, with the all-obliterating rain descending pitilessly upon us, the wind also making itself very objectionable. Yet even in such circumstances, true Celts will always feel in their hearts as

> "We tread the miry road, the rain-drenched heather;
>   We are the men—we battle, we endure;
> God's pity on you, exiles, in your weather
>   Of swooning winds, calm seas, and skies demure!"

On our way we passed all that remained, in these days, of the walls of the house that sheltered the Prince—a building of very considerable size, its foundations now overgrown with ferns and foxgloves. Shortly after we passed this historic ruin, the track began to descend, until we found ourselves upon the rough shores of the bay from which the Prince had embarked for the mainland. Had the rain only allowed us to see more than a few yards ahead, we should have certainly looked upon a gloriously wild scene, but even the rain could not veil the majesty of the great precipitous cliffs which faced us when we emerged from a narrow gully cutting through them on the right to another smaller bay. Here the shore was thickly strewn with great slippery boulders, of all shapes and sizes, sometimes piled one upon another, and over this dangerous and difficult going we had carefully to pick our way, sliding alternating with clambering, as we followed our guide. Mackinnon made his way to a point at the foot of the cliff, where he climbed up a few feet, and there waited till we joined him on the shore below. Giving us each in turn a helping hand, we soon stood beside him, to find ourselves in the most beautiful of the many caves I have ever entered, and a most perfect hiding-place. A species of stone-crop, delicate young ferns, and a soft growth of greenery framed the entrance to a large and lofty cave, naturally divided into two compartments, and very different from the usual run of damp, dark, cramped dens in the ground usually associated with the Prince's hiding. Beneath a boulder on the right was a small spring, and the left hand chamber of the cave culminated in a long and high but narrow passage, while the entrance to the cave was masked by a wall of rock rising to a height of a few feet.

Elsewhere on this same coast, but obviously level with the shore, is another cave which tradition says was the scene of the incident to which it is alleged the Mackinnon coat-of-arms owes the charge on its first quartering, as also their crest. A chief of Mackinnon was cooking venison inside the cave when a boar, rushing in, charged full at him. At this, Mackinnon thrust a large bone, off which he was cutting slices, down the boar's throat; thence the crest is still "a boar's head erased, holding in its mouth the shank bone of a deer proper." It is curious that, with the exception of this charge on the first quartering, of the others, two are for Macdonald and one for Macleod, shewing how very closely the Mackinnons have allied themselves with the two greater clans of the island.

PART III

THE SUPREMACY OF SLIGACHAN

NEAR the Post Office at Broadford is *Goir a' Bhlair,* the
" field of battle," where one of the most decisive Norse
battles was fought: but the interest of the royal road from
Broadford to Sligachan for me always began in the gipsies,
or tinkers, as they are called locally, who never encamp
except in beautiful surroundings. Those that abound in
the Highlands appear to be of a type distinct from those
found in England. They usually travel about the country
with a horse and light cart in which to carry their tents
and household possessions, and their favourite pitch is in
some sheltered part of the moorland, or where they may
be had, in woodland glades. Men, women, and children
alike, have a very wild, unkempt appearance, the women's
clothing especially giving the impression of an out-of-date
assortment of rags, which it would be hard to equal in a
city slum. The gipsy tent is constructed on the half-hoop
principle, and I have never seen it covered with anything
more weatherproof than sacking or old bed-ticking. The
pitch of the gipsy encampment is usually advertised by a
great display of the weirdest description of washing, which
adorns the ground or decorates any convenient dyke, trees,
or bushes. Needless to say, these vagrant tribes are not
by any means welcome visitors to the crofters, who
often give the gipsies a very bad name. However
that may be, Skye gipsies are the most persistent of
beggars.

On one occasion I and three friends were walking on the
Sligachan road, about half a mile out of Broadford, when
suddenly there popped out of the heather and bog-myrtle
by the wayside a wild-looking little girl, bare-headed and
bare-legged of course, and as brown as the proverbial
berry. Speaking in a curious, high-pitched monotone, as

though repeating a lesson in a foreign language, learned with difficulty and not understood, she addressed herself to one of my friends: " Please, kind ledy, will you give me a penny; my father's ill, and my mother's deid."

The " kind ledy " addressed unwisely complied with the request, but accompanied the coin with a charge to the child not to beg any more. Having received the penny, the child fled like the wind, disappearing from sight as instantaneously as she had appeared. On our way back, however, up popped the child again, this time reversing the statement, for in piteous tone she wailed that her mother was ill and her father dead! Greatly shocked at the glib untruthfulness of the girl, the " kind ledy," instead of producing the desired coin, sought to impress upon the child the wickedness of lying. But obviously " not heving ta English," and understanding in consequence nothing of what had been said to her, the girl only repeated her parrot strain. Next morning, when we happened to be taking the same road, the familiar little figure shot up for the third time to beg. Although the sarcasm was lost upon the poor child, the exasperated " kind ledy " of the previous day anticipated the youthful beggar's stock sentence by unfeelingly demanding, " Well, is your mother *still* dead this morning?"

I have travelled this road of roads from Broadford to Sligachan often and in all weathers; and such is its magic, that I have enjoyed myself struggling to take tea with a friend in a downpour whilst jolting in a wagonette over the most uneven and broken parts of the road. But, in the words of the Gaelic poet, Duncan MacIntyre,

> " My delight it was to rise
> With the early morning skies
> All aglow—"

and to tramp the road, breakfasting by the lochside opposite Scalpay, the " boat-shaped island." Everything fairest in creation is on this road in summer—the loveliest of flowers—tall foxgloves, yellow iris, and water forget-me-not in thick beds of brilliant blue, the purple heather just beginning to bloom, wild roses of brightest pink, fresh green ferns, wood-ruff, and a riot of golden broom. There are countless birds, both of land and sea—yellow-hammers, stone-chats, pipits, wrens, and gulls of all sorts and kinds, and beautiful herons. As for the mountains and the streamlets, the waterfalls, the islands, the sea, and the moorland, they defy all words. There is an infinite variety, too, in the road. You climb up and down, wind in and out, here striking inland, and again walking by the sea. You pass the old working of a white marble quarry, successor to that of Kilchrist, and all around you see traces of its presence in the white outcrop. You come across herds of beautiful Highland cattle, long of horn and shaggy of coat, of the loveliest colouring—cream, fawn, and a rich brown-red. Here and there on the peat-hags you see women filling their creels, or carrying them along on their backs. It is very few people that you meet on the road itself—one or two crofters, perhaps, and a postman, or the world's freeman, a professional tramp, sound asleep by the roadside, with his boots off and his toes bare, his head cushioned on a stone covered by his cap. Or you may see on one of the many little stone bridges that span the road one or two men at work in true Highland fashion, which has something very attractive about its leisureliness and its seeming upside-down methods.

The first hamlet through which the road actually runs is Luib, " a creek or bending of the shore "—a naming that exactly describes its situation. Just at the top of the hill, however, on the left hand side before you drop down into Luib, is Loch nam Madadh. You see it lying far down in a dark hollow, and its utterly desolate situation and the wild hills beyond are very suggestive of a haunted place. And perhaps the ghost of Prince Charlie may still wander there, for it is probably down by this little loch and through Strath Mor, " the great valley," that he made

THE HAMLET OF LUIB, THE RED COOLIN BEHIND

his rough and difficult journey to Elgol. So lonely and remote did this glen appear to the Prince, accustomed though he was to wanderings in the wilds, that he exclaimed to his companion, " I do not think the devil could find us now ! "

The little hamlet of Luib, set against the barren beauty of the Red Hills, is very picturesque. The thatch of the cottages is weighted down by stone tied on by rough ropes, reaching down to various lengths on the walls, and across the thatch itself lie long poles, to give further security of tenure. Luib is a fishing village, and, just beyond it, where the road follows the shores of Loch Ainort, the scenery reaches the summit of its grandeur. Thereafter you begin climbing a very sheer hill, and you have a good mile of it before you reach the summit and find yourself in Lord Macdonald's deer forest. I have never yet seen a deer about here, and this fact suggests some affinity with the tourist who, on being told what he was passing through, innocently asked of the driver, " But where are the trees ? " only to receive the contemptuous counter-query, " And what would a forest pe toing with trees ? "

After about a mile of descent on the other side of the hill just ascended, there is on your right the picturesquely named *Drum nan cleoc,* the " hill of cloaks," so called because mists like mantles so often veil the scene here. Also on your right you pass the well of Donald Gruamach, where, local tradition has it, he was found dead in 1534. This chief was the father of the famous Donald Gorm, and he under whose leadership the Clan Uisdean (*i.e.,* the Macdonalds of Sleat) had been successful in expelling the Dunvegan chief and his clan from Trotternish, the most northerly district of Skye.

Just before you gain Sconser, you have—on a fine day— a glorious view of the bluffs of Portree, and sometimes of the Old Man of Storr in the further distance. Sconser is the place of which it is no pleasure to record that from it

Macleod wrote to President Forbes on August 17, 1745, saying that Sleat and he could raise between 1,500 and 2,000 men for the service of German George, but that they would require arms. At the end of September of the same year there was a meeting at Sconser Inn (now non-existent) between Sleat, Macleod of Raasay, Kingsburgh, and Captain Malcolm Macleod.   Here Sir Alexander Macdonald proposed to raise 1,000 men for the Prince, giving Raasay command of one company; but the inopportune arrival of a letter from President Forbes caused Sleat to change his tune, never very certain on any occasion.

Sconser is one of the poorest crofting districts in Skye, and, situated under the perpetual frown of overbearing (and ugly) Glamaig that towers above, it gets very little sunshine.   For all that, and despite the fact that the cottages are as poor as they are picturesque, the crofters refused to leave them when, in 1901, they were urged to remove to Loch Eishort, where new homes and many more inducements were offered them.   This is surely a comment on the ignorant denunciations of Radical agents concerned to manufacture party capital out of the alleged callous indifferent of landlords who are Highlanders to the needs of their tenants.

Any discussion of the large and complicated crofter question, with its many difficult problems, does not come within the scope of a non-sociological book.   Every Highlander must have an intense sympathy with every class of the Highland people, not least with those, chiefs and people alike, who have a hard and continuous struggle to live in their several spheres.   But the alien agitator has no claim other than that of impudence to be heard on the subject with which he has generally scarcely even a bowing acquaintance.   He is often a Cockney tourist taking an initial conventional tour of Scotland, charged to make facts, more often fallacies at the best, fit in with the theories

with which his employers have stocked him. As a towns-
man, he is by the mere force of his upbringing incapable
of understanding problems presented by the exigencies of
country life—least of all of Highland country life—since
he has as much in common with a Highlander as a
Hottentot. The life of a crofter is exactly suited to the
Highland temperament, and, when bad days have fallen
upon Skye, in both Lord Macdonald and the Macleod the
crofters have found kindly and sympathetic friends, always
ready with a helping hand. Indeed, in one very bad year,
the then Macleod ruined himself in his efforts to help his
crofters, nor was his fellow-tyrant, Lord Macdonald,
behind in his generosity.

Apart from the interest of the picturesque cottages you
pass, the road under the shadow of Glamaig by the shores
of Loch Sligachan is comparatively uninteresting. And
when you reach the Inn—save a bungalow up the Glen
and a deserted keeper's cottage the only building in the
place—there is nothing outwardly to impress you, but
within, you very soon discovered, it was no ordinary hotel
at which you had arrived. This was in the days when
Mr. Donald Macdonald of Tormore was the ideal
proprietor. As, where clansmen of the same Christian
name and surname are numerous, the rank and file are
distinguished by nicknames—denoting generally personal
characteristics, such as the *gillie breac* (freckled man),
Iain Lom (bare John), so the gentlemen are known simply
by the name of their estate. There is a beautiful tale told
of that celebrated Queen's Counsellor, the late Sir Frank
Lockwood, in this connection. He and his wife were
invited to some function in the Highlands, and hearing
such announcements as "Lochiel and Mrs. Cameron,"
"Ardsheal and Mrs. Stewart," when it came to their turn,
the witty Queen's Counsellor had himself and his partner
announced as "No. 26 Lennox Gardens and Lady
Lockwood."

The most perfect of Highland gentlemen, of incomparable courtly manners, Tormore was a unique host, for he always made it his special care personally to assure himself of the comfort and happiness of each one of his guests. On one occasion, finding I was engaged in putting the finishing touches to a book, he insisted on my occupying a private sitting-room for the purpose; and, knowing my fondness for riding in the rain, on wet days he would ask me if I would be kind enough to exercise such and such a pony for him. No wonder it was said he ran the hotel as a hobby and lost considerably upon it, for you never felt the charges were adequate to all the comforts of home. After a few visits, you became attached to him as to a friend, and he himself was as truly to be numbered amongst the attractions of Sligachan as the mountains themselves. When you arrived, he was always waiting to welcome you; and when you, alas, left, his was the last figure you saw at the Inn door, no matter how early the hour of your departure. And while the Inn maintains its deservedly high reputation, Tormore, by those to whom he was the incarnation of the spirit of Sligachan, will never cease to be missed. May he rest in peace.

His devoted housekeeper, Bella Stewart, comes in the same category of kindly, warm-hearted Highland friends; always so interested in your expeditions, and concerned to give you just what you wanted in the way of provisions (including your favourite jam!), but more than even a large appetite, whetted by the mountain air, demanded.

Of the Sligachan gillies, none is more famous than John Mackenzie, the keen-eyed, sure-footed hero of many a hazardous climb, after whom *Sgurr Mhic Choinnich* [5] is named. In ordinary cases, you deplore the necessity for taking a man, as a nuisance with which you would fain dispense. But when John Mackenzie is the man in question, you welcome the prospect of a day's enhanced

[5] This is simply Mackenzie in its original form, and means the son of Kenneth or " firesprung."

JOHN MACKENZIE, SLIGACHAN—CHIEF OF MOUNTAIN GUIDES

pleasure. Often has it been my good fortune to enjoy his companionship on long tramps over the hills, where the right track is difficult both to find and to keep. A more delightful companion it would be impossible to have, or one whom it is more interesting to question concerning anything about the Coolin. Such is the universal tribute paid to John Mackenzie by all who have any occasion to mention Sligachan as a climbing centre.

In the climbing season the dinner dress of the climbers is quite an interesting study. Apparently the more patches you have on your garments, and the more odd the garments themselves (for coat and knickers must *never* pair), the more exalted is your position as a climber. To be really smartly dressed, it seems to be *de rigueur* that none of the patches should match either coat or knickers, and that they should be sewed on in as obvious a fashion as possible, with enormous stitches and much consequent display of thread. Certainly the whole effect, especially when there is a great variety of tweed in the patching, is most picturesque—and arresting—and I for one would grieve if it were exchanged for the conventional garb, which should be by law restricted to the town that gave its ugliness birth.

The dominating feature of Sligachan is the peaks of Sgurr nan Gillean, the "cliff of the lads," for though Sgurr Alasdair is the highest of the Coolin, and Sgurr nan Gillean, with Sgurr na Banachdich, [6] only fifth in height, yet so forceful a mountain is it that it seems to follow you everywhere. It is perhaps never so arresting, certainly never more beautiful, than when you see it in the glow of sunset, a swathe of mist interposing a belt of filmy beauty between its splintered crests and its base. As the sun stains the hill in a flood of glorious pink, you watch the band of mist passing from its primal roseate hue through

[6] The Small Pox Peak, so called from the pittings that mark it.

every shade of mauve till all colour has faded away, and you sigh to think such radiance should be so fleeting.

There is the river, too,

"Dashing and foaming and leaping with glee,
The child of the mountain, wild and free."

and never so free as when it is in full flood.   Whilst a river in turbulent mood probably finds a natural response in the breasts of many of those physically strong and vigorous, to the clansman rejoicing in strength there is something peculiarly attractive about a river in spate.   The chord of sympathy is at once struck as you watch the tremendous force which is evident in the resistless onslaught of the swollen waters, swirling in the eddies, and sweeping everything before them.   There is a wild beauty in the brown waters and the creaming foam: there is music in the thunder of its voice: to the Highland heart there is borne to the ear the slogan and pibroch, the clash of the claymore, and the roar of battle.   Often while the rain has come deluging down have I stood on the banks of the Sligachan river, held captive by the congenial companionship of the rushing river, and as often have I marvelled at the surprising abatement of its flood, which falls as suddenly as it rises.   In the morning you may be rejoicing with it in all its frenzy of stirring life and turbulence; in the afternoon you may return to find a very subdued stream, quite meekly submitting to the barrier imposed by the banks upon its limits.

The dark moorland about Sligachan is relieved in the summer by the yellow spikes of bog asphodel, and the nodding heads of the fluffy white canna grass, while in the marshier places you find the sundew and the mauve flower of the butterwort.   To the fragrance of the bog-myrtle is added the delicate perfume of the sweet-scented orchis, which, together with the butterfly variety, grows here in profusion.

The outdoor attractions of Sligachan are not confined

to the Glen, though they do indeed culminate in this direction. There is a very fine round of some sixteen miles which can be made by following the track down the far side of Loch Sligachan over to the crofting district of the Braes, continuing on the rough road till, at Peinmore, it turns round to join the main road to Portree.

When you start out on this round, Raasay faces you in the distance, seeming to close in Loch Sligachan, and at its head you used to pass close to a picturesque cottage, having Sgurr nan Gillean as its background. The cottage, now in ruins, attracted me as the subject for a photograph, and consequently I unslung my knapsack and began setting up my camera. When I was thus engaged, the cottage door opened, a very wild-looking man came out, attended by two hungry-looking collies, and, flourishing his arms about, advanced upon me threateningly. He was obviously warning me off, and, vociferating loudly in Gaelic, his objurgations sounded fearful indeed. As I never feel at ease in the neighbourhood of the lean, smooth-haired collies with the sinister pale eyes, so common to them in Skye, I at once and with all speed began to pack up and off to escape the wolf-like animals. On relating the incident to Tormore, he said that the man evidently regarded my camera lens as a peculiarly baleful variety of evil eye, and that, so far from threatening me, he was much more probably exhibiting terror lest I should " overlook " his cottage. This did not argue much faith in the potency of the rowan tree I noted flourishing outside his door. In view of this light on the subject, it occurred to me that on various previous occasions when in places remote from the tourist track, crofters standing at their doors had retreated hastily within at the sight of me erecting the camera, the explanation was the same, and not, as I had thought, mere native shyness.

You follow Loch Sligachan by a stony track, decked with bracken, fern, and heath, and often broken by a small burn—a path that now climbs along the face of the hillside, and then drops down almost to the water's edge. In the loch you may watch seals sporting in the water, or basking on a rock in the sun, and that most patient of fishers, a heron, standing sentinel about its shores. It was on this track that I first saw the *cas chrom,* the foot plough, literally "bended foot," peculiar to the Western Highlands. It was a crofter who was carrying one over his shoulder, and afterwards I saw it in use. The implement looks a very clumsy one, but nothing could be better fitted for the conditions under which it is employed. No plough and team of horses could be used for tilling such rugged ground as that common to the country where the *cas chrom* is found. Not only does the long curved handle afford a powerful lever to dislodge the frequent large stones encountered by the crofter (who works from right to left, walking backwards), but sods can be cut with surprising rapidity with this quaint implement.

The Braes is a very interesting primitive crofting township; the views obtainable from it of the Portree headlands are very striking; and it is rich in both folk and fairy lore associations. The Pretty Hill, for instance, has a *sithean,* from which sounds of the most wonderful elfin music have been heard; and at Achnahannait fairy cattle find pasture. Still further on is M'Queen's Rock, where are some *gruagach* stones, the old representations of the Celtic divinity, over which libations of milk were, and possibly still are, poured. This rock, together with a loch, was named after one *Aodh Mor MacCuinn,* who lived about two miles south of Portree at the beginning of the eighteenth century. M'Queen was not only physically notable, but the Solomon of Skye, to whom the people resorted in cases of perplexity, and landmarks associated with his judgments were named after him. This man was probably a descendant of that MacSween who won the Braes, as hereafter to be related, from Macdonald. The Skye name, MacQueen, popularly thought to be a corruption of MacSween, the " son of Sweyn," is a wrong

USING THE "GAS CHRON"

rendering of Macquien, from Aidhean, little Aodh, or Hugh; and until recently his posterity continued to live in the Braes.

The Portree road is chiefly associated in my mind with pony rides of nine and a half miles to church early on Sunday mornings. It has always been a case of first catch your pony, for the hill ponies are the most cunning little creatures, with strongly pronounced likes and dislikes, and a devoted attachment to the hillside. In the summer it is their frequent duty to carry folk to the foot of Drumhain, and they apparently do not mind going any of the routes up the Glen. But one and all seem to have a rooted objection to taking the Portree road, as I discovered to my cost from many an exasperating experience, which, for lack of a cycle, often had to be repeated. Even when a pony has been caught overnight, and stabled, ready for saddling at 6.45 next morning, it has been impossible to get him to budge more than the few hundred yards to where a gate opens on his beloved hill pastures. Again and again I have been baulked at this point by the pony's obstinacy, which not even the stable gillie's coaxing could overcome. On occasion, another pony has been caught on the hillside by means of a measureful of oats held out as bait, but even on the most successful of occasions this pony ride is not all bliss. The ponies are so accustomed to picking their own way up the Glen, knowing far better than their riders which rock affords the surest footing and which is the best track, that they become quite rebellious if you attempt to dictate to them where they shall go along the road. They also have a very short step, and are quite unaccustomed to sustaining a trot for more than a few hundred yards at a time.

On one occasion, when I had triumphed in getting an unruly pony to Portree, he got his revenge on the way back. After a mile or two, he began stumbling until I was persuaded he had something the matter with one of his legs. Of course I dismounted, and, putting the reins over

my arm, began to investigate. But the cunning little beast
had merely simulated lameness, hoping thus to secure his
freedom; and he did, for, making a dash forward, the
reins, greatly to his delight, broke. Then, to my horror,
I beheld him wheel right round and head for the Portree
direction again, and only by the greatest piece of good
luck did I succeed in manœuvring him back towards
Sligachan. To cut a long story short, I had alternately
to walk and run every inch of the remaining six miles, an
exasperated spectator of the pony's obvious enjoyment.
He would allow me to get within a foot of him, feeding by
the roadside, then off he would trot, the performance being
repeated *ad nauseam,* until I gave up all attempts to
catch him, discontenting myself with keeping my eye on
him some hundred yards ahead till we reached Sligachan.
My friend, waiting for my return, and wondering why I
was so much later than usual, catching sight of a riderless
pony on the brow of the hill alone, at once had visions of
me thrown and left lying unconscious somewhere on the
lonely road, so that my brisk appearance some few minutes
after, quite intact except as regards temper, came as a
considerable relief.

But on the rare occasions when my pony was fairly
tractable, and the day was fine, it was possible to enter
into and enjoy the spirit of the road. You can imagine
the utter loneliness of riding through the moorland, now
climbing up, now dipping down, the only sounds the
plunging of the river, the songs of birds, the plaintive cry
of sheep, and the lowing of cattle. Frequently you meet
these animals straggling across the road, and the fierce-
looking, shaggy-coated Highlanders seemed to be eyeing
you threateningly, as though to contest your right thereon.
But as soon as you are upon them, and appear to be
running the risk of impalement on their huge horns, away
they turn, to canter clumsily over the wide-spreading
moorland. And it is the same with the rams. Occasionally
a collie dashes out at you barking from a cottage, only

to be contemptuously ignored as a nuisance by the pony; more rarely a native appears, looking askance at the Sabbath-breaker riding into Portree.

It is very appropriate that, on the way to S. Columba's Church, you should pass what used to be called Loch Columcille, now Loch Portree, on which is the tiny S. Columba's Isle. Here are the very fragmentary remains of a very small church, which may have been founded by S. Columba himself when he was in Skye, for the building is ancient enough to date back to his day.

I have never enjoyed a meal more than the breakfasts taken by the roadside on the way back from church, though indeed I have sometimes made disconcerting discoveries with regard to my food supply after an extra jolty journey. I remember once, when dear, good Bella insisted on packing my satchel herself overnight. I had not only first to disinter my (brand new) altar manual from amongst a mess of quite superfluous bananas, but I found that my kettle had furrowed a black way into the sandwich stack, so tightly had the roomy satchel been packed with the superabundant supplies considered necessary to sustain me after my riding exertions. Dismounting by a stream, I have tethered my horse to browse while my kettle boiled and I feasted—both literally on my generous supplies, and metaphorically on the scenery, looking over to Port-an-Righ, the King's port, so called after the visit of James V. in the course of his tour amongst the islands. Its original name, however, was Kiltaraglan, after a chapel of one, Tarlorgan, built there.

For all the times I have been to Sligachan, I must confess to having left the corries round Loch Brittle unexplored. Indeed, so lost is my heart to the way up the Glen that, though I have grudgingly torn myself away from it on odd occasions—mostly very wet days—to climb to the head of the Bealach Maim, and to explore Corrie na Creiche, I have only once gone right down into Glen Brittle. Of course, it is speaking with conscious hypercriticism to

say that this place made no very great appeal to me,
i.e., in comparison with *the* Glen, the only outstanding impression left on my mind of a gloriously hot day being the
wealth of giant meadow-rue growing on the deep white
sands of the sea shore.   It was at Glen Brittle that there
lived Mr. D. Cameron, the author of the famous
" Highlandman's Prayer ":

> " O that ta peats would cut themselves,
> And ta fesh shump on ta shore,
> And that we in our peds might lie,
> For aye and for efermore!"

Corrie na Creiche, the " hollow of the spoil," so called
from its being a favourite retreat with the proceeds of a
raid, was, in 1601, the scene of what was probably
the last great clan battle in Skye.   If you look at
Bartholomew's map of Skye, not far below Vaternish Point
in the Macleod Country, you will see marked *Blar
Mhille gearraidh,* the " battle of the spoiling of the
dykes," and beneath, this curious note, " site of conflict
between the Macleods and the Macdonalds."   From this
remark one would naturally conclude that here took
place an event so unique in the chronicles of the island as
to demand special attention, whereas, in point of fact, it
is some meeting of these two clans that did *not* issue in a
fight that would claim the quality of uniqueness and call
for remark.   The sites of their conflicts must cover Skye
almost from end to end.   It seems that the fight in Corrie
na Creiche was provoked by an invasion of Macleod
country in the absence of its famous chief Rory Mor:
others say the Macleods attacked the Macdonalds as a
revenge for the treatment Donald Gorm meted out to his
wife, Margaret, Rory Mor's sister.   Whatever the cause,
however, Rory's brother, Alexander Macleod of Minginish,
in the chief's absence, gathered the clan together, and led
them to this corrie.   Here the next day the Macdonalds,
under Donald Gorm, fell upon them, and the clans fought

till nightfall, when the Macleods were defeated, their leader and three of his chief clansmen being captured.

I have left to the last Glen Sligachan itself. It is not in this case the attraction of association which is the supreme one, and, in admitting this, I hope I am not lacking in reverence to the memory of Prince Charlie who, in his journey to Elgol, passed up the Glen and climbed over the ridge between Glamaig and Marsco. It is rather the fulness of the scope that one finds in this Glen of glens for the capacities both of the body and of the spirit. The Gaelic poet, Duncan MacIntyre, in his " Last Adieu to the Hills," gives exact expression to the experience known to every true Celt who rejoices in glowing health, energy, and sturdy limbs:

"Oh, wildly as the bright day gleamed I climbed the mountain's breast,
  And when I to my home returned the sun was in the west:
  'Twas health and strength, 'twas life and joy, to wander freely there,
  To drink at the fresh mountain stream, to breathe the mountain air."

The mountain lover finds solely amongst the mountains what the sailor finds alone upon the sea—that sense of limitless freedom so essential to the well-being of the free spirit—life in its purest, simplest, physical sense. Nowhere except among the mountains is it possible for the Highlander to give complete expression to every part of his being. The exultant spirit in him, fired by the sight of the mountains, craves to climb: the strength of him welcomes what to another is the painful toil involved in the rough going over the rocky, broken track, the great beds of boulders, the screes, the burns to be crossed, leaping from stone to stone, the bogs similarly to be evaded. Everything in such a progress responds to some need within him. And the mountains—over and above all, the mountains! It is in them that at once the highest and the deepest sense is touched: their majesty, the awe and love alike that inspire, the immutability, speak of the glorious and eternal Trinity in Unity to Whom the yearning spirit stretches out, finding in the mountains exultation and incentive to attain.

One mile of Glen Sligachan is said to be the equivalent of two ordinary miles. But in practice mileage surely resolves itself into a question of interest aroused rather than of measurement. Certainly to a lover of the wild, the monotony of a level stretch of highroad, with its dull even surface, doubles the distance, while the interest of a constantly varied and often ill-defined track, full of surprises and with a marked individuality, seems actually to halve the real distance.

The most strenuous tramp I ever took was one from Sligachan Inn over to Loch Scavaig by Camasunary, and back by Harta Corrie, a round which my expert companion, John MacKenzie, estimated at nineteen miles. But the intense heat of the day, the ever-increasing interest of every step of the way, and the sheer magnificence of the scenery, conspired to make that day's expedition of much less account as a record than lesser tramps taken on highroads. Along the Glen as far as the point where one turns off to the track for the ascent of Drumhain was, of course, very familiar ground. So hot was the day, and so weighted were we with photographic paraphernalia and provisions for the way (supplied by Bella Stewart's liberal hand), that there was scarcely a stream we crossed from which we did not drink, going down on our hands and knees to get as much water as we wanted. Deer were gathered high up on the seamed and barren side of Marsco: below, on the emerald green sward—surely the fairies' playground—countless rabbits scampered: overhead an eagle soared: in every direction large and shimmering dragon flies flashed to and fro. Camasunary being our objective, we kept to the left instead of taking the track to the right for the usual route to Coruisk by Drumhain. It is at the foot of this ridge that the ponies are tethered to a large boulder whilst their burdens complete the ascent—about a mile— on foot. But in whichever direction you go, it is just at

IN GLEN SLIGACHAN—SHEWING IN DISTANCE SITUATION OF HARTA CORRIE

the parting of the ways that you get the most perfect view
of beautiful Blaven, in the sunshine more than ever
justifying its naming whichever be the meaning, for its
blueness imparts a bloom akin to that seen on a fine ripe
plum. Behind Blaven is the splintered top of Clach Ghlas,
also a very fascinating peak, not least as the home of the
sea eagles.

Instead of choosing the usual Camasunary route—to the
left of Loch-an-Athain, John elected to take me round on
the trackless further side, where, so thick and high was the
growth of heather, progress could only be made in a
succession of leaps and bounds till the river had to be
crossed at the end of Loch na Creubhaig. " Brushwood "
grows plentifully about the east side of this loch—hence its
name. It was the easier method to splash boldly through
the water, well over our boot-tops, rather than attempt a
series of leaps so wide apart that, as far as I was
concerned, an undesigned headlong plunge in mid-stream
would have been the inevitable result. Amongst the many
interesting things I learnt during this strenuous progress
one was elicited by a question as to the presence of
adders in the Glen. John told me that there were a few
to be met with occasionally, and that when sheep came
across them, they promptly stamped upon the reptile's head
and so killed it. He also pointed out two seagulls which,
he said, were in pursuit of a sea-eagle, a common object of
attack on their part—a surprising inversion of what one
would have expected.

Camasunary is *Camas fhionnairigh,* " the bay of the
white sheiling," a name that conveys even yet a fair
picture of its nature and setting, where a solitary farmhouse
and bungalow look the picture of loneliness. You cross
the river by some stepping-stones in order to take the
four-mile climb round a steep and rocky headland of Loch
Scavaig, where the scenery reaches the climax of
splendour. A great deal of fuss has been made in guide
books over the difficulties of this route, in the course of

12

which you encounter the " Bad Step." The track is indeed rough going, but the ascent is quite easy, and the " Bad Step " itself—only about fifteen feet above the sea level—requires neither a (technical) climber nor any great courage to tackle it, certainly little enough " head." Otherwise it would never have been crossed by me, who, on the verge of anything very high and sheer, am always tempted to throw myself over.

It is when you have gained a flat, rocky plateau just above the " Bad Step " that you obtain the finest, because the most comprehensive, view of the Coolin and Lochs Coruisk and Scavaig. Far below is the emerald sea, the sun turning the ripples on its surface into dancing diamonds : a rocky islet holds the centre : beyond, rising in tiers, are masses of gabbro, scored, seamed, and rounded ɔy glacial action ; then a narrow streak of water gives a glimpse of Loch Coruisk hiding in the hollow of the hills, which in the distance rise into a vast amphitheatre of ramparts—of rugged splendour and supreme majesty. Not far below this sublime view-point is the " Bad Step " —a traverse of some few yards along the face of a sloping rock. If you take it facing the sea, with your back braced against the wall of rock behind you, it is quite an easy matter, even carrying a knapsack, to work your way along. And, as you do so, it is fascinating to look down through the fissure—only about a foot across at its widest part— at the sea below, and to listen to the hollow gurgling of its ebb and flow. Then you come out on a tumble of sharp-edged rocks, amongst which grows a profusion of large ferns, and you descend over them until you are down on the shore. If it be high tide and a warm day, you appreciate the necessity of taking off boots and stockings to wade the short distance round to the depression through which you pass on your way over to Loch Coruisk.

Of this famous kelpie-haunted loch and its surroundings I am not going to attempt to give any picture where already so many exist—some of which must be familiar to everyone.

BELOW THE "BAD STEP," LOCH SCAVAIG

I will merely say that, having read many of these descriptions, and seen several pictures alleged to represent the scene, they seem to me to be in several particulars not very faithful literal representations. The first impression the loch made upon me was that of being a much smaller sheet of water, surrounded by much lower mountains, than I had been led to anticipate. In all the pictures I have ever seen, the heights literally soar, and are out of all proportion to the reality. The barrenness and loneliness, too, of the place also seem greatly exaggerated by writers. I have been to many another spot where the sense of loneliness and the actual barrenness were much more apparent, such for instance as Corrie na Creiche.

But these criticisms are not intended as a disparagement of the " hollow of the water," which must always exercise a peculiar fascination, increasing with every visit, upon the lover of wild solitudes. I was once on its shores when the day, hitherto beautiful, began to cloud over, and from the distance came threatenings of thunder, rapidly growing more pronounced as it drew nearer. Then through the fretted pinnacles of the peaks reverberated crash after crash, echoing and re-echoing in most awe-inspiring peals, and only lacking the accompaniment of lightning to complete the scene of the vengeful wrath of some angry giant. And later, in the boat which was taking me back the way I came, it was most impressive to hear the thunder travelling over the water, and to watch the frown gathering over the dark face of the mountains.

The climb from Loch Coruisk up the heathery slopes to the top of Drumhain is a very easy one, but it is all too rarely taken in either direction. People who land from a boat seem content to see Coruisk from below, and those who climb Drumhain from Sligachan are satisfied to see the loch and the surrounding scenery from above. But it is a distinct loss to miss the route which first follows the rocky bed of the Allt-a-Choire Riabhaich, where, poised on the very brink of the rocks which form the banks of the stream, great boulders seem to occupy a very perilous position.   And where better can you hear the water telling its tale in the " Song of the Highland River "?

> " Lashing the rocks with my foamy flail,
> Where the black crags frown
> I pour sheer down,
> Into the cauldron boiling and brown."

But, as we were going home by Harta Corrie, our way lay up by the head of Loch Coruisk, and involved another bold splash through the River Scavaig to walk up the west side of the Loch.   The climb [7] up on to the Drumhain ridge by the route we took on this occasion is certainly not without some precarious features.   Following no discernible track, it involved one or two hazardous circumventings of rocks abutting in mid-air from the mountain side where, if you lost your foothold, the fall would probably have proved disastrous.   But we gained the ridge with only a stumble apiece—mine a curious one in which my throat met a stone, and does not mind if it never hits one again.

The view from any part of Drumhain, looking in any direction, is glorious beyond words, for you find yourself high up in a world of broken, splintered, and shattered peaks, close at hand and flung far back: and out at sea gleam the dream islands of Rum and Eigg. No matter how early in the day you gain Drumhain, and how late you leave it, there is never time enough to linger as long as you would up here in the clouds—provided the day is fine and the view is not obscured—especially with the descent into Harta Corrie before you.

Into this wild corrie we made our descent seated, sliding practically from top to bottom on the smooth surface of a succession of slopes of rock until we came down upon the loose stones with which the bottom of the corrie is liberally

[7] Here as elsewhere, I do not, of course, speak as a technical climber.

bestrewn. At the head of this hollow lies Lota Corrie —surely the smallest corrie to be found anywhere, for it is simply a shelf of bare rock on to which you have to climb, and then indeed you find yourself in barrenness and loneliness to which Coruisk is, in comparison, an entire stranger.

It was in Harta Corrie that another fierce encounter took place between the Macdonalds and the Macleods, who fought through an entire day till not one Macleod was left, and the bodies of the slain were piled round the base of the huge rock, topped by a rowan tree, and still called the " Bloody Stone." The fairies, it is said, fashioned their bows and arrows from the ribs of these dead men, since they are buried where the country of three clans meet. Native folklore also tells a grim tale of a cave near by where a man sold his soul for the gold the cave contained. But for all Sgurr nan Uamh, " the peak of the cave," is the height that guards the entrance to Harta Corrie, all trace of the cave and its treasure has been lost.

Having somehow missed me on my return from this tramp, the kindly Bella, encountering John instead, made anxious enquiry about me. John, not as young as he was, and feeling his age after a fairly stiff day, evidently thought that his increasing years rather than my comparative youth merited any concern that was going. In an aggrieved tone, therefore, he answered: " Uch, *she* wass fresh enough! It's *me* you should pe asking after if you wass asking after anyone!"

The healthy mental tiredness, allied to increased mental activity, that follows upon a long day's strenuous exercise is one of the pleasantest of sensations. United to the comfortable feeling of satisfaction at " something attempted, something done," it makes the perfect finish of a perfect day. You come in from twelve hours among the hills, conscious of every muscle in your body. You take a hot bath, a hearty meal, and then look forward to your well-earned bed, though, before you seek it, you may have a dozen plates to change. But at last, lying flat on your bed, and well stretched out, a great content steals over you, and, falling instantly into dreamless slumber, you lie like the proverbial log (not trooper!) to wake up after your customary eight hours, fresher and fitter than ever to spend another day in like fashion.

––––––

PART IV

THE DEMESNE OF DUNVEGAN

As all things must come to an end, so, alas, a visit to Sligachan is no exception to the inexorable rule, and, therefore, Macdonald territory must be left for Dunvegan, the capital, as one may term it, of the Macleod country. It is a distance of twenty-five miles from Sligachan by road, and it recalls one of the wettest drives I ever took. Unfortunately, too, it was the only time I had ever gone on this road further than Struan, which is fourteen miles from Sligachan.

It was at this hamlet that, despite the heavy rain, my friend and I descended to see an eirde, earth, or " Pict's " house, which, we were told, was to be found on the moor at Knock Ullinish, an ancient hill of justice, as this prefix invariably indicates. Setting out over the sodden moor, we came across the fern-grown opening in the side of a bank, but as all but a few feet at the entrance of the passage had fallen in, there was very little to be seen of the actual structure beyond the stone posts supporting the lintel of the doorway. These earth-houses are long, low, narrow underground passages, or galleries, always more or less curved, and gradually expanding, both laterally and vertically, till their termination in a chamber sometimes as much as ten or twelve feet wide and six or seven feet in height. They are generally burrowed in the face of a hill, and are constructed usually with convergent walls, most

commonly made like the drystone dykes of uncemented,
undressed stones, and are roofed with stone flags which
occasionally also form the walls.   Their narrow entrance,
probably originally closed by a stone door, sloped to the
floor level of the chamber at the end; and occasionally
they contained a second door midway, and a second
chamber, circular in shape, branching off.   The purpose
of the eirde-house is still a matter for some conjecture,
but, as they are generally found, as in this case, in
association with a dun or broch, it is probable they were
used as hiding places when the enemy's approach was
signalled from the adjacent fort.   From the low height of
these earth houses, the inference is that their prehistoric
builders must have been a short and small people, which
the Celts were not.   The execrable weather made it impossible for us to explore Dun Beag, the " little fort," on
the hillside above this eirde-house—a forced omission from
our programme we very much regretted, as it is the best
preserved of all the hill forts left in Skye, and may indeed
be a broch.   But, as I shall be describing later both a
typical broch and a dun seen elsewhere, this mere passing
mention of Dun Beag may, under the circumstances, be
forgiven.

There is also at Struan, Dun Gharsainn, where the fairies
used to dance in the moonlight until some foolish mortal
despoiled the fairy bower by taking away some of its
stones, and so effectually banished for ever the aggrieved
little folk.

This road is reputed to be second only in beauty to that
from Broadford to Sligachan, but unless the second half
is finer than the first (which I have often tramped in fine
weather), beautiful though it is, I would rank higher the
road already described over to Loch Eishort.   After
rejoining our " machine " at Struan, the rain—of the all-
obliterating variety—seemed more determined than ever
that we should see nothing beyond the actual road.   Nor
did we, excepting only well-defined objects just by the

road side, such as the little (Episcopal) church of S. John,
at the head of Loch Caroy, now, alas, disused, by reason
of emigration of the congregation.   We were, of course,
unable to judge for ourselves of the reputed beauty of its
situation, but we did know that between the church and
the loch was the old gathering-ground of the Clan Macleod,
where, in response to the last summons of the Fiery Cross
in Skye, the clansmen gathered in 1745, only to find their
degenerate chief sought—happily in vain—to rally them on
the wrong side.   We could see nothing of Macleod's Tables
on the land by reason of their too much " tablecloth," nor
yet one of his " Maidens," those rocks being quite lost at
sea.   It was most exasperating to know that somewhere
high on the moor to the left, just above Loch Caroy, we
must perforce leave unexplored a prehistoric cemetery—
notably two huge prehistoric tumuli, in reality chambered
cairns, though traditionally alleged locally to have been
raised to cover the fallen of the Macdonalds and the
Macleods, respectively, in their reputed last clan battle,
fought in the mist.

Not before we were thoroughly soaked to the skin, the
rain having at last triumphed over our oilskins, did we
reach the Inn of Dunvegan, the " little fort," and next
morning, again in the rain, we set out to see all we might
of the ancient seat, originally of the Macdonalds, but
for many more years of the Macleods of Harris, or
Siol Tormoid.   The name Macleod, meaning " ugly wolf,"
is said to be derived from the clan's progenitor, an
Earl of Orkney, called *Ljotr;* and the Norse origin of the
clan is insisted on by its own older poets.   The Macleods of
Harris (whose seat is Dunvegan) are descended from
Tormod (Thor-protected), the elder son of the founder of
the clan, thence they are known as the " seed of Norman,"
as Tormod is now translated.   Almost inseparably
associated with the Macleods are their hereditary pipers,
the Macrimmons (son of the famed protector), the most
famous of all the players in the Highlands.   As pipers to·

the Macleod, the Macrimmons had a grant of the farm of Borrevaig.

The present chief of Macleod makes emphatic claim to the Mackenzie sett as the Macleod tartan, but other authorities are agreed this is a misappropriation due to a confusion initially attributable to the Lord Macleod, who, in 1778, raised the " Macleod " Highlanders. Being himself a Mackenzie, his title merely a confusing courtesy one accorded to the eldest son of the Earl of Cromarty, he put his " Macleod " Highlanders into his own clan tartan— the Mackenzie. Hence its frequent mistaken adoption by the Macleods.

How Dunvegan Castle passed from the Macdonalds to the Macleods is told in the following legend, which, however, it is difficult to reconcile with the accepted statement that this was effected through the marriage of one of the clan with Macraild Armine, the Dane,[8] whose name does not appear in any Macdonald genealogy. According to the legend, the old chief Macdonald had no heir, and his only daughter, marrying Macleod of Harris, had a son whom she was most anxious should succeed to Dunvegan. One day the old man put out in his galley from Skye to visit his son-in-law over in Harris, and Macleod, aware of this intention, went out to meet him in a much larger galley, himself at the helm and his wife seated beside him. Soon a mist rose over the sea, and Macleod, seeing he was in danger of running down Macdonald's barge, made to alter the course. But his wife caught at his arm, and, grasping it tightly, whispered in his ear: " Macleod, Macleod, there is only that galley between you and Dunvegan!" The chief, taking the unnatural daughter's hint, deliberately collided with Macdonald's barge, sank it, and allowed his father-in-law to drown. Then when Dunvegan was reached, Macleod, without mentioning his part in it, related the accident that had cost Macdonald his life, and his wife claimed the castle in her son's name.

---

[8] Macraild or MacHarold is now one of the Macleod sept names.

You pass through the most beautiful woods—non-existent in Dr. Johnson's time—reminding you of those surrounding the castle of the rival clan at Armadale; past the waterfall which is known as " Rory Mor's Nurse," because that famous chief sought its lullabies to soothe his slumbers; over the Fairy Bridge, to the oldest inhabited castle in Great Britain.   Then you come upon the modernized landward approach, now the front entrance to Dunvegan, where, on the left, the " Fairy Tower," built by Alasdair Crotach, " Alexander the Humpbacked," the sixteenth century chief, faces you.   The oldest part of the castle, the keep, dating from the fourteenth century, is incorporated in the building crowned by the high modern tower that lies to the right.   The intervening building is attributed to Sir Roderick Macleod, more familiarly known as Rory Mor, " big Roderick," who was knighted by James VI., and Iain Breac (freckled John) carried on but did not live to finish his work.   The rocky side of the castle is entirely detached from the mainland by a natural chasm, now permanently bridged, but it is only from the sea front that you gain a proper impression of the strength and dignity of the castle, situated on Loch Follart, an arm of Dunvegan Loch.

It is a gaunt, grim, grey pile, well fitted to weather the tempest, that there confronts you, a formidable bulwark to contest the landing of any sea-borne invader.   To the right, there are low, rugged cliffs, topped by Scots firs, and they, together with the boulder-strewn beach and the sea itself lapping at the base of the castle, make the perfection of settings to the bold upstanding outline of the fortress. It was into Dunvegan Loch that James V. sailed with his fleet in the course of his visitation.   The castle was yielded to him, and he took Alastair Crotach, the then chief, prisoner as a hostage.

Dunvegan, chosen by the Royalists as the meeting place for a council of war after their defeat at Lochgarry in 1654, became, on the eve of Culloden, a refuge for the other side of politics, sheltering Forbes and Loudon.

On the sea front there is still to be seen, opening on to the rocks, the ancient door which was the original entrance to the castle. You can still see within the doorway the grooves in which the portcullis ran, and in the wall the hole, ten feet deep, for the great beam to bar the doorway from within. A passage, fifty feet long, but only from five to seven feet wide, slopes gradually upward, with steps at intervals, to the platform of the rock; and to the right, off the centre of the passage, is the ancient well. Inside the courtyard, reared against the sea wall, is the stone effigy of a woman, whose costume, though somewhat suggestive of the " milkmaid " style, is very indeterminate as to date, and might range from the reign of James VI. to the Commonwealth, or even later. And in view of the general persistence of fashions in remote places long after they had become obsolete elsewhere, it is always unsafe to date a West Highland figure from its costume. This effigy is most popularly supposed to represent Isabella, the wife of Rory Mor, and with every probability. Indeed, one authority states that upon his tower were placed curious effigies of himself and his lady, " the last of which still exists, but is thrown from its original position." One writer confidently asserts his opinion, however, both that it is the effigy of Flora, the wife of Iain Breac, and that it came from the chapel, now a complete ruin, outside the castle, but his arguments do not appear to me to be sound.

It would be a disappointment indeed to find there were no tales associated with Dunvegan Castle, for it invites them. The invitation, however, has met with the heartiest response, and it is more likely to be a case of satiety than of disappointment with the reader. There is the favourite story of the Macleod who, as he sat one night comfortably within the walls of the castle while a great storm raged outside, exclaimed, " If my bitterest foe were at the foot of those rocks demanding shelter on such a night, I could not refuse it!" And, as though to put his words to the proof, there followed the news that there was wrecked in

Loch Dunvegan, Donald Gorm Macdonald, who had treated his wife, Rory Mor's sister, with the greatest possible indignity. Having fallen in love with another woman, Donald wished to be rid of his wife, who, it seems, had but one eye. Therefore, with every sign of contempt, Donald drove her forth from his castle of Duntulm, mounting her, so it is said, on a one-eyed horse, led by a one-eyed boy, and followed by a one-eyed dog. It may be judged, then, that when the perpetrator of this grim joke appeared at Dunvegan claiming shelter, he put a very severe strain upon Macleod's hospitality. A meal, however, was laid in the hall, but when the Macdonalds entered, the chief noticed upon the table a boar's head,[9] which was of ill omen to the Macdonalds. So, suspecting treachery, and thinking it as well to put as great a distance as possible between himself and his host, Donald Gorm passed with his men below the salt. The Macleod, however, courteously made room at his side for his chief guest, but Donald rudely refused the position, saying, " Thanks, I'll remain where I am; but, mark you, wherever Macdonald of Sleat is, that's the head of the table!" [10]

His advance thus repelled, the host turned the conversation to hunting, and handed round his handsome dirk for admiration. As Donald Gorm passed it on in silence, the more genial Macleod enquired, " Why shew ye not your dirk, Donald? I hear it is very fine." Whipping out his *biodag* on the instant, the Macdonald flourished it

[9] The Macleod crest, see p. 202.

[10] The same anecdote is related of Donald Gormeson, this chief's son, who lived in Elizabeth's reign. Present in London at a Lord Mayor's banquet, the chief was given, in ignorance of his native position, a seat llow down the table. When the mistake was discovered, a message of apology was sent to Gormeson, and he was requested to come up and sit by the Lord Mayor. But Gormeson replied: "Tell his lordship not to be troubling himself. Wherever Macdonald is sitting, that will be the head of the table." It is not unlikely that Gormeson may have heard of the incident at Dunvegan, and thought that neither it, nor the proverbial " swagger " of the Macdonalds would lose by repetition.

in the air, exclaiming, " Here it is, Macleod, and in the best hand for pushing it home in all the twenty-four islands of the Hebrides!" Provocative though this speech was, Macleod sought to turn it off by fishing for a compliment, so he asked, " And where is the second best hand in the Hebrides to drive home a dirk?" " Here!" exclaimed the proud chief of Sleat instantly, changing over the dagger into his left hand, and brandishing it in his host's face.

But if Donald Gorm was blunt and aggressive in his conversation, the open hostility he shewed was at least more commendable than the smooth speech with which Macleod veiled intended treachery, for the events of the night did not end with these churlish episodes. A Macleod maiden who was in love with one of Donald Gorm's men begged him not to sleep in the barn, declaring that none who passed the night there would live to see the morning. The Macdonald follower told his chief of the intended treachery, so that, when Macleod informed Donald that he had prepared for him a room next his own, and had made up beds of heather for his men in a barn, Macdonald, refusing the bed-chamber, announced his intention of sleeping amongst his clansmen. This suited his host's villainous plan equally well, and both Donald Gorm and his men were followed by Macleod eyes into the barn. But, unknown to the Macleods, their guests crept forth silently at midnight, and took shelter under a large rock not very far distant. They had not long made their escape, when signs of a fire were observed, and soon the sky was aglow with the flames kindled by the heather intended for the last bed of the Macdonalds. And to the confusion of the Macleods, early in the morning the Macdonalds marched past Dunvegan, their piper playing, " Macleod, Macleod of Dunvegan! I drove my dirk into your father's heart, and, in payment of last night's hospitality, I'll drive it to the hilt in the heart of his son!"

While to this day hatred of the Campbell clan is in the blood of most true and virile Macdonalds, for all the ancient feuds between the Macdonalds and the Macleods, not a trace of ill-feeling survives between these two clans. The difference must lie in the fact that in the one case there was a fundamental opposition of principles, a difference that cut too deeply for healing, in the other merely clan feuds, involving no matter of political or religious difference. For whilst the Macleods were with the Macdonalds in the maintenance of Royalist principles, even if they do not stand out as champions of the Church, the Campbells, on the other hand, were opposed to both as the protagonists of Presbytery, which was best calculated to advance alike the interests and the proverbial " greed of the Campbells."

The plans of the ground and first floors of Dunvegan Castle may help to a better understanding of its arrangement, especially when one passes within. The hall of the old keep is now the drawing-room—its walls nine feet thick, its original window slits enlarged into huge embrasures. It was probably in this hall that there took place the hideous tragedy which was the culmination of many ghastly crimes of which Iain Dubh Macleod was the perpetrator. This man was the unnatural son of Iain the Fairhaired, a relative of William the ninth chief of Macleod; and in the absence of the late chief's two brothers, he was elected to succeed him. After a series of treacherous murders, Iain Dubh, taking advantage of his brother, Donald Breac's, absence at their father's funeral, seized Dunvegan Castle, killed its warders, and imprisoned his brother Tormod's widow. Thus, when the mourners returned from the burial, they found the castle closed against them, and were confronted by Iain Dubh, fully armed, at the head of the narrow staircase of the seaward entrance. In the hand-to-hand encounter that followed, Donald was slain by Iain, who, to make a clean sweep of his family, killed Tormod's three sons, and imprisoned his remaining brothers with several others of the clan in the dungeons of the castle.

The entrace to the only dungeon extant, a narrow one,

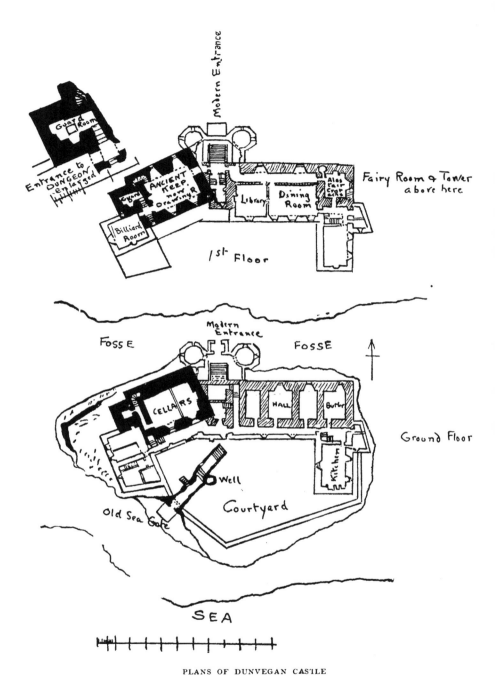

PLANS OF DUNVEGAN CASTLE

(By permission of MacGibbon & Ross' *Castellated and Domestic Architecture of Scotland*,
with several names inserted by M. E. M. D.)

13

4 feet 4 inches by 6 feet, cut in the castle rock to a depth of 16 feet, is in a windowless room adjoining the present drawing room. A flagstone covers the hole in the floor through which the prisoners were lowered, and the only light that reaches the dungeon comes through a narrow loophole set high in the wall. While Iain Dubh's victim's languished in prison, the Argyll Campbells saw fit to intervene on the ground that they were the guardians of Mary, William the ninth chief's only child. They apparently considered that she had been dispossessed of her rights by Iain Dubh, if indeed she was not numbered amongst his captives. A strong Campbell force landed at Roag, and there met Iain Dubh by agreement at the adjacent church of Kilmuir, where he pretended to accept their terms. He then invited eleven Campbell chiefs to a banquet at Dunvegan, where each guest was sandwiched between two Macleods. When the feast was over, a cup of blood was set before each guest as the signal for their stabbing by their neighbours, Iain himself killing the highest in rank. In 1559, however, the second brother of William the ninth chief, Torquil, who, unlike his brother, had escaped Iain's dagger, managed with the co-operation of a warder of Dunvegan to get the better at last of Iain, who escaped to sea in his galley, to meet ultimately with a horrible fate in Ireland.

It is not surprising after all these fearful happenings that there should be in the " Fairy Tower " a haunted room, but by whose ghost of all the many one supposes might well haunt it, I have not been able to discover. Both Dr. Johnson and Sir Walter Scott slept in this chamber, and the poet named it the " Fairy Room." Above it is Alasdair Crotach's chamber, where the family muniments are now kept. The cellars which are now beneath the drawing-room have walls 11 feet thick, and used to be the kitchen.

Of relics, Dunvegan Castle has a goodly share, including some of wide fame. The greatest of these is the

Bratach Shìth, or Fairy Banner, of yellow silk worked with red spots, quite possibly of Saracen origin. But the most general tale is that a Macleod chief married a fairy, and, after twenty years, her alloted span of life, she was summoned to leave him at the Fairy Bridge, which is about three miles from Dunvegan. As she flew away, she dropped part of her silken attire, which the chief found and cherished as the " Fairy Flag." It is endued with power to succour the clan—on three occasions only—when it is waved. Twice has its power been invoked, once to avert the vengeance taken by the fairy giver herself upon Macleod's country when the chief had proved false to her memory by marrying a mortal wife: and secondly, to overcome the Macdonalds on one of the many occasions when they were getting the better of the Macleods.

Another legend has it that on the occasion of the birth of an heir, there were great festivities in the castle, and the nurse, being anxious to share in them, slipped away and left the infant alone. He, being restless, threw off all his clothes, but the fairies were watching over him, and, to protect him from cold, wrapped him about in the flag. Meanwhile the clansmen clamoured to see the young heir, and, slipping back into the nursery, the nurse caught up the child just as he was, and, as she carried him into the hall, an invisible choir chanted of the magic properties of the banner.

There is, too, a third tale, which accredits the flag with having been the girdle of a she-devil who haunted a wild pass in the Holy Land. A Crusading Macleod, taking the precautions urged upon him by a hermit, slew this evil spirit, and found his reward in the magic properties of her belt, which he used as a banner.

There was a hereditary keeper of the banner, who held the key of the iron chest which guarded it, and who alone might unfurl the banner in the hour of need. In such sacred esteem was the banner held, that the chief, who was bound to guard it with his life, stood in front of it when it was unfurled. Twelve of the best of the clan, the highest born and the most renowned, were called upon to support the standard when it was raised, each grasping the staff with one hand and holding a drawn sword in the other. The first of the hereditary keepers (because he had occasion to unfurl the banner) was buried on Iona in the same grave as his chief: the second had a most extraordinary burial privilege accorded to him, which was continued to his successors in the office.

Now, in view of the tattered frailty of the banner, it is scarcely within the possibilities to wave it for the third occasion. When Dr. Norman Macleod, the celebrated Established minister, visited Dunvegan in 1799, the flag, it would appear, was kept inviolate in an iron chest, the key of which was supposed to be lost. It is in connection with the opening of this chest, at which he was present, that Dr. Macleod relates a prophecy of *Coinneach Odhar* [11] *Fiosaiche,* Kenneth the ochre-coloured Seer, better known as the Brahan Seer, who flourished in the seventeenth century. Kenneth Mackenzie, the most famous of all second-sighted Highlanders, has to his credit very many fulfilled prophecies, including the making of the Caledonian Canal, and the coming of the " chariot without horse or bridle," the " iron horse," to Ross-shire. Dr. Macleod vouches for it that of the prophecy, at least a hundred years old, concerning Dunvegan, much was fulfilled on the occasion of his visit.

The Brahan Seer had foretold that " when Norman the third Norman," " the son of a hard-boned English lady," would perish by an accidental death: when " Macleod's Maidens " became the property of a Campbell: when a fox had cubs in one of the turrets of the castle: and, particularly, when the Fairy Banner should be exhibited for the last time, then the glory of the Macleod family

[11] This, a deep or dark cream colour, is generally wrongly rendered " dun," which, however, in Gaelic is *donn.*

should depart; a great part of the estate should be sold, so that a *curach* would carry all the gentlemen of Macleod over Loch Dunvegan; but the time would come when another Iain Breac should arise who should redeem their estates, and raise the power and honours of the house to a higher pinnacle than ever.   Dr. Macleod then proceeds to relate how, under the pledge of the strictest secrecy, he was present when a smith prised open the iron chest in which the Fairy Flag was kept, but how this circumstance could be construed into its " exhibition " for the last time Dr. Macleod does not explain.   Probably " exhibition " does not convey the proper meaning of the Gaelic word so translated.   After describing the flag, however, Dr. Macleod states that " on this occasion " the news of the death of the heir, " Norman the third Norman," a lieutenant of *H.M.S. Queen Charlotte,* blown up at sea, reached the castle.   In the course of the same week, " Macleod's Maidens " were sold to a Campbell, and a fox in the possession of a Lieut. Maclean, occupying a room in the West Turret, had cubs there.   These Dr. Macleod himself handled, and he claims, therefore, that so far the Brahan Seer's prophecy was fulfilled.   But the rest contingent upon these happenings happily did not and has not yet come to pass.

The second heirloom is Rory Mor's drinking horn, holding about two pints, which each chief was expected to drain at a single draught, grasping the ox-horn by the mouth, and letting it curl round the arm.   It has around the top a deep silver band ornamented with Celtic tracery.

The third treasure kept in the drawing-room is the Dunvegan Cup, of Irish origin, quadrangular in shape, made of dark wood covered with filagree silver work.   It has an inscription round the four sides of the rim, and from the constant repetition of the Sacred Monogram inside, it has possibly been used as a chalice.   This, called by the family the " cup of Neil Glundubh," [12] is alleged to have

[12] Black Knee.

come into the family possession in the time of Malcolm the third chief.

In other glass cases are displayed autograph letters of Dr. Johnson and Sir Walter Scott, with other literary relics; but it is to the dining-room one must go for the Jacobite treasures. Here is a lock, silky and yellow, of Prince Charlie's hair, cut off by Flora Macdonald at Kingsburgh, and brought by her daughter's marriage into the Macleod family. There is, too, the Prince's well-worn waistcoat of embroidered cream silk given him by Flora's family, and worn by him at Holyrood ball before Prestonpans; his drinking-glass: her stays (which do *not* stir the emotions), and her pincushion, worked with the names of those who suffered after Culloden. Out in the corridor, amongst many weapons, is Rory Mor's two-handed claymore and the basket-hilted sword used by the chief who led a thousand of his clan to fight for the King at Worcester. Other famous relics have disappeared, the harp of Roderick Morrison, Iain Breac's blind harper: Rory Mor's great bow, and his fine oaken bed.

It will be agreed that no one can complain of dearth of interest in connection with Dunvegan, nor is the interest exhausted by historical associations. Other tales attach to the place, such as the following, told as a Highlander tells it. A man of God was one day reading the Holy Book on a knoll near Dunvegan Castle. The fairy knoll opened when, as the natives say, " there was no opening at all," and out came one of the little folk. " That is a good book thou art reading," observed the fairy, and the reader replied, " It is the book of God." " And is there any hope for us in the Book?" questioned the little woman in green. Now the man, although his heart was in heaven, yet had his head on earth, so he told the truth, yet not without art. " There is hope in the Book for the whole seed of Adam," he answered. Scarcely were the words out of his mouth than the fairy gave a shriek of perdition, and vanished instantly. But for a long time afterwards came a voice of wailing from the knoll: " Not of the seed of Adam we—not of the seed of Adam we!"

Of the esteem in which the MacCrimmons were held the following tale witnesses. Two night wanderers were passing a wood near Dunvegan Castle, and one said to the other: " Are they not the two beautiful things, the moon in the sky, and the music of the mavis in yonder wood?" But the second rejoined scornfully, " Not the mavis at all. It is Padruig Mor Maccruimein and the warbling of the mavis in his fingers." There is an allusion here to the third part of the fairy enchantment that had been cast upon this great piper. After he had been endowed with the gift of being the finest player, and the best of company, the fairy decreed that his playing should be at its best at the full moon, thus allying it to madness.

Like many another clan, the Macleods have a clan proverb, coined after an incident in which some Dunvegan man was killed by a cat; so that now " as fond as the Macleods are of cats " is expressive of Highland aversion.

Never shall I forget the unique ride on the " coach " which conveyed us from Dunvegan to Portree. No incident could better illustrate the leisureliness and indifference to the passage of time, the easy adaptability, and the imperturbable good nature that characterizes the Highlander. We had decided at the last moment to leave Dunvegan earlier than originally intended, taking Saturday's mail coach instead of Monday morning's boat. We were told the mail left at 5 P.M., and, being warned to be at the Post Office in good time, we arrived considerably before that hour, but saw no sign either of a coach or of other passengers. To pass the time, we strolled along the road, and remarked on a derelict vehicle of archaic appearance stranded by the roadside. Imagine our surprise when at 6.30 P.M. we beheld this same archaic chariot drawn up outside the Post Office! The box, which had accommodation for two persons beside the driver, rose high above the open interior—a well-like arrangement, with seats facing each other to accommodate three people on either side, while behind was an unenclosed platform, evidently designed for luggage. None of the seats had backs to them, and were innocent of any attempt at upholstery, whilst paint was a thing of the remote past. Already the " coach " looked fairly full with all the luggage it had on board. Two huge baskets, the post bags, our modest luggage, and sundry odd—mostly *very* odd—packages were stacked towering upon the platform in the rear, whilst other nondescript bundles were disposed in the well itself, and at the driver's feet. Climbing up over this baggage, I gained one of the box seats, to be followed by two natives, who, as if it were the most natural proceeding in the world, gently insinuated themselves with a squash beside me. Within the well, my poor friend shared the six seats with seven other people, and with the postman driving and another man perched on the baskets behind, the three horses, harnessed abreast, set out on their perilous twenty-three mile journey.

Before the first mile was passed, however, the " coach " drew up at the signal of a girl of about eighteen, waiting by the wayside. It seemed impossible that, for all the " coach's " proved elasticity, space could be found for another creature. But the driver made no trouble about it, cheerfully hauling the girl up to share his seat—or, rather, to oust him from it—for, for the rest of the time he occupied the rail running out from the box. Again a little further along the coach stopped, and this time a woman and child were picked up, to be disposed amongst the parcels and upon the feet of the suffering passengers packed together in the well. But the limit of accommodation had not yet been reached. The coach swung, gaily rocking, along the road, seeming in imminent danger of upsetting on every hill slope, when, with the appearance of a man with a horse at the end of a rope, the driver at once pulled up. Obviously here was someone from a distance expecting a parcel or package by the coach,

thought I.   But not a bit of it: we were taking on board
another passenger.   Where, to the traveller inexperienced
in this " coach," there was not a crevice where another
person could possibly be bestowed, the practised eye of the
newcomer at once found a place.   Therefore, behold him
scrambling up beside the man on the top of the baskets
behind, allowing his horse to trail contentedly in the wake
of the coach, his hoofs going " *kloop, kloop, kloop, kloop,*"
all the way.

At the foot of every considerable hill, which occurred
on an average at half-hour intervals, we all with cheerful
accord disentangled ourselves from each other and
descended, though I did wonder how all the pieces of the
puzzle would get fitted together into their places again
when we reached the top of the hill.   When we came to
Edinbane, where the arrival of the mail coach must be
the event of the day, not a soul was to be seen about the
inn, outside which the horses drew up.   Thereupon several
passengers were dispatched in various directions to hunt
up some one to water the horses and to serve famished
travellers.   At last the landlord was discovered some
distance off, and made a leisurely appearance, quite unconscious of there being anything strange about his
absence.   Upon enquiry, the only refreshment he could
offer us was the incongruous combination of very sweet
biscuits and a glass of ale.

Loading up again, still with the full complement of
passengers, but mercifully no more, shedding not a soul
nor even spilling one accidentally, we resumed our swaying
journey till Portree was reached.   Of course, all the way
along we had stopped at the various Post Offices on the
road, and now whenever at long intervals a big house
was passed, the postman-driver blew his whistle, and a
man or woman would appear at the gate to hand up letters
for the post, often with money for stamps and other Post
Office commissions; or the postman would descend from
his perch on the rail to clear the nondescript wooden letter

The DUNVEGAN MAIL COACH

Initial drawing by I.B. caricatured
and re-faced by M.S.M.D.

boxes of *very* unofficial pattern, often obvious makeshifts
fixed in odd places, to serve the convenience of the various
small crofting communities through which we passed.   It
is not uncommon for these wayside post boxes to take the
form of a small cupboard in which parcels can be placed,
and a friend has seen an old oven so employed.   Money is
placed on top of the parcels so deposited to pay for their
postage, and I have never heard of it being stolen.

On the appearance of the coach on the outskirts of the
most considerable of the hamlets, there darted out from
the primitive cottages dotting the hillsides girl after girl,
arrayed in prevailing town fashions, ready to escort the
men on their walk up the coming hill.   At the top, each
said good-bye to her partner, and ran back home again
across the moorland.

Through the beautiful Highland summer night, with its
scarcely diminished daylight, this unique journey proceeded.   We did regret the lateness of the hour—it must
have been nearly eleven—when we reached Skeabost, for
its associations with S. Columba appealed for a halt. I am
certain none of the passengers, and least of all the driver,
would have made the slightest objection to pulling up here
and awaiting our return from an exploration, had we so
desired.   But we felt it was *rather* late in the day, and
besides we were ravenous.

Here at the mouth of the River Snizort you can see from
the road S. Columba's Island, on which are scattered
broadcast the ruins of several churches, two of them fairly
complete shells. The island is reached by stepping-stones.
The smaller ruin is that dedicated to S. Columba, possibly
built in his day.   In the larger and entirely uninteresting
building is the remains of a font, and in the burial ground
some sculptured stones.   On the left of the roadside
we could just discern the isolated stone from which
S. Columba is traditionally said to have preached the
Catholic Faith to the heathen Celts in the days when Skye
was a thickly wooded island.   The mouth of the river is

also the traditional place associated with the prophecy of
S. Columba, as related by Adamnan, his biographer, in
immediate fulfilment of which Artbrannan, an old chief
who had kept his natural innocence, landed to seek Holy
Baptism from the saint, and, dying almost immediately
afterwards, was buried where he had landed.

We did not reach Portree till well after midnight, having
been told at Dunvegan we were due there " just about nine
o'clock," and I fear we succeeded in disturbing a good few
slumbers before we managed to rouse our hotel.

———

PART V

FROM PORTREE—NORTHWARD BY LAND AND SOUTHWARD BY SEA.

SINCE Uig, fifteen miles distant from Portree, was to be
our next centre, my friend thought she would like to try
a dog-cart as likely to prove a less sensational means of
locomotion than the Uig mail cart, assuming it to be of
kin to the Dunvegan vehicle.   But while she found the
front seat a decided improvement upon the accommodation
she   had   endured   from   Dunvegan,   my   outstanding
recollection of this method of progress (which took place
on another very wet day) was the limpet-like quality
required to keep attached to the very narrow back seat in
the course of our ascents of the very frequent and often
very steep hills.

In order to give a consecutive account of the famous
adventures of Prince Charlie in this district, I shall reserve
all reference to them for the way back, devoting the
journey to Uig and beyond, to places or matters of interest
unconnected with them.   The road itself is uninteresting
until just before reaching Uig—the brown moorland
through which it passes being uniformly dull and
monotonous.   The first object to arouse interest is the

house of Macdonald of Kingsburgh—to be seen in the distance through the trees—though now a few trees are all that mark the site of the famous old house, the new house replacing it having no historical associations. It was to the old Kingsburgh House that in 1557 the infamous Iain Dubh Macleod went to visit Donald the elder brother of William the ninth chief, Donald having retired here upon the second election of Iain the Fairhaired, Iain Dubh's father, as William's successor. On the pretext of planning a way to enforce Donald's prior claims to the chiefship, the unfilial Iain Dubh, despite his black reputation, actually induced Donald to meet him secretly at midnight. As the natural consequence of this foolish agreement, Donald was added to the list of Iain Dubh's victims.

Of much more intrinsic interest than Kingsburgh is the ruin of the old farm house of Peindun, about two miles further on, and, like Kingsburgh, considerably off the road —almost, indeed, on the shores of Loch Snizort. Gaunt, grim, and four-square rise the roofless walls of the house in which died the greatest Highland heroine of all time, *Fionghal nighean Raonuill 'ic Aonghais Oig* (Flora, the daughter of Ranald, the son of young Angus), as Flora Macdonald is called in the Gaelic. Shrouded in one of the sheets in which the Prince had slept, Flora was borne by night from her friend's house to the old mansion of Kingsburgh, her coffin carried high on the shoulders of stalwart youths. An awful storm was raging, the night was very dark, and the swollen waters of the Hinnisdale were only crossed with the utmost difficulty. For a week Flora lay in state at Kingsburgh, her body an object of devoted pilgrimage from every quarter of the island. All about and around the walls of Peindun are the ruins of smaller, more primitive-looking buildings—the whole constituting as mournful a spectacle of ruin and decay as any on the island.

Flora Macdonald, born in 1722 in South Uist, was of the ancient line of the Clanranald chiefs, and of her, as truly as of them, is the panegyric deserved that Alasdair Mac Mhaighstir Alasdair wrote on the clan:

> "Clan Ranald, ever-glorious victorious nobility,
> A people proud and fearless, of peerless ability,
> Fresh honours ever gaining, disdaining servility,
> Attacks can never move them but prove their ability.
> High of spirit, they inherit merit, capability,
> Skill, discreetness, strength and featness, fleetness and agility;
> Shields to batter, swords to shatter, scatter with ability
> Whosoever brave their ire and their fierce hostility."

At the time Flora became famous, she was twenty-four years of age, of medium height, good-looking, and intelligent; and she had a kind step-father in Hugh Macdonald of Armadale. Unfortunately, the family of Sleat, to which he belonged, had not the unblemished record of devotion to the Stewarts as that of the Clanranalds. Yet, for all he was in command of one of the companies of militia engaged in hunting the Prince, his heart obviously reproached him, and, if he proved unreliable to his alien employers, he was at least not unresponsive to the truer instinct of the Macdonalds. For, influenced by his step-daughter's persuasiveness, he proved a good friend to the Royal Fugitive, not only suggesting the plan whereby he evaded his pursuers, but actually himself abetting it. Armadale, being in Arisaig on the occasion of the Prince's first landing, had been the first to kiss his hand, and this, quite as much as his step-daughter's influence, would account for the assistance he rendered. Armadale's proposal was that Flora, under the pretext of being nervous at the presence of so many soldiers about Milton, her home on South Uist, should cross to her mother in Skye, taking with her the Prince disguised as her Irish maid, and Neil MacEachainn as escort. Once in Skye, the making of further plans was to be entrusted to Lady Margaret Macdonald, the Jacobite wife of the Hanoverian Sir Alexander Macdonald of Sleat, then absent at Fort Augustus.

Not a mile beyond Peindun, on a rock by the sea, are the remains of Caisteal Uisdein (Hugh's Castle), built but never completed by Hugh *MacGhilleasbuig* (Hugh, son of the servant of the bishop), a relative and next-of-kin of Donald Gorm. It is typical of what the man had to fear that he built his tower without any windows, the only opening being a small door high up in the wall, through which a ladder, drawn up after use, gave access. It was here to Hugh, his uncle, that the notorious Iain Dubh fled for refuge when, after his murder of Donald Macleod at Kingsburgh, his arrest was ordered by the chief and his father, Iain the Fairhaired. Like apparently attracted like, for of such evil repute was Hugh that a contemporary song asks why his nurse did not kill in infancy such an embryo monster.

Uig Bay, with its huge ramparts of basaltic cliff, is a noble harbour, and its naming—a " nook or retired cove," a singularly happy one for this secluded corner with its picturesque village and two beautifully wooded glens. It is surely one of the last places in Skye where you would expect belief in witchcraft to have survived; yet, no further back than the autumn of 1880, the principal Free Kirkers of Uig preferred a charge of witchcraft against a mother and five daughters. Before Mr. Fraser of Kilmuir, they charged these women of having by evil arts taken milk from the neighbours' cows. The recommended antidote was to turn the affected cows sunwise, and to tie a red thread round each tail, the charge being 5s. per cow!

The main attraction of Uig for me was its convenience as a centre of a country of intense historical and archæo-logical interest. I was, therefore, greatly disgusted when the one day available for the northward expedition of nine miles to Duntulm turned out, in its best parts, dull, drear, and misty, and, at its worst, as wet as ever rain can be in Skye. The one consolation was that under the most favourable conditions the road is not remarkable for its scenery, its attractions being almost wholly confined to

14

the objects of other interest found on the route, all, with one exception, on your left, between the road and the shore.

The first object to take you off the road is just about a mile beyond Uig—Dun Skudiburg, which I had seen on the previous day, fortunately in sunshine. There is little enough remaining of its ancient fort, now practically a shapeless mass of tumbled stones, but its situation, crowning a height, steep and rocky on the landward side, and overlooking the sea, is very fine. The seaward front is guarded by a wall enclosing a beautiful stretch of inter-vening greensward, and from the summit you have a magnificent view of the cliffs along the coast, and notably of Prince Charlie's Point, marking the site of his landing in Kilbride Bay. Down in the depths below rises from the sea the Stack of Skudiburg, a magnificent basaltic pillar, of great size and lichen covered, whilst near by is a reef over which the waves break with foam and roar.

Regaining the road, after a couple of miles you can see, half way to the shore, and scarcely sheltered by a few meagre trees, the lonely and very ugly building of Mugstot House. This curious name which seems so alien to Skye, is of Norse origin, is also written Mugstat, and on the maps, Monkstadt. There is nothing to be gained by a nearer approach to this " Monk's place," which served as the seat of the Macdonalds of Sleat between their evacuation of Duntulm and their entry into Armadale Castle. The house takes its name from its nearness to Loch Columcille—just about a mile north—where, on what used to be an island, there are some intensely interesting ruins thought to date back to the days of S. Columba himself. After having become a marsh, the loch was ultimately successfully drained, and, in the course of these operations, two very interesting canoes were disinterred. The first local opinion identified with the ferry boat of the monastery. It was made out of one piece of oak, each end being respectively strengthened by two and three very strong iron bands. The second canoe, hollowed by axes out of a tree-trunk, was extremely shallow, and may have been of prehistoric origin. Unfortunately, both canoes have disappeared.

From the road, you look down upon an unutterably dreary hollow, and think of the abomination of desolation. Indeed a spirit of melancholy settles upon you as you make your way through the boggy ground to the ruins, for they seem as a wordless parable, eloquently conveyed in a picture, of the result of the spiritual labours of S. Columba as seen to-day. For not only in the Highlands, but throughout Scotland, owing to Calvinist persecutions, only a " faithful remnant " of the people to whom he brought the Faith remain in his succession. You proceed across the moorland for a little over a mile, before you gain what was originally the island of the loch—a surface of some three acres, littered with rude lichen-covered stones—the remains of the monastic settlement. These probably afford us the best example now extant of the plan of the most famous of Columban monasteries—the mother foundation on Iona itself. Here, indeed, the remains are of stone, whilst on Iona the buildings were of wood and wattle. But there is evidence here of a ground plan similar to that which, as we gather from Adamnan, characterized the monastery on Iona, in the grouping of the small beehive cells of the monks round a central church and refectory, the whole being surrounded by an outer enclosing wall, cashel, or *vallum*. To describe the remains on Loch Columcille in detail might be wearisome to the general reader, so it is probably enough to say that the church dedicated to S. Columba is only 21 feet 10 inches by 12 feet 2 inches, and of its walls only 8 feet of the height are left, and that near by are the ruins of another rectangular building—possibly the refectory.

At *Blar a' Bhuailte,* the " field of the stricken," in Kilmuir, the Norsemen made their last stand in Skye. But when the defeated took to their galleys for Norway, one, singularly daring and powerful, stayed behind with

a small band of followers and entrenched himself in these
monastery ruins. This man, *Arco Brann Mhor,* or Arco
the corpulent, then sallied forth from his island fortress
to rob the neighbourhood, thus rousing in the chief
Macdonald a determination to be rid of him and his
company. He promised one Macsween, a renowned Celtic
warrior, that if he should succeed, he should receive in
return for Arco's head, the land of the Braes. Inspection
of the fortress proving it to be impregnable, Macsween
resorted to artifice, and, disguising himself as a beggar,
was ferried across to Arco's stronghold, where he was
allowed, on some specious pretext, to stay the night.
Macsween entertained Arco by relating tale after tale till
the Norseman fell asleep, when the " beggar " promptly
and silently despatched him with his dirk, cut off his head,
and succeeded in escaping with it to Macdonald, after
which exploit Macsween retired to the Braes, which his
prowess had won for him. But once again Kilmuir was
troubled by the Norsemen when one of their galleys
infested its shores. On this occasion a famous young
archer undertook to account for it, picking off the
Norsemen one by one as they landed. The survivors put
to sea with all haste, and never again returned.

Before regaining the road, there is Carn Liath, the
" grey cairn," to be seen just above the loch—a tumulus,
15 yards in diameter, having a chamber 6 feet deep in its
centre, and what is probably another at one side. These
chambered cairns had compartments for holding cinerary
urns which, when covered by slabs of stone, had smaller
stones piled upon them until they assumed a conical shape.
Just below the cairn is one of these small cyclopean
buildings—probably a sleeping place—so often found in
association with duns. In this case, Dun Liath is just
about a mile north of it, right on the edge of the sea,
and the building in question is roughly circular, and
only 4 feet high, with a smaller building leading out
of it.

Joining the road once more (and it is a good two miles across the moor from Dun Liath), you should come out near Kilvaxter Post Office, and then after about one and a half miles you take a road on your right to the old churchyard of Kilmuir.[13] Nothing now remains of the church, but there is the all too usual spectacle of neglected burial places in the Western Highlands, a reproach common alike to Catholic and Calvinistic districts, but which in this case seems particularly blameworthy. For here, amidst a rank growth of nettles and weeds, in the now pitiable wilderness of *Reileig Mhor Chloinn Domhnaill,* the burial place of the Macdonalds of the Isles, rests the body of Flora Macdonald. So many thousands attended her funeral that the procession was over a mile long.   Of the MacArthurs, hereditary pipers to the Macdonalds, and the MacCrimmons, there were from their respective colleges on this island, about a dozen who played the coronach over the devoted Jacobite woman's grave. But many years passed before any worthy memorial was placed over her last resting place.   At last her son, Colonel John Macdonald of Exeter, sent for the purpose a thin marble slab set in freestone, but, unfortunately, it was cracked whilst being landed from the ship. Despite the accident, it was placed over her grave, but in a few months every fragment had been carried off by relic-hunting tourists devoid of all sense of decency. This slab, after

---

[13] Local traditional pronunciation proves that this is neither a dedication to S. Maelrubha nor, as is commonly asserted, to Our Lady. It is not, in fact, a dedication at all, but simply means, like Kilmore, near Oban, the " big church," in contra-distinction to Kilbeg, the " little church." Such naming of a church is not in accord either with common Celtic or mediæval use and wont, but seems more analogous to Protestant nomenclature. In this, the principal church of the town became the " High " church, the old dedication being dropped, as, *e.g.*, in the case of Stirling, whose church originally honoured S. Modon. The mediæval name, *Eaglais bhreac,* or " church of mottled stone," was not, of course, a substitute for, but co-existed with the dedication, again to S. Modan ; but the place, Falkirk, has taken this name from the description of its church, instead of, as usual, from its patron saint.

enumerating the names of all the Macdonalds of Kingsburgh who were buried at Kilmuir, concluded with that of
Flora " who died March, 1790, aged 68, a name that will
be mentioned in history, and if courage and fidelity be
virtues, be mentioned with honour." Ill-fate seems to have
pursued poor Flora's gravestones, for, when in recent years
the present large Iona cross and slab of Inverness granite
were erected by public subscription, a storm speedily broke
the cross in two. The damage was none too skilfully
repaired, and only in 1913 was there any appeal made to
rail in the grave, with what result I do not know.

On a clear day you are able to see the coasts of North
Uist and Harris from the churchyard, but by the time I
had reached this point of my pilgrimage, the rain was so
heavy that only with difficulty could I identify Ru Bornaskitaig, which guards the south of Score Bay, and is the
headland which legend asserts to be the place on which
the bloody hand was cast ashore as already related.

The two-mile road by the shore of Score Bay to Duntulm
is a very fine one, and not even the worst downpour can
detract from the landward aspect—the wild beauty of the
pillared cliffs rising on the right, with masses of fallen
rocks tumbled about their base—probably accounting for
the name of " Rock (*sgor*) Bay." Almost savage in its
grandeur, this road makes a fitting ascent to the majestic
red cliff crowned by the shattered shell of what was once
the proud fortress of Duntulm, the seat of the Macdonalds
of the Isles. Like the ancient line of its lords, the great,
rudely columnar cliff presents an uncompromising face,
rising in a sheer precipice to a great height above the sea,
and bidding a bold defiance to the world alike " by land
and by sea." Its predecessor on the site was *Dun
Daibhidh,* a fort seized by a Viking from its Celtic builders.
Now, as you walk over the grass and climb the fence
towards the fragments of what the foundation lines shew
was once a large fortress, you find there is very little to be
seen in the meagre ruins, no part of which are of greater

DUNTULM CASTLE, SKYE

age, however, than the beginning of the seventeenth century. There is a broken gable, the remains of a windowed wall, a hollow in the ground, one or two broken masses of masonry, and that is all—the most complete and eloquent monument imaginable to *sic transit gloria mundi* —when you remember the wide sovereign power wielded by those Lords of the Isles, who successfully opposed themselves to kings.

In the twelfth century it is curious to find a chief so interested in the pursuits belonging to peace as to seek to increase the fertility of his garden by actually importing soil from seven kingdoms—England, Ireland, France, Spain, Norway, Denmark, and Germany. But there is no trace of the fertility in the surroundings of the bleak and barren site of the ancient castle, and, when you descend to the shore, you obtain even a stronger impression of naked strength in the castle rock, apparently wholly impervious to the savage smiting of the sea, however furiously it rage. To the right of the castle, facing seaward, there is on the shore a small shelter cut out in the turf of the cove for the galley of the chief, and on the face of the rock you can still see the rut said to have been worn by the passage of the keel. A tale in connection with this rut has given rise to a Gaelic proverb. It is said that on an occasion when one, Iain Garbh, wished to cross to Harris, he was thwarted by an old man, Gillies, who, with his back to the stern, successfully resisted Iain's every attempt to launch the galley. As Iain at last desisted, he called Gillies a *bodach,* whereupon the old man retorted, " Gillies is not a churl to everybody ! "

Duntulm, no less than Dunvegan, provides you with many thrills of horror. There is the tale of the end of the infamous Hugh Macghilleasbuig—obviously oft-told by reason of its many variations. As in every other case where there are differing accounts of the same story, I shall give the tale as it was told me on the spot by a native.

Hugh, coveting the chiefship, was anxious to remove the famous Donald Gorm, who had wrested Duntulm from the temporary possession of the Macleods. To this end, Hugh took a neighbour into his confidence, and entered into a conspiracy with him. Instead, however, of sending their guilty compact to his fellow-conspirator, he sent it to one Martin, a cattle-dealer, in error for a redeemed bond. The cattle-dealer took the letter to Donald Gorm, who, with incredible magnanimity, actually forgave Hugh. Thereupon Hugh wrote again to Donald, vowing eternal gratitude, and simultaneously proceeded to enter into a new plot with his old fellow-conspirator against the chief's life. By a second mistake, the letters were reversed, Donald getting that intended for Hugh's abettor, whereupon Donald, determining to make an end to such treachery, cordially invited Hugh to be his guest at Duntulm. All unsuspecting that his plot had again miscarried, Hugh accepted the invitation, to be courteously received by Donald, who at once shewed him to the quarters prepared for his reception—in the dungeon! Here he was kept without food till he was ravenous, when a huge piece of salt beef was flung down to him. When Hugh was raging with the thirst produced by his devouring of the meat, a pitcher was slowly lowered to him, but when his eagerly-outstretched hands at last grasped it, it was only to find the vessel empty. In the madness that ensued, the victim vainly endeavoured to scrape a way out of his prison, cut from the solid rock, by using the shin bone of beef, and failing, in despair he tore into the pewter plate with his teeth before he succumbed.

After the death of Donald Gorm, his ghost, together with those of two companions, appeared on the road leading to Duntulm, but, when they were accosted, they all passed mysteriously into the castle, their passage being unnoticed. A wise man was consulted in the matter, and he counselled those who sought him to prepare seven staves of pine, and, according to others, seven spindles of oak,

" with fire at their points," and, thus guarded, they might enter the room into which the ghosts daily disappeared. The old man's advice was followed, and the phantoms were discovered drinking.   On seeing the intruders, Donald's ghost thus addressed them:

> " I was in Edinburgh last night,
> I am in my own mansion to-night;
> And worth of mote in the sunbeam,
> I have not in me of strength."

After telling the intruders where they would find a lost document which was of greatest importance to his nephew and successor, Donald Gorm Og, the phantom disappeared, saying :   :

> " If it were not the slender lance of pine,
> This would be to thy hurt, young Donald Gorm."

Another tale that is told of the castle relates of an occasion when it nearly fell into the hands of the Macleods. The chief was from home, and had left the fortress in charge of his son, a lad of eighteen, with a handful of old retainers under him.   Hearing of this situation, and seeing in it the chance of a splendid capture, Macleod set out with his warriors from Dunvegan.   The boy, observing this strong force advancing against Duntulm, and not knowing what to do, appealed to the jester, who advised him to resort to the stratagem Somerled had successfully employed on a like occasion.   This was to summon from a village two miles distant all men and boys capable of walking and of piping to gather together, and to march them as quickly as possible, piping, in a continuous procession round Cnoc Roill near by, and so to give the impression of great numbers.   This the lad did, and had the satisfaction of outwitting the invaders, who, seeing before them a force far outnumbering, as they thought, their own, beat a hasty retreat home.

James V. sailed into Score Bay in the course of his island visitation, and greatly admired the strength of Duntulm, at which date the chief was a mere child.

Again I tell a tale of the eighteenth century as it was told me locally, of an infant heir whom a nurse let fall out of one of the castle windows overlooking the sea. Despite the fact that a solitary bush growing out of and half-way down the rock caught in the child's clothing and saved it from destruction, the chief decreed the death of the careless nursemaid, condemning her to be tied to the tail of a boat and towed out to sea to drown. The usual book version of this story has it that the poor woman was turned adrift in a boat pierced with holes.

One of the last chiefs to have lived at Duntulm was Sir Donald of the War, the fourth Baronet of Sleat, who fought with great distinction at Killiecrankie. It was through him, so tradition says, that the lost red tartan of the Isles was recovered. He heard an old woman singing a Gaelic song of the Battle of Harlaw, in which she described the tartan worn there by Donald of Isla (or Harlaw). Since it was the custom of weavers of the tartan to sing of the deeds which each line of colour represented, Sir Donald summoned a weaver to him and bade him weave the fabric as the woman sang. The same baronet gave at Duntulm, about 1715, a famous ball at which, amongst others, the traitor Lord Lovat was present. Not long after, Duntulm, haunted by the restless ghost of Donald Gorm, was deserted. Its lordly stones were taken by the crofters to build their humble cots until the day when the present chief of Sleat, to mark the continuity of the new building he was rearing for his home with the old stronghold, incorporated its stones, too, in his work on the site of the abode of the hereditary physician of the Macdonalds.

Around the castle of Duntulm are three *cnocs*—the Hill of Judgment or Pleas (Ru Meanish), of Counsel, and of Hanging. In the old clan days here, as elsewhere, it was on such *cnocs* that the chief sat in state, dispensing advice, justice, and punishment. Clad in his coat of mail, or *lùireach,* with conical helmet bearing the three eagle's plumes and the badge of his clan, the chief was enthroned, his right hand resting on the pommel of his claymore thrust upright into the ground beside him. There, occupying the hill proper to the specific matter in hand, he meted out stern justice as he sat—a terrible figure of inviolable majesty, well calculated to strike awe to the hearts of the clansmen.

Here at Duntulm there is the tale to be told of the guilty couple who were doomed to expiate their sin by being buried alive, and it was down Cnoc Roill, the hill of punishment, that descends from the castle, that another culprit was rolled in a spiked barrel. Hence the hill—the same that served in the jester's strategy—is called the " Barrel Hill " to this day.

The return journey from Duntulm resolved itself into a following in the footsteps of Prince Charlie and Flora Macdonald, and it is necessary to preface the account of this by remarking that Macgregor's *Life* of the heroine, which seems to be the best known, abounds in so many inaccuracies that it is of little value as an historical record. It is regrettable that one is obliged to place in the same category the favourite and spirited version of the tuneful " Skye Boat Song," but those who know it will soon discover where a romantic fancy has reversed the true facts of the case.

Flora in Uist had obtained from her step-father a passport for herself, a man-servant, Neil MacEachainn, and an Irish spinning maid, " Betty Burke," together with an open letter from Armadale to her mother, plausibly accounting alike for her journey and her companions. Just before embarkation, the Prince had to don the garments specially made for him in which to sustain his character of " Betty Burke." " The gown was of calico, a light-coloured, printed petticoat, a mantle of dun camlet made after the Irish fashion, with a cap to cover his royal highness' whole head and face, with a suitable headdress, shoes, stockings, etc." Always, under the most adverse circumstances, ready to make the most of any occasion for humour, Charles proceeded with much jestings and laughter to transform himself into an Irish maid under the critical supervision of Flora. Then, when she was satisfied with his appearance, they, attended by four faithful followers as rowers, scrambled into their boat and left Loch Uskavagh, Benbecula, at 8 P.M. on Saturday, June 28, 1746. Rain, mist, and adverse winds were encountered during the voyage; and it was not Flora who kept watch over the Prince, but Charles who, with every tenderness and solicitude, devoted himself to care of her. In all the story of the Prince's wanderings, throughout which he is consistently seen as one made increasingly great by adversity, a hero who attained a lofty height, there is perhaps no incident where the simple charm and true royalty of his character is more touchingly evidenced than in the details of this voyage. First he sang Jacobite songs to Flora, and when, exhausted after the long day's exertion, she fell asleep, he kept gracious and continuous ward over her till, waking, she found the Prince bending over her, sheltering her head with his hands.

In order to rest the exhausted rowers, an hour's landing was made at Vaternish Point, and, after the party had refreshed themselves, the voyage across Loch Snizort was resumed. Then it was that the fugitives were seen by the militia, who fired but without effect at the boat, and afterwards made as though to launch off in pursuit, but for some unexplained reason stopped short with the appearance of so doing. It was about 11 o'clock on Sunday morning that, very cautiously, the boat was steered into a small cove in Kilbride Bay, and then, leaving the Prince in the care of the crew, Flora, attended by the devoted MacEachainn, made for the adjacent Mugstat House. Here she hoped Charles might find refuge, but, to her dismay, she found an officer of militia was in the house. But Lady Margaret Macdonald was already taking counsel as to what was best to be done with the Prince, and amongst others sharing in her consultations was Macdonald of Kingsburgh. He, fearful for Charles' safety so near the militia, as a preliminary precaution, sent MacEachainn to take Charles to a more secure place, now unindentifiable, near Dun Skudiburg, proposing himself to join the Prince there later. Local tradition has it that, whilst there, " Betty Burke " was seen by one of Sir Alexander's herds-men, and so uncouth a figure did the " maid " present, that the herdsman took fright, and, running into the servants' hall at Mugstat, exclaimed: " Lord preserve us! I saw a large female quickly crossing the fields betwixt this and the *dun,* with a long stick in her hand, with a curious hood on her head, and with a remarkable dress on her person. Undoubtedly, she must be one of those whom the fairies had locked up in the chambers of the *dun* and who managed to escape. I never saw anyone in the shape of an earthly creature to be compared with her!" [14]

It was this strange female figure, flourishing her stick, who advanced to meet Kingsburgh on his approach. Assured, however, of his identity, the Prince greeted him most cordially, and soon they were seated together discussing the plans made for the Prince's crossing to Raasay, whilst Charles refreshed himself with some pro-visions that Kingsburgh had brought. When MacEachainn appeared, he was sent back to take Flora to Kingsburgh House, where Charles was to pass the night.

It was late that evening when the Prince and Kingsburgh started on their seven-mile walk by the old road through Uig, and they were soon overtaken by Flora and the loyal party from Mugstat, all mounted on horses. The country folk were going home from service, and the appearance of " Betty Burke " caused quite a sensation amongst them, shocking them alike by her clumsy deportment and her

[14] " She " also had the reputation of being a fine Gaelic speaker. " But it is not the same as our Gaelic whatever," averred the Skyeman; " We can understand every word she says, but not what they mean ! "

bold impudence in daring to walk alongside no less a person than Kingsburgh himself! But when the party came to ford the river Hinnisdal, which ran knee-deep, mere shock gave place to grave scandal, " to see Burke take up her pettycoats so high when she entered the water. The poor fellows were quite confounded at the last sight." " Your enemies call you a pretender," said Kingsburgh; " but if you be, you are the worst at your trade that I ever saw." Indeed, so obviously ill-fitted was the Prince to play his part that, alarmed by all the inquisitive attention his awkward manipulation of his dress was attracting to him, Flora contrived with the company that Charles and Kingsburgh were left in the rear to reach Kingsburgh House by a route off the road. It was here, midway between Peindun and Kingsburgh that Charles stopped to drink at a small spring of water, still known as *Tobar a' Phrionnsa,* but when I sought the well, it had been trampled out of recognizable existence by cattle.

Between the hours of ten and eleven that Sunday night, the Royal Fugitive reached Kingsburgh House just as Mrs. Macdonald, tired and sleepy, was going to bed. Sending a message to Flora, begging to be excused, and telling her and her company to make free of all in the house, the hostess got into bed, only to be disturbed by her daughter Ann. This lady, who had married Colonel Ronald MacAlister of Loup, was evidently paying a visit to her parents at this time, and, darting into the bedroom, she exclaimed: " Oh, mother, my father has brought in a very odd, muckle ill-shaken-up wife as ever I saw! I never saw the like of her, and he has gone into the hall with her." Ann was almost immediately followed by her father, who bade his wife get up to prepare supper for their visitors, though he refused to tell her who they were. Dressing, and going downstairs, Mrs. Macdonald, too, was scared by the sight that " Betty Burke " presented, and then, when his identity was disclosed, she expressed

herself at a loss to know how to behave in the presence of
Royalty. But Charles soon put her completely at her ease,
and, with his inimitable grace, setting her on his left hand
with Flora on his right, he settled down to the merriest of
royal banquets, feasting on " roasted eggs, collops, and
plenty of bread and butter." After smoking his pipe and
drinking toddy with his host, Charles, provided with a clean
night-cap, retired to sleep between sheets for the first time
for many long weeks.

When, well on in the morning, the Prince made no
appearance, Kingsburgh went to awaken him; but, finding
him very soundly asleep, had not the heart to disturb his
slumbers. Later, when Charles was known to be awake,
Mrs. Macdonald suggested that Flora should go to his
room to request a lock of his hair. Flora's strict sense of
the proprieties was shocked at such a suggestion. But
Mrs. Macdonald caught her by the hand and knocked at
the Prince's door. When he answered, she said, " Sir,
it is I, and I am importuning Miss Flora to come in and
get a lock of your hair for me, and she refuses to do it."
" Pray," said the Prince, " desire Miss Macdonald to come
in. What could make her afraid to come where I am?"

No longer could Flora hesitate, but, accompanied by
her hostess, entered the room where Charles was still in
bed. The Prince, requesting her to sit down beside him,
put his head in her lap, and she then cut off the lock of
hair that is now treasured in Dunvegan Castle.

Before he could set out for Portree, Charles, to avoid
discovery in leaving the house, had again to assume his
female attire, and retain it till he was clear of Kingsburgh.
Again he bubbled over with mirth and merriment as,
assisted by Mrs. Macdonald and Ann, as well as
Flora, he made his ridiculous toilet for the second time.
Flora having left for Portree in advance, the Prince,
bidding courtly farewell to his hostess about 8 P.M., made
for the cover of a wood near by, in which Kingsburgh met

him with the belted plaid of the red tartan of the Isles. Then, from an unprepossessing Irishwoman, Charles was speedily transformed into a handsome young Highlander, armed with a broadsword. Kingsburgh had provided a lad, M'Queen, to guide both Charles and MacEachainn safely through to the capital, for Neil did not know Skye well, and the country was beset by soldiers.

Very affecting was the Prince's parting with Kingsburgh, whom he affectionately embraced, thanking him with tears in his eyes for his great services. Kingsburgh had become so attached to the Prince that he, too, wept, and shewed himself greatly concerned at the emotion evidenced by Charles. Kingsburgh had thrust Charles' discarded garments into a bush, being anxious to treasure them as sacred relics, but, with so much inquisition afoot on the island, he eventually considered it too dangerous. Thus everything was burnt, except the gown and brogues, and, whilst Kingsburgh himself kept the undistinctive brogues, pieces of the gown, an ordinary print with purple sprigs, were attached to Vol. III. of Bishop Forbes' compilation of Jacobite relics known as the *Lyon in Mourning*.

Heavy rain fell as the fugitives made their way to Portree, and, arrived at the capital, Charles sent M'Queen (who was quite unaware of his identity) to enquire at the Royal Hotel if one Captain Donald Roy Macdonald were there, and, if so, to request him to meet a gentleman outside. The gallant captain, who, with Flora, had been anxiously awaiting Charles' arrival, was only too glad to receive the message, and, meeting the Prince as requested, was affectionately embraced by him, for he was still suffering from a wound received at Culloden. When Charles had obtained a promise that he should be treated without ceremony, they entered the Inn, and Charles, cold, wet, and shivering, at once called for a dram. So soaked was he indeed that the water dripped from his plaid as he stood, and he was at last persuaded, despite the presence of Flora, which he urged as the reason for non-compliance with the suggestion, to change his dress for the dry clothes that his friends thrust upon him. Then, without coat or waistcoat, he sat down to a humble meal of bread, butter, cheese, and roasted fish. The room that the Prince occupied throughout these happenings is still shewn in the Royal Hotel.

His farewell to his heroic rescuer and to the no less devoted MacEachainn followed upon the meal, and in the simplest and most surprisingly undramatic fashion the most romantic incident in all his adventurings came to an end. Donald Roy relates how that the Prince, turning to Flora, said " ' I believe, Madam, I owe you a crown of borrowed money.' She told him it was only half-a-crown, which accordingly he paid her with thanks. He then saluted her, and expressed himself in these or the like words: ' For all that has happened, I hope, Madam, we shall meet in S. James's yet.' He then bad farewel to honest MacKechan, who staid that night with Miss Macdonald at Portree, and attended her next day to the place she intended to go to."

Shortly after midnight on June 30, Charles, after a stay of two hours, left the Inn at Portree to join the boat that was to carry him over to Raasay in the Macleod country. Sgeir Mhor is the point where, according to tradition, he left Skye.

In the handsome (Episcopal) church of S. Columba at Portree, the heroism of Flora Macdonald, perhaps an " Episcopalian," is fittingly commemorated in the west window and brass tablet beneath, erected to her immortal memory by one of her great-grandchildren. Tradition has it that Flora's last words were: *" Chriosd 's Ailean 's Tearlach Og."* (" Christ and Allan [her husband] and young Charles.")

You feel that the Jacobite sentiments of Hogg, despite their alien dialect and phrasing, give true expressions to

the feelings which must have animated Flora Macdonald
after the Prince's departure:

> " The target is torn from the arms of the just,
> The helmet is cleft on the brow of the brave,
> The claymore for ever in darkness must rust,
> But red is the sword of the stranger and slave.
> The hoof of the horse and the foot of the proud,
> Have trod o'er the plumes on the bonnets of blue,
> Why slept the red bolt in the breast of the cloud,
> When tyranny revell'd in blood of the true?
> Farewell, my young hero, the gallant and good,
> The crown of thy fathers is torn from thy brow!"

And who more fittingly interprets the passionate attraction
of the Highlands for the Prince, than Aytoun, when
he makes Charles soliloquize:

> " Backwards—backwards let me wander
> To the noble northern land:
> Let me feel the breezes blowing
> Fresh along the mountain-side:
> Let me see the purple heather,
> Let me hear the thundering tide:
> Be it hoarse as Corrievreckan,
> Spouting when the storm is high—
> Give me but one hour of Scotland—
> Let me see it ere I die!
>
> .   .   .   .   .   .
>
> Give me back my trusty comrades—
> Give me back my Highland maid,
> Nowhere beats the heart so kindly
> As beneath the tartan plaid!"

And the islanders, too, would welcome him back, for at
the fulling they sing:

> "Beauteous Morag of the clustering locks.
> To sing of thee is my intent,
> If thou hast gone beyond the sea,
> Prithee hasten home to me!"

Portree has never been more than a half-way house, or
a port of call, for me, so that my reference to the Royal
Hotel and S. Columba's Church practically exhausts all
that I have seen of the capital of Skye.

Though comfort may be sacrificed, there is great gain both in interest and amusement in taking a " mixed boat " (*i.e.,* of passengers, cattle, and cargo generally) rather than the " swift mail steamer " from Portree.   The slower sail down the Sound of Raasay allows of a longer companying with the Coolin, and then when, because of the intervention of Soay, the intercourse is broken—after a last glimpse of them, more alluring than ever, in the enchanted distance at the head of the narrow length of Loch Sligachan—there is always other interesting company to be found on board the boat itself.

On one such voyage, I added to the cherished list of my Celtic acquaintances one of the most handsome men it would be possible to see.   He was a tall, stalwart, old Highlander in a kilt, erect as one of his native pine trees, and with a presence and courtesy that would have dignified a chief.   His tartan proclaimed him a Macdonald, but it was the captain of the boat who told me, in the clansman's absence, that Angus Macdonald was, or had been, in his day, a champion piper.   The worthy seaman then produced from his cabin a very shabby set of pipes, which he put down on a seat beside me, saying, " Just wait you here a whiley till I fetch Macdonald."   I waited, and presently the Lowlander returned with the Highlander.

" Now then, Angus, here the pipes !   Let the leddy hear hoo ye can play ! "

But Angus was regarding the instrument with more than merely obvious disfavour.   To the ordinary eye, they presented a sorry enough appearance: in the sight of a Macdonald, they were contaminated; for, faded as was the ribbon tied about them, there was no disguising *that* tartan from Highland eyes.   At sight of the sett of the great enemy clan, Angus' eye flashed fire.   Drawing himself up, and speaking with great dignity, obviously under severe restraint, he exclaimed, slowly and with emphasis:

" No, Captain, no !   I wass fery sorry not to pe opliching you and ta laady, fery sorry inteed !   I would pe

toing anything that wass possible to pe pleasing you, put
with those, it wass never at aall possible!   No, inteed!"

And if contempt could wither, those pipes, or rather the
tartan that entwined them, would have been shrivelled into
nothingness.

Before I had realized it, we were drawing into Kyle
Akin, commonly interpreted as the " Channel of Haco "
after the King of Norway, who is popularly supposed to
have anchored his fleet here on his way to the Battle of
Largs.   But a study of the sagas proves that these narrows
can have no connection with Haco, who sailed round by
the west of Skye.   It is named after Acunn, who, with his
brother, Readh, were heroes of an earlier age.   Of them
I shall write in the next chapter.

The vista where the mountains of the mainland mingle
with the hills of Skye is one of the loveliest stretches of
the sail, and the bold rocky foreground, with the fragments
of Castle Maol standing sentinel by the sea, heightens the
effect.   It is said that Nicolson, a name common in Skye,
is derived from one Andrew Nicolson, Haco's chief
commander.

Castle Maol, castle of the " mull or promontory," in
Gaelic, *Caisteal na Maoile,* only so called after its
desertion, since Dunakyne was its earlier name, was a
fortress of the Mackinnons.   Tradition says it was built by
one " Saucy Mary," a Norse king's daughter who married
a Mackinnon, and that her object was to exact toll from
vessels passing through the channel, and was attained, so
legend asserts, by stretching a chain across to the opposite
shore of the mainland.   But, judging from the style of the
keep, which was probably originally three stories high at
least, the castle belongs to the thirteenth century—evidence
which rather rules out the popular tradition.   The detached
mass of rock, on the edge of which the walls, 9 feet thick,
are built, is surrounded on three sides by the sea, and the
original internal dimensions of the castle were $30\frac{1}{2}$ feet by

17 feet. Here a meeting of chiefs was held after Flodden to decide who was the successor to the Lordship of the Isles, and Sir Donald of the Isles, of Lochalsh, was duly proclaimed.

I was on shore taking a view including the remains of the old fortress when an excited voice speaking English with the soft drawl of the Celt, came from behind me.

" Uch, Mem, you wass chust tekking ta fery same sketch as Mr. MacGreusich no less—ta fery same wan ass he himself did pent from my shed!"

Turning, I saw a sturdy old man with a short square beard, obviously keenly interested in my repetition of some previous famous performance. I greeted him and asked for enlightenment regarding the artist.

" It wass Fearchar MacGreusich I wass saying, Mem. You will pe knowing him, ta fery greatest sketcher that efer wass, for wass he not porn on ta island herself? Well, he wass penting yon view—chust that. You'll maype hev seen ta fery picture herself no less? Uch, it wass chust a peautiful sketch—you could not pe seeing wan that wass finer—not wan—no, no!"

The old man, who was a boatwright, spoke with keen enthusiasm and fervour remarkable in one of his years. From being friendly, he became confiding, and, taking me by the arm, he said:

" Now, you'll chust pe seeing for yourself ta peautiful thing I can pe making," and led me into his shed. Going towards some partially concealed object, he removed a sailcloth, and disclosed—not some triumph of his craft to sail the sea, but—a coffin covered in black cloth!

" Wass she not peautiful now?" said the old fellow, moving back a step or two, and viewing it with obvious pride, his face beaming. " It will pe for ta createst musicaner that efer wass, and he wass tying on *Eilean a' Cheo* herself, moreofer. You should chust hev been hearing him play ta pipes! Uch, it wass chust hefenly!"

And, if it was not quite heavenly, at least it was with the music of the pipes floating over the water and echoing back from the hills that I turned my unwilling back on Skye that year for Kyle of Lochalsh on the mainland opposite.

———

P.S. on the parting of the Prince from Flora.

Charles probably gave Flora the gold locket containing his miniature before he left the Inn. Sgeir Mhor, on the north side of Portree harbour, is about half a mile from the Inn, and, though it was still very wet, Flora followed the Prince, who, before he embarked, clasped her hand for the last time. Overcome with emotion, he could not speak, whilst she could not restrain her tears as he gazed silently at her. At last, doffing his bonnet, Charles reverently kissed Flora twice upon her brow. Then the poor fugitive entered the boat, leaving his heroic deliverer seated on a rock and following with her eyes the vessel's course till the boat was lost to sight.

CHAPTER III

FROM THE CASTLE OF EILEAN DONNAN TO THE BROCHS OF GLENELG

PART I

EILEAN DONNAN AND TOTAIG

*A*S in the case of Mallaig, so with Kyle of Lochalsh, the coming of the railway has *not* conferred distinction on the scenery. On the contrary, it has been responsible for depositing there an untidy collection of debris, called a terminus, that is an eyesore without excuse. Thus we pondered as our mixed boat drew up to the pier, but when she had been made fast, for the next two hours our initial disgust gave place to amusement in the scenes of activity witnessed—despite the fact that it poured persistently the whole time. According to the time-table, we had just a quarter of an hour to wait at the Kyle, but time is a detail, an unconsidered trifle, that never hampers the voyage of a Highland boat. The pier seemed to be one stacked mass of cargo and cattle. There were railway and other trucks piled high with all kinds of more or less concealed commodities: bales of goods, sacks, barrels, and live stock were littered everywhere.

Our boat, which had already on board a fair amount of cargo, now prepared to receive a fresh relay of passengers, including several Lovat Scouts bound for their annual camp. With fascinated eye, we watched a flock of sheep disappearing through a hole

191

in the pier, as it seemed, to emerge lower down through the side and pass over a gangway into the steerage.   Then the crane with noisy demonstrations announced that it was going to get to work, and we saw several horses belted round and swung out, one after the other over the side of the pier, suspended in mid-air, to be lowered slowly into some vacant spot on the lower deck.   It was a fascinating performance, but scarcely more curious than the cargo that followed.   Of course, after seeing animals dangling in the air, bales of hay and straw in their place were dull to watch, but when a sofa, a bicycle, a fender, a table, a rocking-horse, chairs, and a pony-trap followed, and to them succeeded a coal-scuttle, bedsteads, two fire-grates, bedding, blankets, a kitchener, oil-cans, a plough, a hen-coop, a sewing machine, several pails, a garden roller, harness, and saddles, some spades and cartwheels, and all without a vestige of packing, we wondered, first, if we were witnessing the plenishing of a branch of the Army & Navy or some such stores, to be opened somewhere in the islands, and then where all the goods could possibly be bestowed. It was our experience of the Dunvegan mail coach all over again.   Even as we wondered, some crates of hens arrived on board, in their wake some Highland cattle, evidently holding cabin tickets, since they kept us company on the upper decklet, and from below we heard the squealing of newly-arrived pigs.   To compress what we saw in those two hours into two minutes' description, before we left the Kyle, the boat could hardly be seen for its cargo, and were there any Plimsoll line, it must have been far below the water, for we had made a clean sweep of the litter of goods, and in consequence we seemed to be leaving behind us a different pier from that into which we had steamed.

On occasions on which I have landed at the Kyle, which is in Ross-shire and the country of the Mackenzies of Kintail, it was to walk the eleven miles to Eilean Donnan Castle at the mouth of Loch Duich, which takes its name from S. Duthac, an eleventh century bishop in Ross.   The first seven miles are hilly, and constitute the only part of the walk where the scenery is both picturesque and interesting. After passing Balmacara, the charming old-world village in what may be termed a rocky setting, the road is absolutely level and the surrounding country quite ordinary, except for the singularly fine growth of tall and handsome thistles, which seem to flourish in abundance here. Associated, however, with Lochalsh, through which one passes, is one of the fulfilled prophecies of the Brahan Seer. He foretold, in days when it seemed a most unlikely thing ever to come to pass, that " a Lochalsh woman shall weep over the grave of a Frenchman in the burying-place of Lochalsh." This happened when, more than a hundred years after Coinneach's day, a native of Lochalsh married a French footman, who shortly afterwards died and was buried at Lochalsh. Another of the Seer's prophecies yet to be fulfilled concerns Ardelve, further on. " A severe battle will be fought in the Ardelve market stance in Lochalsh, when the slaughter will be so great that people can cross the ferry over dead men's bodies. The battle will finally be decided by a powerful man and his five sons who will come across from the Strath."

At Aird Ferry the point is reached where Loch Alsh, Loch Long, and Loch Duich meet, and here the views in all directions were a revelation of beauty which nothing on the way had anticipated. But, alas, in the interval of my visits, in one important respect the scene was sadly changed. On the first occasion we had been delighted and held by a picture perfect in every detail, for confronting us was the magnificent ruin of the Castle of Eilean Donnan, *then* the most picturesque of any I have ever seen on the castle-strewn shores of the west coast. It was low tide, and on the smooth green waters of the lochs lazily floated seawrack, golden brown; and in the clear portions it seemed as if the clouds, billows of snow, had fallen. Ferrying across to Dornie opposite, the picture of the castle, as here shewn, was secured, but no such view is any longer obtainable. For, returning several years later, I was horrified and repelled by the ruined picture which obtruded itself on the outraged surroundings, the remains of the castle being in the throes of a rebuilding which must permanently disfigure the landscape. In any modern rebuilding operations, the end no less than the means to the end are alike hideous. From start to finish of the proceedings, everything is ugly; and one can only marvel at a taste which finds any satisfaction in transforming a picturesque ruin which harmonizes so completely with its surroundings into a permanent blot on the landscape. For a modern mansion-house must in the nature of things be aggressive in its pretentiousness, and especially if it is to be connected with the mainland by a bridge, as is reported. How any one identified with the country by reason of his clan can thus choose to identify himself with a proceeding usually associated with Americans or vulgarians, passes comprehension. I have not given expression merely to my personal opinion regarding the havoc wrought on Eilean Donnan Castle, for I have heard identical views spontaneously, and quite as forcibly, expressed by men and women who knew the ruin before violent hands had been laid upon it.

The naturally strong position of the small rocky island on whose commanding summit Eilean Donnan Castle was built in the thirteenth century, was originally the site of a vitrified fort. All mention of S. Donnan I shall leave till we come to his own island of Eigg, since of his connection here his name is the only memory.

Ignoring insupported traditions, there is extant a charter shewing that the lands of Kintail, together with its Castle of Eilean Donnan, were granted in 1342 by William, Earl of Ross, to Reginald, son of Roderick of the Isles. In 1331 Randolph, Earl of Moray, the then warden of Scotland, hung the heads of fifty victims from the castle walls as an act of retributive justice. It is not till the fifteenth century, however, that there is any record of the fortress being in association with the name Mackenzie. Then, after being taken in the insurrection of 1504 by Huntly, representing the King's forces, it reverted to the Mackenzies of Kintail. About the middle of the fourteenth century an old Ross-shire clan, known as the " Wild Macraes," had migrated into Kintail and become devoted followers of Clan Mackenzie, so much so that, serving as the bodyguard of the chief, they were known as " Mackenzie's shirt-of-mail." Some credit the Macraes with an ecclesiastical origin, for the name translated is " son of grace "—temporal and spiritual, as Mackenzie, or MacCoinneach, the son of Kenneth, is by complete interpretation into English, the " son of the fair one." The Macraes became chamberlains of Kintail; they were frequently vicars of the parish, and in 1520 the chief was constable of Eilean Donnan Castle under the Mackenzies; but that office was never hereditary, for when, in 1539, the castle was attacked by the famous chief of Clan Uisdean, Donald Gorm, i.e., the Blue, John Dubh Matheson of Fernaig was the constable. This clan, the "sons of the bear," who have a history lost in antiquity, belonged to the district of Lochalsh. It is said that when, with fifty galleys, Donald Gorm, assisted by the Mackinnons of Strath, came against the castle, there were only three men in the garrison; and that Matheson was killed by an arrow[1] which entered the window by which he was standing. One Duncan MacGilchrist, Macrae, and a watchman, who were the three defenders, were nearly exhausted, and their ammunition also, when Macrae observed Donald Gorm going round the walls of the castle to decide on the best point for a final assault. Fitting the last arrow, a barbed

---

[1] In view of the prominent part archery played in this siege, it may be of general interest to give some details of the equipment of the Gael in this respect. His arrows (saighead) were made of yew, winged with eagles' feathers affixed by wax or resin, and carried in quivers made generally of badgers' skins. His bow was sometimes made of birch (beith) but more usually of yew, hence the bow itself was called iubar, and was often stained red; whilst the bow-string (tarfead) was sometimes of silk, sometimes of hemp.

one, into his bow, Macrae took aim at Donald Gorm, striking him in the master vein of the foot, and Donald, angrily plucking at it, severed in so doing a main artery. His followers conveyed him, bleeding profusely, to an islet or reef out of reach of the castle, and here a hut was hastily extemporized to shelter him. But the only medical help available was unequal to stopping the bleeding, so that there Donald died, and to this day the spot is still known as *Larach Tigh Mhic Dhomhnuill*—the " site of Macdonald's house."

There is also another tale told of the castle, this time in connection with the Macdonells [2] of Glengarry, and their chief, the " Black Raven," as he was called, from the Glengarry crest, a raven perched on a rock. This clan was hated by the Mackenzies of Kintail, and in the days of a very old Black Raven, Kintail thought he saw his chance of annihilating the Glengarrys. As he dared not tackle them unaided, Kintail, by the exercise of much subtlety, succeeded in banding together all the neighbouring chiefs against Glengarry, and for the purpose of considering how their design could best be undertaken, he summoned all his confederates to a council in Eilean Donnan Castle. The old Black Raven heard of this, and, realizing he could not hope successfully to resist so formidable an alliance, he absolved his clansmen from their allegiance, and bade them, together with his only surviving son, take refuge in flight. This the clan scorned to do; but, to their contemptuous surprise, young Glengarry, bidding his father farewell, took to the hills, armed to the teeth. His destination, however, was not some safe hiding-place but the lion's den, and, by donning the Mackenzie tartan both as a

---

[2] In 1660, Angus, chief of Glengarry, was created " Lord Macdonell and Aros," and, though the peerage died out, the clan have continued this orthography, no doubt initially due to the faulty or phonetic spelling and ambiguous script which then prevailed so extensively, and gave, for instance, "Argyle " for "Argyll."

EILEAN DONNAN CASTLE—AS IT WAS

disguise and a certain passport into Eilean Donnan Castle, he succeeded in obtaining an entry without his identity being suspected.   Entering the banqueting hall, where Kintail sat at the head of the council, young Glengarry boldly marched up, took the chief unaware, and seizing him by the throat, threatened him with instant death at the dagger's point if he or anyone else in the hall stirred. Then, while Kintail was at his mercy, young Glengarry made first the chief conspirator and then his allies swear that they would never again molest his father nor any of the clan.   For a Highland story, this has a unique conclusion.   The tale goes that after young Glengarry had released Kintail, he was urged to join the company in the feast that followed upon the arrested council, and that he not only complied but spent the night in the castle, parting the next day on the best of terms with his former enemies.

Following the rising of 1715, William Mackenzie, fifth Earl of Seaforth, held the castle with the Earl Marischal, the Marquis of Tullibardine, and a company of Spaniards. On May 10, 1719, three British men-of-war, the *Worcester, Flamborough,* and *Enterprise,* sailed up Loch Alsh from the sea, and, after the surrender of the Spanish garrison, blew up the castle.

The present state of the castle does not, of course, permit of any plan, old or new, being given, and, if it did, such a one would have no permanent interest.   Had the present proprietor restricted his energies to legitimate excavation and true restoration, he would have earned the gratitude, instead of the groans, of all who venerate an ancient building.

A friend and myself were landed one fearfully wet day on the north of the island, and noting, in passing, the foundation of some building discovered outside the castle, we made our way over the wealth of debris into the interior.   Here we first went to investigate the remarkable feature of this fortress—the hexagonal tower, at a considerably lower level than the courtyard, and still containing

16

some feet of stagnant water.   This, probably a water tank,
is said always to have been open to the sky, and a local
tradition has it that some treasure was once hidden there,
but recent search has discovered nothing.   Entering the
keep, excavation has revealed on the left a barrel vaulted
chamber, probably the guard room, having a fine
embrasured window with a stone seat on either side, and
a three-stepped window sill.   To the right of the guard
room steps lead up on the left, and after the first flight
separate to right and left, some descending, and those
ascending opening into a *garde robe*.   The rest of the
castle was in such a state of chaos that it was impossible
to make out more than that, on the west side, the narrow
passage leading into the courtyard now disclosed the flight
of stone steps down to the sea.

By the shores of whichever loch you elect to walk, you
pass the most picturesque of the old world Highland
cottages, thatched in straw, heather, or bracken, the
brilliant colour of which is very striking.   At low tide you
may see the " swimming cows of Loch Duich " cross the
water from the pasturage on Eilean Tioram to Aird Point
or *vice versa,* and at any time you may hear the raucous
voice of the tin horn blown at Totaig to signify that the
ferry boat from Aird is wanted there.   Directly across the
channel at Dornie, the same summons is conveyed by a bell
erected at the head of the landing-stage, but since the
ferries are within easy sight of each other, there is seldom
any occasion to ring it.   I shall not attempt any description
of the magnificent scenery, more especially of Loch Duich
side, for the simple reason that the rain has never allowed
me to see it properly, but has always promptly and deter-
minedly drawn an obliterating veil over the mountains and
lochs whenever I have sought their acquaintance.   Yet—

> " Though hails may beat us and the great mists blind us,
>   And lightning rend the pine-tree on the hill.
> Yet are we strong—yet shall the morning find us.
>   Children of tempest, all unshaken still."

Only in heavy showers and a raging wind were my friend and I able to cross to Totaig to see the broch there. This, however, no weather nor tempestuous crossing would have kept us from exploring.

Brochs are dry-stone buildings peculiar to Scotland, and the unique feature which distinguishes them from the more ordinary hill-forts is their series of intra-mural galleries. These buildings were obviously for the protection of persons and possessions, built, for all their popular naming of " Picts' towers," probably by Celts, who secured their object in an original and most ingenious manner by " turning the house outside in, as it were," as Dr. Joseph Anderson, the great authority on brochs, has well said. Thus the broch is a building of which the walls, within which are galleries, are built round a circle some forty to fifty feet in diameter, upon which the windows open. It is therefore practically a roofless, tapering tower, rising to some fifty feet, presenting outwardly a wall unbroken by any opening whatsoever save only by an entrance doorway. This was of the nature of a narrow tunnel through the thickness— some twelve feet—of the walls; a door, probably a stone slab, being set about midway, and a guard-cell securing the courtyard. The narrowness of the passage would at once prevent the entrance of more than one person at a time, and ensure the door against attack by levers. But before any enemy could gain the doorway, he would have to face the attacks of the garrison. They would man the top of the wall, which was gained by a spiral stairway in the thickness of the wall; and in the loose stones at their feet, the defenders would be provided with practically an endless supply of missiles with which to keep the enemy at bay. But even supposing the garrison were caught napping, and the enemy forced a way inside, the intruders would find themselves trapped and helpless, as it were at the bottom of a well, and at the mercy of an attack of stones from the windows which commanded every quarter of the enclosure.

Wells are not often found within brochs nor are they always even near any water-supply, hence it is improbable they were designed with any view to a prolonged siege, but only as temporary refuges.

So alike is one broch to another, that it has been seriously suggested that they were built in the Iron Age all at the same time from one plan.

That of Totaig is known locally as Caisteal Grúgaig, where the mother of the two giants of Glenelg is said to have lived.   Caisteal Grúgaig is situated half a mile west of Totaig Ferry, on the extreme east of Loch Alsh, and is most picturesquely placed on the hillside at the foot of a precipitous rock called Onag, and at the side of a demonstrative mountain burn.   The highest point to the south-west of the broch is aptly known as *Faire-an-Duin,* or the " watching-place of the fort."

Totaig presents a broch complete as far as the circumference is concerned, the wall still rising above the lintel of the entrance, and nothing could be more picturesque than the approach to this fascinating building.   Over the fallen stones at the entrance moss has thickly grown; and the hoary wall of huge stones, a great triangular block surmounting the doorway, is as beautiful a piece of primitive architecture as can be seen anywhere in the Highlands.   You pass through the doorway, which is only $4\frac{3}{4}$ feet high by $3\frac{1}{2}$ feet wide at the base, through the deep entrance passage, on the right side of which is a bar hole and on the left a guard chamber choked up with fallen stones, to the grass-grown courtyard.   Immediately facing you is the lower portion of a stairway and window, from which now grow ferns, and making the circuit of the broch by working from the entrance round to the right, you may observe various indications in the thickness of the walls of a cell, the entrance to which is choked up.   Then, passing the window, you come to what may be called a lobby, from which the stairway runs into the gallery.   Five steps lead

ENTRANCE TO THE BROCH AT TOTAIG

up into this, which is quite complete for a distance of several yards, as far as the window, whence five further steps rise, and then are blocked by the fall of the roof. One remaining step leads down to the scarcement from the window, to which, in order to complete the circuit of the broch, you retrace your steps, passing the lobby, to a small round cell next to it. It is worth while to obtain a light to examine the clever construction of the roof, where one big stone at the centre caps the overlapping stones. The top of the broch wall is easily gained from many points, and so broad is it that a horse and cart could easily drive round it. This broch differs from those to be described at Glenelg by reason of this very much thicker wall, the larger stones of which it is built, the triangular block over the doorway, and its complete circumference of walls, roughly 180 feet, measured 6 feet from ground.

The ferry-boat was to have returned for us from Aird at 6 P.M., but, when we got to Totaig Ferry, five minutes late, there was no sign of the boat on the very rough and turbulent waters. Consequently, after waiting twenty minutes, still without any sign of the boat, I tried to use the tin horn, but not a sound could my lusty lungs produce. A man, however, who just then made an opportune appearance, made a fearsome noise with the instrument, not, however, before we thought we descried the ferry-boat in the distance, obviously battling with the cross currents, for it was wholly out of its course. It seemed to stay in the same position for the next quarter of an hour—making no headway at all, and—to cut a long wait short—it did not get into the landing-stage till just on 7 o'clock, the two experienced boys who rowed it declaring they had almost been beaten in their attempt. However, we returned much more easily than we anticipated over the most difficult of the many ferries we have crossed in the West Highlands. I have never seen elsewhere a counterpart of the big ferry-boat here, on which carts, cattle, etc., are taken, for, in addition to the usual sweeps, it has a sail that imparts to it a picturesqueness that its modern counterparts with their motors can never claim.

- - - - -

PART II

GLENELG AND ITS BROCHS

IT is no far cry from Balmacara to Glenelg, and since I was very eager to see the famous so-called " Pictish Towers " there, on our sail southward, after we had passed through the narrow Kyle Rhea, we climbed down into the ferry boat which put out to the steamer. Archæology alone having taken me to Glenelg, I found, as I have invariably found when archæological considerations have dictated my movements, natural attractions in abundance; for in every direction the scenery reaches a very high standard.

One of the earliest possessions of the Macleods, Glenelg is the locality whence, according to tradition, they derived their crest. It is said that Malcolm, the third chief, encountered in the woods a wild bull which was a terror to the inhabitants. Though he was only armed with a dagger, Malcolm seized the animal by the horns, and holding fast to them, cut off the bull's head. Hence the bull's head caboshed became the crest of the Macleods, and their motto " Hold fast." This legend also states that Malcolm removed one of the horns (which nevertheless appears in the crest), and that this became Rory Mor's horn, though why his instead of Malcolm's, you are left to conjecture.

Of the old church of Glenelg, apparently dedicated to S. Comgan, there is now no trace. It is amusing to read of Glenelg in the report of a Whig on the state of the Highlands in 1750 that " the people are much civilized and polished by the Barracks of Bernera." These huge ungainly ruins, although in certain aspects they are picturesque enough, are the reverse of attractive to any patriotic Highlander, in view of their origin and purpose. For they were built by the foreign house of Hanover to subdue the native clans, and the contractor of 1722 secured part of his material by robbing one of the neighbouring brochs of $7\frac{1}{2}$ feet of its height.   In these barracks there died in 1746 of pneumonia Sir Alexander Macdonald of Sleat, the " Rebel of the North," a chief hated by his clansmen as apostate and renegade.   Though he was known to be a Jacobite at heart, the seventh baronet alienated himself from his clansmen by identifying himself with the Hanoverians, their enemies, and thus when he died, this epitaph was written for him:

> " If Heaven be pleased when sinners cease to sin,
> If Hell be pleased when sinners enter in,
> If Earth be pleased to quit a truckling knave,
> Then all are pleased—Macdonald's in his grave!"

From the Barracks a walk of about $3\frac{1}{2}$ miles takes you to Kyle Rhea, and in that short distance are compressed a remarkable number of very interesting antiquities.   On your way you pass Angalltair, and on the corner of the height above the hamlet is a prehistoric fort of stone and earth, called " Macleod's Castle," but, as there is now practically nothing to be seen, it is not worth the climb up.   Constant local tradition has it that Alasdair Crotach lived here until his child perished by falling over the precipitous rock, when the chief abandoned " Macleod's Castle " as his hunting seat for Dalla Mor on the site of the present Free Manse.

Some distance further along on the right hand side, I noted two large grass-grown mounds, which, on examination, were very suggestive of chambered burial-cairns. I was told that the second one was used as the burial-place for unbaptised children; but this would obviously have been merely a secondary use.

On the opposite side of the road, along the edge of the grass-grown beach, is a long ridge, and, since from here,

in the course of excavations undertaken nearly a generation
ago, large skeletons were uncovered, the name *Iomair nam
fear mora,* or the " ridge of big men," is certainly substantiated.   This is the traditional burying-place of those
heroes of the Fianna, Acunn and Riadh, after whom Kyle
Akin and Kyle Rhea respectively are said to be called.
According to one legend, these brothers lived in two strong
towers at Glenelg.   They were great friends, and nothing
occurred to mar their friendship until one day when the
younger brother returned home to find a black hearth.
As the day was bitterly cold, Rhea went to his brother's
tower, where the fire was smouldering.   Kindling it into
a blaze, he took home with him a burning peat to relight
his own fire.   Presumably this seemingly natural enough
action must have taken place either on New Year's or
S. Bride's Days, Beltane, or Lammas, when to give fire out
of the house, even to a neighbour whose fire had gone out,
was held to take *toradh* or profit (milk) from the cows
in favour of him to whom the fire went.   This fact would
account for the conclusion of the legend that when Acunn
returned and discovered the theft—how is not related--he
was furious.   A fight thereupon ensued between the
brothers, and the stones that are found scattered broadcast
over the plain which encircles the bay are witness to this
day of that fight.

Just a little beyond *Iomair nam fear mora,* a gate crosses
the road, and, if you pass through this and, turning at right
angles, keep up by the side of a small hazel wood, you may,
or may not, come across the large slab of natural rock on
which are still faintly to be discovered some " fairy's foot-
prints."   How these came to be made, a very attractive and
highly intelligent girl of Glenelg told me.

Her grandmother lived in one of the cottages, the ruin
of which can still be seen just outside the wood.   One
night, when she was alone with her children, a little man
and a big woman came in, and my informant's grandmother
gave them gruel.   The little man was very ill, but at cock-

crow they both disappeared, leaving behind them, however, the impress of their footmarks on the stone in the wood. The stone shews cup marks connected with channels, and so weathered is it that it takes but a little imagination to see in them tiny footprints such as the little folk might make if only they were heavy enough thus to impress the stone.

In connection with this and other stories, the question naturally arises as to how a " big woman " comes to be associated with the fairies, the " little folk." In a recent book on *The East of Arran,* the author, Mr. Scott, has an extremely interesting chapter in which he builds up a convincing theory as to the origin of Highland fairy lore. He attributes it to a medley of muddled memories which have survived of the prehistoric and Norse races, and very cleverly and completely he works it out. The imagination of the Celt must account for the strange remains of a former age—the little cists of the chambered cairns, the earth houses, and the great monoliths alike—with which they were so familiar. Thus, the Highlanders came to think of the cairns and earth houses as the dwellings of a " little people "; but it could only be " big " men and women who could raise such huge stones, and so there were giants amongst the fairy folk. The flint arrows and spearheads of the Stone Age became the elf shots of the " little people," and since the discovery in the Iron Age of the use of this metal shewed its vast superiority over all previously known materials for weapons, iron in any form became the unfailing charm against the maliciousness of some of the fairies. In the attributes of the different classes of little people, Mr. Scott finds the varying conduct likely to obtain amongst an enslaved race, where some would become devoted and others dour and spiteful servants. Thus, as one of these masters might be kept in a good humour by the present of a bannock when he happened to pass a dwelling of the superseded race when a baking was in progress, so the fairies might be propitiated by having the last cake of the baking left for them.   The propitiatory offerings which the prehistoric races made to the spirits in whom they believed are perpetuated in such ceremonies as the pouring of milk over *grugach* stones. To the kidnappings with which the fairies are credited, Mr. Scott finds a parallel in supposititious stealings of the children of the conquerors by the superseded race, who took this means of propagating themselves when threatened with extinction as a separate race.   The lure of the water-horse and its kin Mr. Scott derives from the Norsemen and their belief in such monsters as Odin's night horse. Following upon these lines, it is easy to find analogies in the remote past for every phase of Highland fairy lore and the ritual observed by the people in relation to the " little folk." [3]

Continuing along to the ferry across to Skye, the road, growing wilder, becomes more beautiful, and in springtime the right side of the road is bordered with masses of prim-roses having very large blossoms.   How Kyle Rhea came by its name is soon told.   Riadh, one day hunting in Skye, attempted to leap the strait in pursuit of a knightly errand, and, falling short, was drowned in the swiftly flowing and dangerous cross currents.

As I have mentioned that Riadh was one of the Fianna, and I shall have further occasion to mention these heroes, it will be well to say something about them here.   While some hold that the existence of the Fianna is only the Gaelic expression of a world-wide myth, and that conse-quently Fingal and his faithless wife, Graine, find an exact counterpart in Arthur and his queen, as Diarmad in Launcelot, others emphatically maintain that there was truly a time when " Fingal lived and Ossian sang."   These, supported by such an authority as O'Curry, say that the Celtic heroes, the Fianna, or followers of Fionn Alba, were the chief amongst the early Gaelic inhabitants of Alba,

[3] See *The East of Arran*, by A. Boyd Scott, M.C., B.D. (Gardner, Paisley).

living in the second or third century, that they fought with Romans, Danes, and one another, and finally struggled against Christianity.

One peculiarly beautiful day I felt impelled to take the road over the Mam Ratagan Pass, the summit of which is gained after a long, rough climb of about 6½ miles. In order to accompany me, my friend conceived the brilliant idea of chartering a pony for the expedition, but, as a pony was not to be had, we secured instead a highly-recommended cob. The satchel with our provisions for the day was strapped on to the saddle, my friend mounted, and we set off. Going through the little village of Glenelg, the inhabitants came out to watch us pass, for we had tied as many as possible of our picnic things on to the saddle, and the horse looked rather comical. This he seemed to resent, and all at once broke into such a jerky trot that one after the other the appendages came flying off, and I had to run in his wake picking up first the tea-kettle, then some sandwiches, then a book, whilst, judging from the sounds that floated back, my friend seemed to be enjoying herself.

Almost at once the pony conceived a violent attachment for me. I was walking ahead, and he insisted on dogging my footsteps. Vainly did my friend try to keep him on the other side of the road: he would have none of it, but, however erratic my course, faithfully followed in my train, so that at last, for my friend's sake, I had to abandon all deviations from the road.

" Clearly it is a case of Naomi and Ruth, for the pony plainly declares, ' Whither thou goest, I will go!' " exclaimed my friend, and henceforth, and despite his sex, we called the animal " Ruth." And, unfortunately, as all the midges and flies of the country side had arranged to accompany us for the day, we had to devote our energies to them and allow Ruth to shadow me.

It was a very hot day, a very rough road, and a very stiff climb up through wild, monotonous moorland, so that, when we gained the top of the pass, to see spread before us the most superb view of Shiel Bridge [4] nestling in the distance on the shimmering waters of Loch Duich at the foot of a magnificent range of mountains, my friend slid from her saddle into the heather and bequeathed Ruth to me. I wanted to photograph, and, as there was no rock or tree to which the animal could be tethered, I tried putting up my camera with him still in close attendance. Photography, however, had to be ruled out of the programme, as Ruth wished to pose in every view and would not keep to heel, and by this time I felt that tea was an urgent necessity. It should have been ideal having tea on that moorland roadside with such a wonderful view, but it proved the very opposite. Taking tea was as fraught with difficulties as taking photographs. Ruth elected to take a stand behind me with his head over my shoulder, only jerking it now and then when my cup was raised to my mouth. After a little while of this, as he stood so quietly, I let the rein go, and for a few blissful minutes forgot all about him. Suddenly, "Where's Ruth?" asked my friend, and we looked round to behold him trotting gleefully down the road on his way home, and after him we had to fly, teacups in one hand and sandwiches in the other. Fortunately, the animal stopped to graze for a little on a patch of grass by the roadside, when my friend mounted him again and we returned to Glenelg. That day-horse quite put in the shade all my previous nightmares, and from having had a particular (metaphorical) attachment to horses, the literal attachment to which I had been subjected all that day made me feel I never wanted to have anything to do with a horse any more, and he therefore did *not* play Ruth to my Naomi again.

[4] Travellers through Glen Shiel have practical experience of the tyranny of alien proprietors. Thanks to the action of the laird in 1907, Shiel Inn was closed—that the deer might not be disturbed by anyone taking shelter for the night, and thus " sport " be made to suffer! Now the nearest shelter open to the traveller after Clunie Inn is twenty-two miles distant, whereas the Shiel Inn was only ten.

On a second occasion I had ample opportunity to note the many objects of interest on the road, several of which had been pointed out to me by the wife of the Established minister.   I and the friend who was then with me had called at the Manse seeking information regarding several local features of interest.   From both the ideally courteous minister and his charming wife we received not only the information we sought, but unaffected kindness and hospitality, so that they are woven into my happiest associations, and I think of them, both so tolerant of and sympathetic to " black Prelacy," as of highest rank amongst Highlanders, where, indeed, low rank is almost non-existent.

It was in the late afternoon that we began our homeward journey from the summit of the Mam Ratagan Pass, and soon we arrived at a point from which you can see, in the far distance on your left, a pool, as it seems, gleaming in the hollow of the hills.   This small sheet of water at Suardalan is known as " John MacInnes' Loch," to which attaches the story of a water horse, which I will tell as it was told me by the minister's wife.

One day John MacInnes saw a beautiful horse by the lochside, and, consulting a wise man as to whether he might use it, he was told he might do so if he blessed it and remembered never to ride on it.   So he appropriated the horse, which worked splendidly, and all went well until one day when MacInnes, finding the animal very quiet, and being very tired, mounted it.   No sooner had he done so than at once the horse's character changed, and into the loch he plunged with MacInnes on his back, leaving as sole trace of the tragedy the lungs of the poor man, which were found afloat on the water.

When " John MacInnes' Loch " is lost to sight, you exchange it for a view down the glen, which, seen in the early evening against the light, makes a magnificent picture.   The dark hillside on your left is in purple shadow; below it the river, like a thread of molten silver, curves in and out on its course to the sea. The middle distance is broken by the dignified outline of the group of stately trees which mark the site of Scallisaig; behind lies the sea, and beyond the sea rise the great hills of Skye.

Further down the road, in the angle formed by it and a lower road, I counted the ruins of no less than thirteen houses, all clustered together. On enquiring about them, I was told that this was the once-flourishing hamlet of Knockfin (White Hill), whose story epitomizes what happened up and down the Highlands, when alien proprietors, having no territorial claims on the land, evicted those who had—in favour of sheep:

> "When the bold kindred, in the time long vanish'd,
>   Conquer'd the soil and fortified the keep—
> No seer foretold the children would be banish'd,
>   That a degenerate laird might boast his sheep."

These cruel evictions took place all over Glenelg about eighty years ago, when, in order that the evicted might not return, the thatched roofs were set on fire and the doors locked against the crofters. I was told of one case where a widow, with a family of six, refused to leave her home, whereupon the factor, one Stafford, with his own hands turned her out, and, locking her own door behind her and taking the key, left her and her children by the wayside to fare as they could. The minister told me that where, between these forked roads and the Manse, a distance a little over three miles, there used to be eleven hamlets, there are now only eleven inhabited houses.

In view of such iniquities, how the Highlanders generally did not rise in rebellion passes comprehension. On the eve of the English invasion that culminated on the fatal field of Flodden, the clansmen were incited to

> "Plunge them in the swelling rivers,
>   With their gear and with their goods;
> Spare, while breath remains, no Saxon,
>   Drown them in the roaring floods!"

But when Lowland sheep came to oust Highland men, they submitted. As a reward for their patient endurance of wrongs, their first claims for consideration were, and are still, contemptuously ignored, especially in the clamant matter of transport, by Governments which treated rebel Ireland and her fancied grievances like a spoilt child, giving her everything for which she chose to scream.

If I have digressed from the Mam Ratagan route, it is successive British Governments that are to blame, not I; and, having delivered my Tory soul on the subject of the callous Radical treatment of natives by aliens, let us resume the route just above Scallisaig. There, on the sky-line of the hill on the right, is poised a boulder which looks as if a push would send it toppling down the hillside. It is of this boulder that the Brahan Seer prophesied that it would one day fall and kill a man, and locally they say it will be a John Macrae mounted on a white horse who will meet this fate.

Of a shepherd who used to be employed at Scallisaig Farm House, the minister's wife told a very curious story. This man was given to the use of very strong language, and one day when a farm hand came along and, telling him of a dead sheep he had come across on the hill, asked him if he would fetch it, the shepherd replied: "May the devil take me if I go." His master asked him to recover the sheep and got the same reply; but when his mistress requested him to go, the shepherd yielded. On his way back, he saw by the river a lovely grey pony, which, how-ever, changed first into a grey hound and then into a black man. This was the "bad one," who thus addressed the shepherd: "You have often called upon me: now come with me." The shepherd begged for time to say good-bye to his people, and this request was granted on the condition that he kept an appointment to meet the devil next evening. He did so, when, after being beaten black and blue, he was thrown into the river. Several times the shepherd was compelled to keep similar appointments, always with the same results. The shepherd found when he took the Bible with him that it afforded him no protection, but when other people accompanied him, nothing happened. At last, to be rid of the devil, the shepherd moved to Glen Urquhart, but the devil followed him there—which thing is an allegory, surely, and the moral is plain to see.

Just below Scallisaig House, quite near the road, within the wall on the left, we were introduced for the first time to a "serpent mound," a subject of which neither of us had had any previous knowledge. We were told that the natives called this a fairy mound, but I noticed that it was associated with raised beaches. On looking the matter up, I discovered that the "wild fancies of some amateur archæologists" had dubbed some natural geological formations, gravel banks known as escars, or in Scotland "kames," "serpent mounds," attributing their construction to Phœnicians and a serpent worship which never had any existence in fact. When, as my companion shrewdly observed at Scallisaig, it would be difficult to find any place in these Highlands out of sight of a peak and not near a river, the inventors of these antiquities have gravely mentioned these two features as tokens by which the serpent mounds may be distinguished. On the top of this escar at Scallisaig, we saw a cist that had been opened and was found to contain an urn with human remains.

Crowning the green hill across the road, exactly opposite the Manse, is one of those forts locally known by the apparently Irish name of *baghan,* the *Baghan Burblach.* The walls, which are partly grass-grown, surround a boat-shaped enclosure of great size, within which are traces of various buildings, which, however, the growth of bracken made it very difficult to find. The view from this fort down the valley, ablaze with the gold of gorse, and across to the mountains of Skye is superb, and the hill, therefore, quite repays the climb, apart from the remains, which would well repay excavation. The site on his glebe of what the minister thought might be a broch, locally known as

an dun I did, with his kind permission and the vigorous
assistance of his wife, attack with spade and pick
sufficiently to make certain it was *not* a broch.

On the left hand side of the track to Ardintoul on Loch
Duich, just before the summit of the first ascent is reached,
there is on the top of the first of three hillocks, *Baghan
Gallda*.   This, which is smaller than the other, has
two entrances, and shews traces of two circular huts within,
and was to us more interesting in its present condition than
the *Baghan Burblach,* because there was more to be seen.

But the wealth of archæological remains I have indicated
from Kyle Rhea through Glenmore are as nothing to the
treasure of Glenbeg, where the two famous brochs of
Glenelg are situated.   With the exception of the broch of
Mousa, Shetland, these two brochs are said to be the most
complete extant, though I should couple with them that
of Totaig, and all lovers of ancient buildings rejoiced when
they were scheduled under the Act of Parliament designed
for the protection and preservation of such priceless
archæological monuments.

The walk from Glenelg up Glenbeg is very beautiful.
Just before leaving the sea shore to turn inland at Ellanreoch, the view round the corner, with great fallen rocks in
the foreground, and the rugged side of Beinn a Chapuill in
the distance, is quite arresting.   All the way through the
valley, the twisting and turning of the Glenbeg river, the
many rocks on its banks, the woodland, in spring thickly
carpeted by masses of primroses and a wealth of wild
hyacinths, and, all around the hills, make up a succession
of perfectly glorious pictures, whose colouring is
marvellous.   Such is the setting in which the brochs of
Glenelg are found, two of them said to be named after sons
of the lady who lived at Caisteal Grùgag, Totaig.   Just
before the first of these, Dun Telve, is reached, you may be
able to identify on the left hand side of the road, near a
sheep fank, a hill which shews the overgrown remains of
a third broch, or what is said to be such.

When, on my first visit to Glenelg, I arrived at the first of the two brochs, that of Dun Telve, the larger, which stands in a field on the right, entered by a white gate, I found a mason at work on the initial stages of restoration. The details of the work so successfully carried out are not only intensely interesting, but they afford so admirable an example of true restoration as opposed to ruinous rebuilding operations miscalled " restoration," that I give them as kindly detailed to me by the young architect to whose art, approaching genius, and ingenuity the broch's preservation is due. He found that the ends of the broch had been pinned up in cement, and promptly cut away this obscuration and negation of the distinctive feature of drystone buildings. In such danger of falling was this broch that it had been shored up with heavy timbers, and, after careful examination and prolonged consideration, it was resolved to consolidate the building by grouting in cement that part which was in the greatest danger of collapse. But in order that there might appear no trace of the use of cement, the joints of the section to be grouted were previously carefully packed with clay. Thus, when the cement was poured in at certain points, it found no outlet, and when the clay was thereafter washed away, there was no outward indication anywhere visible of the extremely clever and most artistic method of restoration adopted. Then, when the shoring could safely be removed, the broch was excavated; and, besides foundations of some out-buildings being brought to light, several stone cups and whorls were discovered.

Several years after, on returning to Glenelg, I saw this perfect restoration completed, as well as that of the second broch, untouched when I had previously seen it; and whenever I think of these fascinating works of art, the delight which I experienced in hovering about them at once returns to me.

The architect's plan, which is reproduced by kind permission of the Society of Antiquaries of Scotland, will give

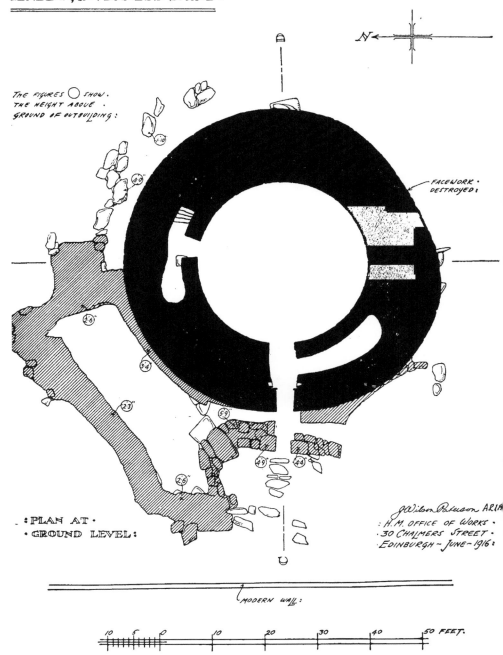

ROCH DUN TELVE·
LENBEG, INVERNESS-SHIRE:

N

THE FIGURES ◯ SHOW·
THE HEIGHT ABOVE·
GROUND OF OUTBUILDING:

1·10

4·0

FACEWORK·
DESTROYED:

2·6"

5·4

2·3"

5·9

4·9

4·4

2·6"

:PLAN AT·
·GROUND LEVEL:

J Wilson Paterson ARIBA
:H.M. OFFICE OF WORKS·
·30 CHALMERS STREET·
·EDINBURGH – JUNE – 1916:

MODERN WALL:

10 5 0   10   20   30   40   50 FEET·

PLAN OF BROCH OF DUN TELVE, GLENELG
(By kind permission of the Society of Antiquaries of Scotland)

a general idea of the plan of this broch quite sufficient for the general reader who does not wish to be overloaded with archæological technicalities.   Taking the plan as guide, and making for the entrance to the broch, the remains of outbuildings on the left are thought to indicate the provision made for the flocks and herds of the inhabitants. You enter the broch between some large stones, probably the remains of a wall designed to strengthen the approach, and pass through a passage 13½ feet long, and just about 5 feet high.   This passage, which varies from 3 feet to 5¼ feet in width, as shewn on the plan, has, beside the usual door-checks and bar-socket holes on both sides, the guard chamber, now roofless, on the right.   The courtyard, upon which the passage opens, is 32 feet in diameter, and, opposite you, only the ground level of the broch walls is to be seen.   But behind you about a third of the circumference remains, the wall here rising to 32½ feet at its highest point.   Turning round to look at this, you at once see the feature which constitutes the peculiarity of the brochs, for you find yourself faced by a section of an upright concave wall coursed by galleries which are intersected by two windows.   These galleries as they ascended became narrower, gradually tapering, until at the summit the double is merged into a single wall.   Passing round to the left, there is an entrance which opens on the left into a chamber in the thickness of the walls and on the right to the stair, still shewing seventeen steps which used to lead into the galleries but now open on to the top of the wall. Only four galleries and a portion of the fifth now remain, and two of these, judging from their height and superior interior masonry, were probably intended for human habitation, especially as the first gallery has a walled-off chamber in it.   This chamber is not lit from the courtyard, but has two entrances into it from the floor of the gallery above.   Perhaps, therefore, it served as a prison. The remaining galleries from their lowness were clearly never designed for living places, but seem obviously to have served some architectural purposes to relieve the thrust and to reduce the weight of the walls. Running round the basement, and again 29½ feet from the base, are two mysterious stone ledges or scarcements, the common use of which in brochs is only one of the many puzzles they present.

On the way to the second broch, Dun Troddan, I noticed at the end of a field not far from Dun Telve, and quite near the river, a stone circle or oval which, as far as I can ascertain, seems to have escaped previous attention. It is small, both as regards the circumference and the size of the majority of the remaining stones, but, as it was deluging, I had to content myself with such observation as was possible from the roadside. Thus, as far as I could make out, the stones were confined to the outer edge of the oval, a large monolith and a smaller being in the centre, and quite a cluster of stones at the side nearest Dun Telve. I counted twelve stones in all.

The second broch, Dun Troddan, stands just opposite the farm of Corrary, on a small natural platform, set on the beautifully wooded hillside. As you approach the broch, you get the impression of a circular tower, of which about one third of the circumference only remains, rising, when I first saw it, to some 25 feet, and leaning inwards. Climbing up behind it, you not only get the most picturesque view of the broch, the top of its irregularly broken wall covered with vegetable growth, and set in the beautiful background of the further hillside; but you obtain the best idea of how the tower must have looked when it was complete. You are faced by a wall whose surface is unbroken, and you marvel at the skill and the patience which were responsible for such a masterpiece of architecture constructed out of stones, quite small for the most part, laid in regular courses, and beautifully fitted together without appreciable gaps in spite of the absence of mortar.

The photograph shews the broch before its excavation,

THE BROCH OF DUN TRODDAN FROM THE BACK—BEFORE EXCAVATION

which gave about six feet more to its height and resulted in disclosing, not only the entrance passage (from which, however, the lintel is gone), and on the left, with its lintel, the guard chamber, still partially roofed, but also a second cell in the same opening as the stairway, of which thirteen steps remain, and a hearth in the middle of the courtyard. As this shews signs of successive occupations, it is wisely intended to leave it so that its various layers may be observed.

I will not go into any further details of Dun Troddan, as readers not specially interested in archæology would only consider them a wearisome repetition when I have already said so much about brochs. Continuing the beautiful walk by the meandering river through Glenbeg with the intention of finding another reputed broch, Dun Grugaig or Castle Chonil, I noticed on the right by the roadside some great heaps of stone, very suggestive of chambered cairns. Further on, just short of Balvraid farm, on the left of the road and near some ruined cottages, I was told that a gentleman I had met and whom I knew to be an enthusiastic archæologist, had located what he thought to be an earth house. What I saw was not very suggestive of an underground dwelling, but I may have quite well been looking at the wrong place. Certainly both here and elsewhere in the district of Glenelg, only the pick and the spade can disclose the nature of much that is at present hidden from view—a treasure-house of archæological wealth, as I believe.

Passing onward, my companion and I made our way by a path up the hillside on the right until we reached a point where, leaving the track, we could cut across the hilly moorland on the right to Dun Grugaig. This structure crowns a precipitous height towering above the beautiful ravine through which, at a great depth here, the river courses. We had both seen plans, drawings, and their accompanying descriptions (of date 1895) of the " broch-like " fort; but neither of us were able to make out many of the features given alike in the plan and letterpress. Even the early growth of bracken was obscuring, and quite probably the debris had increased in twenty-five years, so that what seemed to us but a chamber in the thickness of the wall might have really been part of a gallery running right the way round.   We did make out the semi-circular plan of the fort, but little else, although this was quite sufficient to make us feel that excavation would certainly reveal many very interesting features.   Indeed, of all the baghans and forts we visited in this district, Dun Grugaig proved, in our estimation, quite the most interesting, and we hope it may receive attention at the hands of qualified archæologists.

Glenelg cannot be left without some words with regard to the road to Arnisdale.   While the route up Glenmore to the Mam Ratagan Pass is popularly accepted as affording the finest views, my companion on the walk towards Arnisdale agreed with me that this latter route is incomparably finer.   You climb up and down a very rough, lonely road on the hillside where, if the view in retrospect, looking up the narrows of Kyle Rhea is very beautiful, those presently revealed at the twists and turns of the road beyond Sandaig are simply sublime.   It was a day in spring on which we took this glorious walk; and on the brown heather by the roadside stonechats and whinchats, busy with their nesting, perched, chattering noisily. Unfortunately, of the Coolin, the peaks of Rum, and of Eigg, we only caught a transitory glimpse, for the mist soon swallowed them up, and held them in its mantle.   But no mists obscured Ben Screel and other great peaks which, crowned with snow, held our eyes from the moment they came in view, by reason of their dominating splendour. Leaving the roadway, some seven miles from Glenelg, in order to obtain a view of Loch Hourn, that which our viewpoint afforded us suggested the culmination of grandeur, and we went no further, spending the rest of the time in contemplation of the loch in its sublime setting of mountains.

It is impossible to write of the Highlands with any pretention to completeness and to avoid the subject of religion, for nothing has left its impress so profoundly on the character of the Highlander. It will be a surprise to the vast majority of Sasunnachs, Lowlanders no less than English, to realize some facts that have been sedulously suppressed in sectarian interests. Yet it is demonstrable even from the bare admissions of Presbytery [5] records that it was only because Presbyterianism was forced upon the people of Lochalsh and Glenelg, as upon district after district of the Highlands, where the natives were originally either Episcopalians or Roman Catholics, that in the course of years Calvinism became the dominant religion. Probably, indeed, in no district in Scotland was the Presbyterian settlement delayed so long as in the west of Ross, where the population were entirely Episcopalian or Roman Catholic. Against them Presbyterianism, by virtue of its parliament-conferred status, based upon a perversion of facts, carried on an aggressive and exterminating crusade. For, contrary to and NOT supported by " the inclination of the people," on which Presbyterianism, in its " fundamental charter," based its claim to represent the Scottish nation, the parliamentary Establishment appealed both to the law and to the force of arms to entrench itself, wherever it was rejected by the people. For instance, the Gairloch Presbytery Register records how " the Presbytery had no access to meet in their own bounds, since they had been rabbled at Lochalsh, 16 September, 1724," and speaks of " the great opposition to the gospell

---

[5] For the information of English readers, a Presbytery, formed by the ministers of all the parishes comprised within it, may be compared to a Ruri-decanal Chapter having executive powers. A Synod is the court next above the Presbyteries and comprising them, in the same way as an Arch-deaconry comprises Rural Deaneries. The General Assembly is the supreme Presbyterian Court.

(*i.e.,* Calvinism) met with therein," noting also " the violent opposition given by the enemies of the present Establishment." Again the Presbytery, finding that " Mr. Alex. M'Lennan, nonjuror, Episcopal intruder [the Presbyterian cuckoo's epithet for the Episcopalian robin who did but claim his own nest] diverts the people of Lochalsh and Kintail from hearing the Brethren sent to supply these parishes, appoint Mr. David Beton to write to Sir Robert Munro of Foulis, Sheriff Principal of the shire of Ross, to put the laws in execution against the said intruder."

Then the Presbyterian Synod of Glenelg in the year 1725 approved of an overture authorising some of its members to proceed to Inverness to invoke the aid of " George Wade, Esq., Commander in Chief of His Majesty's Forces in Scotland," and crave his " concurrence and assistance towards redressing the said grievances and strengthening our hands in the Lord's work "—of forcing an alien religion upon an unwilling people! Missionaries were sent out by the Presbyteries to attempt to " supply " in the vacant parishes, but, according to the Gairloch Register, they met with " very barbarous and rude treat- ment," and later in the year the Presbytery speaks of " insuperable difficulties " attending the " planting of their vacancies." The General Assembly ordered five ministers to labour for a short mission, but only one faced the labour, and short indeed was his mission, for after three weeks he abandoned it. When, after some time, seven parishes in the west of Ross were settled with their first Presbyterian ministers, it was done in each of the seven cases by appoint- ment of the Presbytery, because there were no Presby- terians in any of the parishes to make the appointments! [6] One minister, intruded in 1726, had to carry arms in self-

[6] Yet Dr. John Mackay, in his book on the *Church in the Highlands,* says:—" It has been a principle of the Church (*i.e.,* Presbyterianism) from the Reformation, ' that it appertaineth to the people and to every several congregation to elect their own minister.' "

defence against his "parishioners," and in 1734 he had only one family in regular attendance on his ministrations. In Kintail no settlement whatever could be effected till 1730, forty-two years after the revolution which made Presbyterianism the State religion, and, even then, it was again the Presbytery that forced an unwanted minister upon a people who were strongly anti-Presbyterian.

These few instances, out of legion, sufficiently demonstrate what were the real "inclinations of the people," and exhibit Presbyterianism as an entirely exotic system, introduced by ministers of State on principles of political expediency, and shew how it was dragooned upon the West Highlanders by such methods as the inviting of General Wade to take military action, and the assistance of the factors of the forfeited estates of the native chiefs! Well then did Carlyle of Inveresk in his *Autobiography* make the following statement, saying " that when Presbytery was re-established in Scotland at the revolution, after the reign of Episcopacy for twenty-nine years, more than *two-thirds* of the people of the country and *most part* of the gentry were Episcopals; the restoration of Presbytery by King William being chiefly owing to the Duke of Argyle, Marchmont, Stair,[7] and other leading nobles who had suffered under Charles and James, and who had promoted the Revolution with all their interest and power." This testimony, borne by a Presbyterian divine, is amply substantiated by local records and constant tradition all over the Highlands, and by other equally sound evidence.

[7] One of the chief promoters, if not *the* chief instigator, of the Massacre of Glencoe.

CHAPTER IV

THE ISLAND OF EIGG [1]

PART I

THE ISLAND AND ITS PEOPLE

" Whither away, whither away,
  Over the billows bright?
We're bound for the island of cliff and foam
Where the moors lie bare, where the sea-winds roam,
  And the lone bird calls in the night."

S O wrote my friend as we sat in the stern of the *Gael,* sailing over to Eigg from Glenelg. It was an ideal day of smiling sunshine, and a playful breeze frisked over the surface of a sea of azure. As you see the island in the distance—a long, low body, gracefully stretched out on the bosom of the waters, the head held serenely erect, the attitude of calm strength irresistibly suggests the lions at the base of the Nelson Monument in Trafalgar Square. The Sgurr is an excellent sentinel on bright days, when it can always be trusted to remain at its post, but in dull weather it too often retreats into the mist as into a sentry box, and then Eigg seems to have suffered decapitation.

As you look at the island from a distance on a clear day, there may be observed a curious feature in its configuration,

[1] The devotion that the islanders feel is unalienably due to Clanranald was touchingly shewn some years ago when the late Admiral Macdonald visited the realms of his forefathers. Though these possessions had been so long in the hands of strangers, the natives crowded around Clanranald, kissed his hands, and shewed him every sign of affection. The Macdonalds of Morar were for many years considerable landowners in Eigg.

All the translations of the beautiful rùns, croons, etc., of Eigg in this chapter I owe to one of its most devoted and talented sons. Rev. Kenneth Macleod, parish minister of Colonsay.

to which possibly it owes its name. *Eag* is a notch or hollow, nick or hack, and there is a suggestion of these in the angles formed by the wedge-like construction of the island. Seen from the north shore of Ardnamurchan, this peculiarity of structure becomes striking, and testifies to that happy descriptive genius which usually characterizes Gaelic naming. There is a ridiculous story that derives the name from an exclamation of some Norse pirates who troubled the Western Islands in early days. The natives tell you that one dark night a company of these marauders were making their way southwards, and, being well aware of the dangerous nature of the seas, had posted a special look-out. Off the coast of Eigg, this man realized they were running into the shore, and shouted warningly, "*Aige!*" ("At it!" *i.e.*, the land). The ships' course was accordingly altered, but soon there came a second cry, "*A ris aige!*" ("At it again!") and Aige or Eigg the island was called thenceforward. If any such absurd origin for a place-name could be accepted, the cry rather suggests Arisaig, opposite Eigg. But in either case no derivation could well be more fanciful, especially in view of the fact that Gaelic was *not* the language of the Norsemen.

Of the old days, it is said that the natives, when at sea, never dared speak of Eigg directly, so they referred to the island indirectly as the "Isle of Big Women," a name thought to have reference to the queen who ordered the martyrdom of S. Donnan; and to this day the loch nearest the Sgurr is called Loch nam Ban Mora—the loch of big women. There is possibly some affinity between this curious fact and that of the fear of arousing the ill-will of the fairies by speaking of them by their own name.

The island came into the possession of the Clanranald in 1309, when it was given by Robert the Bruce to Roderick the son of Allan in return for the service of a ship of twenty-six oars, with its complement of men and provisions. The island was always a favourite meeting

place for the men of the Isles, and in 1545 the council of
Donald Dubh met here and drew up " A Commission from
the Lord of the Isles to treat with the King of England."

Clanranald, as sung by the bards, is elevated to an
eminence as lofty as his own Sgurr of Eigg:

> "My treasure, my treasure, Clanranald;
> Stag among the deer of the bens,
> Salmon among the trout of the streams,
> Loveliest amongst the swans,
> Loftiest ship that makes the harbour."

In 1615, the people of Eigg had an opportunity of
shewing in what estimation they held a chieftain of Clan
Donald. Accompanied by several of the men of Sleat in
Skye, Sir James Macdonald, in a large boat, sailed for
Eigg, and would probably land at Kildonan. Once on
the island, he met there Coll Macgillespic, or " Old
Colkitto," and his followers; and very enthusiastic was
the reception they accorded their visitor. Standing with
his men in a place apart, Sir James was surrounded by
Coll and his men, who marched round them, firing volleys
of small arms into the air for half-an-hour. After this
reception, every one of Coll's men came forward and shook
hands with Sir James.

Eigg remained in the possession of Clanranald until
1828, when Professor Macpherson bought it. Since his
death, however, it has passed entirely out of Highland
hands, and may only too truly be classed once more
amongst the many modern Innse Ghall—" isles of the
strangers."

The island loses none of its attractiveness when the boat
brings you to closer quarters. Indeed, only when under
its lee do you realize how beautifully it is clothed in green.
Beyond the snug little harbour naturally formed by Eilean
a' Chaisteil,[2] the road from the tiny stone pier climbs up

---

[2] The " Castle Island," so called because of the *dun* or hill fort it once
possessed.

the hill until it is lost in the only real wood of the island. Above the trees you see the Sgurr, but its changed aspect startles you. No longer serene, it now seems to frown, rising abruptly and standing haughtily aloof with a suggestion of superiority over the moorlands, which stretch invitingly out in tier after tier on the lower heights of the island. You wish the ferry boat were not quite so leisurely in its journey over to the steamer, for you long to be landed on this isle of enchantment.

It is always amusing to watch the attitude of the conventional tourists taking the regulation trip between Mallaig and Oban, when the steamer slows down at Eigg and prepares to receive the ferry boat. Women, fashionably clad in garments quite unsuited to the Highlands, and some of the men little less absurdly dressed, cluster round the rails and wonder who can possibly be going to land in such rough fashion at such an unheard-of place. The sailors throw our luggage into the boat as though it were rubbish of which the steamer was well rid, and, truth to tell, our traps, from long experience of similar treatment, do look as if they had seen better days. We tumble down on the top of our belongings, and push off from the steamer under the pitying glance of the passengers, who are obviously thanking their stars that they are at least bound for a place mentioned in every guide book.

When the tide is low, there is an element of excitement in the landing, which can only be effected by a process of slipping and sliding, aided by dexterous balancing efforts on seaweed-covered boulders, prior to a sheer clamber up on to the stone landing-stage. There we are met by an old ramshackle pony-trap to convey both ourselves and our luggage over to the " hotel " (now, alas, no more). The marvel always was to see the same antiquated " machine " turn up unfailingly every year, for one would suppose it could not survive another journey of jolting up stiff hills and over ill-made roads, culminating in a voyage over a rough field. But the ancient chariots that one finds on daily service in the Highlands seem to be endowed with an eternal old age on which no amount of hard usage makes any impression.

The drive over to Laig has not only the charm of novelty from the point of view of the nature both of the conveyance and the roads over which it takes you, but the rare beauty of its course enthralls you, for it can have no superior in any part of the Highlands. You climb up the hill midway between two plantations, and gain the one main road passing through the moorland, which on one side rises to the heights and on the other first slopes and then falls down to the sea, with the blue mountains of the mainland shimmering in the distance. Just where a little burn crosses the road, after tinkling over the stones of its bed by the roadside, the imperious, ever-dominating Sgurr takes on a new face—that of a squat Norman tower of an old English village church. You rattle past a small cluster of fir trees, still through the brown, scented moorland, still with the mountains glistering across the sea, till, a little past the school-house, the ground unkindly rises and hides them from your sight. Just beyond the school on the right is a roadside or resting cairn, erected to commemorate the last journey of a much-loved parish priest. For, though about half of the present population are Protestants, with the usual division between followers of the Establishment and the Wee Frees, those islanders whose families have belonged to Eigg for generations are still Roman Catholics.

You are just upon the Post Office when the glorious peaks of Rum first rise into sight, and begin to weave that spell which they never fail to cast over you. In the old days, we always called a halt here to greet Mairi of the Post Office, whom we were happy to number amongst the first of our island friends. Of all the Highland women I ever met, she was perhaps the most attractive, and not only in appearance, for her face, and especially her eyes, spoke of a spirit which roamed in a rare atmosphere.

Young, and with fine dark hair, she had the most beautiful large dark eyes, alit from the soul within, and her voice had all the softness of a deep and swiftly-flowing burn. To hear her speak was to listen to music; and her charm of manner, in which a simple shyness was blended with a real warmth, was irresistible. It was one of my chief delights to coax her into telling me the tales of the island, and to watch her grace of movement and the expressive play of features as I listened to her soft voice. One felt that here was a veritable queen of the island, occupying by right of nature a throne to which no amount of money or advertisement could exalt any alien, proclaim they their purchase never so loudly in the Press and out of it.

One of the tales that Mairi told me was of Cuagach, which you reach shortly after leaving the Post Office to continue your way to the " hotel." Here is a small water-fall, where a little woman with beautiful hands may be seen washing, washing; but woe betide the mortal rash enough to ask her what it is she washes. One day, however, a man who saw her, rashly put the fatal question, and, since he insisted upon having an answer, the little woman replied, " It is thy shroud I wash!" Indeed, the very sight of the *bean nighe* (washing woman), who haunts many a Highland waterfall, betokens a death, for it is always a shroud she washes.

At the bottom of the hill of Cuagach, the pony trap turns in at a gate on the left, and for the rest of the way you go jolting along a rough and deeply-rutted track, on your right a burn, thick with huge burdock leaves, running into the sea. Finally, you rumble in your springless convey-ance over a field running parallel with and just above the sands of Laig Bay, and, after crossing a bridge of wooden planks, you climb up a grassy hill, where there is not even the pretence of a regular track, to be deposited outside Laig House. The nucleus of this hotel of happy memories began life as a farm house, where Alasdair Mac Mhaighstir Alasdair's eldest son, Ronald, himself a poet, lived; the farm remaining in his family till the emigration of the poet's great grandson to United States of America about 1850.[3] The conversion of the farm house into a hotel began when a " tin " Post Office that used to be on the shore was moved up and tacked on to it. Since I first knew it, further out-buildings of the same temporary nature were added, so that the finished article presented one of the oddest pieces of construction imaginable. But for all that, and the cramped quarters, and poor lighting of the rooms, the kindness and capability of the charming girl-manager, who supplied every comfort, made Laig House a real home which we were always loath to leave and to which we ever eagerly returned. Catriona was another friend, for hers was a sweet nature of a rare innocence and beautiful simplicity. And in all intercourse with both her and Mairi of the Post Office, you felt how well they exemplified in their own persons that Run of Hospitality which belongs to Eigg:

> " I saw a stranger here yest're'en.
> I put food in the eating place,
> Drink in the drinking place,
> Music in the listening place.
> In the Sacred Name of the Triune.
> He blessed myself and my house.
> My cattle and my dear ones,
> And the lark said in her song:—
>   ' Often, often, often,
> Goes the Christ in the stranger's guise;
>   Often, often, often,
> Goes the Christ in the stranger's guise.' "

[3] Another poet, John Macdonald—or *Iain Dubh Mac Iain 'Ic Ailean* (John of the Black Locks)—born in 1665, also lived in Eigg, where he held the farm of Gruline. He fought at Sheriffmuir.

Part II

THE BAY OF LAIG, AND ROUND THE COAST TO KILDONAN

At Laig House, the room of my choice was an outhousie, round whose door a whole farmyard used to gather: a family of hens and their grown-up children; a smooth-haired collie pup; a beautiful milk-white cat; and two calves. One morning early I heard the handle of my door rattle, and great sniffs through the keyhole: a little later, more sniffs of investigation—this time at the window, through which I beheld the enquiring visage of one of the calves! Once when I came in. I was greeted on the threshold by a fine fat toad! There was a further novelty attaching to the occupancy of this room, for every time one wished to take a bath, in order to reach the bathroom, located in the original building, a climb of an outside wall and a walk across the grass in one's night attire was involved.

" Laig " means " Surf Bay," and the wealth and variety of the attractions which its shore possesses, not to mention the various archæological relics it has yielded, are some of the many wonders of the island. If you would realize what a unique shore it is, try to visualize it. Think of a bay with strange cliffs; the most beautiful of white sands; weirdly-shaped rocks, often so deeply pitted as to resemble huge sponges; and rock terraces on a foreground crossed by many little burns; and beyond the deep green and purple patches of the sea, the ever-glorious peaks of Rum. So curious are the sandstone formations that they cannot but beget an interest in geology even where previously there was none—as in my own case. A geologist who knows the shore gave me to understand that in remote ages it formed part of the bed of a great river that flowed over here from Skye. The surf has been responsible for some most remarkable sculpturing. There is a series of deep ditches, from one to twelve feet wide, whose parallel sides separate ramparts rising above them on either hand, and slope outwardly, after having formed a projecting rim. These are the remains of trap dykes, which have now wholly disappeared, leaving only their moulds behind to shew where they once existed. Even more curious, perhaps, are the phenomena of petrified puff-balls presented by many of the sandstone forms; others with tops resembling two or three contiguous circles. In these cases, the matrices have been worn away, leaving these large concretionary masses standing, though many of them have become detached and lie about the shore like huge cannon-balls. Many of these stone " shots," too, may be noticed embedded in the cliffs—very vividly suggesting a bombardment by artillery.

Above the sands are fields of wild flowers, and all around and above the bay they bloom in amazing profusion. Our Lady here may find her bedstraw, mantle and fingers: there are dwarf roses, gentians, tutsan, bird's-foot trefoil, banks of tufted vetch, sea-holly growing amongst greater meadow-rue, the bright blue brook-lime, water forget-me-nots, heart's-ease, flowers of Parnassus, queen-of-the-meadows, hemp agrimony, valerian, water parsnip and its kin, Canterbury-bells, evergreen alkanet, and both sweet and meadow orchis—all these growing to a great size in this wild botanical garden. All sense of time is lost on this wonderful shore, for there you yourself are lost amongst its manifold interests. Scrambling about in the warm sunshine amongst the clear pools, in which green and purple seaweeds float, or in which fleecy clouds are mirrored, you can watch the movements of the various tiny little armoured inhabitants who people them. With clear voice of silver, many a baby burn takes a tumble over a low ridge of sandstone to become a tiny waterfall, which tinkles merrily down over the rocks until it is lost in the sea. It is possible that amongst these little pools beneath the waterfalls either *Tobar an Tuirc,* the " well

SANDSTONE FORMATIONS, LAIG BAY, ISLE OF EIGG

of the boar " or *Tobar nan Eun,* the " well of the birds,"
are numbered.   These two wells, which are said to be a
mile apart, have been associated with incidents in a tale
of the Féinne; but I have never heard in what part of the
island they are supposed to be.

Then there are the birds.   Oyster-catchers run about,
piping on the wet sands; above them scream the seagulls,
not so " common " as their name suggests; rock-pipits
flit from stone to stone; and the curlew with haunting
cry flies across on its way to the moorland.   But were I
asked what most of all I loved on this shore, I would say
a sunset; for nowhere else can the dying sun shew better
the supremacy of his art.   If in a day on the hills the
delights of physical well-being predominate, you are only
sensible of spirit as you watch the illumination of Rum
by the hand of the master-painter.   First he uses his most
delicately radiant colours, and the island glows in palest
yellow or pink that quivers into mauve.   Then he gilds
the tall peaks, and ruddy and yet more ruddy gleams the
gold until it leaps into living fire, and, lo, the whole island
is aflame.   For a breathless space you watch it, fiercely
flaming, and then, very slowly, the fire wanes, and dies
down: the red passes into orange, the orange into yellow
till that, too, fades away, for the sun, slowly vacating his
throne, has now descended the last step, and night has
succeeded to take up the abnegated sceptre of sovereignty.
And as she wields it, a soft grey veil descends upon Rum,
and its mysterious hollows fade away as the mantle is
folded about it, that for a few hours the island may be lost
in sleep.   As you stand, seeing again in memory the
wonderful picture that just passed before your eyes,
" Ossian's Address to the Setting Sun " provides you with
a fitting apostrophe:

> " Hast thou left thy blue course in the sky,
> Blameless son, of the gold-yellow locks?
> The doors of the night open before thee,
> And the pavilion of thy repose is in the west.

> The billows crowd slowly around
> To view thy bright cheeks:
> They lift their heads in fear when they behold thee
> So lovely in thy sleep, and
> Shrink away with awe from thy side.
> Sleep thou on in thy cave, O Sun,
> And let thy return be with joy."

When the tide is low, you can continue scrambling and climbing round by the shore, but most people will prefer in any case to walk over the cliffs to the next bay, where are the alleged " Singing " or " Musical " Sands discovered by Hugh Miller. I always wonder how much this discovery was due to his imagination; for I still remember the keen disappointment I originally experienced when expecting to hear something really in the nature of music result from walking over them. The only thing we could extract from them was a squeak with little of melody in it, and that only by scuffling one's boots vigorously in the bone-dry sand.

Continuing northward, near the north-west point of the island is Aoineadh Mor, " the great steep promontory," and it was in a cave in its face that there hid one of the only three women who escaped from the massacre of the Macdonalds on the island. When she was discovered, the Macleods told her that though they would not have her blood on their heads, yet they would starve her, which, one had supposed, was in spirit the same thing. To accomplish this, it is said that they ploughed up the sands of Laig for a mile in length in order to remove the sword fish upon which she was living. I have not been able to discover the *rationale* of this process, but still upon the shores of Laig you can see grass-covered furrows which are said to have been made by this ploughing. But, apparently, the old woman was independent of the sword fish, for she answered the Macleods: " If I get the shell fish of Sloc (a pool), the dulse of Laig, and the tender water-cresses from the great well of Tolain, I shall not want."

When you turn the corner of Aoineadh Mor, your eyes
are gladdened once more by the sight of the long stretch
of the Coolin which then bursts upon you.   Climbing up
gradually, you find yourself upon a wonderful terrace,
several feet above the sea, with towering cliffs on the
landward side.   You have to make your way by twisting
in and out amongst the enormous boulders, hart's tongue
fern growing profusely in their shade, and rabbits popping
about everywhere over the green sward.   It was here that
I remarked the only wild white rabbit I have ever seen.
Kestrels nest in the great cliffs above, and their cry is
exactly like that of a cat, while their flight is one of the
most fascinating of any to watch, for they sail through
the air on their distinctively ruddy widespread wings
without, apparently, the slightest effort.

Out to sea, there are rocky islets covered with birds,
and it was one of these reefs for which I was told to steer
when I had enquired how I might identify *Uamh Mhic 'ic
Ailein,* the cave where the chief of Clanranald, as its name
signifies, spent one night after Culloden.   He was accompanied by one John M'Lellan, and the story goes that the
chief had only a stone for a pillow, and, not finding it very
restful, he asked his follower for a turf instead.   The
answer he is alleged to have received may be unexception-
able in the Gaelic, but, translated into English, it
sounds distinctly disrespectful — if not rude—certainly
utterly unlike the speech of a clansman to a chief: " How
fond you are of ease!" M'Lellan is reported to have
replied.   " Will the stone not suffice the head that you
may lose before morning?"   The boy who cleaned our
boots at the hotel was a direct descendant of this M'Lellan,
so Catriona informed me.

" Clanranald's Cave " is the largest one of the many
honey-combing the base of Sgurr Sgaileach—the " rock
that casts a deep shadow "; and the broken columns which
lie about its base are so large, numerous, and close together
that it is most difficult to climb over them and get into the

cave without disaster.   There is nothing calling for special remark about this cave, and the same applies to the rest, amongst which, presumably, is *Uamh Chloinn Diridh,* said to be near the north of the island.   I was not, however, able to identify this particular " cave of the ascending slope," where, it is said, a fugitive from the Macleod country took refuge, for what reason is not recorded.   He has a descendant still on the island in the genial person of Donald Macleod, the gamekeeper.   In the same cave, one *Am Piobair Mor* (the great piper) made his first home when he fled from Rum to escape the tyranny of the *Creidimh a' Bhata Bhuide.*   This " religion of the yellow stick " is the Highlanders' name for Presbyterianism, and the term is derived from the fact that Maclean of Coll, to shew how thorough was his perversion, barred the way to the Roman Catholic church by standing in the road leading to it armed with a cane, wherewith to belabour the Faithful into submitting to Protestantism.

Sgurr Sgaileach itself is a very striking cliff of columnar construction, noble in its proportions, and very reminiscent of Staffa, more especially as it is an isolated headland suggesting the island.   When you have rounded the precipice, and after you have crossed a boggy plain, you come out upon the rough talus of the wild and desolate east coast of the island, where walking must be done with the greatest caution if you are to escape a broken leg. For the scree of large rocks, often tightly packed together, is for miles overgrown with bracken, heather, and stunted dwarf-trees, natural man-traps, in which you may easily find yourself uneasily imprisoned waist-deep, if your foot is misplaced.

Like huge ramparts, towering to 500 feet, rise the sheer cliffs, home of eagles, falcons, buzzards, kestrels, rock-pigeons, and endless sea-birds, including shear-waters. These apparently none too common birds breed on the island, and a lady, who used to be taken out by the game-keeper when he found anything of special interest in bird-

A LITTLE WEST HIGHLANDER

life, told me about a nest which she had seen on the top of these east cliffs. The shear-water (which the islanders call a " puffin ") nests on the ground, either using a disused rabbit's burrow or making a hole for itself, and in this it lays a solitary egg, pure white and nearly round. The lady described how the gamekeeper had dug out the great fat baby bird so that she might see it properly. Evidently the shear-water is of a very placid temperament, for the birds never stir, even when treated in this fashion. When it is time for the baby bird to take to flight, the mother feeds it on sorrel leaves, the neighbourhood of which she is careful to select for the place of her nest. Hitherto, the nestling has been fed exclusively on oily fish; and so, in order that it may be able, first to get out of its hole, which it fills completely, then to fly, the baby bird has to submit to a course of reducing diet.

PART III

KILDONAN AND ITS MEMORIES

AFTER walking by the coast from Laig over $7\frac{1}{2}$ of the roughest miles it would be possible to encounter anywhere, you come out on the plain, marked on the ordnance map, *Crois Mhor,* on which is the ruined church of S. Donnan. There is no trace of either great or little cross to be found here now, but the naming possibly has reference to one of a chain of crosses which were said to have traversed the island, to link it from sea to sea with the shrine of its patron saint. S. Donnan, or Donan, was the head of an independent mission of Irish monks who occupied Eigg in the latter years of S. Columba's lifetime. Very little is known of him, and even as to the manner of his martyrdom there are conflicting accounts. When S. Donnan asked S. Columba to be his " soul's friend," or confessor, the

Abbat of Iona predicted he would come to " red martyrdom " (*i.e.*, death, in contrast to " white martyrdom " or suffering short of death as a confessor); and in the annals of Tighernac, burning is indicated as the manner in which he and his fifty-two companions met their death. But other sources ascribe the martyrdom to pirates, urged thereto by the Queen of the island, possibly because her own people refused to undertake the murder. The *Acta Sanctorum* relates that when the pirates came to Kildonan, they found the monks singing their office in the Oratory, where they were powerless to hurt them; but the Abbot said to his companions, " Let us go to the Refectory, where we are wont to live after the flesh, and there we can be slain, for we cannot die so long as we remain where we were in the habit of pleasing God. But where we have been accustomed to nourish the flesh, there we can be loosed from the flesh." And so, on Easter night, in the Refectory they were slain.

It is said that Easter here is a mistake, because the Queen of Festivals that year fell on April 3rd, whilst the date of the martyrdom was Sunday, April 17, 617. But quite possibly the calculator forgot that the Celts reckoned their Easter differently from the rest of Christendom, and hence, ascertaining the date of the Roman Easter in this year, wrongly assumed it was that observed in Scotland.

Told me by an old man since dead, a beautiful legend has it that, on the first night of the death-sleep of S. Donnan and his family, a blessed light was seen to be hallowing their grave, and voices of holy ones were heard chanting a death croon:

" Early gives the sun greeting to Donnan,
Early sings the bird the greatness of Donnan,
Early grows the grass on the grave of Donnan—
The warm Eye of Christ on the grave,
The stars of the heavens on the grave—
No harm, no harm, to Donnan's dust."

The death croon originated in the Celtic Church, and was originally sung by the soul-friend, or confessor of the dying person, assisted by three chanters.   Ultimately the rite was performed by the *bean tuiridh,* the mourning woman, as a part of her duty prior to laying out the dead. Here is a beautiful croon which Mr. Kenneth Macleod has preserved:

THE SOUL-FRIEND:

Home thou art going to-night to the Winter Ever-house,
The Autumn, Summer, and Springtide Ever-house;
Home art going to-night on music of cantors;
White Angels thee await on the shores of the river.
>   *God the Father with thee in sleep,*
>   *Jesus Christ with thee in sleep,*
>   *God the Spirit with thee in sleep.*

THE CANTORS:

Softly sleep, softly sleep.

THE SOUL-FRIEND

Sleep, oh love, on Mother's bosom,
Sleep while she sings soft lullings to thee,
The sleep of the Son on Mary's bosom,
Sleep and put off from thee every woe.

ALL :

Sleep and put off from thee every woe.
Sleep and put off from thee every woe.

THE SOUL-FRIEND:

>   *Youth-sleep of Jesus,*
>   *Life-sleep of Jesus,*
>   *Glory-sleep of Jesus,*
>   *Love-sleep of Jesus,*
>   *Joy-sleep of Jesus,*
>   *Peace-sleep of Jesus.*

ALL:

Sleep and put off from thee thy every woe,
Sleep and put off from thee thy every woe.

*   *   *   *

THE SOUL-FRIEND:

Dream of Mary, and God in her side,
Dream of Columba in sainted isle,
Dream of the One That was ever a Child.

ALL:

All these dreamings, dear love, be thine;
All these dreamings, dear love, be thine;
All these dreamings, dear love, be thine.

THE SOUL-FRIEND:

The dusk of the death sleep is, love, in thine eye.

ALL:

But softly thou'lt sleep,
But softly thou'lt sleep.

THE SOUL-FRIEND:

In name of the Three-in-One, peace to thy pain,
The Christ is come, thou'rt at peace from all pain,
O, the Christ is come, thou'rt at peace from all pain.

ALL:

Softly to sleep, softly to sleep,
Softly to sleep, softly to sleep.

The musical setting of this beautiful croon is to be found, with many another of equal interest, in the *Songs of the Hebrides*, by Mrs. Kennedy-Fraser and Mr. Macleod.

The island cannot long have been left without religious, for the Annals of Ulster record the death in 724 of

Oan, Superior of Eigg. Regarding the relics of S. Donnan and his fifty-two companions, there is great uncertainty, not unnaturally in view of the lapse of so many centuries. In the *Old Statistical Account of Scotland* (published 1796), it is stated that the stone under which the saint's remains were buried having been exposed by the plough, was taken up some years previous (*i.e.*, before 1796), examined, and then buried at a distance of a few yards from where it had formerly lain. Why it was not returned to its original place is not stated. Now, about sixty yards north of the little ruined church is a long, slender, oval-shaped, water-worn boulder, under which is a stone basin covered with a thin, flat stone. This basin contains bones mingled with earth—the alleged remains of the martyrdom; but if S. Donnan were indeed burnt or his relics were translated to Auchterless in Aberdeenshire, as tradition avows, to save them from desecration by Norse invaders, it is difficult to accept this statement. The islanders are very much opposed to any interference with this alleged burial place of S. Donnan, not apparently so much for veneration of his relics, but because they say if the stone covering the mouth of the basin is turned, bad weather results. Thus S. Donnan of Eigg and S. Swithun of Winchester are evidently kindred spirits! S. Donnan was one of the most popular saints in Scotland, judging from the many places named after him, including Eilean Donnan in Kintail.

Tradition has a good deal to say about the successive churches of the island reared on this spot. Two were said to have been burnt down by Norse raiders—and on the occasion of the massacre of the Macdonalds in *Uaimh Fhraing*, the Macleods destroyed the succeeding building, apparently built by *Iain Mùdeartach*, chief of Clan-ranald, to whom is also credited the church at Arisaig. " Kildonan," unspecified as to locality, is a church included in the list of seven built grudgingly, as before related, by Allan nan Creach. The present church is said to have been similarly built in fulfilment of a vow, in return for help received from heaven by Allan, the son and successor of *Iain Mùdeartach*. But such was the character of this chief that he considered himself under no sort of obligation to exceed the bare terms of his vow, for he stopped short at the church walls, and thus the building has remained to this day, so it is said, no one having been sufficiently devout to add a roof. If this story be true, the date of the church must be before 1593, when the chief in question died, and, as one might suppose from the character of its builder, it is a poor, mean, little structure of the plainest and most badly-lit variety. Within, let into the wall on the north side of the altar, is the strange and puzzling duplicate, even to the same date, of the tomb at Arisaig which has been already described. It is said to contain the remains of the prince of pipers, *Raonull Mac Ailein Oig,* the author of the most celebrated pipe music in existence, who died on Eigg in 1641. Beyond this tomb and one sculptured stone of quite ordinary design, nothing is to be seen, a pillar tombstone two feet high, having with a circle an incised cross, having now, alas, no existence except in some printed records.

It was at Kildonan, probably in the vicinity of the church, that Donald of Harlaw, according to legend, was inaugurated Lord of the Isles. The *Red Book of Clanranald* says: " Ranald, the son of John, was the high steward of Innsegall (the isles of the stranger). . . . He called a meeting of nobles of Innsegall and his brethren to one place, and gave the Staff of Lordship to his brother at Kildonan in Eigg, and he was nominated Mac Domnall and Donald of Isla, contrary to the opinion of the men of Innsegall." The straight white wand, the delivery of which seems to have been the only feature of the ceremony on this particular occasion, was an emblem of the purity and rectitude which should distinguish the rule of him so invested.

There is S. Donnan's well at Kildonan, but it is one of the many on the island which no one now seems able to identify, though, a quarter of a mile west of the church, there is the well of S. Donnan's altar, where he was said to have celebrated the Eucharist.   There is also somewhere here *Tobar nan Ceann* (well of the head), where was found dead *Am Piobar Mor,* already mentioned, who had gone to live at Kildonan; and, in view of his name, may be identical with the " great piper " buried in the church.   Beneath the little waterfall made by the small burn that crosses the hollow just below the ruined church is a pool which, though it is not one's exact conception of a well, yet, in view of others on the island like it, may conceivably be either that of S. Donnan or of " the head."   It was in *tumuli* all near the ruins that in Professor Macpherson's time were discovered the very considerable Viking antiquities that he presented to the National Museum in Edinburgh.   Other cairns were subsequently opened up, disclosing cists.   In the hill above Kildonan are several chasms in which cattle have been lost, and into one of these, it is said, a horse fell, but, managing to make his way out, came to light in Skye!

PART IV

THROUGH THE PEATY HOLLOW TO CLEADALE

HAVING exhausted Kildonan, if one can ever be said to exhaust any part of Eigg, you take the road that, running up diagonally inland, joins the main road just below the school-house.   Coming up from Cuagach or Cleadale— what may now be called the residential quarter of the island—you may see the islanders leading ponies equipped for gathering peats, instead of, as in less favoured quarters of the Highlands, the people themselves shouldering the burden.   Eigg is famous for its ponies and horses, and I remember, when first I stayed at Laig, seeing any number of beautiful little Shetlanders, now no longer bred on the island, browsing on its shores. Many of the islanders have their own horse or pony, and these with ropes, often of straw, for bridles, are saddled with panniers on each side when a supply of fuel is wanted from the peat-cuttings. The spectacle of these comfortably-circumstanced crofters with their well-conditioned animals is both pleasing and highly picturesque. The first I ever met was a stout and compactly-built woman, with a white kerchief tied round her head, the embodiment of good nature, health, and contentment, riding leisurely along, seated between the panniers on the back of a sturdy cob.

Just through the gate where you leave the road for the short cut down the cliffs to Laig House, and enter the peat cutting of *Blar Dubh* (black moor), the prospect outspread before you is entrancing. You look beyond the fore-ground, where bracken mingles with tall foxgloves, over the wide sweep of moorland—in late summer a mass of purple heath—which rises in successive terraces till it is crowned by the Sgurr—from this point a low, elongated crest. In the middle distance a herd of fine Highland cattle often browse, very handsome in their long horns and richly-coloured, shaggy coats, and quite irresistible when they include little woolly calves in their company. Once seeing such a herd in the distance, they appealed so much to my camera that I resolved to stalk them, since, for all the fierceness of their appearance, they are so shy that to make a near approach is very difficult. I spent the whole of a very hot morning in making futile attempts, for, in spite of all my strategy and painful crawling over the unkindly ground, no sooner did the head of my standcamera cautiously appear above the giant brackens in which I was completely hidden, than off the cattle would scamper.

To get over to Laig House from the gate, you must cross by plank a burn, which is most beautifully flower-bedecked. It has cut for itself a deep path through the peat, which colours its waters a rich dark brown. In them grows a

TAKING THE PEATS HOME ON THE ISLE OF EIGG

curious plant, which is perhaps the yellow marsh-dock, and a tall handsome thistle with a smooth stem and a large head whose species I have been quite unable to identify. Amongst the wealth of flowers and ferns which thickly fringe its banks are valerian, meadowsweet, and golden clumps of the marsh marigold, called in Gaelic the " shoe of the water horse " from the shape of its leaves. The beautiful hollow that this burn crosses is guarded by the peaks of Rum, which rear their heads in the distance over a ridge of moorland. Wrens, which are specially numerous here, flit about the hollow, which they seem to share with the redbreast. In the Highlands the wren is accounted the king of birds, for did he not soar higher than the eagle on the day when there was a contest amongst the birds for the supremacy of the air? The wren challenged the eagle's right to claim the kingship, and, all unknown to the eagle, settled upon his back when he began his flight. When the eagle had soared as high as he could go, he called out, " Where are you now, brown wren?" whereupon the wren at once flew off and upward, and called out, " Far, far above you!" Hence the wren has twelve eggs and the eagle only two, though I am afraid this part of the legend is scarcely in accord with the facts of natural history.

Crossing the peaty burn by a plank, and climbing up through the bracken, it is not long before you meet with a fence to scale, prior to descending a very slippery, broken slope down the side of the great basaltic cliffs. In a small, dark hollow on your left lies a lochan, shaped like a foot, its waters scarcely visible under the mass of water weeds which grow in and around it. The islanders tell you that this loch marks the spot where a giant from Moidart set his foot on Eigg. And there, across the fields, lies little Laig House, snugly tucked away in a sheltered hollow, a burn crossed by some rude planks running behind the hillocks on which the building is set, and the pillared cliffs rising high above.

In the fertile plain which lies in the hollow formed by the great rocky rampart cleaving the north of the island from north to south in a sweeping curve, lies the crofting hamlet of Cleadale—from the Norse for " cliff dale." It would be impossible to imagine any natural structure more like the outline of a huge castle than the remarkable range of cliffs that guards this hollow. The face of the walls is weathered into rugged buttresses, above which rise turrets and towers, bastion and bartisan, its head fretted here and there with slender pinnacles. At the northern extremity of the curve of this great fortification, and close against it, snuggles Tolain (the hollow under the hill), where is the " great well " to which the old woman who escaped the massacre looked for sustenance.

In Cleadale there are three more wells, the most famous associated with S. Columba himself and called after him —a pool in the stream that flows through the plain, and is situated at the base of a group of rocks. Only tradition, however, records that S. Columba was ever on Eigg. Other wells I could not locate. One is called *Cnoc Oillteig,* after the fearful hag who haunted it, and another *Tobar Lon nan Gruagach,* said to be near *Tobar Chaluim Chille,* in which event it may be an adjacent pool. Martin, one of the earliest to give a record of his pilgrimage amongst the Isles, mentions a " Five Pennies Well." It was a Norse custom to measure land by its rental, and hence in older accounts of the Highlands, it is common to read of " four penny lands," etc.: hence probably the name of " Five Pennies Well." From Martin's reference to it, it is possibly in Cleadale, and may be but another name for one of those already mentioned. He states that it had the property of curing any person of his first disease, merely by drinking copiously of its waters for two or three days. He further asserts that there had often been put to the proof another property of this well which made it unique. If any stranger lay down by it in the night time, he would be afflicted with a deformity in some part of his body, but the natives were always immune from incurring any such affliction. Martin also mentions a heap of stones, called after S. Martin, " round which the natives obliged themselves to go *deisul*," but he gives no reason for this curious observance. Folk lore is further represented amongst the islanders by the *Eun Ban nan Corp*— the " white bird of corpses," which is the size of a seagull, and has been identified with a white or grey owl. It is only seen in the evening flying near the ground, though it occasionally rests on houses, and its coming always betokens a death. There is also *Cnoc na Piobaireachd,* the Knock of the Piper, where all the lads of the island used to gather on beautiful moonlight nights. By putting their ears to the knoll they would hear the most wonderful reels, and laments that " would draw tears from the eyes of a corpse." In the words of the native again, " in one night a lad of music would hear as many reels and laments as would marry and bury all the people of Eigg and in the whole country of Clanranald indeed." Such is the marvel of the *ceol brugha,* or fairy music.

I remember a very old man, since dead, whom I met when I first came to Eigg, telling me that, if a woman bewailed anyone that was drowned, her tears fell in blood drops on the heart of her loved one in *Tir fo Thuinn.* This, " the land under the waves," is where the drowned await the coming of the white ship of the golden rudder, the silver masts, and the silken sails, to bear them back to *Tir nam Beò,* the land of the living. The old man, who had spoken to me of the women sorrowing for their drowned, concluded by saying: " Wass it not ta sad thing, now, that a woman should pe drowning her man ta second time by ta tears she wass shedding?"

Very few of the old thatched cottages survive on Eigg, though there are still a good few cattle sheds of this type dotted about the island. The cottages are mostly substantial but ugly, whitewashed buildings, with abominations in the shape of corrugated iron roofs painted a dull red, cheap—in the days when they were imposed—and hideous. In Cleadale is the little modern church of S. Donnan, which serves the Roman Catholic portion of the population, and was served when I knew the island by a gentle and kindly priest who has since taken the tonsure at Fort Augustus. So charitable a man was he indeed, that when I had on one occasion been the object of a gratuitous attack by the then Established minister, and the incident had become known, the good Father immediately called expressly to say all he could in extenuation of the minister's aggressive conduct. In that minister's immediate successor, however, the priest must have been glad to find a kindred spirit in one as kindly as himself, and of natural geniality.

To vary the old tales by a modern incident, I may here relate what the factor told me of one of the crofters. This was a girl, with very little English, who wrote to a Glasgow ironmonger a letter, so involved and badly spelt, that he could not make out the order he presumed it to contain. After much puzzling, the order was discovered to be for a pair of *boots,* " size four, sharp and tight," evidently with the idea of being " smart " and in the fashion rather than for service anywhere on Eigg.

PART V

ON THE HEIGHTS OF EIGG, AND DOWN BY GRULINE AND GARMISDALE

RETURNING from Cleadale by the shores of Laig, to climb up on to the moors on the heights of the island, my friend again sings:

> " Whither away, whither away,
> Over the sands so white?
> We're bound for the reefs around the bay
> Where the wavelets are dancing all the day,
> But sleep in the pale moonlight.

" Whither away, whither away,
    Over the wandering streams?
We're bound for the home of the moorland flowers,
And the birth-place of beautiful wingéd hours,
    For this is the Island of Dreams."

There is the same sense of physical enjoyment to be gained on the moorland heights of Eigg as amongst the Coolin, and it is just as lonely; yet there is nowhere where the Highlander can be sensible of so much companionship. The most interesting course to take to the lochs is to follow the Charadale burn, for it reveals to you on its banks the most unexpected delights, notably in masses of yellow and brown honey-suckle with its intoxicating perfume, and welcome refreshment in luxuriant strawberry beds. The burn itself has a succession of waterfalls, which tumble down over the rocks between beautifully mossy banks decked with many kinds of fern, amongst which may be found the delicate beech and oak varieties. It was in the process of sliding inadvertently down one of the banks that I discovered a bed of staghorn moss, which I have never found when I have been looking for it.

At the head of the burn, you strike to the right for Loch nam Beinn Tighe, and you have to walk through waist-high ling and bracken, in which it is very easy to get your feet entangled—with obvious consequences. If on this or any other expedition you see, as so often happens, a heron in flight, it becomes an anxious matter to observe what direction he is taking, for, according to Eigg weather lore,

" When the heron seeks the sea,
Good weather it will be;
When the heron seeks the hill,
Good weather it will spill."

Loch nam Beinn Tighe, as seen from the south-east approach, shews some remarkable features. The barren hills, with rounded heads and rugged slopes, shut in the loch on each side: at its extremity it appears to narrow almost to a point, and beyond seemingly the merest ridge of land lies a small expanse of sea, backed by three peaks of the island of Rum.   There is no suggestion of any land, much less half a mile of it, intervening between the loch and the sea, nor yet of the sea being on a lower level than the loch, whereas it is actually some three hundred feet below.

-To the Celt, the deep, dark lochs hidden in the heart of the hills speak of death and dark deeds.   Of one of the hill lochs of Eigg the following tale is told, and well illustrates the weird fancy of the Celtic incantations and spells.   A priest was up on the heights, making his way to the shore, when he was caught in a fearful storm. Seeking the nearest shelter, he stood up under a rock, and, in a flash of lightning, saw that before him were the dark waters of a loch set between two precipices.   On the edge of the loch lay a man in his death throes, and above him stood three wizards crooning over him.   First a lean, black wizard chanted:

> " Torture, torture, man that be!
> Over there, over there,
> Thou shalt be bound, thou shalt be bound,
> Wasps to-day, midges to-morrow.
> Eating thee, itching thee, tumouring thee,
> Over there, over there.
> Man that be."

A bald, grey wizard took up the croon:

> " Torture, torture, man that be!
> Over there, over there,
> Thou shalt be bound, thou shalt be bound,
> A raven above thee, a thistle in thine eye,
> A venom-serpent coming nigh, coming nigh,
> Over there, over there,
> Man that be."

The last, a sleek, yellow wizard finished the spell:

> " Torture, torture, man that be!
> Over there, over there,
> Thou shalt be bound, thou shalt be bound,
> Wind afreezing through the willows,
> Stinging cold like scalding water,
> Over there, over there,
> Man that *was*."

A MINIATURE PASS ON THE HEIGHTS OF EIGG

20

In order to protect himself against these unholy rites, the priest made round himself the sacred circle, signing it with the cross, and blessing it in the name of the Three-One, and at cock-crow the wizards vanished.

Proceeding along the hollow of the heights, you climb up from one lochan to another, lovely little sheets of water, hidden amongst the hills; and beside them strange cliffs of curved pillars, regular in form and lichen-covered. It is amongst them that you obtain some of the wildest views on the island. Within a short distance of Loch Nighean Dughaill there is on the left, between two of these rounded masses of cliffs, a miniature pass which is truly magnificent. In the foreground lie broken fragments of pillars, amongst which grow hummocks of heather, and beyond the weathered sides of the cliffs, across the middle distance, are the ever-irresistible peaks of Rum.

From Loch Nighean Dughaill rises a stream, imprisoned beneath the scree of the cliff, and in its hollow voice there is a weird music very much in keeping with the legend of the dark sheet of water through which it passes. The maiden from whom the loch takes its name was one day herding on the hill when she was joined by a handsome youth. They sat conversing together, and, after a while, he laid his head on her lap and fell asleep. But, to her horror, as she toyed with his hair, she saw that growing among it were leaves of fresh water plants, by which sign she knew that her companion was the dreaded water-horse. He had a piece of her dress in his grasp, but the trembling maiden managed both to cut this out and to remove his head from her lap without disturbing him, so that she was able to flee. As she ran, however, she heard his angry voice declaring he would have her yet. She reached home in safety, but, later on, as she was spending Sunday afternoon with the people of Gruline on the top of a hillock, the water-horse appeared and seized *an Nighean Dughaill*. Men of the company ran to her rescue, but when they reached the loch a bit of her dress and pieces of lung made it only too evident that the water-horse had devoured his victim.

On the hillock beside this fearsome loch, white heather grows; also, what is as rare—and I think much prettier— white bell heath. Even when the heather is not in bloom, you can readily distinguish the white from the ordinary plant by reason of its finer foliage and much more vivid green. Loch nam Ban Mora, not very far distant, has in its centre the remains of a *crannog* which one quaint local tradition says was inhabited by women of such unique proportions that the stepping-stones by which they gained the island were set so wide apart that they were of no use to anyone else. From the end of the loch you get an imposing view of the whole length of the Sgurr—an irregular wall about one and a half miles long—across as rough a stretch of moorland as any you may encounter, and thickly strewn with boulders. This remarkable rampart is entirely columnar from end to end, one fiery layer after another having risen in tiers to a height of four hundred and seventy feet above the remains of a pine forest, for fossils of the *Pinites Eiggensis* have been found beneath the pitch stone. The chasm that separates this highest portion of the Sgurr from the remainder has fragments of a dry-stone dyke, shewing that in pre-historic times it was the site of a hill-fort.

It was in the locality of the Sgurr, probably in some of its many crevices, that the second old woman who escaped from the massacre was said to have hidden herself. And in the same neighbourhood, some two or three hundred years ago, a Norwegian had a still where he and his son made, according to a secret recipe, a liquor resembling Benedictine from the heather flowers. The islanders were determined to find out the secret of the liquor, so they went to the elder Norwegian, demanding to be told it. The man replied, " If you will kill my son, I will tell you "; and when they returned to him, saying his son was killed, he said, " Now you can kill me, for I will never tell

you: I feared my son might do so under threats."
R. L. Stevenson has a poem on an incident similar to this,
the scene of which he places in Wigtonshire, but the story
was told me when I first landed on the island in the
company of the then parish priest, Father Macmillan. He
told me the location of the still was yet pointed out by
the islanders; but a man who places the preservation of
a trade secret above his own life, not to mention that of
his son, is not at all a convincing character.

On the south side of the Sgurr lies the extremely
interesting district of Gruline, a name thought to be
derived from the Norse *gyot,* stones, and therefore
meaning " stony land." If for " stony " you read
" rocky," you gain a good description of this part of the
island, for the enormous crags and boulders of unique
formation, which are the features of the south side of the
Sgurr, are most striking, and it is fascinating to wander
amongst them. Judging from the numbers of ruins
scattered about on the slope between the great boulders,
Gruline must have been at one time the site of a considerable hamlet, and one might conjecture that it may have
been the particular quarter whose buildings suffered
destruction by the Macleods at the time of the massacre.

If you look at the map, you will see very prominently
marked on Gruline the site of *Crois Moraig,* from which
one would naturally conclude this was, or had been, a
monument of note. But the oldest inhabitant, whom I
questioned, had never heard of the existence of such a
cross, and there is no mention of any such monument in
any account of or reference to Eigg that I have discovered.
Conceivably it may have been one of the crosses which
were said to have formed a chain from S. Donnan's church
across the island, as previously mentioned. I could only
discover at the approximate site, as arrived at by the map,
a heap of stones, which, if indeed they indicate any
archæological remains, rather suggest the second heap of
stones spoken of by Martin as dedicated to the Blessed

Virgin Mary. Morag, though generally translated " Sarah " is literally " little Mary," or Marion, though indeed *Moire* is the word used exclusively for the Holy Mother of God.

There are two more wells in this quarter of the island, and regarding their identity there is considerable dispute; but the only approach to a well I could find anywhere in Gruline was a tiny picturesque swamp thickly covered with forget-me-nots: and Gruline, the natives say, is the place of *Tobar nan Ban,* or the well of holy women.

Leaving Gruline on your way to the famous cave of the massacre, you have a very fine and unique view of the Sgurr just a few hundred yards beyond the point where the rough road, going eastward, begins. If you turn round at the point on your left, where, by the roadside, is a rude cairn of rough stones—said to mark the grave of two giants, one of whom lived on Castle Island—you will discover that the great cliff has assumed almost a pyramidical aspect. Continuing down the road, you pass on the right Garmisdale House,[4] and in a bank, near the end of and opposite the wall which encloses it, there is a small well which the natives say is that of S. Katharine. This well, alleged to be beneficial to all diseases, was consecrated by a Father Hugh, who made the islanders carry stones as a penance and lay them in a great heap at the head of the well. Then the priest, after saying Mass and consecrating the well, gave each of the people a candle to light, with which they walked *deiseil* round the well. Martin says this was always done on April 15th— why on that date does not appear, since it is not any of the many S. Katharine's days, the nearest one, that of S. Catherine of Sienna, being on April 30th. Martin also says that from the time of the consecration it was counted unlawful for any meat to be boiled in water taken from

---

[4] Called in old titles Callumscoull, which is thought to be a corruption of Columba's school or hole.

THE SGURR, FROM GRULINE, ISLE OF EIGG

the well. Up to the middle of the last century, this well was held to be good for the falling sickness, but none that were whole would drink from it, fearing that thereby the diseases of those who were healed would be communicated to them. This Garmisdale spring, however, now shews no trace of any heap of stones, and, though they might have been removed subsequently in course of road making, it is difficult to see, in view of the situation of the well, how it could have been ever perambulated. Indeed, details of the consecration ceremony rather indicate the well at Gruline; near the heap of stones I. have identified with the site of *Crois Moraig,* since these may have been those piled together for penance.

PART VI

THE MASSACRE OF EIGG

IT is by entering a gate nearly opposite that which leads through the plantation surrounding the Lodge that you climb up through a field and strike off westward for Uaimh Fhraing, rendered phonetically the "Cave of Francis." The name of this celebrated cave, which is locally called the Human, Man, or Bone Cave, perhaps means the "Ribbed Cave" from *roing,* a boat rib. After you have walked over the top of the cliffs for about half a mile, you descend by a steep, narrow, and broken slope, and, turning sharply to the left, find yourself on a beautiful stretch of shore in front of Uaimh Fhraing. Above the beach is a grassy bank, in which the growth of yellow iris and the handsome marsh plume thistle is specially noticeable, and in the face of the cliff is an angular opening about 3 feet high. You enter a narrow passage about 12 feet long which takes you over rough, damp stones, then opens out into a roomy cave, of which the average dimensions are

213 feet by 22 feet by 17 feet.   As you grope your way onward and upward, you feel the darkness as though it were a palpable thing pressing in upon you from every quarter—a darkness which a candle fails to dissipate.   By an extensive use of magnesium ribbon, however, I was able to look about this gruesome cave, black and damp, and having a smell suggesting both properties.   On the floor of the cavern the remains of the massacred Macdonalds were allowed to moulder undisturbed; then they became the prey of relic-hunters, until the last fragments were gathered together and buried under a heap of stones by a late proprietor.

The versions of the account of the massacre are endless, and, as one always anticipates where incidents of Highland history are concerned, contradictory in many particulars. Mairi of the Post Office is accountable for the following version.   Some of the Macleods came to Eigg for Isabella Macdonald, the chief's daughter, whom one of them wished to marry.   The islanders, however, refused to give her up, and, seizing the Macleods, bound them hand and foot and sent them adrift in their boats.   Being discovered thus at sea by some of their fellow clansmen, these made for Eigg, determined to punish the islanders.   The Macdonalds, however, seeing the approach of the avengers, betook themselves to Uamh Fhraing, and for two days evaded discovery, when the Macleods, thinking their enemies had fled to the mainland, abandoned the search, and took to their galleys.   But the Macdonalds' impatience to ascertain if the coast were clear proved their undoing.   Snow lay on the ground; and they rashly sent out a scout to the top of the cliffs just above Castle Island.   From this height the envoy discovered that the Macleods were just setting sail outside the islet; and they, seeing him too, returned and followed his tracks in the snow.   Mairi was particular to tell me that the scout had designedly walked backwards to mislead the Macleods in the event of their following him—a delightfully Gotham-like proceeding!

When the enemy gained the mouth of the cave, they first of all diverted the stream which ran down from above over its mouth, and they held parley with the Macdonalds within. They demanded the surrender of Isabella, threatening if she were refused them to kill all the Macdonalds. Apparently Isabella herself conducted the parleying on the Macdonald side, for it was she who, as the condition of her surrender, bargained that with her should go out a friend for every finger and toe. The Macleods, fearing that thus the tables would be turned upon them, refused, whereupon the Macdonalds challenged their foes to do their worst. And they did, for the refugees in the cave were smoked to death by a fire kindled at its mouth from the ruins of the houses which the Macleods destroyed. Here ended Mairi's narrative.

This massacre took place in 1577, and there perished 395 Macdonalds, representing all the inhabitants of the island save three old women, who hid elsewhere, and a boat's crew absent in Glasgow. The more usual account of the origin of the massacre is that Alasdair Crotach [5] and some of his clansmen, returning from Glasgow, put in at Eigg, where they grossly maltreated some women tending cattle on Castle Island. The islanders, in revenge, fell upon the Macleods as they bivouacked on the shores of Laig, and, breaking their backs, sent them adrift in their boats. This is quite a likely origin for Alasdair's title of " humpback "; though, after such brutal treatment, it is highly improbable he would be able himself to return to be avenged on the islanders. It is more likely, therefore, that Iain Dubh, as others conjecture, was the leader of the Macleods on this occasion, especially in view of Iain's practised hand, as evidenced by his murderous record. The other versions, into which no Isabella enters, state that the Macleods offered

[5] At this date, however, Alasdair Crotach had been dead about thirty years. He is said to have gained his name of " hump-back " from an injury received in infancy, when a careless nurse let him fall.

to spare the Macdonalds if the murderers of their clansmen were surrendered to them; and that, believing themselves secure against attack, the Macdonalds refused. It is also asserted in a Macleod account that the Macleod chief kindled the fire of heather and brush-wood when the wind was blowing away from the mouth of the cave, being determined to accept whether the wind veered or remained constant as the judgment of heaven, to decree either the destruction or the salvation of the Macdonalds. It is said that the chief of the islanders in 1577 was Angus John Mac Mudzartsone—a title which smacks loudly of Sasunnach rendition.

It is a curious fact that though tradition is continuous and persistent, there is no contemporary record of this massacre, but there is of another eleven years later. In 1588 Maclean of Duart, obtaining 100 mercenaries from the *Florida,* a ship of the Spanish Armada, ravaged the island as well as Rum, Muck, and Canna. It has been objected, with a view to discounting the traditional massacre, that in so short a time two massacres would have been impossible. But the bones found in the cave substantiate tradition, and the repopulation of Eigg, which obviously must have taken place, surely could have occurred in the interval.

The only other relic of the massacre is a huge basaltic column from the Sgurr, which lies on the moor a few yards off the road, to the west of the small clump of firs about the centre of the island. It is said to have been dropped there by a man who was conveying it to the churchyard when the Macleods landed.

PART VII

CONCLUSION

COMING out of the fatal Uaimh Fhraing, a beautiful picture of the distant mainland is framed in the mouth of the cave, where graceful plants grow in the foreground, with the broken and rugged shore beyond, and the sea in the middle distance. Turning to the right, it is but a short way over a very difficult stretch of irregular boulders to *Uamh a' Chràbhaidh,* or the "Cave of Devotion." Entering beneath a very fine and lofty arch, you find yourself in a cavern which is the very antithesis of Uaimh Fhraing—fresh, clean, and sweet. Here the Roman Catholics secretly assembled to offer on a ledge of rock the Holy Sacrifice, and you wonder if here, too, was ever sung the exquisitely tender song of the Holy Mother of God, the " Christ Child's Lullaby ":

> " *My love, my dear, my darling Thou,*
> *My treasure new, my gladness Thou,*
> *My comely, beauteous Babe-Son Thou,*
> *Unworthy I to tend to Thee.*
>
> *I the nurse of the King of greatness!*
> *I the Mother of the God of glory!*
> *Am I not the glad-to-be-envied one?*
> *Oh, my heart is full of rapture!*
>
> *   *   *   *   *   *
>
> *Art King of kings, art Saint of saints,*
> *God the Son of eternal age,*
> *Art my God and my gentle Babe,*
> *Art the King—Chief of humankind.*
>
> *The fair white sun of hope Thou art,*
> *Putting the darkness into exile,*
> *Bringing mankind from a state of woe*
> *To knowledge, light, and holiness.*

Hosanna to the Son of David,
My King, my Lord, and my Saviour!
Great my joy to be song-lulling Thee—
Blessed among the women I."

In Eigg this carol is said to have originated from a step-mother's harsh treatment of her stepson, a strange boy, who ultimately was driven from home by her chidings. That night, however, thinking of her stepson on the hills, the woman could get no rest, so she got up and went out of doors.   There she saw, sitting on a knoll, the most gracious of ladies, lulling to sleep with the sweetest music in all the world her infant son upon her lap, and at her feet, entranced, sat the poor outcast orphan.   The sight of this so rebuked the stepmother that she fell upon her knees, and wept the warm tears of a true mother, and, when again she looked up, she was left alone with her stepson to cherish.

As you wander over the island, you become conscious of permeation by the pilgrim spirit, which a sense of some danger in one's progress quickens, and to the need which this consciousness awakens, the " Pilgrim's Run of Eigg " gives beautiful expression:

" King of the elements—Love—Father of Bliss—
In the pilgrimage from airt to airt,
From airt to airt,
May each evil be a good to me,
May each sorrow be a gladness to me,
And may Thy Son be my Foster-Brother,
Oh may Thy Son be my Foster-Brother,
Holy Spirit—Spirit of Light—
A pilgrim I through the night,
Through the night;
Lave my heart pure as the stars,
Lave my heart pure as the stars,
Nor fear I then the spells of evil,
The spells of evil.

SUNSET OVER THE ISLE OF RUM, FROM LAIG BAY, ISLE OF EIGG

Jesu, Son of the Virgin pure,
Be Thou my Pilgrim Staff throughout the lands,
    Throughout the lands;
Thy love is all my thoughts, Thy likeness in my face,
May I heart-warm to others, and they heart-warm to me
    For love of the love of Thee,
    For love of the love of Thee.
O Father, Son, and Holy Spirit,
Be the Three-One with me by day, by night,
    By day, by night,
On the crest of the waves, on the side of the bens,
May our Mother be there, may her arm be under my
    head,
    O may our Mother be there,
    And her arm under my head! "

It is of course being very hypercritical to say that westward from Laig the coast is the least interesting of the island. The cliffs are very sheer, and the scree close to their base is, even at low tide, almost impassable at points, so that I could never get to the " Pigeon's Cave," which, I was told, was situate round the corner. But I always think gratefully of the grassy slopes of Laig, for to lie out there on a bed of heather under the canopy of the sky in fine warm weather is to experience a night of nights.

Naturally, sleep is not to be thought of when there is so much to be seen in the constantly changing face of the night, nor would one miss the cry of lone birds which rise from the shore or moorland from time to time. Of course, so far north it is never really dark: the darkest hour only veils itself in a misty grey, and soon casts off even that for a lighter shade. I never saw anything more fascinating than the unfolding beauties of the dawn following upon the pale night. Rum and Skye both looked like dream fortresses of grey stone, and the plaint of the sea-birds came across the waters like the cry from a world of spirits.

I think only for about half an hour was there perfect silence, when even the irritating voice of the corncrake was not heard, and for that one half-hour the world seemed wrapped about in awe.

One day before we left Eigg, the kindly tenant of Kildonan Farm offered to take us over to the island of Muck, and we gladly availed ourselves of the chance. Much more interesting than the manufacture of cheeses, or the rather uninteresting island itself, however, was the tale we were told of the adventure that had just befallen the children of the lobster-catcher of the island. It was the Lowland factor, a most unimaginative man, who told us the story, and he vouched for the truth of it.

Three little boys, aged from five to nine, went out to play on the shore as usual, but, as they failed to return when they were expected, an elder sister went out to find them. She came across all three of them sitting on a rock, and gazing with rapt faces out to sea. They did not take the least notice of her, but sat motionless till she came right up to the rock, when they started, and, when questioned, told her the following tale. They had come down to the sea, and, finding a pot of green paint upon the shore, they were trying to hammer it open, when a beautiful little boy, wearing a green vest, appeared, and invited them to go aboard his boat. They saw the little boat, and looked into its cabin, the walls of which were covered with beautiful pictures; but into it they would not go. Then a lovely little girl appeared, and offered them biscuits of the size of a fingernail, and these the children ate. After this they saw the little boat sail away out to sea, and were watching it when their sister appeared. Their father was very angry when he heard this tale; but, despite questionings and examination by various people, each child separately persisted in the same story, and differed in no single detail. They had *never* heard any fairy tales, and when their mother remarked to them that they must have seen the " little green people," *i.e.,* the fairies, the children were very frightened, and would not again go near the place where they had met with their experience.

In view of the manifold attractions, the romance, and the wonder of Eigg, is it surprising that once, when we were tearing ourselves away from its beloved shores, my friend exclaimed:

> " There's beauty here for every sense,
> And exercise for leg;
> We are not vegetarians,
> But we could live on Eigg!"

P.S.—A Jacobite Incident.

As the islanders had fought for the Prince at Culloden, Captain Duff, of the *Terror,* landed on Eigg in June, 1746, to obtain their weapons, of which, however, only sufficient were surrendered to secure, as the Jacobites thought, their safety. But Dr. John Macdonald of Kinlochmoidart was in hiding on the island, and Duff was joined by Captain Ferguson, of the *Furnace,* to search with him. During the search, the Hanoverians discovered that the islesmen still retained some arms, and when the doctor surrendered, he was forced by Ferguson to tell his fellows that if they did not give up all their weapons, their horses and cattle would be destroyed. This announcement secured the desired effect, but not the expected immunity for the Jacobites. Macdonald was seized, imprisoned, and shamefully treated, and, the names of the Jacobite islanders being found upon him, they were all taken prisoners by a trick, and the island given over to rapine, pillage, and destruction. Those prisoners who did not die of starvation on the voyage to London, were shipped as slaves to America.

CHAPTER V

THROUGH LOCHABER TO THE COUNTRY OF THE MACDONALDS

PART I

IN LOCHABER [1]

FORT WILLIAM (or *An Gearasdan* (the garrison), as the country people still call it), initially handicapped by the unhappy associations of its modern re-naming after an alien and callous prince, is one of those few places in the Highlands to which you only go so that you may get away from it and on to somewhere else with all possible speed. As usual, it is because man in his handiwork shews himself indifferent to God's endowment of natural beauty that the ugly little town, compacted of hideous buildings, incongruously defaces the landscape.

Landed on one occasion in this uncongenial town with several hours to wait in drenching rain, I bethought myself to beguile the time by visiting Inverlochy Castle. You reach the castle, just $1\frac{3}{4}$ miles out of Fort William, through a field on the left which was the site of the second, if not the first, battle of Inverlochy, and a portion of which is

---

[1] This is the *Stagnum Aporum*, Aporic Lake (hence, Lochaber, " the loch of marshes ") of Adamnan; probably at that time a name applied to part of Loch Eil itself, instead of, as now, to the district about it. Adamnan writes about " Nesan the crooked," and again of " a certain very poor peasant," both of whom " lived in the region bordering on Lake Aporum."

now, appropriately enough, an old burial ground. It was here in 1431 that Donald Balloch, a cousin of the Lord of the Isles, in order to give fitting expression to his feelings regarding the imprisonment of his chief, attacked the lieutenants of James I. of Scotland. They, the Earls of Mar and Caithness, were not only defeated with great slaughter, but Caithness was killed and Mar had to flee for his life. The most celebrated of all pipe marches, the " Pibroch of Donald Dhu," though it has been, and still is, claimed for the Camerons, is now admitted properly to belong to the Macdonalds, by whom it is called " Black Donald of the Isles March," since it was written to commemorate his victory at Inverlochy.

But this battle, decisive as it was for the Macdonalds, was as nothing in comparison to the great " Day of Inverlochy," of which *Iain Lom,* the celebrated Bard of Keppoch, exultantly sang after Montrose's splendid triumph on Sunday, February 2nd, 1645. " John the Bare," so called from his cheeks, was also known, from a physical defect, as "John the Stammerer," but this affliction proved no great obstacle to the fierce torrents of incisive eloquence which his poems exhibit, whence he was also known as " John the Biting." As a reward for his services to the Stewart cause, he was made Gaelic Poet Laureate to Charles II.—the first and last to hold that office.

It was *Iain Lom* who, overtaking Montrose at Kilcuimin ("Church of S. Cumine," as Fort Augustus was then called), told him that the Covenanting army was encamped at Inverlochy, and it was under the bard's guidance that one of the most amazing marches recorded in military history was undertaken in order to fall upon the rebels. As Montrose's army was made up of various divisions of the great clan Donald, Camerons, and Stewarts of Appin, so, too, the Covenanting host was practically composed exclusively of Campbells under Argyll (*Maccailin*), their chief. The incentive afforded by this knowledge was undoubtedly a main factor in the great achievement of the

men under the gallant Graeme. Avoiding the direct route,
Montrose's army advanced totally unexpectedly by devious
and hitherto untrodden ways from Kilcuimin down upon
Inverlochy. This feat, which would have been a sufficiently
remarkable accomplishment for half a dozen men keeping
together on a favourable summer day, more than a
thousand men, including even some cavalry, achieved in
the depth of winter—under the Great Marquis. Wearing
the same dress as his Highlanders, climbing the rough,
trackless mountains on foot, side by side with them; faring
no better than they on *drammoch* (oatmeal and water);
who would not forgo a night's rest and follow, even
through the darkness, where, with consummate genius,
Montrose led? In such fashion was the impossible made
possible, and the march begun on the morning of January
31st was executed with incredible speed. With little food
and no rest, having not only traversed the wildest solitudes
of the mountains, but plunged through the icy waters of
raging torrents, on the night of February 1st, the Royalist
Army came down to fall upon the hated foe at Inverlochy.

As soon as his scouts brought him news of Montrose's
advance, Argyll made haste to secure the possession most
precious to him in the world—his own personal safety. On
the plea of an injured shoulder (dislocated three weeks
previously), he took to his galley, nicknamed by the
Macdonalds *An Dubh Luidneach* (the black, clumsy
one),[3] and in the moonlight anchored well out on the waters
of Loch Eil. It is urged in defence of this conduct of the
" gley-eyed marquis " that he was persuaded not to risk
his valuable life, but on such a plea no commander would
ever enter a battle. Relegating his position to Campbell
of Auchenbreck, Argyll, at a safe distance, was content to
be a spectator of the fight; he, " the great chief of the
Campbells," thus becoming " a smaller figure at this crisis
than the meanest of his clansmen." He heard the trumpets

---

[3] Or according to others, *Dubh Luideach*, the ragged, or slovenly, black one.

of the Great Marquis salute the unfurling of the Royal Standard, heralding the dawn; he saw the Campbells, augmented by some Lowlanders, altogether some three thousand men strong, drawn up in battle array, opposed by only one-third of their own number. Out over the water, allied with the war-cry of the Macdonalds, carried the fierce invitation of the Camerons, " Sons of the hound, come hither and get flesh!" And awful was the response of Montrose's Highlanders when, loosed from the leash, they charged in long pent up fury against their ancient enemy, withholding their shot until they could fire " into the beards " of the foe.

The dispositions of a clan in battle are of interest. The chief was posted in the centre of the column beside the colours, and stood between two brothers, cousins german, or other relations. His wider bodyguard was drawn from each clan company, which supplied two of its best men, consanguinity always being taken into account. Relationship also ruled in the positions allocated to the clansmen— father, son, and brother standing shoulder to shoulder.

The Highlanders' method of fighting consisted in advancing in an impetuous rush, firing when almost upon the enemy, and then flinging away pistols or dags. Drawing their swords, and holding a dirk in the left hand along with the targe, where the two-handed claymore was not used, the clansmen swept down impetuously upon the enemy. When within reach of the opposing weapons, be it sword or, as later, the bayonet, the Highlanders bent the left knee to receive the thrust of the enemy's arms upon their targes. Then, rising and exerting their great strength, with their targes they hurled aside the arrested or captive blades, so that they could rush in upon a disarmed foe. One blow generally sufficed to fell an opponent to the ground, and then, breaking into the enemy lines, thrusting right and left with every stroke of the claymore, wielded by both hands, the execution was terrible.

At Inverlochy the onslaught of the Royalists was irresistible, and soon the Campbells, breaking before it, fled for their lives over the snow, and the fight became a rout. Pursuing the fleeing foe well inland, and following after them waist-high into the waters of Loch Eil, the Macdonalds fought on relentlessly until no less than half the men who followed Argyll were slain. Amongst them were Auchenbreck and fourteen lairds of the Campbell clan, while twenty-two were taken prisoners, and this overwhelming victory only cost Montrose, incredible as it may seem, four killed, including one man of note, and a hundred wounded.

Iain Lom, installed in one of the towers of Inverlochy Castle that from this point of vantage he might the better be able subsequently to chronicle the victory, wrote of the Campbells on the " Day of Inverlochy ":

> "Warm your welcome was at Lochy,
> With blows and buffets thickening round you,
> And Clan Donald's groovèd claymore,
> Flashing terror to confound you,
> On the wings of idle rumour,
> Far and wide the tale is flying,
> How the slippery knaves the Campbells,
> With their cloven skulls are lying."

and again,

> "Fallen race of Diarmid, disloyal, untrue,
> No harp in the Highlands will sorrow for you!"

It was probably in ironical imitation of the Scriptural phraseology and allusions beloved by the Covenanters that, after this victory, Montrose wrote to King Charles I. this letter:

> " Give me leave, after I have reduced this country and vanquished from Dan to Beersheba, to say to your Majesty as David's general said to him, ' Come thou thyself lest this country be called by my name.' "

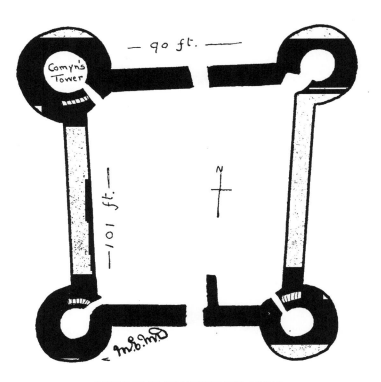

ROUGH PLAN OF INVERLOCHY CASTLE

Long before even the earlier battle, Inverlochy finds a name in history, for in early chronicles a city is mentioned as being situated there, and the tragic ends of remote chiefs and kings, whose names convey nothing to us, are associated with it. While it is difficult to think of any extensive city ever having existed at Inverlochy, the statement that both French and Spanish merchants came to the district for salmon and herring has more semblance of likelihood, in view of the fact that both fish are still plentiful there. Charlemagne is credited with having visited a Pictish king at the alleged earlier castle, and with having signed a treaty with him there.

There is quite as much romance but of another sort attaching to the present ruins. Viewed from the banks of the River Lochy, the remains of the castle make a fine old-world picture, especially when stray mists curl about the mountains in the background. Tradition has it that the Comyns, after whom the north-west tower takes its name, were the builders of the fortress, Sir John the Black, Lord of Badenoch, and the Lord of Lochaber being generally credited with its erection. But the architecture proclaims the castle to have been built later—possibly in the latter half of the fifteenth century by George, the second Earl of Huntly, and it is stated to have been still unfinished in the reign of Charles II. In whatever direction you approach the fortress, you can see that it is a quadrangular building with a tower at each angle, and having walls that are now reduced to 20-25 feet in height. These walls, which were probably originally 30 feet high, are 9 feet thick, without opening, and enclose a great courtyard, 101 feet from north to south, and 90 feet from east to west. The principal gateway is on the river or south side, and another exactly opposite is a somewhat unusual feature. Both gates were provided with a portcullis, as grooves, still remaining, prove. The riverside entrance shews traces of having had a gate house, within which was probably provided an aperture for pouring down boiling

oil or lead upon any enemy who penetrated as far. Every
tower has a stairway in the thickness of the walls, and,
with the exception of Comyn's Tower, which is larger than
the others, they are all the same size, and three have sally
ports, while all communicate with the centre of the building
as well as with the ramparts. The whole castle was surrounded by a moat which did not, however, wash the walls,
but was situated about 40 feet from the building, and was
probably supplied by the river. The position of the moat
can be located by the marshy depression in the ground
around the castle, and on the south front, where the ground
between the towers is raised above the general level and
has formed a platform with a retaining wall, the site of
the drawbridge is indicated by some remains of masonry.

Most mercifully, an English owner's scheme for the
" renovation " or " reconstruction " of the fine old building
was frustrated by his timely death, and one has not,
therefore, to deplore the irretrievable ruin of yet another
old-time relic. In the course of the " restoration " proceedings, which, though never continued, were yet begun,
the workmen made the not unusual discovery of a complete
male skeleton walled up in the northern extremity of the
parapet passage.

Returning to Fort William, there proved to be a good
deal of waiting to be done before the public motor was
ready to start, and it was a natural transition from
Inverlochy reminiscences to the reminiscence of the cruel
and cowardly revenge taken by the beaten clan during the
siege of Fort William by the Jacobites in March, 1746.
More than half the garrison were Campbells under a
Campbell as governor, and they were supported by English
warships on the loch. Under the protection of the naval
guns, the Campbells found an excellent opportunity safely
to avenge themselves upon their ancient enemies, the
Macdonalds and Camerons. Sallying forth, this Fort
William garrison ravaged women and children, burnt
every house they came across, and carried off all the cattle,

sheep, and provisions they could find. In a letter written by Keppoch and Lochiel to Stewart of Fasnacloich, there occurs the paragraph:

" In spite of all the clemency that a prince (Charles) could shew or promise, the Campbells have openly appeared, with their wonted zeal for rebellion and usurpation, in the most oppressive manner. Nor could we form a thought to ourselves, that any men endowed with reason or commonsense could use their fellow-creatures with such inhumanity and barbarity as they do; of which we have daily proofs, by their burning houses, stripping of women and children, and exposing them in the open field to the severity of the weather, houghing of cattle and killing of horses; to enumerate the whole would be too tedious at this time."

The hours of waiting spent at Inverlochy seemed to fly, but when it was time for the car to start, even quicker sped the glorious journey down the shores of Loch Linnhe to Ballachulish, for all the way along, and increasingly, the scenery is a feast of good things; and whether it be the sea, the distant mountains, or the road itself, every prospect delights your heart. At Onich you still may see a few last survivors of the old-world thatched cottages with the smoke curling lazily up through the centre of the roof itself, there being no chimney other than that suggested by a slight peak in the thatching.

Here, too, standing in a field by the shores of Loch Linnhe, is the noteworthy perforated standing stone called Clach a' Charra, 6 feet 8 inches high and 3 feet 10 inches at its widest part. This, an irregularly-shaped monolith, as the drawing shows, has every appearance of having been obtained from the bed of some river which, aided by the action of stones, has worn part of the surface into a hollow and at two points into holes about 2¼ inches in diameter. Probably the stone was already perforated when set up, possibly with the purpose of serving as a guide to Ballachulish ferry. There is on Mull a remarkable chain of standing stones which clearly were set up as a guide to the ferry for Iona, and therefore the suggestion that this stone was similarly designed can scarcely be ignored, particularly as the ferry is clearly envisaged by the top perforation. But Clach a' Charra is not only simply interpreted as the " stone pillar," but as the " stone of retribution or vengeance," although enquiries locally elicited nothing more illuminating than that " my father that is dead knew all about it." Scarcely more satisfactory is an article in an early volume of the *Proceedings of the Society of Antiquaries of Scotland,* since it is not only rambling but singularly confused and entirely vague. As far as it is possible to make anything out of this paper, it would appear that Comyn, the Lord of Badenoch, demanded the surrender of some native women to his own two sons, and that the natives, outraged by the suggestion, rose and killed the two sons, the father escaping. Thus the stone was raised to commemorate the act of retribution which overtook a tyrant.

At North Ballachulish you may see in the summer glorious fields starred with the white and gold of ox-eyes and corncockles, and framed with the vividly bright pink of the wild rose, furrows of meadow-sweet beyond the sparkling waters of the loch, and everywhere the towering mountains stretching far up through Glencoe to the wild and lonely expanse of the moor of Rannoch, and to the head of Loch Leven. Here is the Forest of Mamore, the desolate region where Fr. Mackonochie, of S. Alban's, Holborn, lost his life.

Just about a mile short of North Ballachulish ferry, you pass at the foot of the craggy hillside the beautiful little church of S. Bride. Built in 1875 by a member of the Douglas family, Lady Ewing, wife of a Bishop of Argyll and the Isles, S. Bride's Church, dedicated to the patron saint of the Douglas family, has been associated

CLACH-A-CHARRA, ONICH

with many notable churchmen.   At the west end of the church, outside, there is a cenotaph cross of native slate, erected to the memory of Fr. Mackonochie.   On December 15, 1887, this devoted priest, when a guest of the late Bishop of Argyll and the Isles, was found dead in the snow, with the Bishop's two faithful dogs, Righ and Speireag, keeping watch over the body.   By the path, close to the door of the church, is an exact replica of the graceful crucifix found outside the entrance to the Priory Church on the island of Oronsay.   This covers the grave of the " holy bishop," as the late Dr. Chinnery-Haldane, who died February 16th, 1906, was called by the natives, who, irrespective of their creed and despite his uncompromising Churchmanship, both loved and reverenced him to an extraordinary degree.   A simple, kindly, unaffected gentleman, the late Bishop, whose home was Alltshellach, at no great distance from S. Bride's, loved to move amongst his humble neighbours, and for gipsies he had a special affection, always filling his pockets with something for the children.   Still far and wide on both sides of Loch Leven he is spoken of with the utmost affection, and always with a sigh of regret for his passing.

Within S. Bride's, Dr. Chinnery-Haldane is commemorated by a window representing him as S. Columba, and indeed one is conscious of his influence still pervading the church.   As members of his family come in, there will follow sedately in their wake a terrier or spaniel, to take a recognized place beneath their master's seat, there to remain with perfect decorum throughout the service, while in the porch other dogs not quite so pious will quietly await their owners.   I have been to the Three Hours' Service on a wet Good Friday at S. Bride's, and it has been a lesson to see the reverent intentness of a goodly congregation of Highlanders, mostly men, nearly all of whom were present throughout the devotion.

These Highlanders are in the true succession of their heroically enduring forefathers, who, despite relentless persecution, kept true to the faith of the Church. For in a field near the present Loch Leven Hotel is Carnglas, supposed to have been once the site of a Columban church, and here the forefathers of the present Faithful Remnant used to assemble secretly to receive the Blessed Sacrament. The officiating itinerant priest disguised himself in a grey suit, and a sentinel was posted on an eminence commanding the Fort William road, to give warning if any soldiers were seen approaching.

It is a far cry from these days to those of the Norsemen who, over a thousand years ago, troubled these shores; but, side by side with the reminiscences of persecuted Episcopacy, here are those of pagan Scandinavians. For, in November, 1880, some workmen, digging in peat on the grounds of Alltshellach, came across unique treasure trove. This was a grotesque female image, nearly life size and of great antiquity, which looked as if it had been carved out of a trunk of oak. Competent authorities consider this to be an idol representing a deity of the ancient Scandinavians, set up by them in the prow of a galley, as is suggested by a pedestal in which the feet are sunk. From the very significant fact that in the vicinity there are both Fridda's Field and Fridda's Bay, the idol quite likely is intended to represent the wife of Odin, Frigga, the northern Venus. The figure was presented by Dr. Chinnery-Haldane to the Society of Antiquaries of Scotland, in whose museum in Edinburgh it is to be seen.

There is also to be told a story I have read that some of those who escaped from Inverlochy in 1645 fled down the shores of Loch Linnhe until they reached " Ottanach, a little to the west of the Sound of MacPatrick." " Ottanach " I have been unable to identify, but it is evidently somewhere in the vicinity of Rudha Cuilcheanna that is intended, because the tale relates that the fugitives were ferried across, landing, as it would appear subsequently, near the " Bear's Point." Now Rudha Bhad Bheithe is just opposite Cuilcheanna, and while it seems to

IMAGE OF OAK FROM BALLACHULISH PEAT MOSS
4-ft. 6-in. high

(By kind permission of the Society of Antiquaries of Scotland)

mean the "point of the cluster of *birches*" (*beithe*), the name might have been, or mistaken for, *beithir,* which can mean a bear. Stewart of Ballachulish saw the fugitives landing, and observed they were Campbells. But, remarking that they had already suffered at the place whence they fled, he magnanimously spared them. But some Weirs and MacColls of Laroch were less merciful, and, falling upon their hereditary foes, slew them all and buried them on the shore near the Bear's Point, whence the place was called the "Campbell's burying ground."

———

PART II

BALLACHULISH

FERRYING across Loch Linnhe is not the straightforward journey that might be supposed, but is altogether dependent for its length upon the strength of the currents which obtain at the time of crossing. The ferry itself is known as *Caolas-Mhic-Pharuig,* or the "channel of Patrick's son," called after a Norse pirate who lost his son whilst passing through this strait. At low tide there can be seen, close in to the Argyllshire shore, an insignificant boulder, still called *Clach Pharuig,* by clutching which it is said the Norseman succeeded in saving his own life though he failed to rescue his son. A further tale, to account for the not very obvious splitting of *Clach Pharuig,* was told me by my kind friend, the Rev. Dugald Macdonald, late Rector of Ballachulish, who, as a native of Glencoe, is full of the old tales and traditions of the country. His versions, therefore, I quote in preference to others, where such exist, since it is impossible to give all.

A young chief of Lochiel was full of fun and liveliness, and, being on a visit to Aberdeen when a friend was getting married there, he thought he would attend the ceremony. So he went to the church, and, with a willow wand that was in his hand, he repeatedly struck a skull that was on the window-sill beside him, making indeed the responses with his wand as the marriage service proceeded. After going to bed that night, Lochiel felt very ill and in a strange state, and presently an old hag appeared to him, so ancient that she was toothless and as hairless as a milestone. She said to Lochiel: " I am your wife: we were married, exactly as those two were married in church yesterday." After this apparition, Lochiel could hardly sleep, and getting up in the morning, prepared to leave for Inverness. But on the doorstep the old hag met him with " Huh!" and set out on his journey with him. Saying, " Step it out, Lochiel," the hag walked with him, and " A step for a step, old woman!" Lochiel replied, never halting till, exhausted, he reached Inverness. The next morning, however, Lochiel set forth again, and again was met at the door by the witch. Together they walked as before, until, after seventy-eight and a half miles, they reached Ballachulish Ferry. Lochiel got into the ferry boat and pushed off from the shore. The old woman thought he was going to escape her, so she said, " My sincere wishes to you, Ewan!" Lochiel replied: " Your sincere wishes be on your sides and on yon grey stone," whereupon *Clach Pharuig* split into two.

On the knoll, *Cnap Chaolais Mhic Pharuig,* beside the Hotel, is a peculiarly hideous monument, " erected in 1911 to the memory of James Stewart of Acharn or ' of the Glens,' executed on this spot, November 8th, 1752, for a crime of which he was not guilty." *Kidnapped* has made famous—with many fictitious details—the Appin murder, the true story of which will be detailed in the next chapter.

The first island, flat and grassy, that you pass on your way to Ballachulish is *Eilean Choinnich,* on which a duel was fought by two swordsmen of great repute, and it is after Mackenzie, the man who fell, that the island is named. From this island, a great nesting place for a colony of terns which lay their eggs just amongst the

EVENING ON LOCH LEVEN, SHEWING BALLACHULISH FERRY

coarse grass, I have seen some most wonderful sunsets over the mountains of Morven. While all the way along the scenery has been most beautiful, particularly in retrospect, and in the views across the loch over to the mountains, the road itself attracts chief attention when it enters upon a lovely little length of woodland, flanked by a steep and towering glen. Indeed, the national and native poet might have been describing this particular stretch of the road by the lochside when he sang:

> " Sweet is the sound where rock and water meet,
> Sweet are the light winds softly murmuring;
> Sweet are the lonely heron's notes, and sweet
> The voice of birds amid the woods of spring."

Halfway between the ferry and the present church is *Lagan-a-bhainne,* a deep secluded " milky " hollow, one of the many in the district where the Eucharist was celebrated secretly while men kept watch, their swords at their sides.

Just beyond the woodlands with their rock-strewn, grassy foreground, you pass the graveyard and modern church of S. John, Ballachulish, built 1842, where the liturgical services of the Church are still, as in the past, said in Gaelic by a priest who is most appropriately a Macdonald of Glencoe. Even to a Celt who has no Gaelic, there is nothing which so surely induces a worshipful spirit than the recital of the offices of the Church in the Highland language. I can never forget the fervour of the *Te Deum* as sung and the Litany as said in Gaelic at S. John's, for it made me keenly sensible that Gaelic was pre-eminently the language for the expression of the deepest devotion.

From Glencoe to Appin constitutes one of the few districts of the Western Highlands where the native Episcopalian tradition has survived persecution. As will have been gathered from what has already been said in a previous chapter, the Scottish (Episcopal) Church is no importation from England as is popularly (and ignorantly) supposed, but the Church of native origin, claiming to be the lineal successor of the Church of S. Columba. It is just as absurd to refer to her as the " English " Church, as is commonly done, as it would be to call her the " American " Church, though all are comprised within the Anglican communion. There is nothing that the descendants of the old families of this district more bitterly resent than any reference to their Church as the " English " Church. They retort that it ill becomes the Continental cuckoo to apply any alien term to the native robin whom, in too many cases, the superior strength of the said cuckoo has ousted from its own nest. Further, these patriotic Churchmen maintain that for Presbyterians to persist in talking of the " English " Church in the Highlands, lays them open to the charge of a refusal to face distasteful, but none the less historic, facts.

In Ballachulish, the Scottish Episcopal Church has been continuous from time immemorial, and the silver altar vessels, inscribed " Parish of Appine, 1723," are still in use there. It was from this raised paten and the chalice that many of those loyal clansmen who fell at Culloden received their viaticum at the hands of the Rev. John MacLauchlan. But from the Revolution to 1810, the Faithful were dependent upon the secret ministrations of itinerant priests in secluded hollows of the hills. Political expediency had dictated the establishment of Presbyterianism in place of the Church, and, consequently, on June 7th, 1690, an Act of Parliament created a new " Church of Scotland " to replace the old. Hence in the district where there was no settled Presbyterian ministry before 1861, Presbyterianism is still known as the " Parliamentary Church," [4] or *Eaglais nam Mionnan*

---

[4] Hope, the Dean of Faculty, in 1826, said: " The Presbyterian religion and the Presbyterian form of government are in this country the creatures of the State, and both derive their existence and their doctrines, as well as their powers, from Parliament, and it is impossible they should derive it from any other source."

Eithich, " the Church of the False Oaths." Who has not heard of the persecution of the Covenanters which, however, they largely brought upon themselves by a refusal to tolerate anything but their own intolerance? But who knows anything of the persecution and proscription of the suffering Episcopalians by Presbyterians backed by the State? And yet, had the persecuted Episcopalians followed the aggressive and irreconcilable example of the Covenanters, instead of nobly enduring all pains and penalties in silence, all Scotland would have rung with their sufferings. Places such as Gairloch in Ross-shire, Glenorchy, etc., where there were riots when Presbyterian ministers were forced upon the people, were so remote in those days that news of happenings there were successfully kept from obtaining an undue publicity.

Instances have already been given of the way in which Presbyterianism was forced upon parishes where its ministrations were rejected. The worship of the Church was also proscribed, hence the many well-chosen hollows of the Holy Feast, where in the dark days of the Church the Faithful resorted in secret, coming as many as twelve or fifteen miles, fasting, to receive the Blessed Sacrament. The journals of the Episcopal visitations of Bishop Forbes both in 1762 and 1770 bear most valuable witness to the strength of the attachment of the natives to the Church. It was in a " Store House " near the present church that, in 1770, the Bishop preached to the people, who came in such numbers that both the prelate and the itinerant priest were obliged to officiate in the doorway to be heard of the overflowing multitude on the grass. On this occasion the Bishop baptised " between 60 and 70 " and " confirmed 170 " persons. Shortly afterwards, in the time of the Rev. Paul MacColl, the storehouse was converted into a church, and so remained until it was succeeded by the present building, when it became a barn, and may still be seen near S. John's. Some ideas of the numbers of the Episcopalians may be gathered from the fact that this itinerant priest, " Mr. Paul," as he was familiarly called, baptised over 10,000 persons in his lifetime ; but, in 1852, the local community was considerably depleted when 300 people emigrated to Australia.

After the battle of Culloden, where it was not considered safe to burn down churches, the brutal Butcher actually compelled congregations to pay for the destruction of their own churches.   That is the reason why there are so very few old churches belonging to the Scottish (Episcopal) Church to be found in the historic Episcopalian country, but her members may truly address their venerable spiritual mother thus :

> " They've robbed thee of thine altars,
> They've ta'en thine ancient name,
> But thou'rt the Church of Scotland
> Till Scotland melt in flame !"

It is because of the relentless and merciless persecution and punishment, both by imprisonment and transportation, which the Scottish (Episcopal) Church suffered that her members were reduced to the " shadow of a shade," and those who remained true to her became honourably distinguished as the " Faithful Remnant."

The Rev. Donald MacColl, a native of Appin, was the first priest to pray for the Hanoverian King in a thatched house, then used for service at Brecklet, a hamlet of Ballachulish, above Laroch Bridge.   An old dame, a Stewart, thereupon threatened to throw a stool if he did not desist and pray for the Stewarts, exclaiming as her protest: " *San as leth an diabhail a thubhairt thu e!* "— " It was on behalf of the devil you said it ! "

The slate quarries of Ballachulish used to be a far greater industry than they are at present, though the Government has begun their revival.   Near the shore in front of the quarries is *Rudha-na-glaistig,* the " promontory of the fairy," and this was one of the best known of all the hollows of the Holy Feast.   Eighty years ago, church people living as far away as Kingshouse would set out on the evening of the day before some festival, and, arriving here in the early hours of the morning, would receive the Blessed Sacrament. Then they would obtain some refreshment from friends in the village, possibly stay on for another service later in the morning, and in the afternoon return to Kingshouse.

In connection with Ballachulish in old days, I heard some most interesting stories both from Mr. Macdonald, the Rector of Ballachulish and another native of Glencoe, overflowing with tales of the district. These, and subsequent tales of the occult, are examples of various kinds of that " second-sight " for which the Highlands are famous. There is absolutely nothing in common between these simple experiences, invariably unsought and gained unexpectedly, and the complex jugglery of modern materialistic " séances," deliberately prepared for with an elaborate paraphernalia of mediums and other properties. Second-sight that is simply prophetic, as in the instances previously given of the Brahan Seer's prophecies, permits of the obvious test. Of the many authentic instances of Highlanders having seen things before they came to pass— too trivial to be thought of as " prophecies "—I attempt no explanation, but I accept them unreservedly. Other instances of the appearances of spirits present no difficulty whatever to anyone who believes that the world of spirit is all round about us, rather than in some far distant sphere, and that some persons have a special faculty, lacking in others, for communion with that world. To a Catholic, such cannot be other than a lawful communion, since it is due to the unconscious exercise of a natural gift, and has no sort of affinity with the " psychic gifts " of those who deliberately and of set purpose attempt to wrest information from the departed by what, to a Catholic, are unlawful means. A Catholic cannot accept as a " religion " what, at best, are experiments in the purely scientific sphere.

Now to begin my stories. There was one Ewan Mor MacColl of Brecklet who was gifted with the second-sight. Once at the quarry, trimming slates which a boy at his side was splitting, Ewan suddenly became extremely agitated, and, stooping, seized the boy's legs and removed them out of the pathway, exclaiming, " The spirits of the living are too strong ! " A friend of Ewan's came up, and, seeing how pale and upset he was, asked him if he were ill. He replied that he was quite well, but that there was an awful fate in store for a mutual friend of theirs in the quarry on a certain day. Asked if he could not avert the evil by detaining the friend from going to work in the quarry on the fateful day, Ewan said it was impossible. Not long afterwards, in the course of the quarrying operations, a great stone came rolling down the hill and fell upon a man, crushing him to a pulp. At the very, spot where Ewan and the boy had been working, as MacColl had foreseen, men rushing along to the rescue, carrying an oaken lever to remove the stone from the body, crossed the path which he had cleared of the boy's legs. The truth of this tale was vouched for by my informant's father, from whom he had it.

Two other tales of Ewan Mor MacColl are worth repeating. He had a son who was similarly gifted with the second-sight, and a second son who was fulfilling some contract over the hills at Glencreran. One night the old man called out to his son, " You must go over now to Glencreran if you would see your brother alive again," to which the son replied, " I know it already, father : I have my kilt on." He went and found his brother just at the point of death, following upon an accident.

Some years ago an Australian wrote to someone in the district, enclosing some papers. This colonial said his father had been an innkeeper at Ballachulish, and that Ewan would often come in and foretell happenings, of which the innkeeper made careful note. He sealed these notes up in an envelope, which the son found on his father's death, and now wanted to know if any of the predictions had come true. My informant stated that every one of them was verified as having been fulfilled.

Another intensely interesting tale that I was told was of the *Duine Mor* (Big Man), some impersonal apparition that appeared from time to time in Ballachulish, generally when any disaster was impending to any of the landed gentlepeople of the district. My informant's father was very anxious to see *An Duine Mor,* for he was curious to know what he was like. One day, when out with a friend, he expressed this desire, but the friend exclaimed: " I hope to God we do not meet him!" They had not walked very far, however, when *An Duine Mor* appeared, to the great terror of the friend. His companion, not in the least perturbed, cut across the road obliquely to stop the ghost, but never addressed him, as a spirit must always be the first to speak. My informant said his father was 5 feet 9½ inches, but *An Duine Mor* was a great deal taller, and that he vanished slowly like the mist. His father described to him in great exactness the chain armour which the ghost wore, and which the father had never seen in his life before. Indeed, my informant said he saw it for the first time on a subsequent visit to the Tower, and that he recognized it from his father's description as that *An Duine Mor* had worn. An interesting fact that I had from the Rector is that several natives had repeatedly heard the train passing through Ballachulish long before there was any talk of the line being laid.

PART III

EILEAN MUNDE AND GLENCOE

JUST opposite the slate quarries is Eilean Munde, a beautiful little rocky islet, wooded with fir trees, called after S. Mundus, Mun, or Fintan Munnu, who is called " the torch with the ascending flame," and " pure tested gold." He was an Irishman who took the habit on Iona under S. Columba in 597, and, living on Loch Leven, died in 635.

The first time I ever walked through Ballachulish, being very anxious to explore this, " the Macdonalds' Burial Isle," I was directed to the cottage of the possessor of a boat in which I might cross. It turned out that this man was thoroughly well versed in all the lore and history of the district, concerning which he was a great enthusiast. On the way down to the boat, he suddenly turned on me, and, stopping short, abruptly enquired, as the nearly forgotten but necessary preliminary to any further inter-course, if I were a Campbell, expectorating after every mention of the name, as indeed he did on every occasion of its use. But his apologies were profuse on my indignant repudiation of the stigma, and, there being no obstacle of clan, we proceeded to embark. Halfway across, catching sight of the cross I was wearing, the boatman, resting on his oars, again enquired, " Wass you a Popery—or an Episcopaalian?" On my telling him, his enthusiasm was great, and, regardless of what happened to the oars—or the boat—he insisted on shaking hands with one who, like himself, was " an Episcopaalian and a Mactonald." For the rest of the way over to the island his conversation gave proof of the strength of his convictions; and I thought it a curious point that, while he ardently supported, from regular personal experience, the practice of Sacramental Confession previous to the reception of the Blessed Sacrament, he was very much opposed to the use of flowers in church. This is the inversion of one's usual experience, for people will accept decorations for æsthetic reasons whilst rejecting discipline because it makes unpleasant demands upon them. So simple a man was he that he was surprised to hear that for all I had been in London, I had never seen there either the late or the present Rector of Glencoe on the occasions of their visits to the metropolis.

When we landed on the island, some of the information

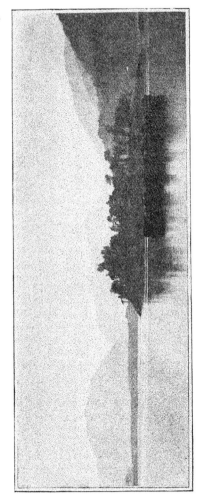

EILEAN MUNDE FROM TAYFUIRST, BALLACHULISH

he gave me was most curious, probably all the more so because he was not much at home in English. For instance, he explained the island's name by saying that the "Poperies" (as he called the Roman Catholics) gave a "Church" name in the Sacrament of Confirmation, hence Mun, but the family name was Mungo! Taking me to see the lesser memorials of the island first, he brought me to a stone sculptured with a Stewart coat-of-arms, having for crest a dove with a leaf in its beak, the stone being erected to one " who departed this life, aged 18." This slate, he said, covered the body of a man who was shot on going into the quarry, and he evidently took the coat-of-arms to be a symbolical representation of the tragedy. Thus he explained the dexter supporter, a savage shouldering a club, as the man with a gun who had shot the victim, and the bird to be a pigeon which had flown with a leaf, to cover with it the wound on the dead man's head! Bishop Ewing wrote of this slate, " There is also a carved stone, commemorative of the descent of a white dove upon the bosom of a quarryman, as he lay mortally wounded by a shot from the quarries." But in this case the puzzle of the crest still remains, unless it be a West Highland heraldic license which has made a crest to illustrate the incident.

From one grave to another was I taken, my interesting escort enthusiastically imparting quaint information, much of which, in consequence of its complex English, I was unable to apprehend. Notwithstanding that I had told him I had never been on the island before, at every grave where we halted he prefaced his remarks by asking me, " Wass you knowing whose grave that wass now?" and was always disappointed when I had, of course, to confess entire ignorance every time. But when on the western edge of the island he halted at a grave, whose headstone was a gable taken from the chief's house that was burnt down because he had risen in the '15, his fervent emotion was most touching to observe. Standing reverently by the grave, cap in one hand, and the other on his heart, he told me that here was buried the last of the Macdonalds of Glencoe, and asked me if I would take his photograph as he stood there.

As we were leaving the island, my companion told me that only at his proper landing place might a body be landed for burial, for a man must follow in the footsteps of his father and none other. Questioning him on this point, I gathered that did the weather prevent a Glencoe man from being landed at the Glencoe landing place, the coffin must be taken back to await a propitious day, for that, however easily a landing might be accomplished elsewhere, the body could not be taken ashore at the Ballachulish or Callart landing place. Camerons of Callart as well as Macdonalds have the right of burial on the island.

I refrain from recording his observations on the subject of the Campbells, alien land owners, Presbyterians, and Roman Catholics, merely observing that his language was so forcible that over and over again his English entirely failed him, and he had to finish in the Gaelic. Despite the fact that he was out of work, not only did my escort absolutely refuse to accept any money from " a Macdonald and an Episcopaalian," but he insisted on my coming back to his cottage for milk and scones, and could hardly be dissuaded from carrying my camera up to the little Hotel at Clachaig where I was spending the night. (I may here mention, in passing, that my luggage only arrived at 8.30 P.M., and I had just unpacked it when I was told that if it was to go with me next morning on the boat, it would have to be ready to leave the hotel at 9 P.M. !)

On the second occasion of my landing on Eilean Munde, the Rector of Ballachulish was my escort, and he observed that no one could compute the money that was in the island. He did not refer to any unexploited natural resources, however, but to the old Highland custom of dropping money into the graves to requite the hospitality of Mother Earth. He said that still people of the old families did it, and that, when he was taking funerals, a coin was often quietly dropped in when it was thought he did not see the act.

The Rector also told me the curious story of the burning of the church of the island, said to have been one of the seven built as a reparation by Allan Breac Cameron, the same church in which the Chief Maclain who perished in the massacre is alleged to be buried. In his *Costumes of the Clans,* Maclain writes:

> " Glenco was a man of gigantic size and muscular frame, and his bones are yet to be seen in an open niche of the ruined chapel of S. Munn, the size of which are evidence of the fact. We would suggest the propriety of having these relics placed in a more becoming receptacle."

There is certainly no sign of these bones now, nor even a trace of the " niche " above mentioned. It is just the simple structure common to most West Highland churches, a plain, small, rectangular building, without any division between nave and chancel, and now there are only the walls and gables left standing. It is said that the shell-mortar of these old churches was made with boiling water. It was on S. Barnabas Day, 1495, that the church was last used, under the following circumstances. A man had his cow bewitched, and consulted a local wise man, who said he was not powerful enough, and referred his consulter to the Dalness wise man. The Dalness seer told the enquirer to take a quern (stone for grinding corn) and place it above the church door on the coming Sunday, and he was to repeat as every man came out of church, " *Priobaid air do shuil, a dhuine,*" which, translated literally, is, " Twinkle on thine eye, my man," but the sense of which is conveyed by, " Disaster fall on thee, man of the evil eye!" This was all done in due course, and, as one particular man came out, the quern fell on him, thus proving him to be the man guilty of bewitching the cow. The cow's owner promptly attacked the indicted man, and, the congregation taking sides, a hot fight ensued till one man twisted a handful of hay into a torch, set the thatched roof of the church on fire, and thus destroyed it, burning within it the priest, a Macdonald. On the hillside above Eilean Munde a white stone marks the site of the old priest's croft where the priest serving the island lived.

There is also a tale told of a young Cameron buried on Eilean Munde, who was not allowed to rest because of a false vow he had made. He had fallen in love with a Macdonald girl, and swore to be true to her so long as his head was upon his shoulders. But his affection proved fickle, and he threw over his first love for another. Not long, however, did he enjoy his new attachment, for he caught a fever that ended fatally. After his burial, the peace which usually reigned on Eilean Munde was rudely disturbed, for piercing shrieks issued from its shores and continued day after day. At last one man, bolder than his fellows, landed on the island to discover the origin of the cries, and beheld, to his astonishment, the young man of the fickle affections buried indeed, but with his head above ground! The unquiet spirit besought his visitor to draw his sword and behead him that he might thus have rest, and the request being granted, peace was once more restored to the spirit and to the island.

From the island it is no very great distance to the village of Glencoe, a name which does *not* mean the "vale of weeping," as Macaulay, other fictions, and the guide books have it. No one can say what is the meaning.

I heard in Glencoe a very interesting and well authenticated story of second-sight which is worth recounting. My informant, wanting a small job done, was looking out for the return of the carpenter from Kinlochleven one Saturday afternoon, to ask him to do the work. The carpenter and two brothers worked at Kinlochleven all the week, and when it was time for the boat to be in,

THE RUINED CHURCH ON EILEAN MUNDE

my informant went up to his bedroom, which had two windows commanding the road in two stretches. Soon through the first he saw the three men advancing in a certain order, one carrying a brown paper parcel under his arm. When they took the turn of the road out of sight of the first window, my informant moved on to the second, but though he waited for ample time to allow them to reappear, they never did, although there was no other road for them to take. The narrator came downstairs, went outside, and asked of a woman opposite if *she* had seen the carpenter and his brothers passing. She said she had not, but, about two hours later, my informant saw them again on the road. This time, being determined not to miss them, he went out and, sure enough, they did at last come up to him. The carpenter explained that they were just ten yards off the boat at Kinlochleven when the " beast of a captain," refusing to wait for them, steamed off. So they had to hire a machine to drive all the way on the other side and be ferried over. They were very annoyed at the loss of their afternoon, and, on questioning them, my informant found that had they caught the boat, they must have passed his house exactly when he first saw them. When he *did* see them the second time, they were in precisely the same order as on the first occasion, and one of the men was carrying the parcel the narrator had previously seen.

It is but a little way from the Church of S. Mary to Invercoe, where the old Bridge of Coe spans the river. It was here, under the beautiful fir trees, that there was held the open air Evensong taken by the Rev. Donald Mackenzie which made such an impression upon Bishop Ewing. He writes: " The keys of the kingdom were delivered in Gaelic, and the whole service was in the same language. There were about two hundred worshippers, and, as I looked upon them, every knee bent on the grassy moss and every head bowed low, repeating the words of our venerable liturgy, I felt myself rebuked by the earnestness of their devotion."

PART IV

THE MASSACRE OF GLENCOE

UNDER the same trees let us call a halt to summarize briefly the history of one of the most treacherous and brutal incidents recorded in British annals. So cunningly and callously planned in cold blood was the massacre of Glencoe, that all of those responsible are branded for all time as criminals of the basest type, in spite of the fact that honours were bestowed on some instead of the punishment that was due to all alike.

With the death of the gallant and glorious Graeme on the field of his crowning triumph at Killiecrankie, the cause of James was irretrievably lost, but, nevertheless, the loyal Highlanders still held themselves bound by their oath of allegiance to James VII. Thus, when the Dutchman, imported to usurp his throne, demanded of them that they should transfer their allegiance to him, requiring of them an oath to this effect by December 31st, 1691, the loyal chiefs sent to St. Germain, requesting of James permission to take this. To Campbell of Breadalbane, a man endowed with no small share of the cunning crookedness of his clan,[5] was entrusted the task of reconciliation, and, throughout, his conduct of affairs was characterized by double-dealing and hypocrisy. Three other Campbells, as will presently appear, share with him in the infamy of the massacre, so that it is surely no wonder that to this day the clan is execrated in Glencoe by all the native families who still remain, and that the Campbells have been accounted accursed not only by every true Macdonald, but by the many other loyal clans who have fallen victims to their

[5] It is not without significance that a magpie or pyet (*pioghaid*) is called in the Highlands the " messenger of the Campbells," the same phrase being also used to designate any person who is " garrulous, lying, and interfering with everybody."

rapacious cunning and scheming. Others who shared in the chief responsibility for the massacre were, beside the Dutchman himself, his Secretary of State for Scotland, Dalrymple, Master of Stair, and Livingstone, commander of the forces in Scotland. The Lowlander, Dalrymple, however, was the ceaselessly moving spirit, and it was to him, jointly with Breadalbane, that the idea of the massacre owes its inception. Dalrymple's action was evidently animated by his religious prejudices, for he stated in one of his numerous letters, urging on various officers to their bloody part, that the men of Glencoe were " all papists,"[6] and therefore fit subjects for vengeance.

By December 30th, Alexander Macdonald of Glencoe [7] and Glengarry at least had not taken the oath to William because they were not then in receipt of James' permission to do so, which, however, had reached all the other chiefs. According to contemporary evidence, Maclain was " a person of great integrity, honour, good-nature, and courage," also " strong, active, and of the biggest size, loved by his neighbours, and blameless in conduct."

On December 31st, Maclain, apprised at last of his release from his allegiance to James, presented himself to Colonel Hill, commanding at Fort William,[8] and expressed

---

[6] It is emphatically asserted in Glencoe that the MacIains were Episcopalians, and that the Roman Catholics, like the Presbyterians, only appeared in the district when the natives became augmented by people from other parts. There is a letter of October 20, 1782, to Bishop Petrie requesting him to appoint a Gaelic priest for the Episcopalians of Appin, and this is signed amongst others by " John M'Donald of Glenco." But to Presbyterians, Episcopalians and Roman Catholics were alike, "all papists."

[7] The Macdonalds of Glencoe were more usually called the MacIains, or Clan Iain Abrach (of Lochaber), their progenitor being *Iain Og an Fhraoich,* or young John of the Heather, hence his race became the " Sons of John." This " young John " was a son of Angus, Lord of the Isles, by the daughter of one Dugal MacEanruig (hence Henderson) of Glencoe, which thus became a Macdonald possession, and the style "Abrach" was derived from the fact that one of the earlier chiefs was fostered in Lochaber.

[8] The room in the Governor's house, in which this interview took place, is still shewn.

his readiness to take the oath to William. To his dismay, however, he found that he should have betaken himself to the Sheriff of Argyll at Inveraray, but he succeeded in persuading Colonel Hill to give him a letter to Campbell of Ardkinglass, the Sheriff in question. Not only did Hill do this, asking Ardkinglass to receive Glencoe as " a lost sheep," but he gave the chief a personal protection, pledging himself that no proceedings should be taken against Maclain till his case had been investigated by William. But so anxious was Maclain to comply with the literal requirements of the Government that, despite his age, the snow, and the rigorous journey of over sixty miles, he set out at once for Inveraray, not even stopping for refreshment at his own house, near which he passed.

Having been detained on his way for twenty-four hours at Balcardine, in Appin, by Captain Drummond, it was January 3rd before he reached Inveraray, only to find the Sheriff absent. Not till January 6th did the weather permit of Ardkinglass's return, and then he scrupled about receiving MacIain's oath because it was too late. Ultimately, however, he was prevailed upon to do so, and sent it, together with Hill's letter, to Colin Campbell, Sheriff Clerk of Argyll, at Edinburgh. This perfidious man defaced the certificate, so that Dalrymple, who knew that this had been done, in conjunction with Breadalbane, delighted for any chance to avenge himself on a personal enemy, had the way clear to pursue the murderous designs against the Macdonalds of Glencoe. For Breadalbane sometime previously had proposed to Dalrymple a " scheme of mauling them," and Dalrymple, in a letter to Lieut.-Colonel Hamilton, *dated a month before the amnesty expired,* was already gleefully planning the massacre. He wrote:

" The winter is the only season in which we are sure the Highlanders cannot escape us, nor carry their wives, bairns, and cattle to the mountains."

And in another letter, written by him only two days later, he observes:

"It is the only time they cannot escape you. . . This is the proper season to maule them in the cold long nights."

Next he wrote in January to Livingstone:

"I hope the soldiers will not trouble the Government with prisoners."

And afterwards, when the false report came to him as a blow:

"I am sorry that Keppoch and Maclain of Glencoe are safe."

But when this information was contradicted, he hastened to write again to Livingstone:

"At this news I rejoice: it's a great work of charity to root out that damnable sect—the worst in all the Highlands."

Whether by "sect" he referred to their being "Papists" or really meant "sept," cannot now be determined.

Then from William, given under his own hand, and dated January 16th, came the supreme order sanctioning the massacre:

"If M'Ean of Glencoe and that tribe can be well separated from the rest, it will be a proper vindication of the public justice to extirpate that set of thieves."

With this authorization, Dalrymple lost no time in setting his bloodhounds loose, and, beginning with Livingstone, the order for the massacre passed from him to Lieut.-Colonel Hamilton. But Dalrymple, fearful lest his ghastly schemings should lack sufficient urging, also wrote Hill to the same effect as he had already written to Livingstone, telling Hill in addition that Argyll and

Breadalbane, fitting confederates, had promised to ensure that no fugitives should escape into their territories. Thus Hill, heedless of the promise he had given Maclain, wrote to Hamilton, delegating to him his orders to march on Glencoe; Hamilton transmitted them to Major Duncanson, a noted adherent of the house of Argyll, adding in a postscript the instruction for a guard to secure the ferry at Ballachulish and to keep all the boats on the farther side.

Finally Duncanson gathered up the previous letters into the following, which he sent to a man innately fitted in every way to play the part of a Judas:

" BALLACHOLIS,
12th February, 1692.

SIR,

You are hereby ordered to fall upon the rebels, the McDonalds of Glencoe, and putt all to the sword under seventy. You are to have a special care that the old fox and his sons doe upon no account escape your hands. You are to secure all the avenues, that no man escape. This you are to put in execution att five o'clock in the morning precisely, and by that time, or very shortly after it, I'll strive to be att you with a stronger party. If I doe not come to you at five, you are not to tarry for me, but to fall on. This is by the king's speciall commands, for the good and safety of the country, that these miscreants be cutt off root and branch. See that this be putt in execution without fear or favour, else you may expect to be treated as not true to the king's government, nor a man fitt to carry a commission in the king's service. Expecting you will not faill in the fulfilling hereof as you love yourself, I subscribe these with my hand.

ROBERT DUNCANSON.

For their Majesty's service.
To Captain Robert Campbell of Glenlyon."

This letter was written in old Ballachulish House, where Duncanson was quartered. Meanwhile Maclain, having, as he thought, made his position secure, returned to Glencoe with a mind at rest. Then, as the first move in the projected butchery, 120 men of Argyll's regiment, under Campbell of Glenlyon, appeared on the scene. John, the elder son of the chief, went out with some of his men to challenge the soldiers, but Glenlyon assured them that they came as friends, seeking quarters only in the peaceful capacity of tax collectors. Indeed, both he and his subalterns, Lieutenant Lindsay and Ensign John Lundie, gave their parole of honour that they came without any hostile intentions whatsoever, so that for the fourteen days they were the recipients of the hospitality of Maclain. Glenlyon, who was quartered at Inveriggan, even succeeded in ingratiating himself with Alexander Macdonald, the chief's younger son, who had married his niece, and in consequence received a warm welcome on his almost daily visit to Alexander's house.

There is no need to stigmatize by any adjectives the character and conduct of Glenlyon and his subalterns: a cold statement of the hideous details of the massacre speaks eloquently for itself, as well as providing an apt comment on the Gaelic proverb: *Cho fad's a bhios slat' an coill, bidh foill ann an Caimbeulach*—"As long as trees are in the wood, a Campbell will be treacherous." On the eve of the massacre, with Duncanson's letter in his pocket, Glenlyon played cards with John and Alexander MacIain, and accepted an invitation to dine with the chief himself next day. Then he went off to make his final preparations for the massacre. The noise made by these aroused John Maclain, who, getting out of bed in alarm, went to Inveriggan to enquire of Glenlyon why the soldiery were stirring. Glenlyon replied that they were about to set out on an expedition against Glengarry, and reproached John for his suspicions, asking him how it was possible to suspect one allied to him by marriage of

designing any harm against them.   His suspicions lulled,
John returned to his house, but his servant refused to be
satisfied and kept his master awake.   Then, before a party
of men gained the house, thanks to this servant's watchful-
ness, John, joined by his brother, managed to escape by
the Devil's Staircase.

In the meantime, at five o'clock, Lieutenant Lindsay went
to the chief's house, obtaining ready admission under the
pretext of making a friendly visit.   Lindsay shot the old
man as he rose out of his bed to receive his visitors, and
he fell back dead into his wife's arms.   Her the soldiers
stripped naked, tore her rings off her fingers with their
teeth, and so ill-used her that she died the next day.   Two
other men were also killed in the chief's house, and a man
from Braemar was wounded there.   At Inveriggan, Glenlyon himself commanded, ordering first his own host to
be shot.   Nine men were seized, bound hand and foot, and
then shot one by one.   A young man of twenty, whom
Glenlyon for some unknown reason would have spared,
Captain Drummond shot.   This same gentleman ran his
dagger through a boy as he clung to Campbell's legs,
imploring mercy.   A woman and a boy of four were also
amongst the victims of this butchering party, who also left
a child's hand behind them.

One, Sergeant Barker was in charge of the slaughter at
the village of Achnacon, where he and his men were billeted.
Nine men seated round a house fire were fired upon, and
amongst them fell the Laird of Achatreachtan, who had in
his pocket a safe conduct from Colonel Hill.   Two or three
others were wounded, and the rest escaped by the back of
the house, with the exception of the Laird's brother, who
begged as a favour of Barker that he might be shot out
of doors, in recognition of the kindness the sergeant had
received at his hands.   Barker consenting, the Laird's
brother threw his plaid in the faces of the soldiers who
were going to shoot him, and so escaped.   In other parts
of the glen people were dragged from their beds and
murdered, including an old man of over eighty.

Between thirty and forty inhabitants of Glencoe were thus massacred, and the whole two hundred would probably have suffered had not the wintry weather prevented Hamilton's arrival until six hours later, so that the way of escape he was to have closed remained open. But, coming across on his march an old man of over seventy, Hamilton did what he could to compensate by shooting him. Nor was he too late to burn down all the houses and to carry off all the cattle and horses, about a thousand head, which were taken to Fort William to be divided amongst the officers of the garrison.

After the burning of the houses, heartrending scenes were witnessed of aged women, mothers and babes, toddling children, all half-naked, struggling to make their way over the snow-clad mountains to some shelter. But as the nearest houses were many miles away, the majority of these poor fugitives perished in the snow. About 160 escaped.

> " Oh, the horror of the tempest,
>   As the flashing drift was blown
>   Crimsoned by the conflagration
>   And the roofs went thundering down!
>   Oh the prayers, the prayers and curses,
>   That together winged their flight
>   From the maddened hearts of many
>   Through that long and woeful night.
>   Till the fires began to dwindle
>   And the shouts grew faint and few,
>   And we heard the foeman's challenge
>   Only in a far haloo.
>   Till the silence once more settled
>   O'er the gorges of the glen,
>   Broken only by the Cona
>   Plunging through its naked den."

Such are the massacre's fearful details of which one may read in any history, and its victims were as truly martyrs as were the Holy Innocents—martyrs in deed though not in will, put to death for their religion.

There is a local tradition which may be added to the above incidents. This states that Iain Mac Raonuill Oig, an old Glencoe bard, was saved from the massacre by his devoted son who bore him away on his back, going by a roundabout and difficult way until he gained a boat on the shore of Loch Leven. In this they crossed to some cousin's at Callart where they hid till they could return to the ruins of their home at Achatreachtan. I think this may be he whose grave on Eilean Munde I had pointed out to me as that of the bard who, at his own request, had been buried at the nearest possible point of the island to Glencoe.

Another bard of Glencoe—famous for its poets—was *Raonull na Sgeithe,* Ranald of the Shield, a son of Allan Macdonald of Achatreachtan, and he perished in the massacre. He had been a distinguished soldier both under Montrose and Dundee, and when he heard of the martyrdom of King Charles, he wrote *Cumha Righ Tearlach a-h-Aon,* a " Lament for King Charles I." His son, Donald, also a bard,[9] escaping from the massacre, very fittingly led the 120 men of Glencoe who, on August 27th, 1745, joined the Prince's forces at Aberchalder.

There is also an instance of *Slinneineach,* or divining forthcoming events from certain markings on a shoulder blade, told in connection with the massacre. On the fatal night a party of Macdonalds were poring over the shoulder blade of an animal slain to afford hospitality to the soldiers. One of these Macdonalds exclaimed: " There is a shedding of blood in the glen!" and another said there was only the stream at the end of the house between them and it. Thereupon the whole party rushed to the door, and, in consequence, were amongst the few to escape.

The *caoineag* is a being quite distinct from the *bean nighe* (see p. 227), since, unlike her, she can be neither approached nor addressed, yet is like in that she always foretells death. Another characteristic is that she sheds

---

[9] Yet another bard, the author of a spirited epic of a battle, and an elegy on Iain Lom, was Aonghas Mac Alastair Ruaidh, who lived about the end of the seventeenth century.

tears for those who fall in fight. It is not often that the *caoineag* is seen, but her lamentations were often heard in the lonely glen, by the fresh water's side, or on the mountains, and a fearful thing it was accounted thus to hear her wailing. Several nights in succession before the massacre her voice was heard sorrowing, and some, heeding it, fled the glen. The following is the verse of a song which used to be current in Glencoe

> "Little *caoineag* of the sorrow
> Is pouring the tears of her eyes,
> Weeping and wailing the fate of Clan Donald,
> Alas, my grief, that ye did not heed her cries!"

It is also traditionally said the march known as " Breadalbane's " and the " Wives of the Glen," was played by Glenlyon's piper early on the morning of the fatal Saturday to warn the MacIains:

> " Wives of wild Cona, Cona Glen, Cona Glen,
> Wives of wild Cona, wake from your slumbers!
> Early I woke this morn,
> Early I woke this morn,
> Woke to alarm you with music's wild numbers!"

Heeding this warning, one woman, it is said, escaped to the hills with her child.

There are other tales of soldiers not so merciless as their officers, who managed to convey indirect warning to individuals. The hint conveyed to a nurse in the house of the Laird of Achatreachtan seems very obscure when translated into English, but it seems to have served its purpose. An old soldier quartered there was seated by the fire on the night before the massacre, and, seeing the nurse and child playing beside him, he called the house dog to him. Stroking its head he said, " Ah, many a good thing may happen, good dog, during the long winter night. Yes, many a good thing may happen, but it may not be so to-morrow!"

At Brecklet, in *Gleann an Fhiodha,* three soldiers were quartered with a family of Robertsons. The father came

in on the day before the massacre and took off his plaid,
whereupon one of the soldiers remarked, " Yours is a good
plaid." To this Robertson replied, " It is not bad." The
soldier continued : " Were this plaid mine, I would put
it on, go out, and look after cattle." As the host ignored
this remark, a second soldier spoke. " No one knows,"
he said, " to whom that plaid may belong to-morrow." At
this, Robertson fired up, exclaiming, " I would like to see
the man who would take my good plaid from me ! "
Looking at him steadily in the face, the soldier said very
deliberately, " Were the plaid mine, I would put it on at
once, take every male child with me, and go and drive
cattle away to a safe place." Robertson took the warning,
and the soldiers, apparently following their instructions,
set the house on fire, but they came back later and
extinguished the flames.

It is said that one of the victims of the massacre cursed
its instigators, and prophesied that their wives should be
for ever childless. It is a remarkable sequel that the
second, third, fourth, sixth, and seventh Earls of Stair all
died without issue, the elder branch becoming extinct with
the death of the seventh Earl in 1840.

A man of Carnach had his arm broken by a shot, but he
managed to escape by jumping the burn at Escan, a place
where it has never been jumped since.

With regard to the history of the Macdonalds of Glencoe
after the massacre, I was told some very interesting facts
which it will be well to preface by some general remarks
on the subject of clan and sept names. There is not a clan
in the Highlands but comprises more or less septs, or sub-
divisions, many of whose names on the surface suggest
little or no association with the main stem itself. I have
already mentioned that the Macdonalds of Glencoe are as
frequently called Maclain, the sons of John, after the
founder of their branch of the great Clan Donald. The
MacEanruigs, or Hendersons, were the hereditary pipers
of the MacIains. Similarly, the MacInnes are known in

the Gaelic as *Clann Aonghais* (sons of Angus), consequently MacAngus occurs amongst their sept names, as
does Johnson [10] amongst those of Glencoe.

The hereditary offices of the clans account for many
another sept name, though not invariably, since some small
dependent clans provide some officers. Taking those
attending in their various capacities at the courts of the
Macdonalds, Lords of the Isles, we get, indicated by an
asterisk, the following sept names of Clan Donald:

Bard—MacVurichs (son of the mariner).

Marshal—Mackinnons (son of the fair born).

Recorder—Macduffies (sons of the black peace) of
Colonsay.

Purse Bearer—Macsporran (sons of the purse) anglicised Purcell.

Physician—Macbeth (son of life) Beaton or Bethune.

Piper—Macarthur (son of Arthur).

Armourer and Smith—Macrury (son of the famed ruler).

Speaker—MacLaverty (son of one bearing dominion).

Isles, as the territorial designation of one family of this
clan, has also become one of its sept names, and from the
Gaelic patronymic of the House of Sleat, *Clann Uisdein,*
comes the literal translation Hughson, then Hewison,
Houston, and other variations. Personal peculiarities also
account for many sept names, as MacGillivantic, a more or
less phonetic rendering of the Gaelic for stammerer. This
is a sept of the Macdonalds of Keppoch, and suggests the
descendants of *Iain Lom.* Other names attached to the
clan are simply Anglicised equivalents of the Gaelic (such
as Donaldson), and others are more obscured through mis-

---

[10] But all Johnsons are not Macdonalds, any more than all Smiths are
goibhean, *i e.,* Smiths of Clan Macpherson.

spelling, syncopation, often phonetic, like Kean for
Maclain, and Kelly for Gille, both Macdonald sept names.

In the case of "broken clans," when the name of the
clan was proscribed, as in the famous case of the
Macgregors, names having no association or connection
with the clan had perforce to be adopted; similarly, in
order to conceal their identity after the '45, many a loyal
clan had to resort to the same artifice to save themselves
from continuous persecution. The Macdonalds of Glencoe
were in like case after the massacre, and I was told on the
best authority, that some who sought refuge in Ayrshire
disguised themselves as Walkers, and others, going to
Dunblane and the borders of Stirling adjacent, simply
translated their name and became "Donaldson."   In this
particular family there is always found an Alasdair and an
Iain amongst the sons.

Many local traditions the Rector of Ballachulish told
me as he took me over the scenes of the massacre, upon
which we will now enter. We were horrified to find the
bridge at Invercoe outraged by an iron notice, erected to
notify motorists—quite wrongly—that this was the scene of
the massacre. The Scottish Automobile Club is responsible for this and similar notices throughout the country
demonstrating the vulgarian spirit of the age, for these
placards show no greater sense of the fitness of things than
that evidenced by those who disfigure beautiful scenery by
advertisements. This labelling of scenery, comparable to
writing a title across some work of art, is surely a matter
which calls for determined action on the part of all those
members of the Scottish Automobile Club who are concerned to free their association from the aspersion of
execrable taste, and sublime scenery from the indignity of
a cast-iron label.[11]

[11] When I was subsequently up the glen, I found on the first occasion that
the offending notice had been moved to indicate roughly one of the true
centres of the massacre. On the second occasion it had been "moved on"
up the glen, and one can only hope it will be soon moved out altogether.

Turning up the track by the near side of the river, you are at Carnach, and there the Rector pointed out a beautiful green field on the right where it is said the first shot in the massacre was fired. Passing further on, you see the graceful slender cross " reverently erected in memory of Maclain, Chief of Glencoe, who fell with his people in the Massacre of Glencoe of February 13th, 1692. Their memory liveth for evermore." And as you stand there, the ancient prayer ascends: "Give them rest, O Lord, in a place of light and refreshment, in green pastures beside the waters of comfort, from which pain, sorrow, and groaning have fled away."

The distinctive crest of the Macdonalds of Glencoe, a dexter hand holding a dagger in pale proper, and their motto, *Nec tempore nec facto,* surmounts the coat-of-arms, identical with that of the Isles, and the cross itself has the most sublime setting in the background of the mountains of Glencoe. The *Suaicheantas,* or Badge, of the men of Glencoe, worn by the clansmen in their bonnets, was in common with the rest of Clan Donald, *Fraoch gorm,* or common heath, and their common war-cry, *Fraoch Eilean* —heather island. While some say that the tartan is that of the ordinary Macdonald, others claim that of Glengarry as that also proper to Iain Abrach. It is recorded that of the " Highland host " who were brought down to subdue the covenanting rebellion were the " Glencoe men . . . who had for their ensigne a faire bush of heath, wel spred and displayed on the head of a staff."

Turning off to the right, the Rector took me to a large boulder known as *Clach Eanruig,* or the Stone of Henry, and told me the tale associated with it. Sports were being held in this field on the eve of the massacre, and a soldier, whose conscience smote him at the thought of the cruel fate in store for the unsuspecting population, thus apostrophized the stone, as the only means whereby he dared convey a warning: " Oh, thou grey stone of the glen, though great be thy right to be here, if thou knewest what would happen to-night, thou wouldst no longer tarry here."

Continuing up by the rough track on this side of the river, a most glorious walk, we came to the site of the old hamlet of Inveriggan, where there is standing the picturesque shell of a house near the sites, still traceable, of several burnt down in the massacre. All are at no great distance from the beautiful burn which cuts its way down to unite with the broad stream of the Coe.

At Inveriggan the Rector had another tale to tell, and I give his version in preference to others which may be found both in verse and prose. During the massacre, a woman at Inveriggan, hearing the soldiers at their bloody work, fled with her baby son wrapped in a blanket. Followed by a little dog, she took refuge under a bridge crossing the burn I have mentioned, which ran just below the house. The baby began to cry, and Glenlyon, hearing it, despatched a soldier to discover if it were a boy, and, if so, to kill him. The soldier found the mother stuffing a corner of the blanket into the baby's mouth to stifle his cries, but, seeing the child smile, the soldier had not the heart to kill him. Knowing, however, Glenlyon might not be denied, the soldier cut off the dog's head and went back to his commander, exhibiting his bloody sword. "That is not human blood," said Glenlyon; "kill the child, or I will kill you." The soldier went back to the child, and, cutting off one of its little fingers, with the blood smeared on the sword satisfied Glenlyon. Years after, the same soldier was travelling in Appin in the depth of winter, and received hospitality at a house, where he begged to be taken in. In the evening as they sat round the fire, his host asked the soldier what was the most terrible scene he had ever witnessed, and the man answered, "The massacre of Glencoe." Later, the host slipped out to see a neighbour, exclaiming, "There is one of those butchers of Glencoe in my house. I will make an end of him before morning!" But the neighbour counselled patience, and

SITE OF MASSACRE AT INVERIGGAN, GLENCOE

both returned together to question the soldier further. Asking him what was the horridest scene he saw in the massacre, the soldier told the tale of the child he had spared at Inveriggan, whereupon his host held up his hand that lacked the little finger!

From Inveriggan we passed on to another ruined hamlet, Achnacon,[12] where scattered remains of houses, their stones blackened by the fire of burning, suggest some lines of Ossian as having peculiar aptness:

" I have seen the walls, but they are desolate. The fire has resounded on the hills, and the voice of the people is heard no more. The thistle shook there its lonely head: the moss whistles on the wind: the rank grass waved about the stones. Desolate is the dwelling: silence is in the house of my fathers."

These pitiful ruins lie round about the stately Signal Rock, but with that execrable taste all too common, alas, amongst Sasunnachs who have acquired by purchase historic possessions in the Highlands, so little regard has been shown for what surely should be for ever a site of inviolable sanctity, that the present proprietor has seen nothing unseemly in the construction here of trout ponds with neat paths winding about them, and seats erected at intervals! *O tempora, O mores!*

The Signal Rock commands the valley in all directions, and from its flat top, tradition says, the signal for the massacre to begin was given—hence its name. From here we gained the road, and, just a little beyond the Clachaig Inn, we took another track leading over the moors to the site of the summer residence of Maclain.

Though the chief had his winter house at Invercoe, for some reason he was occupying this house in *Gleann Leac na Muidhe* in the fatal February of 1692, and here it was

---

[12] "Field of the dogs." A common name in Glencoe and Appin, signifying a place where their celebrated hounds kept for hunting were unleashed.

that he was murdered.   The applicability of the name,
" glen of the slate and churn," is not on the surface
apparent, but the Rector explained it as having reference
to two of its characteristics, the green sward of the glen
itself being smooth as a slate and the burn which courses
it flowing with such impetus over its broken and rocky
bed as to churn its waters.

> " Dark is the green of thy grassy clothing,
>   Soft swell thy hillocks most green and deep,
> The *cannach* 13 blowing, the darnel growing,
>   While the deer troop past to the misty steep."

Past the keeper's house, and on the hillside above a byre,
are the pathetic ruins, whence there is an impressive view
across the glen to a chasm deeply seaming the rugged side
of Beinn Bheag.   Foxgloves and ferns have done their best
to veil from sight what is left of the blackened walls, but
they cannot stifle the cry of the stones which is perpetually
sounding for the ears of all who will hear.   In the atmosphere of this ruined house, the vision of the murdered chief
is conjured up by a passage from Ossian:

" His face is like the beam of the setting moon.   His
robes are of the clouds of the hill.   His eyes are like
two decaying flames.   Dark is the wound of his breast.
The stars dim-twinkled through his form, and his voice
was like the sound of a distant stream."

PART V

CONCLUSION

WITH this visit to the site of the murdered chief's house,
our pilgrimage to the several scenes of the massacre ended,
but not so the Rector's tales.   Of Seonaid Vic Alastair
Macdonald he had already told me in an incident I shall

13 Bog-myrtle.

repeat when we come to Ballachulish House. This woman's old father, Alasdair MacAonghas, son of Macdonald of Achatreachtan, born about 1665, and living at Tigh a' Phuirt, was one of the many bards of Glencoe, and a fervent Jacobite, and, old and frail as he was, he set out after Prince Charlie's men. But he was so infirm that Maclain of Glencoe urged him to return home, and, although he accepted the advice, when he arrived there, he was utterly broken-hearted that he had not been able to join the Prince. His second daughter Seonaid (Janet), having compassion on the old man's sorrow, comforted him by exclaiming, " This is not the end of it ! " and, getting up early the next morning, she saddled their old grey mare, and set her father upon it. Thus he set out a second time for the Jacobite army, but failed to overtake the men of Glencoe and died and was buried at Dunblane,[14] where a tombstone is said to commemorate the incident.

Campbell of Glenfalloch went to Glencoe in pursuit of Jacobites after the battle of Culloden. Going to Invercoe, to the house of the Laird, who had married Stewart of Ardsheal's sister, he only found a fool there, and so spared the house, making compensation by burning the houses at Carnach.

As the ordinary route through Glencoe is so widely known to every tourist, it would be superfluous to attempt any detailed description of it, so that a few remarks will suffice. Before you reach Loch Triochatan, there is a bridge crossing the river, and in connection with this bridge Mr. Macdonald, the Rector, had an experience of the second sight. He told me that, when he was a boy up in

[14] Going to Dunblane in order to find this tombstone, I asked the old man who had charge of the graveyard to direct me to it. With great indignation he answered me, as though I had offered him an insult, " Thirty-three years have I been here, and never did I hear any sic a tale." Though I went carefully all over the stones, I could not discover what I sought, but in view of the crumbling and weathered condition of so very many of them, from which all inscriptions have disappeared, I thought the stone I sought might very well be one of these, for the tradition is persistent.

the Pass, he saw in the distance this bridge very many years
before it was built. When he got nearer, however, he
could see no sign of one, and it was years afterwards that
he saw that a bridge *had* been erected in the very place
where he had seen it as a lad, and that his vision, which
had been very clear, exactly coincided with the bridge as
it then stood in substance.

It is at Loch Triochatan, once famous for its water-bull,
that you enter upon the second phase of Glencoe, in which
it shews a beauty grim and terrible. For the first part is
a gradual climbing up through a fine wooded road, and
in a plantation on the right there was till quite recently
pointed out a hawthorn tree where, it is said, a few
Campbells, whom their intended victims managed to kill,
were buried. From the Loch onward, however, the bleak
and rugged mountains of the wild and narrow glen close
in upon you increasingly, and deeper and deeper grows
the bed of the Coe until it becomes a veritable gorge
through which the river plunges. On the right, opposite
Achatreachatan, high up on the hillside, is the dark opening
known as " Ossian's Cave." Glencoe is the reputed birth-
place of this " little faun," who is alleged to have lived in
the third century. " In the same manner as the name of
David is traditionally associated with the Hebrew Psalter,
or the name of Homer with the Homeric poetry, so is that
of Ossian, the warrior bard, with the classic poems of the
Gael. His name will always be identified with the bardic
literature that celebrates the deeds of the Fianna, even
though scholars cannot affirm with historic certainty that
he actually lived or was the real author of one of the
ballads attributed to him. Few of the oldest existing
Ossianic poems are thought to be older than the eleventh
or twelfth centuries." Thus Professor Magnus Maclean.

The point of the road where the glen reaches its summit,
known to tourists as the " Study " or " Queen's View," is
locally called by the beautifully poetic name of *Innean a'*
Cheathaich, the "anvil of the mist," the flat expanse of rock

to which it has reference being anvil-shaped. The Devil's Staircase, by which the sons of Maclain escaped, and which climbs over to Fort William, is about three miles beyond this point, on the left hand side. The Rector told me that the "Anvil of the Mist" was the scene of the "Bloody Pool." The men of Glencoe were accustomed, just before Christmas, to make request of their richer neighbours for gifts of food to celebrate the festival. This was called "*Faoidh Nollaig*," Christmas hospitality, and the result of the collection was pooled. In 1543 three companies set out in as many different directions on this pursuit, and all agreed to gather at the Black Mount, to divide the gifts into three equal portions. This they did accordingly, and all went well till only a back of cheese was left. One man said, "This should go in this portion," another, "No, in this." The dispute waxed so hot that fighting began, and raged so furiously that at last all but one man was killed. Wondering what delayed the parties, a clansman went in search of them, and found only a piper alive, who just managed to relate the fatal circumstances before he expired at Lochan-na-fala, the "little loch of blood." To this day in Glencoe there is a local saying, "There will be more about it than there was about the back of the cheese," and, if universal local report be true, it is the case regarding the way in which Glencoe was snatched from the Macdonalds. The old natives tell you how a Macdonald of Glencoe, eager to redeem the estate, was travelling back from Canada on the same boat as the Hon. Sir Donald Smith, to whom he confided, to his undoing, his hopes and aspirations. The millionaire, thinking Glencoe seemed a nice place, took the first chance of wiring his man of business to secure the estate for him. So the country of the Macdonalds was alienated from its ancient heritors, although public sentiment was too strong to allow Sir Donald Smith to assume the style of "Lord Glencoe" when he was raised to the peerage, and he had to content himself with the title of Strathcona.

CHAPTER VI

THE COUNTRY OF THE STEWARTS

" We will take the good old way,
We will take the good old way,
We'll take and keep the good old way—
Let them say their will, oh ! "

—SHERIFFMUIR
(" The March of the Stewarts of Appin ").

___

PART I

THE STEWARTS, THEIR CHURCH AND FORTRESS

OF all the clans in the Highlands, none has been more consistently and persistently loyal to the " good old way " alike in Church and State than the Stewarts [1] of Appin, with whom are comprised the cadet families of Ardsheal, Achnacon, Ballachulish, Fasnacloich, and Invernahyle. It is from Sir John Stewart of Bonkyl, who fell in 1298 at the battle of Falkirk, that the Stewarts of Appin are descended. In their coat-of-arms, the galley of Lorne is quartered with the quartering common to all the Stewarts, the fess checky, which probably represents the chess board the accomptants of the King's Office used for calculations. This use of these boards in all likelihood accounts for the name of the Exchequer in which the Stewarts held hereditary office. The galley [2] is a reminder

___

[1] The spelling, " Steuart " and " Stuart," dates from the French alliance with the Scots, and is due to the absence of " w " in the French language.

[2] In every case where the galley is found in armorial bearings, it has been borrowed from its original bearers, the Lords of the Isles, by clans which were originally vassals of that house. Before Appin, for instance, became associated with the Stewarts, it was in the domain of the Lord of the Isles, the lands of Duror having been granted to John of the Isles by David Bruce in 1343. As the eagle on the Macdonald arms signified a royal sovereignty, so, too, the galley symbolised their superiority by sea.

that, following upon the Macdougals, the Stewarts of Appin were Lords of Lorne for sixty years, until Argyll obtained the coveted Lordship by means that did him no credit—to use restrained language.

Whenever the King has called " To me ! " the Stewarts of Appin have always made instant response—in the Wars of Montrose for the Royal Martyr, at Killiecrankie, in the Rising of '15, and foremost on the fatal field of Culloden. Of the chiefs, alike of the main and the cadet branches, the long record is one of unsullied honour, of spirited leadership, and of the devoted attachment of their clansmen. Their motto, " Quhidder will zie?" is a challenge to all who dare oppose them. It asks in effect, " What will you? Peace or War? Make your own choice," and prompt action rather than words has always answered the enemy's reply.

The first of this family of Stewarts to possess Appin, the "abbey" lands of Lismore, was Duncan, to whom many lands were gifted by James IV. It is unfortunate that when the railway was carried through the district of Appin, the name should have been conferred on the station at one extremity of the district called Portnacrois, for such a proceeding tends to an unnecessary confusion in historical geography. Of the character of the Stewarts, the anonymous Whig author of the *Highlands of Scotland in 1750*, praising when he thinks to condemn, writes: " The people of Ardnamurchan [Mac Iains] and the Stewarts of Appin are the most deeply poisoned with disaffection to a Happy Constitution in Church and State of any people I ever saw. They idolize the Non-juring Clergy, and can scarcely keep their temper when speaking of Presbyterians." And again: " The people of this country (Apine) are tall, strong, and well-bodied. They are a kind of Protestants,[3] but, as has been already observed, idolize the Nonjurant Clergy, and are Enthusiastically Mad in their zeal for

[3] Yet a page or so beforehand, the author refers to their very active priest, John M'Lachlan, as "at least half a Papist"!

Restoring the Stewart family. They are not thieves, but are industrious in their Business and Honest in their Private Dealings "—a most condescending admission on the part of the Sasunnach.

It was due to the then Marquis of Carmarthen that the Stewarts of Appin did not share the same fate as the Macdonalds of Glencoe. In a letter of January 7, 1693, from Stair—countersigned by William of Orange—Livingstone, Hamilton, and Hill were all informed of the Government's intention " to destroy entirely the country of Lochaber, Locheil's lands, Keppoch's, Glengarry's, Appin and Glenco." So strongly did Carmarthen remonstrate with the Orangeman that this specific order was withdrawn, though events proved that not every part of Stair's evil designs were thereby thwarted.

About two miles from Appin Station, in the Strath of Appin just below Achnacon House, is a picturesque roofless, ivy-covered ruin which is all that remains of the first Presbyterian place of worship built on the mainland of this district in 1749, as the date over the keystone of the door records. It must, however, mark the site of a church previously built there, and also of an earlier Presbyterian building, from the fact that there are some old Celtic tombstones of an age far anterior to the present building, and also references in the Presbytery records of 1660 to the " new Kirk of Appin." These old gravestones have been so neglected that it is impossible in most cases to make out anything whatever of their sculpturings, worn away by overgrowths. One, on which a rude sword, its handle out of line with the blade, can be traced, shews in a circle below a curious piece of knot work. The first Presbyterian minister of Lismore, it is to be noted, was not settled till the end of 1719, and the Records of the Presbytery of Lorne as early as 1660 speak of the " New Kirk of Appin," possibly a temporary building erected before the present one here. A quaint feature of this ruin

is the series of stone steps built outside at one end
(originally placed at the opposite end), and leading into
the gallery, traces of which are still visible all round the
inside of the building. But by far its most interesting
feature is a blind round arch quite recently, and, one is
bound to say, somewhat incongruously erected to commemorate those who fought and fell with the Stewarts of
Appin at Culloden. Beneath the arch is the old headstone
that commemorated the Appin regiment on the battlefield
before a new one was substituted for it there. The old
stone was fittingly given to Achnacon as the representative
of the eldest cadet family of the Stewarts still retaining
possession of lands in Appin. As always, when in the
presence of any reminder of the pitiful tragedy of the last
battle fought on British soil, there surges up the vain
regret:

> " Ah, my Prince, it were well,
>   Had'st thou to the gods been dear,
> To have fallen where Keppoch fell,
>   With the war-pipe loud in thine ear!"

The memorial, surmounted by a free standing cross,
beneath which is the date of Culloden and the Stewart
war-cry, commemorates the " 92 officers and men of the
Stewarts of Appin who fell in the memorable charge of
the right wing of the Prince's army, April 16, 1746."
These include eighteen different names, only three of which
are septs of the Stewarts, the rest being those of dependent
clans, members of which lived in Appin, and who were
proud to range themselves under the banner of the
Stewarts. Many of these old families, as the MacColls,
Livingstones, Rankins, and M'Innes, recur over and over
again in the records of the Diocese, and some are still
happily found in the district. Although the MacColls are
a sept of the Macdonalds, they seem to have attached
themselves for centuries to the Stewarts, who had no more

devoted supporters than they. So close was the attachment of the MacColls to the Stewarts of Achnacon in particular, that it became a custom for all of that house to be laid to rest with a MacColl standing on either side of the coffin at the time of the funeral. This custom was honoured by its observance on the last sad occasion recently in the churchyard of the Scottish Episcopal Church, Appin, the old graveyard now being disused.

No more beautiful nor fitting emblem for the memory of the Prince and those who fell in his cause at Culloden could have studded the old graveyard than the forget-me-nots of deep " true blue " that literally carpeted the ground all about the memorial when first we saw it.

> "Lost is the Star of the night,
> And the Rose of a day's delight,
>   Fled ' where roses go;'
> But the fragrance and light from afar,
> Born of the Rose and the star,
>   Breathe o'er the years and the snow."

The aforementioned Presbytery Records, it is interesting to note, complain that " Most of the Gentlemen and Heritors of Appin are not of the Communion of our Church, and some of them, particularly the Laird of Appin, never attend ordinances as dispensed by " Campbell the Presbyterian minister. What a contrast do these virile old chiefs in their consistent Episcopalian principles, refusing to have their religion State-dictated, present to most of the aliens in the Highlands, landed proprietors by the power of the purse, who have succeeded to them! Those whose supreme article of faith is, " I believe in any Established Church " never stop to think what inconsistencies consistent adherence to this Erastian principle involves, and, short of a visit to Utah, where they would be faced by Mormonism as the " State religion," they will probably never realize it.

Portnacrois is the village round the station of Appin,

CASTLE STALCAIRE AND LOCH LAICH, APPIN

and, dated from " Portnacroish in Appin," October 20, 1782, a letter was sent to Bishop Petrie, signed by "Alex. Stewart of Invernahyle, Jas. Stewart of Fashnacloich, and John Macdonald of Glenco." It made reference to " such a numerous concourse of people who have so long and so strenuously adhered to the Catholick Church," and urged their claims to a settled Gaelic ministry instead of such infrequent services as they could only obtain from a priest itinerating a large district. But it was not till July 2, 1815, that, with every circumstance of simple dignity, Andrew Macfarlane, Bishop of Ross and Argyll, consecrated the present church of S. Cross at Portnacrois in Appin, of which the Rev. Paul MacColl became the first incumbent, and " Ballecholis," Invernahyle, Fasnacloich, Keil, and Achnacon appear as representatives of the congregation.

A little beyond Appin Station you cross the railway line, and, standing on the shore, you obtain an uninterrupted view of Castle Stalcaire, perched on its rocky base in Loch Laich just about a quarter of a mile out to sea. " The Castle of the Falconer," though roofless, still stands four square, sturdily indifferent to the buffettings of wind and wave alike, a picturesque feature of the landscape, with its crow-stepped gables and outside stone stairway leading up to the main entrance—all set against the low mountains on the far side of the loch. But a mere distant acquaintance with the castle does not content you; a boat is what you seek in order that you come into more intimate terms with Stalcaire Island. You can only land on the tiny shore of a miniature bay at the south-east angle of the islet, where some rude steps hewn in the rock are still traceable. You climb these and walk over the beautiful green sward to ascend the stairs to the doorway. A marble tablet just inside informs you that Castle Stalcaire was " built probably in the 13th century, was owned by Sir John Stewart Lord of Lorne 1320, and repaired about 1450 by Duncan Stewart of Appin as a hunting seat for his kinsman James IV." Duncan, the King's seneschal, is said to have built the castle out of the proceeds of one-third arrears of rent of the Isle of Mull he was collecting for the King from Maclean, added to three years' rent he himself obtained from an estate granted him by James V.

It was Duncan, the seventh chief of Appin who, in a drunken carousal, was prevailed upon to yield the castle to Campbell of Airds, an estate close by, in return for an eight-oared galley. In consequence of this shameful transaction, the clansmen would never follow Duncan in battle again. Duncan sober, however, repented of what had been tricked out of Duncan drunken, but, being a Stewart, he was too honourable to repudiate his unequal barter, and Campbell had not the generosity to release him. But as the Stewarts were the hereditary keepers of the castle for the King, John Stewart of Ardsheal, newly home from leading the clan at Killiecrankie, seized the castle on behalf of young Appin to hold it for King James. At the end of 1689, the " Argyllshire Highlanders," raised to oppose the Jacobite clansmen, were employed under Captain John Campbell of Airds to reduce Castle Stalcaire; but it was not till October, 1690, that on very honourable terms the fortress surrendered to the Earl of Argyll. It was garrisoned by militia in the spring of 1746, but now, most happily, the castle is once more in the hands of those who have the best right to it, for it was regained by purchase in 1908 by Mr. Charles Stewart of Achara, and may it remain in the Stewart possession to the end of time! Unfortunately for Appin itself, Dugald, the tenth chief, was the last of the direct line of Appin, and he in 1765 sold Appin to Seton of Touch, and to this day Appin House is in the possession of strangers, while the representation of the Stewarts of Lorne and Appin has devolved upon the head of the family of Ardsheal. But, happily, both at Achnacon of Appin and at Achara, Stewarts still reign as only clansmen can.

Omitting such lesser details as are unlikely to interest the general reader, I will mention only the principal features of the fortress. Castle Stalcaire consists of a simple rectangular keep about 50 feet by 40 feet, and 4 storeys in height; its main entrance door being, as usual, on the first floor level. This entrance is surmounted by a shield which is said to have borne the Royal Arms, but its charge is now undecipherable. The stone stairway by which the entrance is gained is a later addition, for originally a ladder would have been lowered to admit such as might lawfully enter. To strengthen the defence, the doorway has above it a wide machicolation on two bold corbels on the level of the parapet, this providing openings through which boiling oil, lead, and other warm welcomes might be poured upon any invaders. Through the doorway you enter straightway into the hall, 31 feet by 21 feet, which occupies the whole of the first floor. It has windows on three sides, one of them having stone seats, and a fireplace occupies a space on the fourth side. But to be thrilled, you must cross over to the dark, oblong opening which in the north-west corner still gapes greedily for the prisoners, who have long ceased to occupy its black damp depths hollowed out in the heart of the rock. A wheel stair alongside leads to the second floor, which has a very ornamental fire-place and a *garde-robe* in the thickness —9 feet—of the west walls. The third or top storey, as it now is, was partly in the roof, and was lit by dormer addition to the castle as originally built. These alterations windows: but this upper storey was probably a later and additions were very likely carried out in 1631 when, it is said, the castle was re-roofed and re-floored. There is a solitary angle turret at the south-east which, besides having an ornamental window, has many shot-holes, and has, at the time of the other alterations, been carried up to terminate in a small room that was probably intended for a look-out post since it commands a fine sweep of the loch. Precipitating yourself from the top storey to the basement—an easy transit where there are no floors—you find yourself in a series of vaulted chambers from which a door opens out on to the rock, and is defended, like the main entrance, with a wide machicolation. Passing out this way, you make a tour of the walls, and note on the south side of the tower that there has evidently been a small courtyard from traces discernible of a surrounding wall. In a rock to the west of the keep there is a sluggish pool of water, which is said to have been a tank constructed in connection with a spring which existed there. It does not appear to do so now.

Alexander Stewart, the first Laird of Invernahyle, whose estate was given him after Flodden, lived in Eilean na Stalcaire. He was known as *an Teochail,* or the Peaceful, and early one summer morning he went to contiguous *Eilean na Gall* (Isle of the Stranger), which can be gained on foot at low tide. Not apprehending any danger, *an Teochail* laid down his Lochaber axe. But *Cailean Uaine* [4] (Green Colin), brother of Campbell of Dunstaffnage, with whom the Stewarts had a deadly feud, landed with a party of men and seized the axe, exclaiming: " This is a good axe if it had a good handle to it!" Alexander immediately answered, " Has it not that?" and to shew that he apprehended Colin's sarcasm, his repartee took the practical form of laying his own hand on the weapon.

During the struggle which thereupon ensued, *An Teochail* was basely fallen upon by Colin's men and, the victim of superior numbers, was speedily murdered. Subsequently *Cailean Uaine* put all the family to the sword, an infant only escaping, thanks to the devotion of his nurse. She managed to hide the babe in a hollow of a rock, tying a lump of lard round his neck for subsistence, before she

[4] So called from the preponderance of green in his tartan.

was caught. She was kept a close prisoner for three days, and, as she persisted that she had no knowledge of the child's existence, she was released. She managed, unobserved to regain the child, and finding to her joy that, thanks to the lard, he was alive and well, she escaped with him to her husband, a Macdonald of Moidart, and an armourer. The child thus rescued grew up so powerful as to be known throughout the Highlands as Donald of the Hammer; since he could wield a hammer with each hand for hours together. Ultimately Donald avenged his father by slaying Green Colin and recovering Invernahyle.

As we left Appin to walk back to Duror, we obtained quite the most perfect view possible of Castle Stalcaire and Loch Laich in retrospect. It was a spring day of a marvellous all-prevading blueness, of a depth and intensity such as people are wont to associate only with the Mediterranean, and the sun was shining brilliantly. A very high wind ruffled the waters of the loch, and, looking back, it seemed as if the sturdy old fortress and the islets, all black against the light, were set in a bed of leaping, molten silver. The walk throughout was a delight to the eyes: strikingly beautiful at that point in the road where one looks across the Sound of Shuna to Eilean Shuna, with its small ruined castle perched on its southern extremity; and also further on, where the great head of Ben Nevis rose covered with deep snow.

Just short of Dalnatraid, if you keep a very searching eye on the roadside at the right, besides the many groups of resting cairns, you may discover, half overgrown, the rude shelter provided by two long slabs of stone set on end, within which many a coffin was placed for the night, with another slab to cover it, on its journey to the old chapel and churchyard of *Cillchaluimchille* at Duror. This is across the line at no very great distance from Glen Salachan, a somewhat dreary valley, which, however, may be the " Coire Salchan " mentioned by Adamnan as the district in which S. Columba was staying when " a certain peasant " came to him. The saint, asking the peasant where he lived, and being told by the shores of " the lake Crogreth," predicted the harrying of the poor man's home, but consoled him by saying his family had escaped, all of which prophecy the peasant found true. If this " Lake Cogreth " be, as surmised, Loch Creran just below Appin, " Coire Salchan " is likely to be this Glen Salachan, more especially because of its proximity to Cillchaluimchille of Duror, simply now called Keil. One is generally right in inferring that wherever Keils, Keil, or Kells (*i.e.*, *cill*, a church, cell, or burial-ground) simply occurs, the dedication is to S. Columba, the suffix of the saint's name being considered a redundancy in the case of a church dedicated to him, who is pre-eminently the saint of Scotland. Both chapel and burial ground of Keil of Duror are small and of no interest; what old graven stones there may have been having suffered such violence from weather and lack of care that their sculpturing has practically disappeared.

PART II

THE SOUL-SHRINE OF APPIN

THERE are still, even in these degenerate and vulgar days, some bright spots left in the Highlands, and one of these is Duror. About a mile beyond the station, on the right stands the house of Achara, beyond " the field of the standing stone," whereof the tall monolith set up in striking isolation, is a witness, probably to some fight. It is the house, still most happily the home of Stewarts, where the soul of all that was good in the days that are past is still enshrined. From this centre emanates and radiates that atmosphere with which Duror is permeated, keeping it in spirit as well as in letter a truly Highland village, untainted by the purse-proud vulgarity of some aliens. In Duror, all the naturally fine characteristics of the Highlander, notably his true gentility, can and do thrive. From Achara flows unfailingly spontaneous and unostentatious generosity—not the unconsidered flinging broad-cast of superfluities as an advertisement, but the kindly, pains-taking considerations which only a friend can shew. Here, indeed, a friend is always at hand, hospitality's self, accessible as an equal to the lowliest, for there is the tacit recognition of the claims of the people of Duror upon the " big house " of Duror in all times of stress, need, or trouble. There is never the insult of a condescending patron conferring favours upon inferiors. Here the laird, clad in kilt of Hunting Stewart tartan, and his wife, with their firm hold on Episcopalian principles and in their devout practice of the Faith, are truest Stewarts, taking and keeping the " good old way " of their forefathers, and followed therein by all the families of the district, who worship with them in the little Church of S. Adamnan.

When such an example prevails at Achara, is it any wonder that with the people of Duror it is a case of *noblesse oblige,* that *noblesse* which is common to all true Highlanders? Whether it be the Darby and Joan of the Post Office, the silver-badged postman, the farmers, the late schoolmaster's widow, the proprietor of the one tiny shop of the village, one and all are entirely charming in their simple, unaffected courtesy, kindliness, and friendly spirit. Kindly, gentle, and courteous too, was the late Established minister, who lived on happiest terms with the Rector. Duror, indeed, affords a lesson of agreeing to differ in perfect charity where Church principles are concerned, for there is no compromise in these, yet there is agreeing to unite on social occasions where no such principles are involved. Thus there is no attempt even on " special occasions " at the Jesuitical insincerity, in my opinion (on the Episcopalian side), of " united services,"

but the true spirit of good feeling is shewn when Episcopalians, headed by the Rector, join in *soirées* held by the
Presbyterians in their place of worship.

But if you would know something of Duror, you must
meet that sturdy old Episcopalian, Duncan Rankine,[5] the
embodiment of the district's history, for his forbears fought
at Culloden, bore witness at the Appin trial, and their
name recurs with the utmost regularity in the old Diocesan
registers.   Rankine is also the very personification of good
humour: there is always a smile on his face, a twinkle
in his eye, and the suggestion of some excellent joke up
his sleeve.   A very well-read man, there is nothing in the
history of the district about which he cannot tell you, and
he informs you with pride that not only were the Rankines
pipers to the Macleans, but very fine pipers at that!   His
farm is Inshaig, a white house by the roadside, which was
the old change-house where James of the Glens was
arrested.

As for Duror of Appin itself, think of a big white house [6]
set in an expansive field against a background of high
mountains: a picturesque road running partly alongside
a river where heron patiently fish—a river which winds
and loiters through the woodland home of the squirrel,
or rushes down through undulating moorland to join the
sea: a little line of cottages on the one side, a rather
longer line higher up: beyond them on the same side,
tucked away amongst trees, the Established place of
worship and the Manse: further still, on the opposite side,
beyond the Inn, the Church of S. Adamnan and the
Rectory, which face Glen Duror: mountains all around,

[5] Since this was written, this friend has, to the loss of all who knew
him, died.   May he rest in peace and rise in glory.

[6] Inside the main gateway is one of those neat little roofed boxes you so
often come across in the Highlands, to save passing carts or messengers a
long journey up to the door with such things as bread, etc. Instead, the loaf
is just popped inside the wayside box to be fetched from the house at
leisure.

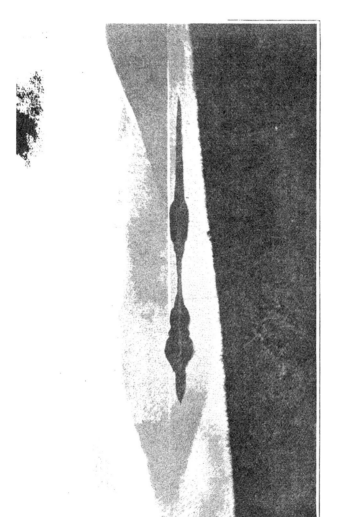

SUNSET ON CUIL BAY, DUROR

chiefest of all the great mass of Ben Vair—this is Duror in baldest outline.

In the spring snow crowns the hill tops, and often mantles their sides: along the base of the mountains across the sea steals stealthily the smoke of the heather burning: over the moor comes the cry of the curlew. If there has been heavy rain, there is thunder in the voice of the river as its swollen stream plunges along on its tortuous course to the sea. Primroses are strewn broadcast, lovely large blossoms, growing in thickest profusion all along the road side, carpeting the banks of the river, under the trees, even in a cleft high up in one of the tallest of the trees— everywhere, except on the moorland. There instead—if heather, broom, bracken, and bog-myrtle alike be as yet lacking—you may stumble on something else. Quite unexpectedly, as you make your way off any track through the marshy grass and stubbly heather, a curlew may rise with lamentations immediately from before you, and at your feet you will discover, laid upon a large tussock of coarse bent grass for nest, four large drab oval eggs, blotched with brown. On the way home in the evening from your wanderings there are sunsets to be seen— wonderful effects of light and shade, glorious displays of tender, quivering colours.

Through Glen Duror you can make your way by elusive and ill-defined tracks both to Glen *Leac-na-Muidhe* and Ballachulish. On the near side of the glen, you can still see the old house of Acharn, now hideous with a corrugated iron roof, where lived James of the Glens after his eviction, and in which, it is said, R. L. Stevenson stayed when he was gathering material for *Kidnapped*. Glen Duror had a *glaistig* or *gruagach,* as it is here indifferently called, who was associated with the farm and not with the individual occupants of Achindarroch, and this being was described as having a face like a lichen-covered slab of stone. So long as a daily libation of milk was poured out for her over the Gruagach Stone, she kept the cows from the calves at night, and once when a new farmer omitted the libation, the cows were found with the calves in the morning. A servant maid who was going down to the burn for water was asked by her fellow-servants if she was not afraid of the *glaistig,* and laughed scornfully at the idea. In consequence, on her way home, she received from an unseen hand a slap on the cheek which twisted her head to one side, but the next evening it was put straight again by a slap on the other cheek!

There is a particular pool in the river up the glen which the Rector told me was associated with the administration of Holy Baptism in the old days, and there is also a *Lag na Feisdean Naomha* (hollow of the Holy Feasts) in Appin. S. Adamnan's Church, just opposite the glen, deserves to be mentioned because it was built in 1848 by the men of the congregation entirely by their own hands, with the exception of the roof which they could not manage, and all at their own cost. The chancel has recently been added as a memorial to Dr. Chinnery-Haldane, since S. Adamnan's was the last church in which he ministered. The east window has a unique tracery, the outline of a thistle having been very effectively introduced.

A little over a mile from the church is a great gash in the side of Ben Vair called *Lag-na-ha* or *Eas-nan-con.* The natural chasm has been widened by quarrying operations at a point some way up the hillside, and it is just above the quarry that Ardsheal's Cave may—or may not—be found. Charles Stewart, fifth of Ardsheal, was a famous swordsman who fought with, and was the only one who ever wounded, Rob Roy. Ardsheal was tutor of young Appin, and led the clan in his stead at Culloden, where the Stewarts suffered heavily. The Carmichaels were the standard-bearers of the clan, and it was predicted by a local wise man that nine Donalds would fall carrying the Stewart standard. The celebrated banner of Appin, of light blue silk with a yellow saltire, still in possession of the Ballachulish branch of the family, was stained by the life blood of its first bearer, Donald Carmichael. After eight others, including a MacColl, had fallen in defence of the flag, it was only saved from capture by the gallantry of one of the corps, *Mac an t-leighe,* Donald Livingstone. He, a boy of eighteen, locally known as Hairy Donald, one of a Stewart sept from Morven, tore the colour from its staff and wrapped it round about his body, ultimately getting away, badly wounded, on horseback, and surrendering the banner to Appin himself.

Wishing to see his family once more before he fled to France, Ardsheal, after Culloden, returned to Appin. First he sought shelter in the Red Pass Cave on the side of Sgurr Dhearg, but it was so small that his discomfort was great. With him were Stewart of Invernahyle and MacColl of Gleann Stocadal; and one, Duncan MacColl, to whom their presence in the neighbourhood was confided, impressed on them the need of extreme caution, Ardsheal House being invested by soldiers from a ship of war. But this warning was not sufficient to keep Ardsheal from his wife, and as she could not come to him, he went to see her one day in a barn. While passing the barn, still standing, as I shall mention, beside where Ardsheal Cottage used to be, I have wondered if it might be the same building, and have pictured the meeting. Presently the retainer on the look-out came in to report that soldiers were making for the barn, and, in order to delude them into supposing Ardsheal was attempting to escape, this man, having delivered his message, took to his heels. While the red-coats pursued him, Ardsheal hid under the hay, and his little girl sat on top of him thus covered. Captain Scott looked in, but only seeing Lady Ardsheal apparently looking after her child playing in the hay, he departed. Then Ardsheal got out of the hay, and, thinking himself safe from discovery, went out with his wife and child into the garden. To their horror, they saw Captain Scott returning, whereupon Ardsheal lay prone amongst the kale whilst his enemy, after conversing with his wife and little daughter, again left the place. After many similar adventures and narrow escapes, he took refuge in the cave of Lag-na-ha. Here he was concealed for three weeks, a little maiden who daily took out a few lambs to the hills bringing food to him, as the absence of the soldiers gave her opportunity. Rankine told me there was a secret place where she left provisions for the chief to fetch when the coast was clear. The district swarmed with English soldiers, and, though all the people knew where their chief was hiding, no reward could induce them to disclose his whereabouts.

Despite the many risks he had run, Ardsheal still persisted in going to see his wife, and one day he only escaped capture by hiding near the head of a small sea loch at Ardsheal, squeezed between a big rock and a precipice, this hiding-place being called the Caigionn. A fool (?) very cleverly managed to feed his chief. The bank where he was hidden was covered with hazel trees, and under pretext of cutting branches for basket-making, the half-witted clansman's presence in the field was soon ignored by the watching soldiers. Whenever he saw his chance, by a clever artifice the fool deftly passed on to Ardsheal the food and the *searrag,* a kind of bottle, he had disposed about his person. Thus sustained, he was enabled to keep in hiding, and at last Captain Scott and his men, thinking their quarry had escaped, withdrew from Ardsheal House, and so the laird was able to regain Lag-na-ha, where he apparently spent a few weeks.

We had great difficulty in finding the cave, for it is not in any case easy to arrive at, and we had received somewhat ambiguous and misleading directions. The water descends through Lag-na-ha in a series of waterfalls, thus forming different " storeys," as it were, that in which the cave is to be found being in the second flight, just above the quarry. The precise waterfall under which the cave is situated is now indicated by an iron pipe which can easily be seen, a landmark which sticks out prominently and is noticeable

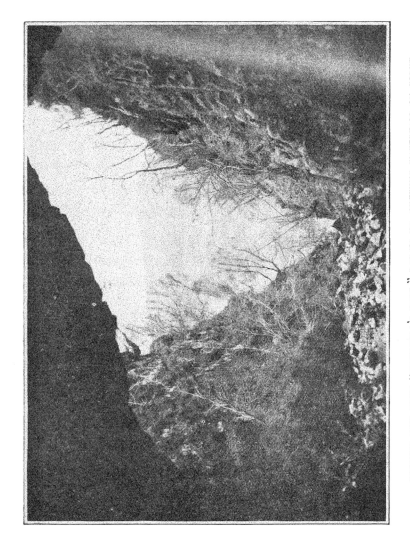

LOOKING OUT FROM "ARDSHEAL'S CAVE," LAG-NA-HA, SHEWING WATERFALL ON RIGHT

for its ugliness. You have a very stiff climb of about a
quarter of a mile up the sheer face of the hill on the Duror
side of the hollow. Then you take, sharp on the left, a
track that leads right to the precipitous edge of the chasm,
and, climbing a dilapidated barbed wire fence which runs
at right angles to it, you cautiously slip and slide down the
slope until you find yourself in the deep dark gash through
which the stream tumbles. Right in front of you, well
ahead, rises the face of a sheer precipice, on to the left
side of which pours down a thin spout of water, clearing
the mouth of the big cave which yawns at you on the right.
Most probably before the stream came in for the attention
of engineers, the water fell over the cave, otherwise it is
difficult to understand how a refugee there could have
escaped any searcher, for once access is gained to this
particular chasm, the whole extent of the cave is plainly
visible to the most casual observer. You scramble up the
rocky bed of the stream to climb into the cave—which is
practically an open shelf in the face of the precipice—a
shelf with ledges and small tunnellings all round the walls,
in which rock pigeons had made their uncomfortable nests,
for we found several untidy heaps of sticks on which lay
their eggs. From the cave, when the trees are bare, as
when we were there, you obtain a very comprehensive and
commanding view of the high road, running hundreds of
feet below like a white band.

It is said that it was in the September of 1746 that
Ardsheal with four other gentlemen managed to escape in
a French ship from Peterhead to the Continent, taking a
pony up Glen Duror, and hiding on the way in a kiln
above the head of Loch Etive. All the while he was in
exile, such was the devotion of his people, that, besides
paying their rents to the Hanoverian factor in charge of
the confiscated estates, they voluntarily assessed themselves
and sent the money out to Ardsheal by the hand of James
of the Glens. Particularly noticeable in this respect were
the M'Robs, a sept of the Stewarts descended from the

natural son of Robert Stewart, son of Dugald, first chief of Appin. This devoted sept latterly held their lands of Glen Duror, Lettermore, and Acharn in Duror from Ardsheal, by whom only a nominal rent was exacted, but the M'Robs actually assessed themselves for the then large sum of one hundred pounds to send to their chief.

And what happened in Appin happened throughout the Highlands amongst the Jacobite clans.

In the December of 1746, Ardsheal House was sacked by the Government troops, and the Lady Ardsheal was obliged to flee for refuge to a hut. From this, too, she was brutally driven on the very night of her confinement, and with her infant and five more children was forced to seek shelter otherwhere from the falling snow.

The most beautiful way to Ardsheal from Duror is round by Cuil Bay, where you take the track that climbs over the moorland and leads through woodland and plantations to the present house of Ardsheal, perfectly situated on high ground, looking far over Loch Linnhe. After having been in possession of Lowlanders, it is a matter for great thankfulness that the estate is once again not only in Highland hands, but in those of a clan which has always been intimately associated with the Stewarts. With Mrs. Cameron of Ardsheal, staunchest of Episcopalians, and herself of Highland family, the traditions of Appin are in safe keeping.

Somewhere on the shore near Ardsheal is *Clach Ruric,* or Ruric's Stone, which was sent crashing down the hillside by the natives upon a band of Norse invaders, killing their chief (hence the name) and several of his following.

You can return to Duror from Ardsheal by way of what is marked on the map as the " Back Settlement." Instead of retracing the track inland over the hillside, you keep round by the shore. Presently you gain the site where once stood Ardsheal Cottage, before its stones were removed and re-erected nearer Ardsheal. Leaving the enclosure by a gate beside an old barn—that to which I have already referred,—right ahead, you soon come across a built-up causeway of beautiful smooth grass, to the left of which, snuggled in the shelter of the low hill slope, are the foundations of two old cottages. To the lawn-like causeway succeeds a rough path which, with jagged rocks rising into a wall on one side, the sea on the other, and, ahead, the crests of the mountains, makes a striking picture. A few hundred yards further on, there is a raised beach, over which has grown the most seductive pasture land where, indeed, you would expect to see fairy cattle browsing instead of ordinary cows and sheep. This fertile plain is a fine smooth expanse, most ideally sheltered by the hills which rise on the left.

In the distance you see a substantially-built cottage, and it is not till you are right upon it that you find, although its slate roof is intact, it is deserted; and beyond it is a large barn, its roof all broken in, while around it are the remains of several rudely-built cottages. Such is what is left of the "Back Settlement," a small hamlet in one of the most perfect settings imaginable, looking over the blue waters of Loch Linnhe to the majestic hills of Morven. Naturally, one wants to know how came this clachan to be deserted, and the old tale is soon retold. After the lands of Appin had fallen into the hands of strangers, they were bought by the then Lord Tweeddale as a speculation, and he sold them, at an excellent profit, to another alien. This new proprietor, despite the fact that he had recently " come into money," was not content to forego any of the rent of his poorest tenants, as in the old days their impoverished chief had done. Far from it. Not only did this alien landlord demand the current rent, but the payment of all arrears, and, since the poor crofters were utterly unable to do this, they had to leave their homes, not only here in the " Back Settlement," but round about Cuil Bay also. Now these ruins remain as an eloquent testimony to the blessings of alien proprietors.

PART III

THE APPIN MURDER

I HAVE kept to the last for a consecutive narration any account of the murder which has, largely through the agency of *Kidnapped,* made the name of Appin famous to a public which knows nothing of its greater claims to distinction. James Stewart, known as *Seumas a' Ghlinne* (James of the Glens), is said to have been a natural brother of that chief of Ardsheal with whom the cave in Lag-na-ha is associated. James of the Glens had originally a farm in Glen Duror, and bore the highest of characters. He was a very charitable man, and had practically adopted the famous Allan Breac Stewart—a wild and wayward fellow.

Such was the partizan diplomacy of the Government that, after prohibiting any Highlander from holding office as factor of Highland estates, they placed as factor of the forfeited estates of Ardsheal, Callart, and Mamore, Colin Campbell of Glenure, known as the Red Fox, a member of that clan which was the hereditary and implacable foe of the Stewarts as of every other clan. Cunningly securing James to serve under him, the policy of Glenure was to turn out as many of the old tenants of the estate as he could, with the two-fold aim of diminishing the rental which they so faithfully paid a second time to their exiled chief, and to feather the nests of his own clansmen by letting them have the farms of the evicted.

In pursuit of this scheming, James of the Glens was evicted from Glenduror on the Whitsunday of 1751, in favour of Campbell of Ballieveolan, and removed to Acharn. Local tradition affirms that James of the Glens once, when inflamed with drink, was heard to say with reference to Glenure that "he would go three miles on his hands and knees to put an end to him"; and indeed one of the witnesses against him bore this evidence.   James also predicted that Glenure would be murdered, adding, " Whoever is the guilty one, I shall be the sufferer." Yet there appears to be evidence that James was on sufficiently good terms with Glenure to serve as his assistant, and it is on record that they met quite amicably on December 31, 1751, at John Breck Mac Combie's Change House at " Kintalline."

Pursuing the road from Glen Duror past Lag-na-ha, you very soon gain the distant view of the stately head of Kentallen Bay, and, as you pass the road on your left, which winds round the beautifully-wooded rocky point to Ardsheal, you will notice nearly opposite the little church a small whitewashed cottage, with a corrugated iron roof painted red.   This is said to be the old " Change House " of " Kentalline," to which reference will again be made.

It was on Thursday, May 14th, 1752, that the Red Fox, accompanied by his servant Mackenzie, Donald Kennedy, Sheriff's Officer of Inveraray, and Mungo Campbell, his nephew, left Fort William for the purpose of evicting tenants in Appin.   Though none of his party were armed, Glenure actually expected to be attacked on their way through Lochaber, and indeed it was only through a miscarriage of plans that he did escape the vengeance of the Camerons there.   Crossing the ferry at Ballachulish in safety, and taking the old road through Leiter More, Kennedy and Mungo Campbell went first, followed by Glenure, his servant riding last.

As you walk through Kentallen by the lovely shores of Loch Linnhe, not far beyond the station, you see distinctly on your right a grass-grown track which obviously repre- sents the old road.   Approaching from the other side, in our attempt to locate the site of the murder, we followed the track, but could see no sign whatever of the cairn that we knew marked the place.   Preferring to make an unaided discovery, we disdained enquiry, and after a lengthy search at last located the cairn, not on the very obvious track, but much higher up the hillside where there was no trace of any road ever having been, and at a very little distance above the Lorne Fever Hospital. Here, then, it was that Glenure was shot in the back by a man hiding behind a holly tree on the hillside, up which he escaped. The tree, with whose curious shape a photograph had made us familiar, we could not identify anywhere within reasonable range or sight of the cairn, and I can only think it has now disappeared. It was between five and six P.M. that Glenure was shot, exclaiming, "Oh, I am dead!" and, after a brave struggle to keep his seat, he fell from his horse, two bullets having entered near the spinal cord and come out in front. While Mackenzie went off to get help, the other two remained apprehensively by Glenure, fearful of a further attack, and when help came the body was borne across the bay in a boat to the Change House at Kentallen.

James of the Glens was sowing oats when he heard of the murder, and, though suspicion at once fell upon Allan Breac as the actual murderer, since his person could not be secured, James was arrested, without warrant,[7] as his accessory the next day, in order that some Stewart might be made to pay the price of a Campbell's life.

To give full details of the trial would only prove tedious to most people, but the outstanding facts of the way in which the judicial murder of James of the Glens was encompassed, are as follows. He was taken to Inveraray, the capital of the Campbell country, for his trial. Of his three judges, the Lord Justice General of Scotland was the Duke of Argyll, the Campbell chief; and Lord Kilkerran, a bitter Whig. The judges had the selection of the fifteen jurors, and Argyll so exerted his influence that of these eleven Campbells were chosen, and no Stewarts were included. James did not have fair treatment as

[7] Though the warrant was signed in Edinburgh on May 17th, it was characteristic of the "justice" meted out to James that it was never heard of till July 6th!

regards his defence, and totally inadequate time in which to prepare his case. Charged only with being accessory to Allan Breac, James of the Glens was found guilty by the packed jury, and on September 25th sentenced to death. In all judicial records it would be hard to beat the sublime effrontery of the cowardly exultation over a fallen and helpless adversary contained in the " judicial " statement of the chief partisan posing as a judge—a judge whose clan had itself always been ready to satiate itself " with the blood of any name or clan to which " it " had an aversion," as, indeed, the actual case in hand exemplifies. And as far as the dispensation of justice was concerned, it was certainly a " mock court of judicature " over which Argyll presided with his packed jury. The Duke of Argyll, addressing the prisoner in his statement after sentence, said:

" If you had been successful in that rebellion, you had been now triumphant with your confederates, trampling upon the laws of your country, the liberties of your fellow subjects, and on the Protestant religion. You might have been giving the law where you now have received the judgment of it; and we, who are this day your judges, might have been tried before one of your mock courts of judicature, and then you might have been satiated with the blood of any name or clan to which you had an aversion. . . . Though you do not now stand accused as a rebel . . . yet . . . this murder has been visibly the effect and consequence of the late rebellion."

Apparently what in a Jacobite was reprobated as revenge was perfectly lawful for a Campbell. Dozens of Macdonalds might be massacred in Glencoe, and those proved guilty of the crime not only allowed to go scot free, but the chief of the criminals promoted to " honour." But where one Campbell's life was concerned, an innocent man must suffer rather than no one, so that a loyal Campbell, who had the hanging of James Stewart flung in his face, could retort with pride that anybody could get a guilty man hanged, but that only *Mac Cailin* a man who was innocent!

On October 5th, James was transferred from Inveraray to Fort William, and on November 7th he was carried thence under a guard of one hundred men of Brockland's Regiment to *Cnap Chaolais Mhic Pharuig,* just past *Tigh a' Chnaip* (the house of the lump), as Ballachulish Hotel is called in the Gaelic.   There, where the inelegant monument erected in 1911 now stands to commemorate the site, James of the Glens, protesting his innocence, proclaiming his faith as an Episcopalian, and repeating aloud as he ascended the scaffold Psalm xxxv.,[8] was hanged on November 8th.   At 5 P.M. his body was suspended in chains from the gibbet, and there it hung for weeks, guarded by soldiers.   The Rector of Ballachulish told me that Isabel, the daughter of " Yellow John," as the then Stewart of Ballachulish was called, used to keep the birds of prey from the poor body.   In January, 1755, it fell, but was not allowed burial, a soldier being actually instructed to wire together the bones, that the skeleton might be replaced on the gibbet!   Not till later in that year did it disappear finally.   It is said that a half-witted character, *Mac a Phi a chuthaich* (MacPhee of the madness), or *Donnchadh - an - t - Seana Chinn* (Duncan, the old fashioned one), urged thereto by some men, cut down the skeleton, and cast the gibbet, some say the body too, into Loch Linnhe.   Down the water the gallows drifted as far as Bunawe, where it came ashore, and was afterwards incorporated in a bridge.   It is stated that the bones were secretly collected and buried by night amongst the Stewarts of Ardsheal [9] in Keil Churchyard, Duror.

No one ever questions the entire innocence of poor

---

[8] Now known throughout the Western Highlands as "*Salm Sheumais a' Ghlinne.*"

[9] Bishop Forbes, in his *Journal,* states that young Stewart of Ballachulish carefully gathered the bones and placed them in the same coffin as that in which rested the body of Mrs. Stewart.

James of the Glens; and Allan Breac, though believed to be an accomplice, is known not to have fired the fatal shot. The identity of the murderer is a well-preserved secret said to be known only to some members of the Stewart family, kept by them evidently for some motives of clan loyalty. It is said the murder was the result of a compact of six leading Stewarts to be rid of Glenure, and that lots were drawn to determine who should take the matter in hand. One man, at least, had to be bound by ropes by his family to prevent him proclaiming the truth from the scaffold on *Cnap Chaolais Mhic Pharuig*. James of the Glens was a noble and heroic man, who apparently was content to suffer unjustly to save a life which he thought of more value than his own. After many years, a young girl, *Seonaid Nic Aonghais* (Janet MacInnes), when tending cattle in Gleann a' Chaolais, behind Ballachulish House, found a gun in the hollow of a large elder tree. She shewed it to old Mr. Stewart of Ballachulish, who exclaimed after examining it: *" 'Se sin gunna dubh a mhi-fhortain, Sheonaid."* (That is the black gun of the misfortune, Janet.) The gun is known locally as *An-t-slinneanach* (of the shoulder-blade), and used to be kept as a relic at a house in Ballachulish.

The first house which you pass after leaving the pier is built on what was known as the Dragon's Rock, and the tale of the destruction of the dragon is so quaint that it may prove amusing. This dragon lived up in Corrie Lia, a hollow above Ballachulish pier, on Ben Gulbin, and, after the fashion of dragons, spent its days in devouring all it could seize until a day when " Charles the Skipper " came along. From his ship anchored out on Loch Linnhe, he constructed a bridge of barrels, duly spiked, and to tempt the dragon to seek prey in a fresh hunting ground, lit a fire on board, at which he roasted a piece of meat. The dragon fell into the trap, and was torn to pieces in the process of attempting to cross the spiked bridge, while the ship moved away from the last barrel. But it left behind a whelp, which had some progeny hidden in a corn stack at the foot of ·Ben Gulbin. In order to be rid of the· dangerous brood, the owner set the stack on fire, and the mother, unable to rescue her litter, lashed herself to death on the rock now known as the " Dragon's," at the foot of the mountain, thenceforth called Ben Vair—the " hill of the dragon."

A little further on the left is the entrance to Ballachulish House, anciently the seat of the Stewarts of that ilk, now fallen from its old dignity to serve as headquarters of some co-operative society. It is not, however, the original house where Duncanson was quartered and signed the ultimate order for the Massacre of Glencoe, but is the house rebuilt after burning in 1746. And this is the story of how the house came to be burnt.

A man of Ballachulish held a colonel's commission in the Hanoverian army, and became very friendly with one of his officers. This man, Captain Scott, was ordered to Ballachulish to terrorise the Jacobites by fire and destruction of their property. The Ballachulish colonel wrote to his sister Sheonaid, telling her that Captain Scott, a friend of his, was coming, and asked her to shew him some attention. Sheonaid, therefore, went to see him, but so homely was her appearance that Scott found difficulty in believing she was whom she represented herself to be. However, when he was satisfied with the truth of her assertion, he promised that, so long as she walked out with him, he would not burn any property. She consented to this bargain, and, setting out forthwith, they walked together as far as *Rudha na Lice* (point of the stone), where the line now crosses the road, and here they met Stewart of Ballachulish. Rashly he greeted her with offensive words: " Well, Sheonaid, are you Captain Scott's mistress to-day?" and Sheonaid replied, " That is a very unfortunate speech." She thereupon bade good-bye to Captain Scott, after asking him to spare Ardsheal House, old Appin House, and Fasnacloich, adding, " But do what you like

SUNSET ON LOCH LEVEN

27

with little Campbell of Ardnachlach." Captain Scott did
as he was requested, but burnt Ballachulish House because
its master had insulted Sheonaid.

Never could a house on fire light up the hills with such
a flame as did the sun in setting over Lochs Linnhe and
Leven one night I remember. I was standing opposite the
point Carnus on the Callart side when King Sol thrust in
his torch amongst the mountains of Morven. They,
instantly responsive, leaped into flames that surged
riotously all about them, and were reflected in quivering
anger on the serene waters of the loch. Here and there
tall pine trees, like dark, impassive giants, stood sentinel
by the shore, keeping a silent watch, undisturbed by any
breath of wind. Then the fire, having expended its fury,
sank into a glow, then died out, leaving the mountains
mantled in softest grey while I took farewell of Appin.

CHAPTER VII

THE HOME OF S. COLUMBA AND THE ISLAND OF STAFFA

"Far on the Pictish coast is seen a sea-girded islet,
Floating amidst the billows: Eo the name that it beareth.
There the saint of the Lord, Columba, rests in the body."
—WALAFRID STRABO.

___

PART I

IONA OF THE TOURIST

"Isle of the past and gone,
  The life from thee has departed;
Thy best is now but a carven stone
  And a memory lonely-hearted!"

MOST famous of all the misspelt names that errors of transcription have perpetuated is that of *I Chaluim Chille*—"the island of the dove of the Church," S. Columba. What is still known to the natives as *I* (*i.e.*, ancient *Hii*), the meaning of which is unknown, was originally written in S. Adamnan's great *Life* of the Saint, *Ioua Insula*. This, the original Pictish name, probably meaning "barley," and bestowed because of the island's notable yield of the then staple grain, was wrongly copied *Iona Insula*, and Iona the island has ever since remained.

Probably no place in Scotland has been more visited by tourists than this little island, three and a quarter miles long and a mile across the centre; yet there is no place of which the spirit has, increasingly of late years, evaded them more completely. Iona and S. Columba are as essentially inseparable in association as Robert the Bruce and Bannockburn; yet one is sensible of a very real divorce that has taken place, which has, in effect, almost succeeded in banishing S. Columba from his own island.

Of this most sad realization, every visitor to Iona, imbued with the true pilgrim spirit, must become acutely conscious. The divorce is doubtless attributable to the fact that, thanks to a late chief of Clan Campbell, the ecclesiastical remains of the island have been placed in the hands of those who are not the spiritual successors of S. Columba, and the consequent alienation and modernizing of the old buildings have dissipated that atmosphere which is proper to Iona and which was its most priceless possession. The only kinship which it is possible for the present trustees successfully to claim with Iona's past is that of a certain affinity with the Danes, who never landed on the island without destroying its buildings. For the trustees have laid violent hands on the remains of the old Abbey church, and, by means of extensive rebuilding operations, miscalled " restoration," have not only irretrievably ruined a once picturesque fabric, but have raised a monument to soullessness.

It is little wonder that the passengers of the *Grenadier* often indicate to one another the wholly modern " United Free " place of worship as the " Cathedral." True restoration, which, with a reverent regard for antiquity, seeks in a conservative spirit to preserve that which still remains, and so to secure continuity with the past, is one thing: a so-called " restoration," evidencing no veneration for the past and consequently no sense of continuity, which lacks alike all sense of art, good taste, and appreciation of the fitness of things, is quite another. It is both revolutionary and vulgar. Ruskin wrote on the subject of the then projected, and now unhappily accomplished, " restoration " of Dunblane ex-Cathedral: " Restorations are always either architects' jobs or ministers' vanities, and they are the worst sort of swindling and boasting." The famous art critic, who goes on to assert that if Dunblane Cathedral were restored it would be " the most vulgar brutality Scotland has committed since the Reformation," would have had something equally forcible to say with regard to the vandalism perpetrated on Iona.

Consider! Who, even in these days of commercial jobbery, would think of restoring, let us say, Leonardo da Vinci's fresco of the Last Supper by employing even the best artist in Europe to renew the faded portions; or the world's first sculptor to " restore " the lost arms of the Venus of Milo, assuming the statue originally had arms? Every decent instinct would cry out against such projected vandalism, and would declare in favour of being content with whatever time has spared of either work of genius, rather than that either masterpiece should be wholly ruined by some " restoration " attempted by modern peddlers of the arts. And architecture is not only one of the arts, but almost a lost art. Thus one can only regard with amaze the spectacle of any modern architect having the audacity to mix up in any mediæval fabric the clumsy, mechanical output of modern builders; and more, to superimpose it upon the beautiful workmanship of the old craftsmen, artists every one.

For any Catholicly-minded person, to the pain of viewing the art of antiquity as outraged on Iona, is added the far keener sorrow experienced in beholding therein obvious tokens of Protestant possession so utterly out of keeping in a shrine designed for Catholic worship.

It is doubtless to these visible signs of the change and to others of the commercialism that has come over Iona, that the apparent absence of tourists sharing in Dr. Johnson's emotion is due. They are rather influenced, however insensibly, by the commercial spirit which is everywhere in evidence, alike in the children offering for a few pence pieces of Iona marble rubbed smooth on some harder stone, and in the various neat little wooden booths where all sorts of wares associated with Iona may be had. And these nice little shops are thought suitable to find a place in the Street of the Dead!

. Indeed, the general lack of that pilgrim spirit, which, one would suppose, would animate all visitors to such a hallowed isle, is as remarkable as it is deplorable. Amongst the two hundred people who, on an average, used perfunctorily to rush round the prescribed route daily, during the one-and-a-half hour available, there predominated that air of boredom which marks the sufferance of a not very congenial task demanded by convention. Even of those who press closest to the official guide —quaintly termed " custodier "—only an occasional individual appears to show anything more than a languid interest in the antiquities—nothing approaching that aroused by the picture post-cards on sale at various points.

A few, however, may be found conscientiously " doing the sights " thoroughly, by themselves, with some guide book, every one of which informs them that Maclean's Cross, one of the latest on the island, of mediæval workmanship, is the oldest in Scotland—which can boast of hundreds far earlier! Other " facts " imparted by these blind leaders of the blind are equally reliable. If any of the tourists give a thought to S. Columba at all, they probably imagine the existing buildings are the remains of his monastery, whereas, according to the best authority, they are not even on its site. Possibly people pass the old shrine where his relics were kept: and probably they see within the Abbey Church itself his actual stone pillow; but this is the whole sum of associations likely to be Columban, as seen by the ordinary daily visitor. Those who follow, like a flock of sheep, in the wake of the custodier, or pore over a guide book, obtain no idea whatsoever of the real Iona. Not only is the tourist route through the " City of Iona "—the smallest in the world, for all it is called by the natives Balla More, the " great town "—so poor in Columban reminiscences, but it presents the least beautiful part of the island to visitors. Quite apart from its historical associations, Iona has a natural charm which few suspect—least of all from the steamer's approach to the island, which presents a flat, barren, and altogether uninteresting appearance. You may better appreciate this fact by a reference to the map, which shows how remote from the landing place, with the exception of Martyr's Bay, are the scenes to which you pass as, for the present, Iona of the tourist is left behind.

PART II

THE OTHER IONA

" O, lone green Isle of the West,
  So oft by the mist enshrouded,
I have seen thee to-day in thy quiet best—
  Not noisily mobbed and crowded:
Seen thee in flooding light,
  Seen thee in perfect calm;
Yet am I sad as at the sight
  Of mummy that men embalm."

MY friends and I set out for S. Columba's landing-place by the shore road, with eyes eager to note on the way the various points of interest we knew we should pass. Walking southward, we soon reached, just short of the Free place of worship, the little sandy inlet known as Port nam Mairtir, or Martyr's Bay. Some say the old Irish ecclesiastical word from which the name is derived is simply the equivalent for " martyr," and, since it was in use in 806, these people identify this bay as the site of the slaughter of the first martyrs of Iona, sixty-eight monks killed by the Danes. Others, however, state that the Irish word denoted the enshrined bones of a saint, and thus suggest that here probably the casket enshrining the relics of S. Columba embarked and disembarked on its various journeyings.

If this interpretation be true, there is some affinity between Martyr's Bay and its alternative but less familiar name of Port nam Marbh, the "bay of the dead." Here it was that the bodies of those brought for burial to Iona were landed, in keeping with the custom of having one specific landing-place for such a purpose upon burial islands. Just opposite the bay is a low grassy mound called *Eala* (probably derived from a word meaning bier), and upon this the bodies were laid before they were borne up the "Street of the Dead" for burial in *Reilig Odhran*. This *Straid nam Marbh* does not follow the course of the present street so named, but was a broad, paved way, which cut up slantwise through the field facing the bay. There used to be an old arch called *Dorus Tratha* (time door), through which it turned to the right, passing between the present nunnery and Cnoc Mor, and to the west of Maclean's Cross, whereas the present road goes round the other side of the cross.

The erratic course taken by the unconventional road we followed by the shore to S. Columba's Bay leads through very pleasant scenes. Varying in width at every few feet in its irregular boundaries, on the right are dotted at intervals the substantially-built cottages of the crofters. These that are not trimly thatched have slate roofs; all are neat and clean in their coats of whitewash, and there is every sign of great fertility in the flourishing fields of corn and hay round about them, enclosed by dry-stone dykes.

While Highland sheep and cattle are everywhere very numerous, what struck us as being the special feature of the island's young life was undoubtedly its energetic pigs. They are of a most athletic breed, and preserve slim and well-proportioned figures by long excursions over the island and extraordinary gymnastics on the sands. Indeed, one day when we were bathing in one of the many bays of whitest sand, of which Iona alone can boast, we were joined by one of the animals, who plunged with great zest into the waves.

Iona, though fairly level in parts, is a land of pleasant prospects, because of its wonderful fertility and rich verdure.   Turning inland, before we left the road at its end to make our way over the wild moorland to the haven of our desire, the general flatness, only relieved by slight elevations, finds its compensation in the charm of the flowers of the road side.   Indeed, in these ditches there is the garden of the island, where grow tall and luxuriously-flowering plants in great variety.   Beside the stately purple loosestrife, you will find the small but equally attractive centaury, with its starlike flowers of brilliant pink.   A curious characteristic of the surface of the whole island is the constantly recurring protrusions of rock which seem just to have managed to break through the earth and no more.   When we came to the cross-roads, we followed the short length to the right, and in a few minutes were climbing up on to the heathery undulations of the moorland, crags alternating with bogs.

There is no sort of track on this side over to S. Columba's Bay: it is simply a case of making for the south of the island and keeping as clear of bogs as possible until you come upon the high-flung beach of marble pebbles, pale green as they near the sea, which identifies the inlet as the famous landing-place.   On our way there, we struck the beautiful headland known as Dugal's Ridge —home of the blue rock pigeon—and then, in the next opening, the now abandoned quarries, which yielded a very handsome green variety of marble.

The " Bay of the Coracle " proper is the eastern half of the rugged haven, which is divided into two by a rocky islet.   Amongst the shingle at the water's edge may be found tiny pebbles of a translucent green stone, upon a reef of which, on the flat rock of the shore of the bay, tradition says Columba first set his foot when, at the age of forty-two, he landed here on Whitsun Eve, May 12th, 563.   While all natives of Iona are reputed to be immune from drowning, possession of one of these serpentine

PORT À' CHURAICH, IONA, FROM THE HILLS

pebbles is held to confer the same immunity upon anyone who wears the stone upon his person.

In the coracle of wicker-work, covered with ox-hide, came twelve companions with S. Columba, and it is said that, on the principle of burning their boats, this coracle was buried in the long, low, grassy mound just above the pebbles at the head of the bay. But when the mound was attacked by the spade several years ago, nothing was found, so that it yet remains for a proper excavation to determine whether it is not indeed a long barrow of prehistoric age.

The native who once sagely remarked to me, " There will be more things in Iona than anyone can be telling you ! " gave expression to a truth which we nowhere realized more vividly than in this quarter of the island, which abounds in antiquities which have never been adequately investigated. At the western end of the pebbly beach of Port a' Churaich, for instance, are many cairns of stones, popularly attributed by vivid Protestant imagination to the performance of monkish penances. More probably they are sepulchral, and may represent the graves of the inhabitants of the adjacent " bay of ruins."

But before we left Port a' Churaich, we searched out at its head *Garadh Eachainn Oig,* " the garden of young Hector," in which are numerous traces of small buildings. At one time Iona was numbered amongst the possessions of Clan Gillean,[1] the " servants of John," or the Macleans of Duart, who, first granted rights there by the Lords of the Isles in return for their fealty, subsequently took the island from the Bishops of the Isles. As befitted a clan renowned for its loyalty to the Stewarts, Macleans fought nobly for the Prince at Culloden, and many an Iona man was numbered with them. It is thus possible that this " garden of young Hector " is associated with that Maclean who fled to Iona after the fatal fight, and, warned by one MacInnes that the red-coats were after him, was taken

---

[1] This name has been rendered variously, but now the broad division is that clansmen attached to the Duart branch spell themselves Maclean, while those of Lochbuie prefer Maclaine.

by MacInnes to a cave where they both hid till escape was possible. This cave, MacInnes afterwards stated, would take the whole of the islanders, but he would never reveal its locality, and to this day it is unknown.

Above Port Laraichean, the " bay of ruins," we came into a beautiful grassy expanse, shut in on all sides except to seaward by high rocks, and we were able to trace the foundations of some six or seven circular stone huts and a larger one of square construction that is built against a rock. These are the oldest remains on the island, but whether they represent the settlement of some other religious after S. Columba's day, or were in existence when he landed, has never been determined. That the island was uninhabited when he landed is probable, for the records, which state that he was met by two bishops already settled there, who demanded his submission, and that he refused because it was revealed to him they were druids in disguise, are too late to be credible. The name sometimes given to Iona of " Island of the Druids " is a misinterpretation due to a mis-spelling of the old name *Innis nan Druineach,* which means " island of cunning workmen," possibly with reference to the Iona school of craftsmen of sculptured stones, or to the embroideresses of Iona.

As you face the sea, on the right of Port a' Churaich is Druim an Aoinidh, and a short climb brought us to Carn Cuil ri Eirinn, or the Cairn of the Back turned to Ireland. The legend of S. Columba having previously landed on Oronsay and leaving it because the land of his birth and of his heart was visible from its shores, is well known. There, too, on an eminence behind the Priory ruins, is a Carn Cuil ri Eirinn, and if there is not a cairn, there is the same legend with regard to Cove, Knapdale, where is a cave associated with the saint. Tradition says that this cairn upon the Ionan height marks the spot whence S. Columba sought for Ireland and was satisfied that his native land was at last out of sight. It goes hard with one

who venerates ancient tradition to be obliged to admit that
it seems an indisputable fact that on some clear days
Ireland may be seen from Iona.

There is an ancient Celtic poem, inscribed " *Columkille
fecit,*" which wonderfully describes the outlook from Carn
Cuil ri Eirinn:

> " Delightful would it be to me to be in Uchd Ailiun,
> On the pinnacle of a rock,
> That I might often see
> The face of the ocean;
> That I might see its heaving waves
> Over the wide ocean.

> " When they chant music to their Father
> Upon the world's course;
> That I might see its level sparkling strand,
> It would be no cause for sorrow;
> That I might hear the song of the wonderful birds,
> Source of happiness;
> That I might hear the thunder of the crowding waves
> Upon the rocks.
>   .   . .   .
> " That my mystical name might be, I say,
> ' Cul ri Eirinu.' "

The outlook over the sea from the rugged hill-top can,
despite the lapse of so many centuries, differ little from
the scene which met the gaze of S. Columba. On a typical
summer day there is outspread before you, beyond the
rocky indentation of the coast-line, the emerald depths of
the sea—its intense green due to the whiteness of the sand
beneath. Many a rock and islet—home of the cormorant
and diving gannet—break its surface, and well out to sea,
on the largest, Soa, probably the seal farm of the
monastery, you may, if your sight is good enough, perhaps
make out some of these fascinating creatures basking in
the sun. Highlanders say that seals are the children of
the King of Lochlann [2] under spells, and that their eyes
tell they are of royal blood. Much nearer to the shore is
Eilean na h-Aon Chaorach, so called because it offers
" pasture " only sufficient for " one sheep."

[2] Scandinavia, the mystical wonderland beyond the seas.

The back is always regretfully turned on this most fascinating part of the island, and on the shaggy cattle which enhance its charm as they browse peacefully on the hills and in their hollows. To be caught in a sea mist here is a very curious experience. You stand surrounded by a perfectly clear expanse of atmosphere, but you notice, steadily advancing towards you from the sea, a sheet of gauze-like mist. It is fascinating to watch its inroad, so carefully planned does it seem, and so deliberate. For a while all immediately about you remains quite clear while gradually the distance is blotted out, and then the mist, stealing inland, obliterates everything it touches, until you yourself are swallowed up in a very ocean of white vapour. And then you are wise to wait until it disperses or you run the risk of many an obvious accident.

Turning round and looking inland, you see nothing but an expanse of heathery uplands, for, excepting near the crofts, there are no trees on the island, nor have there been except in remote pre-historic ages, as shewn by the huge trunks found in the peat bogs of the Lochan Mor.

Making our way back northwards, we followed, when we could find it, the track which does exist on the west side of the island roughly from Port a' Churaich to the Machar, or Plain of Iona. We knew to keep well clear of the very unclean waters of Loch Staonaig (of the slope), more marsh than loch, and the centre of the common grazing land where in the summer the people used to take out their cattle.

Arrived on the verge of the sandy slopes of the uplands, we sat down for a space before descending on to the beautiful silver shore of the Machar Bay.

> " O'er tangled and shell-paved rocks
>   The white sea-gulls are flying;
> And in the sunny coves brown flocks
>   Of wistful seals are lying;
> The waves are breaking low,
>   Hardly their foam you trace;
> All hushed and still, as if they know
>   This is a sacred place."

You may see, too the black and white little birds of S. Bride, the oyster-catchers with their scarlet beaks and orange legs, running over the sands: a dignified heron patiently standing at the water's edge; and a brood of eider ducks sailing out in this " bay of the ocean nook," *Camus-Cuil an-t-Saimh.* It was this shore that was probably the scene of the coming of the crane from Ireland, as told by Adamnan. S. Columba prophesied that this bird would be driven to land by adverse winds, and one of the brethren was sent to await its arrival and to minister to it. Everything happened exactly as the saint had foretold, and the bird, after three days' rest, made again for Ireland. When we descended to the shore, we were fortunate in seeing in action *Uamh an-t-Seididh,* the " Cave of the Puffing," more generally called the " Spouting Cave." This is no very great distance along *Ceann nan Creigh,* the stretch of rocks that bounds the bay on the left as you face the sea. Under certain conditions of wind and tide when the cave is flooded, the water is forced up like the jet of a fountain through a hole on the roof.

The beautiful level plain of the western side of the island was the scene of the labours of the working brothers of the monastery, and here S. Columba took his last farewell of them.

From the Machar we struck the only road that cuts across the island, extending from east to west, if not literally from shore to shore. Soon we reached, on our right, a large, low grassy mound, now generally known as the Sithean Mor, or the Great Fairy Hill. Here apparently took place the celebrations with which the Feast of " gentle Michael of the snow-white steed " was honoured throughout the Western Islands, the blessing of horses being their special feature. But it has a far more beautiful association as *Cnoc Angel,* or the hill of the angels, for here " citizens of the Heavenly Country clad in white garments, flying to him with wonderful swiftness," held

tryst with S. Columba one day as he prayed.   A cunning
prying monk followed after the saint as he went to the
western part of the island, after having enjoined that none
should follow him.   This monk saw the angels and heard
their converse, but, when afterwards taken to task by the
saint, he expressed his contrition for his act of disobedience,
and kept silence regarding both what he had heard and
seen until after S. Columba's death.

When, completing our circuit, we gained the cross-roads
once more, we turned to the left and took our way along
the modern course taken by the " Street of the Dead,"
past the mediæval buildings, until we came to *Traigh Bhan
nam Manach*.   These " sands of the monks," almost as
white and quite as fine as the driven snow, are near the
north end of the sound, and look over to the low flat hill
terraces of Mull.   Even on a dull day, the sea never wholly
loses its emerald hue:

> " The sweet-sounding plash of thy light rippling billows,
>   As they beat on the sand where the white pebbles lie,
> And their shuddering roar when with wheeling commotion
>   They lift their white crests in grim face of the sky."

Do not these last lines suggest a mood of nature in keeping
with the massacre of an abbat and fifteen religious by
Danes from Limerick, of which this bay is the traditional
site?   The martyrdom took place on the Christmas Eve
of 986, and it was on the black rock, known as *Sgeir nam
Mart,* the northern boundary of these sands, that the monks
are said to have been slaughtered.

Before we returned to Balla More, we climbed Dun-I,
that we might finish our day as we had begun it, following
in the footsteps of S. Columba.   This probably is the hill
on which, as Adamnan relates, he used sometimes to be
seated, and the outlook on a calm serene day of summer

is not without its inspiration. And as regards memories
of the Iona of Columba,

"No fitter day than this
    To look at thy mystic beauty,
And brood on memories of the bliss
    Of faith and love and duty,
Of the homes of quiet prayer,
    Of the days of patient toil,
Of the love that always and everywhere
    Burned like a holy oil."

PART III

S. COLUMBA AND HIS IONA

"Lone green Isle of the West,
    Where the monks, their coracle steering,
Could see no more, o'er the wave's white crest,
    Their own loved home in Erin;
Shrouded often in mist,
    And buried in cloud and rain,
Yet once by the light of a glory kissed,
    Which nothing can dim again!"

BEFORE I attempt to give a portrait of S. Columba, or to
indicate what is believed to be the site of the first monastery
and to re-create its plan, it will be well once more to knock
on the head a hydra-headed myth. It is a historical
anachronism to identify either S. Columba or his immediate
followers with the Culdees, who, by the way, were by no
means peculiar to Scotland. The one certain fact about
these severely ascetic, non-literary, non-missionary
"Servants of God" is that they were never heard of
before the eighth century, and do not appear in Iona before
the twelfth. They almost equally certainly had little if
anything in common with S. Columba and his religious.

Now comes the question, "What sort of man was the
Abbat, and what was he like?" In answering this, as
indeed every other question about him, there is only what
is to be gleaned from S. Adamnan's *Life* of the Saint—

a book which every intelligent visitor to Iona should take there with him. The Abbat must clearly have been a strong and vigorous man in view of the physical achievements of his many voyagings. We know he had a singularly clear and penetrating voice of great beauty, and large luminous eyes. He was a true Celt, intensely human, easily moved to tears, full of generous emotions, lovable, sympathetic, and tender equally with man and beast; having also the Celt's hot temper—readily roused, in S. Columba's case, by injustice or wrongs done to others. He had great wisdom, and the humility which goes with true greatness, and was richly endowed with intellectual as well as spiritual gifts, including prophetic vision: he was a skilled scribe and a true poet. In short, S. Columba was a forceful and persuasive personality.

The habits worn by himself and the brethren were of a coarse woollen texture of natural colour, having a hood, and in wet weather a cloak or *amphibalus*. Underneath they wore white tunics, and were shod with sandals. Of the peculiar form of the tonsure, which, together with the method of computing Easter, was the outstanding distinction between Celtic use and that of the rest of western Christendom, there has been much discussion. But Dr. Dowden, the late learned Bishop of Edinburgh, has proved beyond dispute that it was of a form which can be best visualized by supposing just that portion of the head to be shaven which would be covered by a strip of material widening from one inch gradually to two inches in the centre and then gradually decreasing again to one inch, passed over the top of the head from ear to ear.

Having now some idea of the appearance of the figures which wended their way over from Port a' Churaich to the plain by the Sound, there is next to be identified the site they chose for the building of their monastery, the island having been gifted to S. Columba by his kinsman, Conall, King of Dalriada. I hope the accompanying sketch map and picture of the monastery, as constructed from all

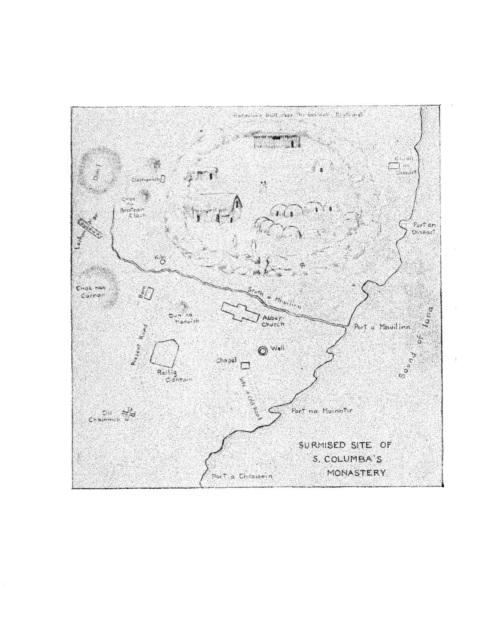

SURMISED SITE OF
S. COLUMBA'S
MONASTERY

details available, will reduce other description to a minimum. Dr. Skene, the supreme authority, considers the monastery to have been situated a quarter of a mile north of the present mediæval ruins, as indicated by the sketch map. The monastery buildings were all built of wood brought over from Mull, and probably thatched with reeds, the whole being surrounded by a *vallum* or rampart of stone and earth, part of which may be identified to-day. The space thus enclosed had on the higher part of the sloping ground, between the monastery buildings and the Abbat's cell, the church of oak, with a small side chamber attached: on the second side there was the wattled guest chamber: on the third, the refectory of considerable size in which, beside the boulder called Blathnat, to be seen to this day, there was a fireplace and vessel of water, and on the fourth, the cells of the monks with their own little courtyard. Within these cells the brethren slept on straw, S. Columba himself having his bed on the bare ground, with a stone for his pillow, in his own hut of planks. This was at some little distance from the others, on the highest part of the ground, and here the Abbat worked in the day, two attendants being at his door.

If you strike out over the wild north-west quarter of the island, called *Sliabh Meanach,* you may come across *Cnoc nam Bràthan,* or the Hill of the Querns—a height having a precipitous face on the west. Not very far off is *Cobhan Cuildeach,* which probably means, *not* the Culdee's Cell, but the " secluded hollow," with reference to the ground, not the cell, of which the circular foundations are still traceable. It is highly probable that this is one of the places to which S. Columba, dispensing with his usual attendant, withdrew himself for times of solitary silent prayer. Adamnan has a description of a place amongst the bushes, perhaps of heather, remote from men, where the Abbat one day, going to pray, saw hosts of demons fighting with darts in the sky over Iona, which exactly suits this place. For it overlooks the sea towards Tiree, and it was in the direction of Tiree that the Abbat saw what was probably the thunder storm dispersed.

Without the *vallum* of the monastery were the granary or barn, the cowhouse, the kiln, and, presumably, a mill. The harbour of the monastery was evidently Port na Muintir, the " port of the community " or family of monks. The religious were divided into seniors, working brothers, and juniors under instruction; and all took the monastic vows of poverty, chastity, and obedience, saluting with prostration their Abbat, who had generally an attendant. They were strict in their observance of the fasts of the Church, keeping every Wednesday as the weekly memorial of the Betrayal, as well as Friday of the Crucifixion, besides Lent, though this rule of fasting was relaxed in honour of visitors. The usual fare of the monks was barley-bread, milk, fish, and eggs, and only rarely did they eat meat. The introduction to an old poem, the *Amra Columcille* states that S. Columba latterly subsisted on nettle pottage without dripping, in consequence of which the marks of his ribs through his tunic could be seen on the sand of the bay where he used to lie at night. This evidently has reference to the saint sleeping out, presumably in summer, on the shores of the little bay, Port an Diseart. Sundays and other festivals were marked by the celebration of the Holy Eucharist, two priests generally ministering jointly at the Altar—a peculiarity of the Celtic rite known as con-celebration. When, however, a bishop was present, though he might be under the jurisdiction of the Abbat, even if the Abbat were but a simple priest like S. Columba, the bishop's higher ministerial order was emphasized by the fact that not only was ordination, in consonance with unbroken Catholic custom, restricted to him, but he celebrated the Eucharist alone. The position of the Celtic bishops was tribal rather than diocesan, for they served in communities, and, unless themselves Abbats, were lacking in that jurisdiction which was exercised by the heads of religious.

The Celtic episcopal position is exactly illustrated by the many modern instances of bishops who are members of Cathedral chapters, in which capacity they are under the jurisdiction of the Dean, even though he be but a priest. If it is remembered that offices in, and orders of, the ministry are distinct things, and that many offices may be held indifferently by either bishop or priest, much confusion of thought will be avoided.

Though the services of the Church on Iona followed the Celtic Use, they were all in Latin. The Canonical hours were observed daily, a bell, probably of the high quadrangular hand type, of which several specimens are still extant, summoning the brethren to worship. They sang the offices vested in white; Sacramental Confession with Absolution and Penance were practised; and the Sign of the Cross was in frequent use. There is no trace whatever of any knowledge, much less any recognition, of even such modest papal claims as were made at this date when, what are now the distinctive doctrines of Rome, had not come into being. While worship was naturally the predominant feature of the life of the community, it did not absorb the whole time of the monks. Iona, besides being renowned for its transcriptions and also for missionary zeal, provided medicines for the body as well as for the soul. The monks, too, were skilled farmers, tilling the land, and keeping not only cattle and sheep but seals. They built boats of different kinds, worked both in wood and metal, and fished in the Sound, still famous for its flounders. Indeed, the folk-lore of Iona attributes to S. Columba himself the wry mouth of that fish.

The tale goes that Columkille met a shoal of flounders one day, and quaintly asked one of them, " Is this a removal, flounder?" "Yes, it is, Columkille, crooked legs," answered the rude fish. " If I have crooked legs," replied the saint, " may you have a crooked mouth," and thus the fish came by this wry feature.

No picture of the true Iona would be complete without

some mention of the first royal hallowing in Great Britain and an account of the last days and death of S. Columba, as so exquisitely related by Adamnan, the ninth Abbat. On the death of his patron, King Conall, S. Columba, instructed in a vision, summóned Aidan, the late King's cousin, to Iona, and there ordained him King by laying on of hands with prayer and benediction.   With regard, however, to the famous Stone of Destiny, now enshrined in the Coronation Chair of Westminster Abbey, Dr. Skene's investigations have proved that not only was it never on Iona, but that it was never anywhere but at Scone.

It was on one day in May that the aged Apostle of Scotland, being desirous of blessing once more the working brothers as they toiled on the Machar, was borne thither in a waggon.   He spoke with the brethren, blessed the island and the islanders, and prophesied that no poison of vipers should have power to harm any of its inhabitants, whether man or beast, so long as the Commandments of Christ were observed.   A few days afterwards, during the Celebration of the Sacred Mysteries, S. Columba had a vision of angels, which brought him great joy, because from them he learned of his early translation, and on the last day of the same week, he, with his faithful attendant Diormit, went forth for the last time.   After blessing the corn in the granary, he foretold his gathering into the world of spirit that same night, and then began his return to the monastery.   Half way back he sat down to rest, and there came up to him his faithful servant, the white horse, which was wont to carry the milk pails.   Laying its head against the saint's breast, the horse began to whinny and to shed tears.   Diormit was for driving the horse away, but S. Columba forbade him, and when of its own accord the faithful creature left him sadly, the Abbat blessed it.[3]

---

[3] In 1906, when a piece of earth-work behind the house Clachanach was being cleared away to permit of a building addition, a skeleton of a small horse, which may have been that of the Abbat's friend, was found firmly embedded six feet deep in the embankment.

Then, resuming the road, S. Columba ascended " the knoll that overlooks the monastery." [4]   With both hands raised, he blessed the home of his community, prophesying:

" Upon this place, small though it be, and mean, not only the kings of the Scotic people, with their peoples, but also the rulers of barbarous and foreign races, with the people subject to them, shall confer great and no common honour: by the Saints also even of other Churches shall no common reverence be accorded to it."

Descending the knoll, he returned to his cell to continue the transcription of the Psalter on which he was engaged. When he came to verse 11 of Psalm xxxiii. in the Vulgate, " But they that seek the Lord shall not want any good thing," he stopped and went over to the church for Vespers. This finished, he returned to his cell, and, sitting up on his bed, gave his last commands by Diormit, enjoining mutual charity amongst the brethren, and promising them the aid of his intercession after he was parted from them in the body.   Then he was silent until the bell rang at midnight for Lauds, when he rose hastily and ran before all others into the church, where he fell upon his knees before the altar.   Diormit, following, saw the whole church suffused with an angelic light, and, groping his way towards the saint, he raised S. Columba's head upon his breast and there tenderly held him.

Meanwhile the brethren had come in with lights, and assembled round their dying father, whose face showed the joy he experienced in the vision of the angels come to bear away his soul.   With an apparent attempt to bless the monks, his children, with the Sign of the Cross, the saint went the way of his fathers, the brethren weeping and bewailing his passing, which took place about midnight, between Saturday and Sunday, June 8th and 9th, 597. But they finished Lauds before they bore the sacred body

----

[4] Probably *Cnoc nam Bristeadh Clach*, a small height behind Clachanach, is Torr Abb.   Dr. Skene has conjectured Dun I, but surely for so old and evidently so infirm a man, this would have been too high a climb.

with singing back to his own cell, where for three days
and nights it lay before burial. Then his " honourable
obsequies " " being ended with sweet praises of God, the
venerable body of our holy and blessed patron, wrapped
in a fair shroud and placed in the tomb prepared for it,
is buried with due reverence, to rise again in resplendent
and eternal brightness."

Unfortunately, the biographer gives no indication where
S. Columba was buried, and the question has given rise to
much speculation. After a careful review of all that has
been written on the subject, it seems most probable that
the monks laid the body of their founder to rest in the old
burial ground of *Cladh an Diseart,* (the " burial-ground
of the hermitage "). Here are two pillar stones, 5 feet
high and 3 feet apart, which Dr. Skene, following
Mr. Drummond, thinks mark the original grave, especially
as at the same place was found the stone, 1 foot 7 inches
long, sculptured with an Irish cross, which is identified with
S. Columba's pillow, recorded by Adamnan as having been
placed upon his grave, and now preserved in the Abbey
Church.

It was probably early in the ninth century that
S. Columba's grave was opened in order that his remains,
as the monastery's most precious possession, might be
gathered and placed in a portable shrine, to be carried
into safety whenever the island was threatened by
sacrilegious invaders. Still, however, S. Columba's dust
is mingled with the soil of Iona, and wherever his bones
ultimately found a resting place after their varied
journeyings, Iona for ever remains the place of his burial.

That his relics, or *marta,* were constantly taken to and
from Ireland is certain. They were first borne there early
in the ninth century, brought back about 818 by Abbat
Dermid, again taken there in 878 to escape Norse invaders,
and brought back about the close of the century—exactly
when is not known. But in 976, the shrine was robbed
by one Donald Mac Murcadha; in 1090 the reliquary was

in Ireland again, and was last heard of at Downpatrick. Kenneth MacAlpine obtained a portion of the relics for the consecration of the church dedicated to S. Columba at Dunkeld about 850; and here, as late as 1500, some of the saint's relics were preserved. What is called " S. Columba's Tomb," a little oratory on the north side of the Abbey Church door, Dr. Skene conjectured was the place where the shrine containing the *marta* of S. Columba was jointly deposited with that of his *minna* —eighteen personal relics, including his cross, *cathach* or " battler " [5] Psalter, cowl or *culebach*, and white tunic. This authority points out how easily both could be hidden by a covering of turf, as related by Walafrid Strabo, to protect them from the depredation of the Danes. Dr. Skene further points out a fact which is not without significance in connecting *Cladh an Diseart* with this " tomb "—that whereas another name for the original burial-place is Cladh Iain, the remains of S. John's Cross are found by the " tomb."

If from Iona of the tourist S. Columba has been banished, his memory is still enshrined alike in the Church and in the folk-lore of the Highlands. For Episcopalians and Roman Catholics alike still observe June 9th as his day, and Thursday is one of the days of the week when the baleful fairies are powerless to work ill, for Thursday is S. Columba's day. There is a Gaelic proverb that says, " When Thursday is dear Columba's day (June 9th), the warp should be prepared and sheep sent to pasture." The pigeon or dove is his bird: S. John's Wort, which is said to break into bloom first on June 9th, is his flower. In the Gaelic it is known as *Achlasan Chaluim Chille,* " the armpit flower of S. Columba." It was said to have been

[5] Relics of saints were often carried as *vexilla,* or standards, to ensure victory in battle, hence the Celtic name of " battlers," of which the chief was S. Columba's psalter. It was borne in battle so late as 1497, and his pastoral staff was similarly used in the tenth century. In consequence, it was known as *"Cath Bhuaidh,"* or battle victory.

given by the saint to a child herding cattle, to place under his armpit as a protection against the perils of the night. Now when the herdsman comes across it, he picks it as a charm, saying, " Unsearched for and unsought, for luck of sheep I pluck thee."

There is also a beautiful legend of S. Columba and a robin, which came and perched beside him one day as he sat in his cell. Looking up with a smile on his face, the Abbat asked : " Hast thou a song upon thee, O red breast?" The robin answered with a song so thrilling that it brought tears to the eyes of Columba, for it was of the Passion of the Redeemer that the little bird sang, and how he himself had come by his ruddy breast. This is his song as a modern mystic has rendered it:

" Holy, Holy, Holy,
   Christ upon the Cross;
My little nest was near,
   Hidden in the moss.

" Holy, Holy, Holy;
   Christ was pale and wan;
His eyes beheld me singing,
   Bron, bron, mo bron! [6]

" Holy, Holy, Holy,
   ' Come near, O wee brown bird!'
Christ spake: and lo, I lighted
   Upon the Living Word.

" Holy, Holy, Holy,
   I heard the mocking scorn!
But *Holy, Holy, Holy,*
   I sang against a thorn!

" Holy, Holy, Holy,
   Ah, His brow was bloody:
Holy, Holy, Holy,
   All my breast was ruddy.

" Holy, Holy, Holy,
   ' Christ's Bird shalt thou be!'
Thus said Mary Virgin
   There on Calvary.

[6] " O grief, grief, my grief!"

" Holy, Holy, Holy,
    A wee brown bird am I;
    But my breast is ruddy
    For I saw Christ die.

" Holy, Holy, Holy,
    By this ruddy feather,
    Colum, call thy monks and
    All the birds together."

The Abbat did as the redbreast asked him. He summoned first all the monks and then all the birds, that together they might worship. In answer to his call, there came to him all the feathered creation of land, sea, and sky—the birds of ocean, gulls, and ducks, the great eagle from the mountain heights, the tiny wren from its lowly bush, and his own dove from the woods. Columba, having put peace upon them all, celebrated the Holy Mysteries, and in perfect stillness the birds waited until the service was ended, when the Abbat let them depart with his blessing. The robin, however, lingered long after the others that he might sing once again his song of the thorn-crowned Christ; and to this day it is said upon Iona that the redbreast still sings, " Peace, peace, peace! In the Name of Christ, peace!"

For the traditional Churchman, all the joy, the beauty, and the glory of Iona are summed up and consummated within the rough-hewn granite walls of the tiny Sanctuary of S. Columba in the House of Retreat on Iona. Here is enshrined the soul of the island, for here in the continuity of the possession of his faith, and in the same sacramental worship so dear to Columba, his spirit pervades the atmosphere. And in outward token of the place where the spirit of S. Columba may still be found, a sculptured figure of the Abbat, pastoral staff in his left hand, his right raised in blessing, looks out over the Sound.

' Thou,' Columkille, the friendly, the kind.
In the Name of the Father, the Son, and the Spirit Holy,
Through the Three-in-One, through the Three,
Encompass us, guard our procession,
Encompass us, guard our procession."

PART IV

POST COLUMBAN IONA

AFTER the death of S. Columba, the community which he founded, inspired by his spirit, carried on his work, and, having converted Scotland, contributed in no small measure to the Christianising of England. Oswald, the heir to the Northumbrian throne, had come as an exile to Iona, and probably there, in the days when Seghine was Abbat (623-652), he and his brother Oswy were baptised. When Oswald came to the throne, he sent to Iona for a bishop. First there was sent to him a stern and severe man, who was so unsuccessful in his mission that he returned to Iona to report his failure. At a council of the monks held to consider the matter, one Aidan, addressing the monk who had failed, suggested to him the reasons for his non-success. So full of wisdom were his words, that the council forthwith agreed that Aidan himself was the missioner most suitable for Northumbria, and, having him consecrated bishop, sent him forth, to be followed on his death by two other Iona monks, Finan and Colman.

Adamnan, the biographer of S. Columba, was the ninth Abbat of Iona, by far the most famous after the founder himself. It was during Adamnan's rule that the monastery, probably the original one, was repaired with wood; and he himself abandoned the Celtic tonsure in favour of the Roman. But although he also became converted to the Catholic Easter, no change was made in this respect on Iona till 716, nor was it till 718 that the community of Iona adopted the Roman tonsure.

In 815, the primacy of the Coarbship of the Columban Order passed from Iona to Kells in Ireland, consequent upon the ravages of the savage and brutal Danes, to which Iona was subjected for over two hundred years. In 795, and again in 798, the island was sacked, though the monks escaped; and in 802, the monastery, probably the original one of S. Columba, was burned to the ground by the same marauders. In 806, the first recorded martyrdom took place on Iona, probably at Martyr's Bay, as already mentioned, and it is likely that the sixty-eight who then suffered represented the entire community of the island.

The monastery was probably resettled from Ireland, for on January 19th, in 825, S. Blathmac and his companions were slaughtered. S. Columba's relics were on Iona at the time, reposing in sanctuary near the altar, and when the approach of invading galleys was discovered, the monks made haste to conceal their greatest treasure. They took the reliquary and hid it in a hollowed tumulus, covering it with thick sod, and Dr. Skene identifies the little oratory now called " S. Columba's tomb " as the site of the hiding. Blathmac was seemingly acting as Superior during the Abbat's absence in Ireland; and was celebrating the Holy Mysteries at the altar of the monastery when the pirates rushed in upon the community, slew the worshipping monks, and demanded the shrine from Blathmac. He refused to yield it up to them, and they thereupon felled him to the ground as he commended his soul to God. S. Blathmac's shrine possibly shared subsequently with that of the founder, " S. Columba's Tomb.'"

In 986 took place the last invasion of the Danes, when *Traigh bhan nam Manach* was the scene of the martyrdom, and apparently then the second monastery was overthrown. It is thought that the monks who escaped on this occasion secured themselves in the round tower, the foundations of which, once called a well, can still be seen outside the door of the Abbey Church. These isolated round towers, rising from 50 to 125 feet, were a distinctive feature of Celtic monasteries, and while many still exist in Ireland, in Scotland there are also two of the same type at Abernethy and Brechin. They were built for the protection of the monks and their treasure in the event of assaults, being only gained by a door high up and reached by a removable ladder.

In 987 the tables were turned upon the invaders, for " by a miracle of God and Columcille," through the agency of the Christian Earl of Orkney, Sigurd, 360 of the plunderers were slain. This was the last heathen raid on Iona.

The wooden monastery that had been burnt down by the Danes was replaced in 818 by one of stone, probably on the site where the present ruins stand; and about the same time Constantine, King of the Picts, nobly built the monks another at Dunkeld. From remains that have been excavated in the present monastic area this later Celtic monastery of Iona still shows traces of several buildings, identified by an orientation different from that of the latest ruins. These seeming remains of an earlier monastery comprise: (1) A small oblong gabled church, 33 feet by 16 feet, standing north of the Abbey Church enclosure: (2) A second building of the same orientation near it, but double in size, probably the refectory: (3) the tiny oratory by the Abbey Church door, now called " S. Columba's Tomb ": (4) a round foundation, 6 feet thick, where now stands a stone coping, representing the base of the round tower: and (5) several beautifully carved stone crosses, only one of which now remains entire. There are also of the same orientation as the first two buildings the remains of a square foundation in front of the Abbey Church, called the Abbat's or Columba's House; also, south of the church, the two ruinous walls of what was S. Mary's Chapel; as well as traces of cells on the west side of the wall enclosing the present cloisters. In order of age, " S. Columba's Tomb " dates from about the ninth century, the round tower must be at least a century older, and the other buildings later still, while the high crosses were probably carved and set up in the tenth century.

It was in 1074 that S. Margaret, Queen of Scotland, restored the monastery; in 1099 the last of the old order of Abbats died, and in 1154 the bishopric of Man and the Isles, to which Iona belonged, passed from the metropolitan supervision of York to that of Trondhjem, consequent upon the Norse possession of the Isles. But in 1156 Somerled, first Lord of the Isles, placed Iona under the Abbat of Derry. In the fourteenth and fifteenth centuries Iona was in the diocese of Dunkeld, but in 1506 it passed back to the bishopric of the Isles, and from that date till the religious revolution overthrew the old order, the Abbey Church was the cathedral of that diocese.

In 1266 the Western Isles passed from Norse dominion into that of Scotland, when Angus Mor was Lord of the Isles, and from 1567 onward the Abbey remained in the possession of the Bishops of the Isles; and *Tigh an Easbuig,* the " bishop's house," another isolated and very fragmentary ruin, north alike of the Abbey ruins and of the millstream, was probably their place of abode. On the death of Bishop Thomas Knox in 1626, however, the Macleans of Duart seized the island, probably on the strength of the footing they had previously obtained in 1390, when, in consideration of their attachment to Donald of the Isles, he granted Lachlan Maclean some land and the right to a certain tribute from Iona. But Charles I., always abhorrent of the alienation of Church property, in 1635, with characteristic piety, ordered the restoration of the island " in absolute possession " to the then Bishop. When, in 1651, the religious revolutionaries passed an Act for the demolition of all monasteries to inaugurate a " reformation," the Marquis of Argyll and the Earl of Glencairn were charged with the conduct of affairs on Iona, and accomplished the wholesale destruction of buildings. The island suffered its final declension when in 1688 it passed into the hands of the family of Argyll.

PART V

SCOTLAND'S MOST FAMOUS BURIAL-GROUND

ONE cannot but regret that the historic square burying-ground of *Reilig Odhran,* with its 1,300 years old burial roll, should continue to be in use as Iona's only cemetery [7] in view of the modern monuments which, to write mildly, are so utterly out of keeping with the old grave stones.

Dr. Reeves seems to accept *Reilig Odhran* without question as the burial-place of S. Columba. But Dr. Skene has pointed out that it could not originally have been called after S. Oran, since, sixty years before the coming of Columba, there is the record of the burial here of the three sons of Erc, who founded the kingdom of Dalriada. Further, he draws attention to the fact that there is no such name as Oran to be found in the list of those twelve who first landed with S. Columba. Thus Oran cannot be identified with the first monk to have died on Iona as recorded by Adamnan.

Nevertheless, the legend of S. Oran is worth recalling if only for its grotesque details. It was in order to allow S. Columba to take possession of the island, or, as others say, to appease the fiend who overthrew in the night all that S. Columba built by day, that Oran of his own free will was buried alive—evidently with his head above ground, as was the fashion of these burials—common in the Middle Ages. After three days, he was dug up, and so horrified S. Columba by declaring that there was neither God nor devil, heaven nor hell, that the Abbat ordered him to be re-interred. Hence has arisen the Gaelic proverb, " Earth to earth on the mouth of Oran, that he may talk no more." The real Oran was an Irish priest who died fifteen years before S. Columba landed on Iona.

---

[7] There are eight other ancient burial-grounds whose names and sites survive.

It is not probable that the popularity of *Reilig Odhran* as a place of burial is due to any belief that S. Columba himself was buried within its confines, because monasteries usually had burying-grounds where only members of the community were laid to rest. But undoubtedly his burial in any part of the island would be considered to hallow the whole of Iona, and thus a grave on its shores was sought after as one in doubly consecrated ground. Desire for burial on Iona was quickened by the Gaelic prediction:

" Seven years before the Judgment
The sea shall sweep o'er Erin at one tide,
And over blue-green Islay;
But the isle of Colum—the cleric—shall swim."

There is the first authentic record of kingly burials in *Reilig Odhran* in 685, when the Pictish King, Brude MacBile, and Egfrid, King of Northumbria, were interred there. After them, equally well authenticated, followed fourteen of the early Scottish Kings, beginning with Kenneth MacAlpine and ending with the " gracious Duncan " killed by Macbeth, then that murderer himself, and finally " Lulach the Fatuous," who died in 1057. After his day, Dunfermline Abbey, built by Queen Margaret, became the place for royal burials.

In old days there used apparently to be in *Reilig Odhran* three round roofed vaults of stone called *Iomaire nan Righ,* or the Ridge of the Kings, inscribed as the tombs respectively of the Kings of Norway, of Scotland, and of Ireland. Of the burial of any Kings of Norway here, however, there seems to be no evidence: the Scottish Kings authentically recorded are limited to the fourteen above mentioned; and of the four alleged Kings of Ireland, only two (who died as monks of Iona) can certainly be identified. A King of France is said to be buried under a rough oblong block of red granite, inscribed with an Irish cross, but there is nothing to authenticate the tradition. But, as will afterwards appear, the dust of many of those who bore the proud title of Lords of the Isles, Macdonalds having regal sway, is fittingly mingled with that of kings who wielded no greater power than they. Indeed, the opinion conceived of the Lords of the Isles is expressed by an epitaph said to be found on Iona, *MacDonuill fato hic,* " Death alone could lay Macdonald here "—akin to the Glencoe motto.

Teampull Odhran, or the Chapel of S. Oran, is the most ancient building left on Iona, a small simple structure, oblong like most West Highland churches, but unlike them in having its door at the west end, and richly carved, and within the unusual embellishment of a triple arch over an altar tomb of the Middle Ages. *Teampull,* a Celtic ecclesiastical word, signifies a stone church, and this one is said to have been built by Queen Margaret about 1074, though the doorway is probably of later date. The fact that there is the greatest shelter on the west, and most exposure on the east probably dictated the architecture, for there is no east window, only two narrow slits in the north and south wall near the east end, and there are gables at both ends, where traces of old roofing are still to be seen. The canopy, already mentioned, on the north wall near the doorway is singular in several respects, and very interesting. It has an outer arch of ogee form with two crochets and a pinnacle at its head within which is a crucifix. The labels in which on both sides the arch terminates seem to be meant to represent lions, the one rampant, the other passant, having beneath him a broken piscina, obviously for use in connection with the altar tomb which was originally beneath the arches. The inner arch is trefoiled, and between it and the outer arch the space has been ornamented with Celtic scroll work, now terribly defaced.

Fr. Trenholme identifies *Reilig Odhran* with the place of special sanctuary on Iona, where any might take refuge from a precipitate foe, and find security in the protection of the Church until his case was lawfully tried.

Before detailing any of the stones, I will supplement the general observations I have already made in a previous chapter on some special features characterizing these beautiful and unique West Highland sculpturings. As regards date, they are generally attributed to the end of the Middle Ages, *i.e.,* roughly from the fourteenth to the beginning of the sixteenth century, and they were probably the work of schools of craftsmen not restricted to Iona, but found in other parts of the West, such as that on Inishail, an island of Loch Awe, which was known, like Iona, as *Innis nan Druineach,* or the island of sculptors. The art of the slabs is distinctively Celtic, and the note of the graceful foliage ornamentation—the elaborate tracery resolving itself into crosses, the basket or plait work, the knots, the grotesque animals of the zoomorphic designs— is its imaginativeness and freedom from conventional treatment. There is, too, a peculiar feature in the carving. With the exception of bosses and effigies in high relief, the chisel has cut deeply into the stone per-pendicularly, making no attempt whatever at rounding or bevelling, thus leaving a flat-surfaced though bold relief, presumably as best calculated to resist the stress of weather. Inscriptions are rare: where they exist they were generally brief, but are now too often illegible.

Of the more general symbols, there are frequent representations of shears like those used for sheep-clipping, probably to suggest the cutting of the thread of life: the round mirror and comb, indicative of a woman's grave: the divergent spiral, the trefoil and triquetra-plait, all emblems of the Holy Trinity. The curious double goblet-shaped chalice, which some writers have taken for an hour-glass, is almost invariably present on a priest's tomb, as his distinctive token; and, to a lesser degree, books, probably representing the primer or missal as those in most constant use, are also found on ecclesiastics' stones.

One of the commonest representations on the slabs is that of a galley or *birlinn,* as indeed it is still on the armorial bearings of so many chiefs, to whom they were the commonest means of transport and often their principal homes. On the stones these galleys are never shewn with their sweeps or oars—which were at least sixteen feet long—as in the later representations in the arms of the chiefs. The galleys, while they vary in the number of sweep-holes shewn, in details of helm, rigging, furled sails, shrouds, and stays, have almost invariably both prow and stern pointed and raised high above the low deck. They often display a shield or fly a banner, and sometimes there is a figure to represent the crew, of which there would be from 30 to 120 men. Originally the galley, as the ship of the Highlands, was possibly introduced as a symbol of the Church.

Perhaps most interesting of all are the effigies of warriors, with the vast majority of whom even tradition associates no specific individual, leaving an obscure past to withhold their identity. It is not safe to assign to any of these effigies the date when the dress, armour, etc., depicted on them generally prevailed, since costume long previously obsolete elsewhere still persisted in the Western Highlands, parts of which are even now extremely isolated. Nor, after careful study of endless numbers of these effigies, do I find it possible positively to assert exactly what garments are intended to be represented on them. There is, however, the same type of bascinet and camail, or gorget of chain mail, as is found on English brasses from 1360 to 1424. The West Highland bascinet, higher and more conical than that found elsewhere, is called the *clogaid,* to which the camail would be laced, as elsewhere, to staples. The camail falls like a tippet over the shoulders of a long garment reaching to the knee, which, when it is shewn divided in front, as in earlier examples, may be intended to represent the hauberk or *luireach,* the shirt of mail, which certainly was worn in the West Highlands. Under the hauberk elsewhere was worn the gambeson or aketon, a quilted or padded garment intended to absorb the shock of blows upon the armour. There is certain evidence that the aketon was worn in the West Highlands, but there is no example in the effigies of any *luireach* being worn over it. I am, therefore, disposed to think that the long garment shewn on the effigies represents the aketon worn alone, though it is almost invariably called a surcoat by other writers, probably because that was the normal uppermost garment worn with that full armour, which would be unobtainable by most West Highland chiefs. There was a suggestion that this long garment may represent the ancient *léine chroich*, an extremely ample yellow shirt worn by persons of distinction in the Highlands, and disused about 1600. This conjecture accounts for the disposal of the twenty-four yards of linen of which this shirt consisted, by supposing it to have been taken up in quilting or padding, but from various descriptions it would appear that the *léine chroich* was much more like the belted plaid. It is not possible absolutely to identify any of these monumental representations of dress with the kilt, though that garment is rather suggested, as already mentioned, on one of the Arisaig fragments of stone.

For the rest of the figures, the legs are usually protected by *chausses* or *jambes,* and the feet encased in sollerets shewn often with spur-straps. Spears are of a fairly uniform type, and shields, usually called " heater-shaped " because their contour is of the shape of the heated stones that were slipped into the old box irons, whose contour is exactly the same as that of a flat-iron.

It would only be wearisome to the general reader if I were to detail all the carved stones of *Reilig Odhran,* and probably by the time I had finished some would have been removed elsewhere, " general post " with the grave stones of Iona being a favourite pastime of the authorities. So, since there are several books in which all the stones are both delineated and fully described, I will mention only those which are most likely to prove of general interest, either by reason of the matter of their carving, or of the person they commemorate.

Going within the chapel first, you see an inscribed grave stone, decorated with a galley and zoomorphic tracery. This is popularly said to have marked the grave of Angus Oig, that Lord of the Isles (the " Ronald " of Sir Walter Scott in his *Lord of the Isles*) mentioned in Chapter I. of this book as he whom Bruce honoured at Bannockburn and after. Angus Oig undoubtedly was buried on Iona in 1326, but the inscription, " Here lies the body of . . . the son of Lord Angus Macdonald of Isla," does not fit one who was himself Lord of the Isles, nor is the space of the obliterated name sufficient to have allowed of it being *Angusii*.

There is in Eucharistic vestments an effigy of one of the Benedictine priors of the monastery, one Christian Macgillrescol, the meaning of which name I cannot resolve.

The stone of " Paul of the Sporan " (or purse) is identified with the only Campbell said to have been buried on the island.

Out of fragments of stone once within the chapel, the late Mr. Romilly Allen, the great authority on Celtic monuments, reconstructed a great cross which he considered of exceptional beauty and resembling exactly the famous cross still standing complete at Kildalton in Islay. The fragments prove this broken Ionan cross to have been seven feet across the arms.

In S. Oran's Chapel there is the effigy of a warrior of the late fifteenth century or early sixteenth century which local tradition asserts to be the tombstone of a Macquarrie (sons of the noble or glorious one) of Ulva. But the blazoning of the shield cannot possibly be identified with any of the quarterings of the coat-of-arms of the Macquarrie chief as now matriculated, for that has no sort of beast as a charge, as this has. If the effigy hereafter to be described in the chapter on the Abbey Church represents a Maclaine of Lochbuie, this, judging from the charges on the shield, is more likely to be another of the same clan. The figure here is shewn wearing the *clogaid* and camail, the sword is thrust through the baldrick or girdle in the usual fashion, and the gauntletted right hand grasps a spear.

Outside in the burial-ground, two long, railed-in, parallel rows of tombstones run down the centre, that on the east being called the Ridge of the Chiefs and the other the Ridge of the Kings. In the Ridge of the Kings, beginning at the south end, you remark a stone of earlier date than the majority, a rude slab of unhewn, uneven outline, incised with an Irish cross inviting, in Irish minuscules, prayers for the soul of Ewan. Then follow some graves of ecclesiastics, of which the first, shewing under abnormally short vestments unmistakably crooked lower limbs, is said to represent Bishop Hugh of the Crooked Legs, otherwise unidentified. He stands under a canopy, one hand raised in blessing, the other grasping his pastoral staff with the crook turned out, said to imply Episcopal jurisdiction in contradistinction to that of an Abbat, one of whom apparently is depicted some stones further on. He is in the same attitude as the bishop, but has a very quaint face, and his crook turns in, implying a jurisdiction limited to his own community. Beneath him, there are the figures of two hooded monks grasping each other's hands in greeting. Then you come to a unique slab which is worth notice. On this, above the usual sword, is a representation of a duly vested priest, a deacon or server behind him, lifting his hands in benediction as, celebrating the Holy Eucharist, he stands before an altar which is vested in a cloth and has upon it a Celtic cross and chalice.

The slab next it has a sword running down the centre, and on one side of the blade what is presumably its sheath: there is a curiously plaited cross on the left of the hilt (which has a little cross on the head of the pommel), and what is said to represent a strong box, an alleged emblem of a founder of a church, at the foot of the stone. This is called the gravestone of Reginald of the Isles, the founder both of the Benedictine monastery and nunnery, of whom it is recorded that he obtained a cross from Jerusalem and was buried on Iona in 1207.

Last of all in this ridge comes the grave of the legendary King of France.

Passing now over to the Ridge of the Chiefs, and also beginning at its south end, the first stone of peculiar interest is that of some chief of Macleod, possibly John of Lewis, who, after an unadventurous life, died about 1532. At the top of the stone under the inscription is a galley with sails furled, and in the middle of the unusual pattern of interlaced tracery is a little figure of the chief in *clogaid* and aketon, armed with a spear, a sword sticking out from his side, and a shield. The next is also an interesting monument of " the Rider," thought to be a Maclean. In this event, judging from the probable date of the stone, it may represent Red Hector of the Battles, the second chief of Duart who, falling at Harlaw in 1411, was buried on Iona. The mounted knight with his spear at charge, is set between an ornamented panel and a kneeling figure, below is a sword flanked by zoomorphic tracery.

An extremely beautiful stone, associated with *Ailean nan Sop,* is next to that of " the Rider." There is an elaborate square cross in tracery above a galley, and, below, further beautiful designs of beasts and foliage. This " Allan of the Wisps " was a Maclean of Duart who obtained his name from the fuel with which he set buildings on fire—his distinguishing exploit. He died about 1551. An effigy in high relief shews a warrior wearing a ridged *clogaid,* a square beard, and otherwise habited and armed, with the exception of having no chain mail, as the alleged Macquarrie of Ulva within the chapel. Local tradition calls him a Maclean. But if one can safely deduce anything from the device of a tower on the shield, and if the dragon be ignored, a Maclaine of Lochbuie is rather indicated, since a tower is the charge of the second quarter of the shield of that chief, who, in 1630, used to have a tower embattled argent for crest.

An extremely ornate and beautiful stone, even in its defacement, is that commemorating the four priors, as specified by its inscription. The effigy of another warrior, traditionally identified with Maclaine of Lochbuie, appears to be buckling on his sword. His dress calls for no special remark, and he has no shield, so that I am inclined to suppose that the local traditions have got a bit mixed, and that, accepting the charge on the shield of the last-mentioned as labelling him of Lochbuie, this may represent the chief of Duart of the early sixteenth century. A warrior called traditionally a Maclean of Coll is clad exactly as the preceding, but he is depicted as drawing his sword. The next slab whose general orna- mentation is very similar to that of " the Rider " is called the gravestone of " Ewan of the Little Head." He was a famous Maclaine, the eldest son of one of the first chiefs of Lochbuie, with whom he quarrelled and struck. The old man thereupon complained to Duart, who was only too pleased to have an excuse to invade Ewan's territory. When Ewan heard Duart was going to attack him, he went to consult a witch, who said that Ewan would prevail in battle if his wife would give him butter without his asking for it. Now Ewan's wife was a termagant, and constantly quarrelling with her husband, with whom she was so angry on the morning of the battle that, far from offering him butter, she provided no breakfast for him! In a towering rage, Ewan, without having tasted any food, mounted his horse and rode off to his death, for very soon one of the enemy smote off his head with a broadsword. In a panic the horse rushed off with his headless rider, and ever since he has always been seen when any of the Lochbuie family were about to die. It was because Ewan died fasting, so says the legend, that he is thus doomed to restless activity. Not a hundred years ago an islander of Iona declared he saw Ewan pass on his black horse with his little head under his arm, but, unfortunately, history omits to relate if in this instance Ewan was a true prophet!

Not even tradition attributes any of the existing stones to the famous Donald of Harlaw, Lord of the Isles, crowned on Eigg, nor to his brother Ranald, progenitor of the Macdonalds of Clanranald, both certainly buried in *Reilig Odhran*. And so with them the paths of glory led not only to the grave, but to a passing into oblivion as far as the identification of their burial-places is concerned.

PART VI

THE MEDIÆVAL MONASTERY AND NUNNERY BUILDINGS: THEIR CROSSES AND THEIR GRAVESTONES

ABOUT 1203, Reginald, Lord of the Isles, founded his monastery of S. Columba on Iona, with its church, dedicated to the Blessed Virgin Mary. Reginald's " black monks," so called from the colour of their habit, were reformed Benedictines known as Tyronenses. Their first Abbat tried to turn out the Celtic community, which, however, successfully resisted his attempts, and ultimately apparently conformed to the Benedictine rule.

The clearest idea of the arrangement of the last monastery will be afforded by reference to the accompanying plan, on which the structures and remains which Dr. Skene identifies with the earlier stone monastery (which the succeeding apparently ousted) are distinctively indicated. The extent of the havoc wrought by the modern rebuilders has not been restricted to the nave and transepts, and when it comes to identifying the different buildings of the monastery and those outlying, architectural and archæological authorities are at great variance. Consequently, they land one in such hopeless confusion as to the precise structure to which they refer, that it is impossible

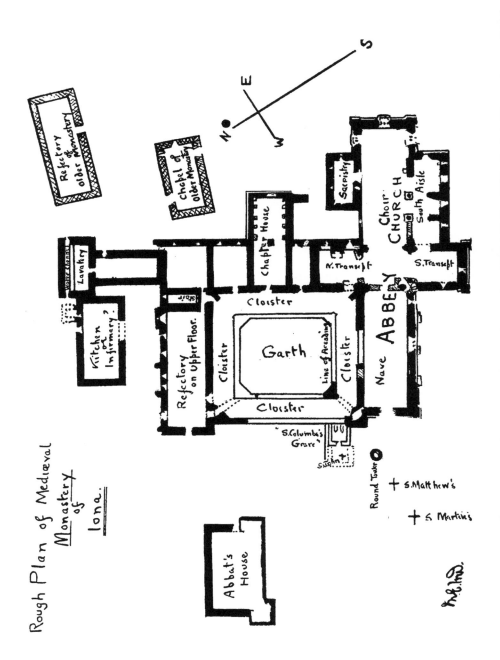

Rough Plan of Mediæval Monastery of Iona.

Refectory of older Monastery

Chapel of older Monastery

Lavatory

Kitchen or Infirmary?

Refectory on Upper Floor.

Stair

Cloister

Cloister

Garth

Line of Arcading

Cloister

Cloister

Chapter House

N. Transept

Sacristy

Choir CHURCH

South Aisle

S. Transept

Nave   ABBEY

"S. Columba's Grave"

S. John †

Round Tower

† S. Matthew's

† S. Martin's

Abbat's House

for anyone who is not an expert and who writes away from Iona to decide between them, for instance, as to whether a particular building was the kitchen or the infirmary. To a lesser extent, there is a divergence of opinion as to the date of the Abbey Church, and the best I can do in both cases is to state, without overburdening, what seem the most likely conjectures, always according to Dr. Skene that pre-eminence his learning, research, and local investigations have won for him.

The Abbey Church of S. Mary is a cruciform building, having a massive central square tower which has, near the top, some unusual plate tracery, square and quatrefoil in design. Though architects now seem fairly agreed that the date of the present building is to be uniformly attributed to the end of the fourteenth century, it is difficult to reconcile this conjecture with the inscription, now mutilated, but which Dr. Reeves was able clearly to note ran as follows, " *Donaldus o' Brolchan fecit hoc opus,*" on the capital of the south-east pier of the tower. Now in the Annals of Ulster the death of one *Domhnall Ua Brolchan* is recorded in 1203, and Dr. Skene, following Dr. Reeves, identifies the two, and conjectures that thus the date at least of this particular part of the building is fixed. And surely the evidence borne by this unambiguous inscription can scarcely be overthrown by the mere conjecture of architects who now refuse to assign so early a date as the twelfth century to any part of the building.

Before entering the church, the little oratory, $10\frac{1}{2}$ feet by $7\frac{1}{2}$ feet, just outside, known as " S. Columba's Tomb," claims attention. Within are two stone receptacles, one of which is universally associated with S. Columba's remains, the other variously conjectured to have contained his *minna,* the shrine of S. Blathmac, or the remains of S. Columba's attendant, Diormit. Immediately in front of the oratory doorway is the broken shaft of S. John's Cross, which apparently occupies its original position on a small rectangular altar, consisting of a stone slab resting upon four upright stones, and having four other slabs serving as panels between them.   Precisely similar altars are still to be seen on the islands off the west coast of Ireland, and in the old days, twelve stones called *Clachan brath* (stones of judgment) were thrice turned round *deiseil* on the circular cavity of the broad flat stone below.   This is still done with similar stones at Innismurray in Ireland, where there is an altar of rubble.   The stone that apparently belonged to the Iona altar seems to have been lost for a time and subsequently dug up in *Reilig Odhran,* and the idea underlying the turning of the stones was the curious one that the end of the world will not come till the stone on which the *clachan brath* stood wore through. Apparently, therefore, those who turned the stones wished to hasten the coming of the Last Day.

Before the oratory doorway, and behind S. John's Cross, lie three pre-Norman gravestones exactly similar to that already described in *Reilig Odhran,* inscribed with Irish crosses, and asking in Irish minuscules for prayers for the souls of those they commemorate.

Now to enter the church.   Passing through the nave, still as the hands of time have left it, and under the tower into the choir, as ruder hands have devastated it,[8] there are several features which must interest everyone, irrespective of their knowledge of architecture.   There are the very arresting capitals of the pillars, both of the tower piers and in the aisle, a curious medley of carvings of beautiful foliage, grotesque animals, religious and fanciful subjects, as well as the ubiquitous warrior.   In the south aisle, curious half-round arches, of the nature of flying buttresses, spring from the ground to give their unique support just above the capitals of the pillars, and there are odd levels on the ground, emphasized by the new flooring, which are thought to be a result of accommodating

[8] Since I was last on the island, the nave, too, has suffered "restoration." I only heard this after this chapter was in print, hence inaccurate references to some parts now rebuilt.

SACRISTRY DOOR, ABBEY CHURCH, IONA

it to the slope of the ground when a crypt was done away with in enlarging the church. Evidences of the existence of this crypt are said to be indicated chiefly by the arcade of two arches in the north wall of the choir, six feet above the present level. " This arcade is thought to have been part of a chapel above a stairway down to the crypt. The choir floor has subsequently been lowered six feet, thus doing away with the crypt." It was usual in a church associated with the life of a saint to have a *confessio,* or place where his relics were enshrined, in front of the High Altar, and this often took the shape of a crypt beneath, in which the shrine reposed. Quite possibly, then, this crypt was designed for the *marta* of S. Columba.

As stated in a previous chapter, the High Altar was made from the white marble of Kilchrist in Skye, and was described in 1688 as being " very noble " and " entire, except for one corner, which has been broken by accident." Eighty-five years later, Dr. Samuel Johnson records its disappearance, destroyed apparently to provide amulets against fire, shipwrecks, etc.

Below one of the arches of the arcade above mentioned is perhaps the greatest atrocity—worse even than the horrible rose window of the north aisle—perpetrated by the rebuilders, the harsh and crude " restoration " of the sacristy door, the original beauty of which has thereby been utterly destroyed. This door was apparently built on the new floor level, and gives entrance into what is supposed to have been originally a chapel at the bottom of the crypt stairs. On the south side of the sanctuary are the sedilia under three fine arches, the pillar supporting one of which, however, has suffered the disfigurement of " restoration." There three seats were built for use of the celebrant and his two assistants, the deacon and sub-deacon, at the high celebration of the Holy Mysteries, and beside the sedilia is a piscina, the receptacle for the rinsings of the sacred vessels at the end of the service. Outside the door in the north transept, which leads into the cloisters, is a holy water stoup; and on the edge of the east wall of the south transept is a cross within a small circle, similar to others still to be found on the outside walls. These are consecration crosses, which were carved or painted, twelve within and twelve without—usually in Scotland—on the walls of a new church, for the bishop to anoint with the sacred oil when he came to consecrate the building.

Of the monuments and carved stones which are now (or were) housed in the Abbey Church, by far the most appealing is the simple stone pillow of S. Columba in its brass cage on a window ledge. Near it is another tapering boulder, also probably a gravestone, since it came from Cill Chainnich. It, too, has an incised cross upon it of the cross crosslet type.

On the north side of the sanctuary, its supporting slab resting on lions, is a recumbent figure of Abbat Mackinnon, who is shown vested in the Eucharistic vestments complete—amice, maniple, and stole all being shown—and wearing a mitre. This, usually restricted to episcopal use, was granted by the Pope as a special honour to certain abbats even if they were only simple priests, though before he died this abbat was consecrated a bishop. The pastoral staff is here broken away, but the inscription is intact, and is thus translated: " Here lies John Macfingon, Abbat of Y, who died in the year of the Lord 15—— on whose soul may the most high God have mercy: Amen." The monument was sculptured in the Abbat's lifetime, leaving a space for the year of his death to be inserted, but this was neglected, though it is known to have taken place in 1509. This same abbat shares with his father in Mackinnon's Cross, now also sheltered here. This " the cross of Lachlan MacFingon and his son John, Abbat of Hy," was " made in the year of the Lord 1489," and the Lachlan commemorated by it was the chief of his clan. The tracery on this cross is very beautiful, especially the zoomorphic design on its reverse side, where interlaced foliage springs from the tail of a very decorative dragon at the base.

Opposite the effigy of Abbat Mackinnon is that of Abbat Kenneth Mackenzie, much more defaced, and without any inscription. He probably preceded Mackinnon at no great distance of time, since their monuments are so similar.

There are two other effigies in high relief. One represents two warriors under a double canopy, one in an aketon, the other in plate armour, unusual in these monuments. Beneath is a galley and an inscription of an unusual character round the border, which is translated: " Here lies John Maclan, Lord of Ardnamurchan, and Mariota Maclan his sister, the wife of Maccolin Macduffie, Lord of Dunevin in Colonsay, bought this stone for her brother." Which of the figures is Maclan does not appear, but the chief in question is probably Sir John MacIan of Ardnamurchan, who was killed in 1518. Possibly the other figure is that of the donor's husband.

The other tombstone is traditionally identified with Neil Maclean of the Ross of Mull, though the rude charge on the shield suspended from his neck, a galley above a lion (?) rampant, taken alone, is not now identical even with a part of the armorial bearings of any chief. With the position of the very common charges reversed, it might be identified as an incomplete attempt to reproduce some of the marshallings of half a dozen chiefs' coats-of-arms, including those of Macdonald of the Isles as well as Maclaine of Lochbuie. Because of the charges on the shield, therefore, I find it difficult to accept this effigy as representing, as alleged, the grandson of the third chief of *Duart* who lived at the end of the fifteenth century, more especially as the Ross of Mull would be in Lochbuie territory. The only features of this monument differing from those previously described are the warrior's curiously curly beard, and a small object, probably a horn, hanging on his right side.

In the floor before the sanctuary is a matrix denoting where a monumental brass has been, though in this case tradition avers the brass to have been of silver, and attributes it as representing one of the Macleods of Harris and Dunvegan, possibly William Dubh Macleod, who was killed in 1480, being the seventh chief, and father of Alastair Crotach.

Before you leave the ex-Abbey Church, you notice in the north-west angle, in the base of what seems to have been a turret, a small chamber, said to have been the porter's lodge, which is entered by a door from the nave.

As you pass out of the ruined doorway, you see, a little to the south, between S. Martin's Cross and the wall of the nave, five feet of the broken shaft, all that remains of S. Matthew's Cross (called by some S. John's), with a representation of the temptation of Adam and Eve figured on one side.

Of the early tenth century, the oldest cross on Iona, so grey with age and broken is the noble monument of S. Martin, that it is difficult to appreciate the fact that it is carved in red granite. On the west face, the central subject is the Holy Mother and her Divine Child, surrounded by four angels. Animals are on the arms of the cross—perhaps as symbols of the evangelists: on the shaft is the conventional representation of Daniel in the lions' den; groups of human figures, bosses, and serpents. The east face is ornamented with beasts, bosses, and serpents. S. Martin of Tours was a friend of S. Ninian, and so highly venerated in the Celtic Church that his name was commemorated in the Celtic Divine Liturgy, which was, of course, the specific Eucharistic service in use on Iona.

There are now the remains of the monastery itself to be seen, and where its plan is not self-explanatory, I will add such details as are likely to be of general interest, though there seem to be no conjectures as to the nature of some of the chambers, and conflicting opinion as to the use of others. Regarding the Chapter House, however, there is no dispute. It is entered from the cloister on the east by what seems like a vestibule, opening into the Chapter

House proper through two rounded arches richly ornamented with dog-tooth work. Although both this and the
substantial round pillars supporting the arches all suggest
late Norman work, we are asked not to let appearances
deceive us, but to attribute the architecture to a later date.
The ornamentation of the capital is very curious, one side
being totally different in style from the other. The arcading
round the walls still indicate where the members of the
Chapter were seated, and over the flat-barrel roof there
is general agreement the library was situated. This was
famous for its priceless treasures before the Religious
Revolution was responsible for their dispersal, if not their
destruction.

The small room, or slype, on the left as you leave the
Chapter House, appears to have been used as a calefactory,
being unique in the possession of a fireplace, the only one
in the monastery, but obviously never appertaining to a
kitchen. Walking northwards, you pass three separate
chambers, concerning the use of which I have heard no
sort of conjecture, and have none to make myself. The
one hazard I have come across as to the site of the
dormitories places them on the floor that originally existed
above these chambers—on the same level as the library.
Traversing the end of the third unidentified room, and
opening into it, is a chamber which seems to have been a
lavatory, for it contains a built-up water-channel running
across its length.

The long building on the north side of the cloister was
the refectory, or dining hall, situated on an upper floor,
and gained by a wide staircase at the east end; being
seemingly built over an earlier one on the ground floor,
where now are low cellars. Parallel with the refectory
on its north side is an almost detached structure, which
most suppose to have been the kitchen, where the fire, as
in the refectory, would have been an open one in the centre
of the floor. One authority, however, thinks it was the
infirmary, and this is the only conjecture I have seen with

regard to Iona which makes any mention of this integral part of a monastery.

The eminence called Torr Abb may take its name from the adjacent Abbot's house. It is not S. Columba's hill.

To the north of the Abbey Church is a small triangular unenclosed space called *Cill na Goibhnean* (the burial-place of the smiths), or *Cill na Meach Iain* (of Soft John), where, in that quarter of the compass always associated with darkness, murderers and the unbaptised were buried in unseemly association.

Leaving this enclosure for the nunnery, just opposite the Abbey, the spur of the hill, called Dun nam Manach, has obviously once been fortified. It is not in itself particularly interesting, but near it, probably next to " S. Columba's Tomb," used to lie the famous " black stones of Iona," so called not from their colour, for they were grey, but from the black doom which would overtake any who swore falsely upon them. " Mack Donald, King of the Isles, deliver'd the Rights of their lands to his vassals in the Isles and continent, with uplifted hands and bended knees on these black stones." No traces of them are to be found now, but an islander who claimed to have seen the black stone says it was destroyed by a madman who thought it bewitched the natives. From his description, it was apparently one specific gravestone, " 5 feet high," having on it in high relief the figure of a priest, which, in view of its contiguity to " S. Columba's Tomb," I think quite probably may have come to be accepted as his actual effigy, as was certainly the case in similar instances, as I shall mention later on. In this event, the peculiar sanctity in which the " Black Stone " was held would be amply accounted for.

On your way to the Nunnery along the present Street of the Dead, you pass Maclean's Cross, probably the latest on the island. Exactly whom it commemorates is not known; and if it be some chief of Maclean, even tradition does not indicate which. The west face of this thin cross

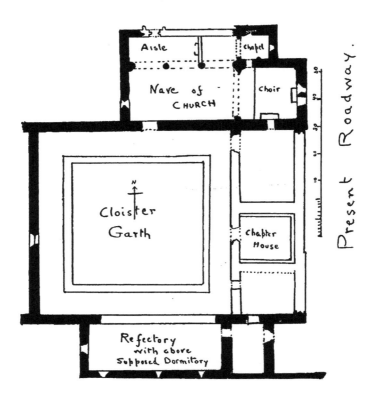

PLAN OF THE NUNNERY, IONA

(By permission from MacGibbon & Ross' *Ecclesiastical Architecture of Scotland*, with several names inserted by M. E. M. D.)

of schist, standing over 10 feet high, has within the solid circle of its head a Crucifixion, and on the shaft, interlaced foliage and tracery similar to that on its east side. This face has suffered so much from weathering that the mounted knight at the bottom, which is clearly shewn in drawings made in 1867, is now hardly discernible.

Behind the cross in the field is the site of *Cill Chainnich,* a church and burial-ground dedicated to a friend and companion of S. Columba, S. Kenneth, by whom, possibly, the church was built.

The Nunnery, dedicated to the Blessed Virgin Mary, was, like the monastery, founded by Reginald of the Isles, who established there a Benedictine Priory, with his sister Bethog, or Beatrice, as its first superior. These religious. like their brothers, were called " black " from their habits, but later they either changed from the Benedictine rule or were replaced by Augustinians. These Austin Canonesses were apparently nurses of the sick, the name implying that they lived by " canon " or rule. Not only was their habit white, but they were singular in wearing the rochet, a sort of surplice with close sleeves, the white vestment of lawn that Anglican bishops wear beneath the black chimere, or their red doctor's habit.

With the Nunnery, as with the Monastery, a plan of the building is the best means of enabling everyone to locate its different parts. There is very little that need be said in amplification of the plan, for it is really self-explanatory. Practically the only remains of general interest are those of the church, where the nave has three round arches of Norman character filled up with solid masonry by a Duke of Argyll to keep out the cattle! The little Lady Chapel in the aisle is vaulted and had an upper story gained by a very narrow stair, part of which still remains.

Of the stones, the principal is the upper half of one sculptured with a figure of the Prioress Anna, who is shewn wearing her rochet above her habit and beneath a mantle. Her head rests on a pillow which two angels are smoothing:

above are the symbols, common to a woman's tomb, of a round mirror and comb; and the figures of two little dogs find a place on either side. Below her feet, and upside down, is the prayer, " Holy Mary, pray for me," having obvious reference to the figure, on the missing half; of the Holy Mother, " crowned and mitred with the Divine Child in her arms." When this unusual stone was intact, the figure of the Prioress faced that of the Blessed Virgin, and the inscription round the edge, as translated, ran, " Here lies Lady Anna, daughter of Donald Tearlach, sometime Prioress of Iona, who died in the year 1583. Her soul we commend to the Most High."

Besides this stone, there should be noticed the slab of mica schist, on which, filling the whole stone, is a pattern ornamented with Stafford (interlaced) knots in double rows; and another very beautiful stone with a unique ornamental cross, graceful and slender, having an octagonal interlaced centre-piece, and two leaf-like extremities with the stem terminating in Stafford knots, and on both sides, above its arms, an ornamental leaf and an animal.

The isolated building to the north of the Nunnery buildings is S. Ronan's Chapel, said to have been the parish church which, with its Rector, was first heard of in 1372. S. Ronan was abbat of the Monastery of Kingarth in Bute in the eighth century, and the bay where now the ferry boats land passengers from the *Grenadier* is also called after him.

A legend states the parish chapel to have been built in the twelfth century by Alexander I. of Scotland, who was driven by wind and tide on to the shores of Iona one day when he was fishing off the coast of Ireland. He is said to have lived for some time in a cave in the north-west at Culburgh.

PART VII

SOME FOLK-LORE OF IONA

THERE are between two and three hundred inhabitants of Iona whose characteristics are those of the Highlander as he has been affected by foreign influences. They are essentially a kindly people, yet you cannot but regret that the bluffness which so often veils the kind heart has replaced the natural charm and instinctive courtesy of the Highlander untouched by outside influences. Many of the crofters take charge of children sent them by the Glasgow Poor Law Authorities to be boarded out, and with them the city children find happy as well as healthy homes. It is probably owing to similar causes that the islanders' Gaelic has suffered, for, as spoken on Iona, it differs very widely from what one hears in Inverness-shire and in Skye, where the best Gaelic is to be heard. Their English, too, is a strange mixture of that spoken by the Highlander and the Lowlander.

Iona is not lacking in folk-lore, and it has its *glaistig,* of whom the following tale is told. The *glaistig* lived on the Staonaig, in a hole amongst the rocks, and as usual the people poured out a libation for her every night on her stone. One very wet day the *glaistig* entered the house of a woman called Livingstone, and found her alone at dinner. Standing before the fire, the *glaistig* held her wet garments outspread to dry, but, unfortunately, they took fire. In consequence of this incident, no woman of the name of Livingstone can succeed in kindling a fire at dinner-time—no great inconvenience after all, one would imagine.

There are two wells on the island to which different attributes were ascribed—a very common feature of Celtic paganism which persisted long after the extinction of its originating genius. *Tobar na h-Aois,* or the Well of the Age, is a small triangular pool on the brow of Dun I which had the reputation of restoring youth to any woman who bathed her face and hands in it at the potent hour before sunrise.   Doubtless some particular incantation would have to accompany the act, but the efficacy of the waters, one would have supposed, would have suffered discredit after the first trial of their powers.   *Tobar na Gaoith Tuaith* invited sailors who wished to sail southward to make their offerings at this " well of the north wind," whereby a breeze from that quarter might be assured. There was apparently also a well of the south wind for use when a sail northward was in contemplation, but no one now is able to indicate its whereabouts.

In the Abbey Church there is a small nook called the " tailor's hole."   Here, it is said, the monks kept the tailor who made their habits, but they made him work so strenuously, and for such long hours, that he began to have horrible visions at night.   Worst of all was a fleshless hand that used to shew itself in the wall and say: " Take a great grey paw that is without meat!"

In connection with one of the *sithean* of the island, the following tale is told; but I do not know whether the reference is to the great or the little fairy mound.   Two young men of Iona were fishing upon the rocks one day, and, returning home, they found one of the *sithean* open. They both went in and joined the fairies in their dance. While, however, one, in order to ward off fairy spells from his person, took the precaution to stick a fish hook in the doorway, the other did not trouble so much as to put down the string of fish he was carrying.   The islander who had guarded himself with an article of iron—most potent of charms against the *sithe*—was able to leave the fairy mound when he wished, but his fellow no longer retained that power.   After a year had passed, the free fisherman returned, to find his companion still dancing with the string of fish in his hand.   The new-comer took the dancer out into the open air, when immediately the fish, all rotten, dropped from the string—not at all as surprising a *dénouement* as apparently one is expected to see in the end of this story.

Part VIII

A DAY AND A NIGHT ON STAFFA

NATURALLY, we did not contemplate leaving Iona without visiting the neighbouring " isle of staves." I wanted to spend a night there, but had to be careful of my two friends who were not so able as myself to rough it.

Knowing that a shepherd was said to have lived upon Staffa, I made enquiries as to whether his hut was still standing. But the replies I received were contradictory; one man said there was no shelter at all on the island outside the caves; another declared there was a hut used by MacBrayne's men when engaged on repairs to the tourist equipment of the island; but all were agreed it was no place for ladies to spend the night.

Thus, in consideration of my friends, I regretfully abandoned the plan of taking the *Grenadier* to Staffa on a day when it called in at Iona first, next day reversing the route, so that we could have returned by it. We arranged instead with one of the islanders to take us over in his boat, and on a beautiful day in early August set sail northward for our six-mile, crossing early in the morning, to allow of our being as long as possible on the island. Our good landlady, the boatman's sister, gave us a huge basket generously packed with the most substantial sandwiches I ever saw, and a large bottle of milk, whilst we equipped ourselves with our kettle, tea, and a spirit lamp. With a second man to help Donald with the boat, we had a most exhilarating sail.

The sea was radiantly green, and, with the sun playing on its surface, it seemed as though we sailed over an ocean of sparkling emeralds and dancing diamonds. Soon Staffa loomed sufficiently large to rivet our attention, and with ever increasing interest we drew nearer to the massive tilted table-land, until we were able to distinguish the three-fold structure of the island, which rises to 144 feet at its greatest height. The sea washes round a base of volcanic agglomerate, above which, curiously aslant, especially at the south-east corner, rise black basaltic columns, the third tier consisting of another basalt, generally shapeless, though showing occasionally a small column.

It was thrilling when, under the lee of the island, we saw yawning before us the dark, elliptical opening of the great cave named after Ossian's hero, Fingal, the King of Selma, which penetrates the island to a distance of 227 feet. We gazed, fascinated, up at the glorious domed arch that rises 60 feet above the sea level at the entrance, and under it our boat was able to sail into the cave, a feat that is not always possible. High above our heads soared the roof of overhanging pillars, some snowy white from their covering of calcareous accretions, and beneath us were the transparent green depths of the sea, with its bed of gleaming, pure white sand. When we pushed out, we did not enter the Boat Cave on our right, being told it is of no particular interest beyond the range of pillars that we could see overhanging it. This cave, which can only be entered by boat, hence its name, is a passage like a mine-gallery, 12 feet wide by 16 feet high and 150 feet deep, hollowed out in the bottom agglomerate.

We landed just outside Fingal's Cave, and took our way carefully over the famous Causeway, the worn tops of the broken columns of which often suggest a tessellated pavement, and along by the Great Face, which is formed of three distinct beds of rock, of unequal thickness. In the columns of this glorious colonnade, hexagonal and pentagonal forms predominate, and after noticing what is said to be the only square stone in the island, half way along, we reached Fingal's Wishing Chair. We all three sat successively in it, and I am sure we all wished the three wishes whose fulfilments are said to be thereby ensured, but, not remembering what mine were, I cannot bear any testimony as to the truth of the chair's claims.

THE HERDSMAN, STAFFA

The Buachaille, or "Herdsman," the conoidal pile of columns which rises out of the sea to a height of 30 feet alongside the Colonnade, from which it is separated only by the narrowest of channels, is very attractive. Opposite it, extremes meet in the hideous stairway painted a glaring red which has been put up to enable tourists easily to gain the heights of the island. Just round the corner from this point is what is called the Clamshell, or Scallop Cave, but all we saw was more like a cove than a cave, having on one side beautifully curved pillars suggestive of the ribs of a ship, and on the other shewing a wall of broken pillar ends suggesting the face of a honeycomb. But there must be more of the cave than we saw, for it is said to be 130 feet long and uninteresting inside.

I was all eagerness to get on the top of the island to see for myself if it afforded any shelter. To my great delight, I soon discovered in a hollow a very rude shed, consisting of a tarpaulin pent roof reared partly over wooden sides and partly on walls of stone piled together in the roughest possible fashion, oblivious of chinks. A makeshift broken door, in which there were more gaps than wood, hung on one crazy hinge, and the hut was lit by a small glass window. Within was a rude wooden table, alongside one wall two wooden bunks end to end, and against another, a small rusty broken stove, with the stove-pipe beside it, a small heap of coal-dust, and an old pail in the corner. This was obviously the carpenters' shelter, erected within the remains of the old shepherd's cottage, and the sight of it filled me with elation. I rejoined my companions, and, in view of my discovery, announced to them my settled determination to spend the night on the island. I had not the least objection to being left alone, but when my friends proved just as eager to stay, my delight was complete. After they had satisfied themselves, as I had done, that no reasonable person could desire a better shelter, we went off to communicate our intentions to Donald, and soon had the supreme satisfaction of seeing our boat sail away leaving us behind, the only human beings on Staffa.

But we were not long left to ourselves, for within an hour the *Grenadier* came in, and discharged its freight of tourists. In one of the boats returning for another load I went off to the steamer, to procure what provisions I could to augment our stock for our extended stay. There were some people on board who had been at our hotel, and when they heard of our intention they most kindly insisted on my taking the loan of their rug for the use of my friends. I inferred that it was only as a favour that I was allowed to obtain—for a consideration—three eggs, a small piece of bread and cheese, a little tea, a modest bottle of milk, and the loan of a knife—all, so it was alleged, that could be spared if the passengers were not to go short. Back I went in the last boat-load with my spoil which, together with the rest of our belongings, we surreptitiously stored in the hut, since we did not court attention from the tourists. When, however, at last the *Grenadier* steamed off, and we were seen in clear-cut outline against the sky, there appeared to be quite an agitation amongst the passengers, who were obviously under the impression we had been left behind by mistake.

We had already had a substantial meal of sandwiches —too liberal in view of the scant remaining store of provisions which, totally incommensurate with our appetites, would yet have to last us till the *Grenadier* called in at noon next day. However, we were in no mood for any anxious considerations for the future, but living in the present only, we retraced our steps to revel again in the stately solitudes of Fingal's Cave, whose spell was still upon us. There we tested its majestic reverberations by chanting Psalm cxiv. (*In exitu Israel*) to the Tonus Pereginus, and the chant never seemed so dignified and stately as when it re-echoed through this unique vault, accompanied by the sonorous swell of the sea.

After tea, involving further inroads on our slender store,

we made a tour of the island, rough grass its only vegetation, gathering on our way for our prospective fire, driftwood, which we garnered into an obliging golf-cape. We were very distressed to see wherever we went the rocks strewn with dead birds, obviously killed and thrown there by the stress of storm and tempest.

Mackinnon's, and the Cormorants' or Scarts' Cave, which are really two caves, can be seen from the top of the island, lying to the south-west, beyond the Boat Cave. I have not discovered the origin of the name Mackinnon, as applied to this cave, but, as the home of so many birds, the others are obvious in their aptness. The cave is noteworthy alike for its overhanging pillars and the striking effect produced by its noble entrance, 58 feet high and 48 feet wide, when these dark portals are seen from the sea. It is 224 feet long, and at its end there is a gravelly beach upon which a boat can be drawn up. There are other caves in the two bays on the west side of the island, where the cliffs drop down to the sea, and there is the Goat Cave at the north-east angle of the island, but none of them are noteworthy either for size or beauty.

We had been eagerly anticipating the glories of a sunset from these cliffs, looking over the sea to the many islands, with a sunrise to follow at dawn, and thus we were filled with dismay when the beautiful day subsided into a dull evening, followed by a drizzle. Emptying the golf-cape of its firewood within the hut, where it made an imposing stack, we next turned our attention to securing a water supply for the kettle and in the pail for washing purposes. Before Donald left, he had shown me the " spring " across a bog and at no great distance from the hut. If I had not thus been introduced to it, I should never have identified it with the mere trickle that dripped in minute drops from the moss into a tiny hollow of mud, and it took half an hour to fill our modest-sized kettle. The pail we afterwards left to fill at its leisure, which proved to be a matter of hours.

The most unique and diverting night any of us ever spent began by clambering over the roof to erect the stove-pipe preparatory to lighting the fire, and smashing the driftwood against the stone wall.   Having lit the fire, we felt we must do some cooking for supper, and, as the eggs were designed for breakfast, the only thing we could cook was the cheese, so we decided on toasting it.   For this purpose we sacrificed our mirror—the lid of a tin box we had with us—but, unfortunately, the cheese so treated proved such a relish (despite some burning and an attachment it contracted to ashes), that we went on to the eggs, and so were left with only a few biscuits for breakfast next morning.   Bedtime followed upon a very entertaining evening, whose length was determined by that of the candle ends we carried in our pockets for use in the caves.   The rain by this time was falling more heavily, and it was pretty cold, so on both counts, and although I had myself a sufficiency of warm things to distribute, we resolved to keep the fire going all night.   My two friends were to occupy the bunks, while I, as stoker, decided that for freedom of action, I should sleep on the table.   With our makeshift pillows and coverings, we all settled down, but, as it turned out, to laugh the night away rather than to sleep, for the situation, even if not remarkable, appealed to our sense of humour on account of its novelty.   The constant creaking of a wickerwork " pillow " tickled the occupant of the other bunk, and my sliding down at, on an average, half-hour intervals to stoke the fire amused both of my friends vastly.   First wood would be thrust into the stove, and then, after slopping some water out of the pail with a board on to a shovelful of dross, that, too, went on.

Throughout the night we were thrilled by the subterranean thunder, like the discharge of mighty guns, which we heard.   It was a most impressive and could be undoubtedly an awe-inspiring sound—the same that, endured night after night, had by its eerieness at last driven away the shepherd from the island.   This noise is due to

THE SHELTER ON STAFFA

the sudden compression of the air by the rolling surge within those caves I have mentioned as lacking in interest. To lie within that hut, the sound of the waves booming against the cliffs, alternating with the dull roar of underground cannon, and, ever and again, the plaintive cry of some sea-bird, was a unique and unforgettable experience.

Suddenly these distant sounds in which we were revelling were overwhelmed by a near noise, suggesting the invasion by an army of rats, but our blood had not quite turned cold before the " rats " took themselves off as suddenly as they had come. Then we realized that it was a large flock of gulls which had alighted for a few moments on our very low roof.

I think it was before six when we all turned out of bed —not at all a difficult matter after a wakeful night. We performed the best toilet we could with makeshift appliances, and, looking out of doors, we saw the dawn was very misty. Returning indoors, we found our meagre breakfast only less unsubstantial than the mist. Though we had been disappointed by our sunset (and with our breakfast), the morning passed very merrily, and at last, just as we caught sight of the *Grenadier,* it broke into a perfectly glorious day. Despite our painstaking toilet, we were conscious of looking a very disreputable trio to join the spruce tourists whom we saw thronging the boats. We tried to slink unobserved down to the boat after the last load had been landed, but it was impossible to escape notice, and we heard afterwards that some imaginative passenger had given an exciting account of the " rescue " of three ladies in a starving condition (this was quite true) who had been shipwrecked on Staffa. I was so intolerably sleepy, that, though there was every inducement to keep awake, I spent the crossing in involuntary slumber. At no great distance from the pier, our kind, good-natured hostess was awaiting the landing, and, as soon as she saw us, she singled me out, wagging her finger at me:

" I ken fine it was you that was at the bottom o' this

jink.   Did ye no think how anxious I would be—no for you, indeed—but for your twa friends?   There was I last night when it began to rain in a fine to-do.   Indeed, I was not sleeping all night for thinking of you—that is, your twa friends.   And I was just asking Donald, that was not without blame to be leaving you—or, I should say, your twa friends—I was asking him what he would be doing if there was a mist in the morn that would be preventing the *Grenadier* calling in for you?   But Donald, he was just as heedless as yourself indeed, for he said ' Never you bother yourself: they'll come back all right.'   And it's thankful I am he was right (though it's no thanks to him or to *you*), and I'm real glad, not to say relieved, to see you all safely back again, even *you* that is the dare-devil."

————

Note.—Since the chapter was originally written, I have heard that the natives of the adjacent island of Gometra attribute the name of Mackinnon's Cave to him who was Abbat of Iona when the Roman Catholics were driven from that island.   Abbat Mackinnon took refuge here, but, finding it too exposed for a good shelter, he crossed to Mull, and gave his name to the cave at Gribun, where he died.

CHAPTER VIII

THE ATTRACTIONS OF ARDNAMURCHAN

PART I

ITS GENERAL HISTORY, AND ITS DESCRIPTION FROM ORMSAIG TO ARDNAMURCHAN POINT

IN reading the history of the Highlands you become impressed with the importance of Mingary Castle, and the impression is heightened when the architectural authority on Scottish castles not only stresses this and its antiquity, but gives an illustration of the fortress which makes you feel that it would make a very interesting acquaintance. Thus it was Mingary Castle which was responsible for taking a friend and myself to Kilchoan, a mile distant; but on getting there, we found that, in our estimation, this castle was very far from being the most interesting feature of an entirely fascinating peninsula.

With the exception of the dignified domination of Ben Hiant, the approach from the sea gives no indication of the wealth of natural beauty possessed by Ardnamurchan. Seen from the steamer heading for Kilchoan, its shores and the interior look bare and void of interest, while Mingary Castle itself presents by no means an imposing appearance and is distinctly disappointing. But no sooner are you landed on the shore of Kilchoan Bay than the charm of Ardnamurchan steals upon you, and with every advance tightens its grip, until you make entire surrender as its willing, nay exultant, captive.

One of the respects in which I found Ardnamurchan singular met us at the outset, and is possibly due to the extirpation of Clan Maclain and the repopulation with strangers in the seventeenth century. The interests of Kilchoan and the district so far exceeded anything that any printed matter generally accessible, such as the *Statistical Accounts,* had led me to expect, that in all directions I found myself thirsting for more and fuller information concerning what we saw. Elsewhere in the Western Highlands, it is unusual to find, at least among the older natives, any who are entirely ignorant of local history and legend. But here none of all those I asked could tell me anything whatever, except an occasional vague and often incorrect reference to the Campbells of Lochnell. Everyone, after pondering the matter, referred me to some one else who would be able to satisfy me, so I was assured. I asked in all about nine people, and the curious point was that not any two of them referred me to the same person. I first sought information from one who, it was confidently affirmed, was so full of local knowledge that when he once began he would never stop. However, when I found this " authority," a know-nothing Lowlander, he never began! Ultimately I was fortunate enough to hear of an accomplished native of the district who proved to be not only a scholar but an authority on very much more than Ardnamurchan, of which he knows practically all there is to know. This gentleman, Mr. Angus Henderson, now of Stirling, most generously placed at my disposal a wealth of local information contained in many interesting articles on Ardnamurchan which from time to time he has contributed to the Celtic Press. Not only so, but Mr. Henderson has read through this chapter, sparing no pains to answer the many questions I asked him on various points, and correcting the Gaelic, so that readers as well as myself are generally indebted to his interest and good offices. He, of course, is not responsible for my opinions and various conjectures.

Ardnamurchan, which if it means either the promontory of the " great " or of the " narrow " seas, is aptly called, originally rejoiced in the name of *Rìoghachd na Sorcha,* literally the " kingdom of eminence," or, practically, the " hilly kingdom." The peninsula, originally one of the possessions of the great Somerled as Lord of Argyll, was ceded by him to Godred the Black in 1156, after an indecisive battle, and in Norse possession it appears to have remained for about a century. There is nothing of any particular interest to relate until Muchdragan Mac Righ Lochlunn comes on the scene *circa* 1270, and of him in association with one of his vassals, Evan Cléireach, who lived near the foot of Ben Hiant, tradition tells the following tale.

The Norseman was one of the worst of tyrants, and when one day he announced his intention of visiting Evan Cléireach, that shrewd individual suspected designs on his beautiful wife. Thus Evan took the precaution of making sundry preparations previously, the principal one being the concealing of his wife and family on the shore at the far side of Ben Hiant. In due course Muchdragan appeared with an escort, to be met by Evan armed only with his *tuaghairm,* or battle axe, and dressed in a long flowing shirt, evidently the *léine chroich* [1] of the Highlanders. While they engaged in conversation, Evan suddenly threw his axe at Muchdragan, cleaving his skull, and fled up the hollow to the summit of Ben Hiant, pursued by the followers of the Norseman. Near the head of the mountain, one of these caught hold of the tail of Evan's shirt which, giving way in his grasp, precipitated him backwards upon his comrades following close behind. Freed in this way from his pursuers, Evan, half-naked, gained the six-oared boat which he had in readiness at Coire-mhuilinn, and, embarking with his wife and family, made for Islay. According to tradition, Evan induced the

[1] See p. 369.

Lord of the Isles to send his son *Iain Sprangach Mac Aonghais Mhoir,* " John the Bold, the (youngest) son of Angus the Great," to take possession of Ardnamurchan, and from him came the MacIains of that ilk, not to be confounded, however, with Clan Iain Abrach.

History records that in 1292 John Baliol, as King of Scotland, conferred **Ardnamurchan** upon Iain Sprangach on the death of his father, Angus Mor, and in the possession of the MacIains the peninsula remained until the seventeenth century when the clutch of the Campbells fastened upon it.   Both the chief, John Mac Iain, the ally of James IV., and his two sons were killed [2] during the invasion of Ardnamurchan by Sir Donald of Lochalsh, and the chief was buried on Iona. [3]

Whatever glory had appertained to the MacIains of Ardnamurchan departed with the chief John.   His successor, being a minor, was placed by the Crown under the guardianship of Argyll, who, as " lieutenant of the Isles " by Lowland appointment, naturally used the position for the aggrandisement of his house.   The young chief was apparently dead before 1538, when his sister, as heiress to her father's lands, resigned Ardnamurchan in favour of Argyll.   But although next year the King paid £5,000 to Argyll for the same lands, the insidious Campbell influence characteristically continued to be exercised variously until the way was clear for taking possession of Ardnamurchan: and, consequently, when at the beginning of the seventeenth century, Clan Iain was weakened by internal broils, Argyll seized his chance. He had previously taken possession of the title-deeds of the heir of Mac Iain, which, so Argyll discovered, had been left with a citizen of Edinburgh as a pledge for debt

[2] They were killed at a place called *Creag an Airgid* (the rock of silver) gained from the road to Sanna, and are said to have been buried on a knoll close under the south-west side of the hill. But diligent search failed to discover the cairn.

[3] See p. 379.

incurred by Mac Iain in educating his son. In 1612, therefore, Argyll sent as his commissioner to Ardna- murchan, Donald Campbell of Barbreck, a man so stern, unconciliatory, and cruel, that in 1618 Clanranald, pitying the thraldom of his kinsmen, sought to drive the Campbells out of the peninsula. But he failed, and, goaded into revolt, the Mac Iains, taking to piracy, became the terror of the west coast. Their misdeeds culminated in 1624, when they manned and armed an English ship they had seized, drawing down upon themselves dire vengeance, issuing in their extirpation as a clan in 1625. Those who remained appear to have attached themselves to Clan- ranald, and were replaced in Ardnamurchan by families of Mac Iains, Hendersons, and MacLachlans, who had already suffered Campbell dominance in Mid-Argyll. Campbell of Barbreck, as a reward for his services to Argyll, was given possession of the peninsula, and on his death the Lochnells succeeded by purchase, in their turn to be followed by various alien proprietors down to the present day.

Landed on the shore of Kilchoan Bay, which in early summer is starred with the soft pink of myriads of sea- thrift, and turning to your left, a short walk takes you to Ormsaig Beg, where is *Caisteal Dubh nan Cliar,* which once gave its name to the parish of Ardnamurchan. Whether you choose the road with its picturesque straw-thatched cottages, or the track which runs near the sea, and some- times past strange rocks and clifflets, you walk all the while in the fragrance yielded by thick carpets of wild hyacinths and runnels filled with deep purple-leaved water mint. On the glorious day that we stood on the shore at Ormsaig Beg, watching the spray rise as the waves broke, we might have sung with literal truth:

" The land is aflush with spring,
The tide runs high in the bay,
The winds have a clarion ring
And the billows a shining ray."

To our left, across the tumbling waters of the bay, Ben Hiant, calm and serene, reared his majestic form: in the middle distance tossed a sailing-boat, unquietly at anchor: at our feet the waves broke with pleasant plash upon the rocks and stones: now and again a gull contributed its unvarying plaint. Passing on through the lush meadow land, its rich green grass mingled with the purple of spotted orchid, marsh mallow, and newly-opening foxglove, while here and there in thick clusters blossomed the little burnet rose yielding its scent of super sweetness. And now and again we came across beautiful little wells, their crystal-clear water sometimes fringed by ferns or yellow flags—always picturesque in their informal settings of stone.

It is on this fascinating shore that the " Black Castle of the Poet Bards " is found—a strange little building of which no one can tell you anything save that its history is lost in the mists of antiquity. And yet its appearance does not impress you with any great sense of age, for its architecture is not cyclopean nor is the building dry-stone, so that it cannot be prehistoric. Amongst the miniature cliffs which at one part of the shore are broken up into tiny gorges, making natural fortifications, is a huge rock of irregular shape. Against the side of this, a sort of small pent-house has been built of cemented stones and boulders. The interior is roofed with six enormous, over-lapping slabs, and on the top of the rock, besides a striking boulder naturally standing erect, are the remains of some brickwork of indeterminate purpose. Forming a rude semi-circle guarding the small and low entrance to *Caisteal Dubh* are traces of an enclosing wall. What purpose this strange little structure can have served other than that of the abode of some " minstrel " of solitary habit I cannot conjecture, nor how it came to be called a " castle," except on the supposition that the " minstrel " was such a supreme master of his art that, in recognition of his skill, his little hovel had this title gracefully conferred upon it.

GREIDEAL FHINN, LOOKING OVER TO MULL

Almost opposite the landing-place at Kilchoan, there is a track by which you can directly gain the megalithic remains of *Greideal Fhinn*, or " Fionn's Griddle." You follow the track past a cottage until at its end you reach two walls at right angles, and, climbing both of these, you gain, on a slight eminence at Ormsaig Mor, what is called on the map, as indeed generally, a " stone circle." What you see outstanding, however, as you approach these most interesting prehistoric remains from this quarter, are two groups of stones. The larger and more arresting group on the right suggests a roofless chamber, with incomplete and irregular walls ending in a tail of stone ; while the smaller on the left looks to the lay eye like nothing so much as a stone trap ready set- to catch some prey. But to anyone familiar with archæology, both groups are recognizable as denuded cists, the remains of a chambered burial cairn, and indeed the *Statistical Account* records that earthenware urns were found here, although it says nothing as to their precise disposition or contents. Examination of the remains seems to indicate that the cairn which originally covered them was surrounded by a circle of standing stones, for in the slight ridge which still marks its circumference there are suggestions of socket holes in which such stones would originally have been set up, ultimately to be removed, like so much more of the structure, as convenient building material by the natives living near by.

What should be said on the subject of these chambered cairns generally will more fittingly find a place in the last chapter ; so, regarding generalities, I shall do no more than observe that, like the cairn of Nether Largie, to be described in that chapter, this, too, seems to have lacked the passage which ran through many cairns to give entrance to the main burial chamber. At least, there is now no trace of the existence of any such passage. For the rest it will be sufficient to give a brief description of the remains at Ormsaig Mor, together with some very interesting conjectures concerning its naming. Mr. Henderson has made the interesting surmise that since the Norseman Keitil Flatnefr is known in Gaelic as *Caiteal Fionn,* this may be the place of his burial, *Cladh,* the word meaning this, having dropped out in the course of time. This Norseman, " Flatnose," at one time exercised something like supreme power in the domain of the Isles, and he is known to have died somewhere in the West of Scotland. Mr. Henderson suggests that Keitil was buried here (though in this event his would obviously be a secondary, not a primary burial), and this gave to the cairn his name, *Cladh Chaitil Fhinn,* which became corrupted into *Greideal Fhinn.* Certainly neither a " griddle " [4] nor a " cradle," either of Finn or of anyone else, is even remotely suggested by the present remains; nor can one see how the stones can at any period have resembled either object. Mr. Symington Grieve, a well-known antiquary, who has written an exhaustive and fascinating monograph on the subject, quotes Dr. Joseph Anderson as characterizing the " Griddle " as " a rare example of a sepulchral construction of the late Stone or early Bronze Age." Mr. Grieve, who thinks *Finn Mac Cumhail,* the great Fingal himself, may be buried here, states of these remains that " it is the only structure of its kind known in Ardnamurchan." I think I have discovered another which I shall describe in due course.

As seen set against the village of Kilchoan, with Ben Hiant in the far distance, the larger chamber presents a very picturesque and striking appearance, especially if the sun catches the top edges of the stones. The chamber stands near the circumference of the circle east and west, with its entrance on the west, and of its construction eight stones remain, including a large stone, its " tail," $3\frac{1}{4}$ feet high and 4 feet 2 inches broad, which stands at an angle

---

[4] But I have heard of a stone circle in the Lowlands, I think in Dumfries-shire, called a "griddle."

running from north-west to south-east outside and at the end of the chamber. The enclosure is 10 feet 2 inches long, 6½ feet wide, and the height of its highest upright stone, that in the centre at the end, is 5 feet 2 inches. Mr. Grieve, who wrote in 1910, says that the large flat stone which partly roofs the chamber had only recently slipped down on its south-east side. This covering slab, which is almost square, is set cornerwise, and measures 6 feet from corner to corner as thus it rests.

The smaller chamber, which lies about 11 feet to the west of the larger, and near the centre of the circle, has its opening on the south-east. This, from the outside ground level, measures 2 feet 11 inches high, the whole chamber standing 1 foot higher, and having within a cist of small stones now filled with debris. The chamber is formed of five stones, and the covering slab or " roof," which is 3 feet 11 inches long, is 2 feet 5 inches wide at the bottom, its broadest part, and 13½ inches thick at its thickest on the south side, but only 7 inches on the north. The enclosing circle has a diameter of about 67 feet from north to south, and about 1 foot less from east to west; outside its radius on the north lies prone a great stone, 6 feet long, while on the south side lies a slab which has beneath it a shallow hollow filled with stones. As far as the over-growing turf permits of measurements, this stone is about 3 feet 8 inches square.

From *Greideal Fhinn* there is a choice of ways of joining the road to Ardnamurchan Point, for you can either follow a cart track and gain the main road by a bridge, or more immediately and directly by crossing the burn (as best you can) opposite the Wee Free buildings. We took the sublime road on S. Columba's Day, deeming it most fitting to celebrate his festival by making pilgrimage to his island just short of Ardnamurchan Point. It was from every point of view a red-letter day of that perfect summer weather we had come to consider inalienable from Ardnamurchan—overhead a blue sky unflecked with clouds, and the sun shining with unvarying zest from morn till eve. As for the road itself, crossing burns by fords, climbing through the moorland between rugged hills, descending to the shores of beautiful Lochan na Crannaig,[5] then turning in and out till it takes a great curve and a huge dip at the picturesque, old-world, little hamlet of Aodann, it is stored in my memory as one of the most glorious of the many glorious Highland roads that run through my heart, and a fitting theme for song. Indeed, what true Celt does not feel like singing as the road unfolds to him increasingly that joy of nature which he finds in its fullness by moorland, water, and mountain, whatever the weather? For he can mould his mood to Nature's—rejoice with her in sunshine, or muse with her as the mist moves over the mountains, and even in rain can he find refreshment—at least until it attains the height of unvaried monotony.

Down in the hollow where the road finds its lowest level, you enter upon a beautiful little stretch of woodland where the blush of the wild rose adds its charm to the landscape, and the long-drawn plaint of the yellow-hammer replaces the soaring song of the lark. Always a handsome bird, the yellow-hammer in these Western Highlands is peculiarly bright in his colouring and is extraordinarily tame. Not so that other handsome little bird, the stone-chat, which we observed in the more open parts of the road, for flitting about restlessly from bracken top to stone and from stone to furze twig, he gives you little enough chance even to admire him at a distance. At the not infrequent wooden gates crossing the road we would stop, even if they were wide open, to admire the ingenious hinges, which, simply contrived out of material literally to hand, interested us greatly. Selecting a suitable sturdy branch of silver birch, this is cut below the fork, its end is neatly rounded, but as

[5] The existence of a " lake dwelling." is plainly inferred by the name, and presumably has reference to the very small islet, as the only one to be seen.

regards its branching ends it is left untrimmed. The crook of the branch is fitted over the top of the gate-post, a knife being used to ease it at any point where the post is prevented from swinging freely round. In this position the twigged end of the branches are placed to lie along the top of the dyke, and to keep them in position there a row of stones is placed on top of them, a covering of turf serves to bind these stones together, and a short piece of galvanised wire makes all secure. I have never elsewhere seen hinges like these—surely the most ingenious and efficient that simplicity ever contrived.

Views of the islands, Muck, Rum, and Eigg, that we should have obtained from various points of the road, a heat-haze unkindly withheld from us; nor from any place all that day could we manage to snatch more than a faint, fleeting, and begrudged glimpse of them—our one disappointment. When the road turns sharply to the left, and so continues, it enters upon a new phase, the barren moorland sweeping over in wide stretches to the hills where Ben na Sealg holds commanding sway. Reaching Girgadale across the wide moorland, you are enchanted with the little cluster of thatched cottages nestling in the hollow of the hills, with the reedy lochan behind them.

It was here that the notorious riever of the 17th century, Mac Iain Ghiòrr (the son of John the Short), had an extensive farm, to which he repaired when deprived of certain lands in his native Appin. Tradition says that he augmented his own very small stock of cattle in the following ingenious manner. He had a clever mare which he would ride out to a distant region where he might tie to her tail any good horse he found grazing on the hills. This done, Mac Iain Ghiòrr's well-trained and sagacious accomplice would lead the stolen horse off home by some out-of-the-way route, while her master would return by a different track. But Mac Iain Ghiòrr did not restrict himself to operations on the land. *"Per mare, per terras,"* was *his* motto as well as that of his race, and equally cunningly did he conduct his campaign by sea amongst the islands. In order to disguise his boat and make detection difficult, he frequently changed both the colour of it and of his sails, and indeed often had them a different colour on either side, so that there is still an old saying—

> " One side white the other black,
> Like the boat of Mac Iain Ghiòrr."

Many tales are told of the craft with which he evaded conviction, substantiating *alibis* which always cleared him of the charges brought against him. After his last trial, he retired from cattle-lifting in favour of farming on legitimate lines, and departed this life about 1650.

Here at Girgadale, just a little short of the goal of our pilgrimage, we most appositely encountered a white horse.
me, as her fellow clanswoman, with milk and a huge scone,
The good wife at the farm near by who generously dowered
was intensely interested in hearing it was S. Columba's
Day, and of the incident, which I then proceeded to tell her, of the white horse and the saint prior to his death. Indeed, such an impression did the familiar story make upon her that on our return we discovered she had already retailed it to two or three people who had looked in to see her.

What can I say of Port na Cairidh that may conjure up even the faintest ghost of the picture of loveliness that it presents, for it is beautiful beyond words—a treasury of silver and of shimmering jewels? Imagine yourself passing through a bed of iris ablaze with its yellow flowers, and looking through a rocky foreground. There, where a small burn trickles down over sea-weed covered stones, Highland cattle stand cooling themselves in the water, or lie upon the sand white as the breast of the sea-swallow which is darting time after time into the water for its food. Dark amethyst and glittering emerald in belts cut across the turquoise of the main body of the sea, the foreground of which is broken with picturesque glimpses of rocks where the slowly receding tide is revealing golden sea-wrack and an ever-increasing expanse of gleaming sands:

> " The sands are a silver sheet
> And the waves a revel of light,
> Where motion and music meet,
> And colour and form unite."

Beyond, the haze dims the outline of Muck, and only when the veil is lifted for a space can you see Rum, island of dreams, and Eigg of all delights.   On the left inshore, however, is another island, and this, a tumble of rocks partially clothed with grass and with sea-weed at the water's edge, is Eilean Chaluim Chille, the tiny rocky islet of S. Columba set in Port na Cairidh.   Local tradition says that when " making a journey through the rough and rocky district which is called Artdamurchol," as recorded by Adamnan, the saint spent a night on the islet, thence called after him, Eilean Chaluim Chille.   Thus our pilgrimage was not consummated until we had waded out to the island and explored it from end to end, without, however, finding anything to record.

On one part of the shore of Port na Cairidh, where it shelves down beside a large rock, the white of the sand yields to a mass of multi-coloured minute shells.   Here you find periwinkles in brown, red, yellow, and green, with opalescent pearly tops, a few cowrie shells, and, most attractive of all, exquisite little scallop-shells of the kind known as " variable," because their colour differs so widely.   Here it is of a bright salmon-pink delicately shading into white.

Before starting on our return journey, we crossed a peat bog to climb a hill whence we could see the lighthouse, as marking the most westerly point of Scotland.   It was when passing Ardnamurchan Point that the incident occurred in the career of Somerled the Great that, according to tradition, gave the Clan Macintyre its name.   Olaf the Red, King of Man and the Isles, had refused his daughter to Somerled, who, determined to have her, accepted the offer of his foster brother, one Maurice MacNeill, to contrive means to force Olaf's consent. Somerled and Olaf were cruising at the time, and Maurice, on board the King's galley, bored holes in its bottom, and filled them with butter, at the same time making pins which would effectually stop up the holes when the butter was washed away. This occurred when Olaf's galley, followed by Somerled's, encountered the stormy seas off Ardnamurchan. Finding his vessel sinking, Olaf called for assistance to Somerled, who refused all help until the King promised him his daughter in marriage. This done Somerled received the Norseman in his galley, whereupon Maurice quickly stopped the holes with the pins he had made, and this saved Olaf's galley from sinking. Hence his descendants are called to this day *Cloinn-an-t-Saoir,* or Macintyres, " sons of the wright," though another version of the origin of this surname attributes more heroic action to the progenitor of the clan, alleging him to have been alone in his boat when it sprang a leak, stopping the hole with his thumb, and cutting it off to free himself for steering the boat into port.

Part II

KILCHOAN, CAMUS NAN GEALL, AND COIRE-MHUILINN

When you are once more opposite Greideal Fhinn, it is merely a matter of minutes before you are through the gate that takes you on to the main road at right angles. This runs along the beautiful shores of Kilchoan Bay, and, turning to the left, it is no great distance to the fine situation on the hillside where is the ancient burial-ground of Kilchoan.

The church of Eilean Finan originally served the whole district of Ardnamurchan, then of greater extent than now, when the River Shiel is its boundary. It was in the 13th century that a large portion of the diocese of Dunkeld was taken away to form the diocese of Argyll. Then the peninsula was divided into three parishes, Ardnamurchan, Arisaig, and Sunart—Eilean Finan first being allocated to Sunart as its church, though afterwards it was included in the parish of Arisaig. Kilmory of Arisaig became the mother church of Arisaig, and Kilchoan of Ardnamurchan.

Kilchoan commemorates S. Comgan, whose day is October 13th. This saint, an eighth century abbat, was the son of an Irish prince, and was the brother of S. Kentigerna and the nephew of S. Fillan. Forced to flee from Ireland, Comgan lived for many years in Lochalsh, and is said to have been buried on Iona. Such are all the very scant details known of the life of the saint to whom the mother parish of Ardnamurchan was dedicated.

Within the ancient burial-ground there is the shell of an entirely uninteresting, featureless building, only dating from the 18th century, probably occupying the site of the old church. No words can be too strong to characterise the condition of the churchyard, the neglect of which is altogether scandalous and without excuse. Rank growths, particularly of nettles growing to a considerable height, have been allowed to obscure the ancient gravestones, and when, at the cost of many stings and much fruitless effort, you at last succeed in getting down to some hidden slab, it is only to find it moss-grown. Two sculptured slate stones of the Middle Ages, which I found lying side by side, are worthy of note and are said to have been " brought " from Iona by the celebrated free-booter of Ardnamurchan, *Mac Iain Ghìorr,* wherewith to mark the graves of his father and mother. The first stone, which is intact, displays at the top a galley with furled sails, flying a flag and shewing a shield. Between the two masts a pair of shears is shewn, a very unusual position for them to occupy.

Below the galley is a charming and unique zoomorphic design, considerably weathered, but sufficiently distinct to allow of its nature being made out.   Four very spirited animals are shewn in pairs *addorsé*, all very much rampant regardant, the partners facing each other, each with one fore and one hind leg bent at right angles to their bodies, and each respectively conjoined.   The tails of the two animals *addorsé* are intertwined.   The usual sword with folaginous tracery on each side runs down the centre of the stone, and beneath it is a very uncommon representation of a man engaged in combat with some beast. Unfortunately, the figure and the associated representatives are too worn to determine certain very interesting details, but the man appears to be wearing a helmet with a long pendant for attachment to the waist, such as is more clearly seen on Macmillan's Cross, Kilmory Knap—all very suggestive of the capuchon with liripipe headdress.   These peculiar helmets, designed to enable the wearer to recover them if struck off in fight, were in vogue at the end of the 13th and beginning of the 14th century.   The warrior is more probably wearing the usual haketon rather than the unusual kilt.   So worn is the stone that it is impossible to identify the curious but indeterminate beast—perhaps a merman—which he appears to be grasping by the throat, while with his left hand he thrusts his sword into it. Alongside, but entirely aloof, there is a very beautifully executed sculpture of a stag.   The second stone has unfortunately the top broken off and is very badly weathered; although the broken piece still shews a very beautiful and uncommon square design of a cross interwoven with four concentric circles.   A fleur de lys enters the surrounding border lines at each angle, and between these, the termination of the arms of the cross, is a Stafford knot. A design of shamrocks runs on either side of the sword which centres the stone, and beasts are shewn on either side of the pommel; while at the foot is a galley.

It is said that John, the only son of the famous Red Comyn, died and was buried at Kilchoan in 1325-26, but of this Mr. Henderson knows nothing.

During the first establishment of Episcopacy, the Bishop of Argyll sent Donald Omey to serve as first reformed priest in Ardnamurchan, and expressed the hope that the chieftains (presumably of Clans Donald and Campbell alike) would respect him.   But on February 12, 1624, Omey reported that on the last Sunday, while he was preaching, a young man armed with a targe, sword, and hackbut came in, and " verie rudlee, with ane awfull and fierce countenance, addresst himself " to the complainer, handing him a letter from Clanranald telling him to begone as he valued his life.   As he *did* value his life, Donald Omey departed, to be succeeded in 1629 by Duncan M'Calman, a priest more fitted to commend the reformed principles of Episcopacy to the Romanist clansmen.   These would not attend the reformed services, but instead occupied themselves in putting the stone outside the church.   Thereupon out came M'Calman, a big strong man, and exhibited a prowess equal to the best of the putters, so impressing the astonished clansmen that they trooped in after him when he re-entered the church to resume his interrupted service.   When Episcopacy was first disestablished in favour of Presbyterianism, M'Calman was excommunicated by the Presbyterians as a Royalist, but surviving the Restoration, he resumed his ministry in 1672 under Episcopacy re-established.

The reversion to the faith of the church of S. Columba thus made in Ardnamurchan unhappily succumbed, as it did elsewhere, to the forcible persuasions of Presbyterianism, which had the State to enforce its claims both with military and money.   Thus when, in 1697, Alexander Macdonald, the famous Maighstir Alasdair, Episcopalian incumbent of Ardnamurchan and father of the celebrated bard, refused to conform to Presbyterianism, he was deposed by the Presbytery of Lorn for " Nonjurancy."

But the people were so devoted to him that no Presbyterian minister dared make an appearance in his lifetime. For all that, the hollow ceremony of declaring the church vacant, in accordance with Presbyterian custom, was gone through, the Presbyterian minister of Ardchattan volunteering to undertake the performance, one doubly congenial to him as a Campbell. This minister, in kilt and armed with sword and pistol, set his back to the wall of Kilchoan Church and defied the people who refused him admittance. Thus was Presbyterianism demonstrated up and down the Highlands to be " most agreeable to the inclinations of the people " !

" Master Alexander " was not only a very remarkable man of parts, " of candour, ingenuity, and conscience," but of immense strength and physical prowess, for living at Dalelea, on Loch Shiel, he would leave home at an early hour on Sunday morning for the church at Kilchoan, walking *via* Gorten, Ockle, and Kilmory. Reaching Kilchoan before mid-day, he would take service and walk back again, regaining Dalelea before midnight, after walking altogether between fifty and sixty miles. This he would do every Sunday and in all weathers. He died somewhere between 1720 and 1725, and was buried on Eilean Finan.

After the Revolution, what is called a " Government Church " was built and endowed for the Presbyterians by the Government. Yet for all the might of Presbytery in erastian alliance with the State, the Synod of Argyll had to record in 1728 that " the people of Ardnamurchan " are " for the most part of different principles to the Church of Scotland," as by Act of Parliament created; and ten years later, the Presbytery of Lorn notes that the inhabitants of the same region are " mostly Papists," and " the rest high-fliers disaffected to Church and State." Thus are described the Episcopalians who were faithful to their principles. The anonymous Whig author of the *Highlands of Scotland in 1750* gives the Ardnamurchan people the same character as those of Appin.[6] Although Roman Catholics, strangely enough, seem to have disappeared entirely from Ardnamurchan proper, S. Mary's, Shiel Bridge, being their nearest church, Episcopacy apparently persisted there later. For in 1835 Sir James Riddell of Ardnamurchan wrote to Bishop Low in quaint terms requesting that a church might be built to accommodate himself, his family, and thirty or forty " pristine mannered poor Episcopalians " in his neighbourhood. The Church of S. Finnan at Kinlochmoidart seems to have been the outcome of this request.

Regaining the main road to make a circular tour of Ben Hiant, in order to reach the exquisite bay of Camus nan Geall and to return by Mingary Castle, the outstanding impression you receive all the way is that King Midas has preceded you. For on all sides there is evident the touch of gold, from the soft sheen of the marsh marigold in which a meadow is asmother, to the blaze of the gorse and broom[7] with which the moorland is agleam, its pungent perfume almost overpowering. Pursuing the road for a matter of two miles, you climb a wire fence and cross by a bridge the Coire-mhuilinn Burn in order to strike the track which is supposed to be plainly visible all the way on this side of Ben Hiant until the road again appears to view. But like many another mountain track, its route is only obvious on the map, and we had to depend almost entirely upon our sense of direction as guide.

Almost the only attraction we found on this tramp was that of the numberless curlews whose haunting cry never fails in its appeal, and in stray deer which from some hollow on the mountain side bounded out to make away at our distant approach. Apart from this, we found little of interest save association with the tale of Muchdragan and Evan. Below Ben Hiant we traversed the base of

[6] See p. 309.

[7] In Gaelic this is *Bealaidh*, the flower sacred to Baal.

Beinn na h-Urchrach, the "hill of the cast or throw," where Evan threw his axe at the Norseman. But there we did *not* see Muchdragan's Cairn, marking the spot where he fell, and we may or may not rightly have identified the exact " hollow of the pursuit," Glac na Toire, up which Evan fled. When at last we descended on to the road running through Cuil Eoghainn,[8] we found it absolutely dull, and were thankful when we gained the bridge for the promise of more interesting scenery beyond. Nor were we disappointed in our hope.

We had not walked very much beyond the bridge when we saw spread out before and far below us in the distance the beautiful shores of Camus nan Geall, our objective. Leaving the road, we made our way over marshy ground and down by a plantation on the far side of Buarblaig into the exquisite little grassy hollow. This secluded paradise is completely sheltered on three sides by the surrounding hills which rise protectingly round its flat, smooth, green sward, yielding at the water's edge to the purest of silver sands. On both sides of the bay, at the base of the hills, are the all too familiar ruins of cottages, speaking dumbly of yet another deserted hamlet, and here and there are a few groups of stately elms. We passed between two of these, the trees in pairs, towards a long line of them, and at the foot of the two nearest I observed a group of large stones, which soon resolved themselves into megalithic remains similar to those of *Greideal Fhinn.*

A cairn of very considerable dimensions is indicated by the remaining stones, which form a segment of a circle. At one end, inconveniently close to the elms, is a large group of five stones forming a chamber resembling the larger of *Greideal Fhinn.* This I cleared of the stones filling it till I reached a slab I could not move by reason of my cramped quarters. This clearance revealed an entrance between two pillar stones, and beyond these

8 The nook of Evan—probably where he lived.

SCULPTURED MONOLITH AT "CLADH CHIARAIN"

another, leaning against a huge stone, formed a roof.   The
fifth stone stands outside the leaning stone.   Of the outlying
stones, that nearest the chamber had apparently fallen out
of the perpendicular over some smaller stones, possibly
from the original cairn.   The other two stones, in juxta-
position, the upright about a foot high, that lying alongside
somewhat larger, were probably the remains of a stone
circle surrounding the cairn.

Leaving these stones, and crossing the wide space of
green sward to where, in the centre, is the small isolated
enclosure of Cladh Chiarain, I at once made for the tall
monolith of unhewn stone which stands facing south on
the side of the sea.   This, set in the circular grass-grown
ridge indicating presumably the original *vallum,* is a pillar
of some rough red granite-like stone of the same variety
as those under the elm trees.   The back of the stone has
no ornament other than lichen, but on the front I made
the intensely interesting discovery not only of a rudely
sculptured irregular cross, with bosses in the angles of the
arms, but above it, of the rude figure of a dog, his long
tail curling over his back.   So far as I can ascertain, both
the megalithic remains under the elm trees and this ancient
pillar cross have hitherto entirely escaped notice.   Dogs,
of course, are quite commonly found in the representations
of hunting scenes on the mediaeval stones, but this
is obviously a very much earlier cross, probably one of
the earliest in Argyllshire, and I cannot recollect any other
example of a similar sculpture of primitive age.

While some hazard Camus nan Gall, the " bay of the
stranger," for Camus nan Geall, as it is now rendered,
Mr. Henderson conjectures that the name originally was
Camus nan Ceall, the " bay of the churches or cells."
According to Ardnamurchan tradition, S. Kiaran, bishop
and abbat, the friend and schoolfellow of S. Columba,
was buried here; hence the enclosure is called *Cladh
Chiarain* after him.   This Irish missionary, after labouring
in Cornwall, where he is known as S. Piran, came to the

West of Scotland, a predecessor of his more famous friend, and settled at Campbeltown, becoming the patron saint of Kintyre. Yet the Irish chronicles say nothing whatever of his migration here, though S. Kiaran gained a high reputation throughout Scotland for his asceticism and sanctity. He is said never to have looked on a woman and never to have told a lie. He founded the great monastery of Clonmacnois in Ireland .S. Columba, in a hymn lauding his memory, calls him " the light of this Isle." There is a very ancient MS. missal, discovered in the 18th century in Drummond Castle, which contains a very beautiful prayer attributed to S. Kiaran. In it the saint prays thus:—

> " O, thou Son of God, have mercy on one devoted to Thy service. Heat and quicken my benumbed soul. should I have quickly failed if Thou hadst not supported Long have Thy visits been denied to my cell. Yet me. I will therefore render Thee the tribute of my highest praise, before the multitude of the people; and place whatever pangs I may endure to the score of my own sin and folly."

When animals are so often associated with the saints, with those of the Celtic Church more especially, I had hoped to find a dog in some way identified with S. Kiaran, in order to be able definitely to connect with him the monolith thus sculptured with his symbol. It is a cow, however, which figures most in connection with S. Kiaran in the Irish lives, and it is not possible even for the most vivid imagination to see the remotest resemblance to a cow in the animal above the cross. Possibly, however, a dog may be intended to represent some attribute of the saint, as, e.g., in the case of S. Bernard the Great. As it was prophesied at his birth that he should be " a faithful watchdog of the House of the Lord," and his life fulfilled the prophecy, S. Bernard is often depicted in art with a dog beside him. But, again, the dog here may simply be intended to imply that a dog was buried with his master.[9]

S. Kiaran died on September 9, 548, at the very early age of thirty-four, and if, never having lived in Ardnamurchan, his body were brought to Camus nan Geall for burial, might not he have given rise to the name of the bay as that of the " stranger "?

But whatever the meaning of the name, the history of Camus nan Geall is by no means exhausted by its connection with S. Kiaran.   Mr. Henderson derives Buarblaig, the name of the adjacent farm, from *muir,* sea, and *bulg,* bulge or eminence; and following Fr. Charles Macdonald, identifies it with the *Muirbolc Paradisi* of Adamnan.

It was whilst " making a journey through the rough and rocky district called Artdamurchol " that S. Columba, hearing his companions, Laisran and Diarmit, speak of two Irish rulers, told them that these chiefs had recently been beheaded, prophesying that some sailors from Ireland would that day confirm his statement.   It was to *Muirbolc Paradisi* that these sailors came, and the reasons for thinking this place Camus nan Geall are more cogent than those which identify it, as is commonly done, with Port Murloch in Lismore.   Whilst Adamnan leaves it vague as to whether *Muirbolc Paradisi* was in Ardnamurchan or within a day's sail of it, the gentle loveliness of this fertile spot, in such striking contrast to the vigorous beauty of the rest of the country as a whole, bold, barren, and rocky, certainly suggests a peaceful paradise, a veritable garden of Eden, quite apart from the evidence of the adjacent Muirbolc.

In Book II. of Adamnan there is a reference to

[9] Whilst this was in the press, my attention was called to a book in which it is asserted that " Ciaran is the son of a female dog-head " (from the alleged translation of his alleged mother's name). Although the book in question is, in more estimates than mine, a mass of valueless, rambling conjectures, this specific quotation is, perhaps, worth giving in connection with the dog on the monolith.

Chambas Art Murchol, which is invariably identified with Camus nan Geall. One, Joan, of royal race, was an evil doer and a spoiler who persecuted a priest, Colman Ela, who was a much-loved friend of S. Columba, devastating his homestead on no less than three separate occasions and carrying off everything discoverable. On the third occasion, as Joan and his followers were returning laden with spoil to their ship, they met S. Columba. But instead of yielding to the persuasions and prayers of the saint, who besought them to relinquish his plunder, Joan sneered at and mocked Columba as he took on board his ill-gotten gains. Thereupon the Abbat followed Joan as far as the sea, and " walking into the crystal waters up to his knees," prayed to Christ with both hands raised. " Then the saint, his prayer ended, returns to the dry land and sits down with his companions on rather high ground," when he prophesied the fate which would overtake Joan on his voyage. This incident seems to suggest that Colman Ela lived at Camus nan Geall, and if so, the conjecture that the name means " bay of cells " is surely thereby strengthened. This Irish bishop, or priest, can only have lived here temporarily, however, for he is known to have died in Ireland; otherwise one might conjecture that the pillar cross marked his grave.

There is a great leap in time from these days to those of the remaining associations of Camus nan Geall as the burial place of the Campbells of Lochnell, who are remarkable as a sept which became, in the eighteenth century, dissociated from their clan generally, both in religious and political principles. For then Colin Campbell of Acharn, the fourth son, brother of Sir Duncan Campbell of Lochnell, became a Roman Catholic, the first to take this step. Subsequently taking Holy Orders and becoming priest of Moidart, he acted as chaplain to the Roman Catholic Jacobites at Culloden, and, wearing the kilt, was killed. Lochnell himself and his third brother, Alexander of Slignish, also fought for the Prince on this fatal field, doubtless inheriting their Jacobitism from their mother, who was the only child of Duncan Stewart of Appin.

Within the outer ancient boundary of Cladh Chiarain is· now a roughly-built enclosing wall shewing trace of neither doors nor windows, nor any indication that it has ever served as a Catholic place of worship. Within at one end, two 18th century tombstones are reared side by side against the wall. Both exhibit the clumsy " art " of their age, and above both are lumpishly executed cherubs' heads set in wings. Beneath this, one stone has just the Lochnell coat of arms, but the other is of real interest, for on it is a representation of the Crucifixion, which, as rarely attempted at this period, is worth describing, especially as it has several curious features. The Sacred Figure, His aureoled Head inclining far over to the left, has His arms stretched straight out along the arms of the cross, which consists of them only, no shaft appearing vertically. Above the head I.N.R.I. appears, and what is probably A. and O. on either side. If there is any inscription on either tombstone, it is illegible. Outside this enclosure, beautiful with a carpet of hyacinths when we saw it, and near the monolith, are two fragments of sandstone slabs, one of which still shews a skull and cross-bones.

Climbing up the hillside on to the main road, I walked towards Ardslignish, to find that " health-giving well called after S. Columba " which Adamnan records is in Artdaib Muirchol, that is, Ardnamurchan, where lived the parents of one Lugucencalad. This infant boy was by his parents presented to the saint for holy baptism at a place where there was no water to be found. Thereupon S. Columba turned aside to the nearest rock, and after praying beside it on his bended knees, rose and blessed the brow of the rock, from which water at once ·bubbled up in abundance, enabling him to baptise the boy. And still, on the left, just a little off the road before it turns round at Ardslignish, S. Columba's Well [10] issues from the base of a rock, forming a pool of beautiful spring water,

and thence trickling down to the road.   There was unfortunately no time to do more than snatch a glimpse of the
entrancing prospect of Loch Sunart as its craggy shores
disclose themselves here, but returning to Camus nan
Geall, the view from the edge of the lower road emphasised
its claim to be called a paradise.   On one side the hill-
slope is wooded, and beneath the trees glowed a purple
haze of hyacinths, but elsewhere the unrelieved emerald
green of the hills holds the hollow in the centre of which is
Cladh Chiarain.   Bathed in sunshine, the sea was dazzling
in its beauty—

> " And ev'n as the waves that swing
>   And swirl on the shining sand,
> The billowy life of the Spring
>   Rolls over the sunlit land."

Once upon that shore of silver, above which the water, as
in the days of Columba, shewed " crystal clear," it was
difficult to leave it.   But home we had to go, and as we had
not appreciated the way we came, and the shore appeared
very attractive, we yielded to its allurements and, taking
our way by the sea, began our return journey to Kilchoan.

The first half provided us with a beautiful walk of
varied interests.   As we looked across the little " bay of
the cells " to the cliffs which rise high on the further
side, we were very impressed by two features of their
formation, both of which it was difficult to believe were
solely due to Nature's talented sculptors.   One, high up
against the sky-line, was a huge stone very suggestive of
a monolith like that at Cladh Chiarain, set up by human
agency ; and the other, lower down, bore a most striking
resemblance to a castle, and yet was simply the result of
weathering.   Our walk curved in and out by the shore,
now taking us over the beach itself, then climbing up over

---

[10] The factor, who shewed me the well, which he said had been certainly
identified by Father Charles, told me that the inhabitants now generally
term S. Columba's Well a trickle issuing from an iron spout on the left hand
side of the road after it turns to the left and descends the hill.

the grassy slopes of the hill-side.   Here we walked past
a hollow breaking up through the hills that lay on our
right; there we passed under the shadow of the cliffs,
which at one point once sheltered a tiny clachan, now in
ruins.

Then we began a climb which continued steadily up to
the point where some Maclean over from Mull has permanently poked his nose into territory to which he never could
lay claim.   The cliffs, which rise here to a considerable
height, are very picturesque with their fretted heads and
chasmed sides, but the going becomes increasingly rough
over the scree for which the cliffs are responsible—huge
fallen rocks plentifully tumbled down the hillside.   Up
to this point, however, there was nothing for a lover of
sturdy exercise to complain of, but when, leaving the fallen
rocks behind, we began the climb over Maclean's Nose,
we left easy exercise behind us.   Our path, now increasing
in steepness, lay over a débris of small loose stones; and,
laden with the very considerable traps appertaining to
painting, photography, and picnicking, we had to toil up
the slippery ascent under the sun's warmest approval.
We would have better appreciated his more modified
approbation as, sliding and slipping, we strove to make
permanent headway and to avoid falling down the precipitous hillside.   At last we did gain the summit and a
superb view over the sunlit sound to Mull rewarded our
struggles, but very soon after, in making our way over
the headland, we lost the track we had hitherto followed
and, plunging into a wood, were again involved in
unpleasant and difficult going.   And so it continued all
the way to Coire-mhuilinn.   We had the choice of literally
pushing our way through a wood where the trees grew both
low and close together and where we were often plunging
through bogs and mud; or else the equally uneasy going
provided by the huge and uneven stones and rocks of the
shore.   Indeed, so exasperating were the difficulties we
encountered in making our way along that we did not

appreciate, as otherwise we should have done, the many attractions of the walk along this singularly beautiful stretch of coast. On the contrary, we were thankful when, on the near side of Coire-mhuilinn, we at last gained the rock of Evan's Nook, where that hero concealed his boat.

This incident, however, is the least distinction of the beautiful "hollow of the mill," for through it flows the stream of which Alasdair Mac Mhaighstir Alasdair has sung in his famous "Sugar Brook," in English an inept and even silly title for the beautiful Gaelic *Allt an t-Siucair*. The poet had a farm on the side of the stream, and in this poem he describes in animated and appreciative language the charm of a lovely summer morning in the setting of this secluded spot. In his walk abroad, the bard misses nothing. He hears the varied songs of the birds, notes the dew glittering as diamonds on blade and leaf, the bees sucking sweetness from the flowers, and the cattle peacefully grazing. There is joy everywhere in the sunshine: the stream dances, the fish leap, the calves and kids frisk in sportive frolic, the herdsman and milkmaid are busy in unhurried labour. The ground is gemmed with flowers of every hue, and on the sea, ships, white-winged, speed on their courses.

So subtle a language is the Gaelic, conveying so much to the Gael that is absolutely untranslateable, that the best of English versions must give an utterly inadequate rendering, failing entirely to convey the beauty of the original. Thus the following extract from the " Sugar Brook " is like a watery version of the rich wine of the Gaelic:—

> "When passing o'er the Sugar Brook
>   One fragrant morn in May,
> The meadows, wet with dew-drops,
>   Shone bright at dawn of day;
> The crimson-breasted robin
>   Was pouring forth his lay,
> The cuckoo's note of gladness
>   Rose from the scented spray.

" Thy limpid waters laving
  Rich banks of bonny green.
Where in its silv'ry splendour
  The salmon oft is seen;
He leaps in all his glory
  To catch the flies at play,
And lashes with his playing
  The waters into spray.

" Thy crystal stream goes flowing
  Through many a grassy lea,
Supplying sap and fragrance
  To every herb and tree;
The honey-bee is roaming
  In yonder flowery dell,
The nectar from the roses
  He stores within his cell.

" How pleasant is the lowing
  Of cattle by the fold,
Their calves around them playing,
  How pleasant to behold!
The milkmaid sings her chorus
  To cattle in the dale,
While they to overflowing
  Soon fill the milking-pail."

This and other poems of the Clanranald bard are thought to have been written between 1725 and 1745. It was in his Presbyterian days that Alasdair Mac Mhaighstir Alasdair served as schoolmaster and catechist at Ardnamurchan and itinerated the district. He settled first at Eilean Finan, moving thence to Kilchoan, and finally to Coire-mhuilinn.

————

PART III

MINGARY CASTLE

As we made our way from the " Sugar Brook " to Mingary, a walk always sufficiently beautiful from the rugged character of the shore along which reefs of rock thrust themselves into the sea, we were brought to a halt by a display of early summer, " decking the fields in holiday array." At our feet lay outspread a bed of globe flower, its pale gold scattered broadcast with royal largesse, while above rose the " faire flow'ring of the hawthorne tree." Passing on, the Castle, sturdily planted on its rocky base, soon dominated the landscape—rocks fretting the sea at its foot, broken rugged moorland in the foreground, and mountains rising in gradually receding planes behind—the whole tremulous in the limpid gold with which Nature suffuses her pictures against the light. We first came upon the Castle, however, in the morning, approaching it from behind and from the other side. Passing round the encircling wall, we stood in a field where hyacinths in countless numbers made a mass of purple blue in the foreground, and stretched out in all directions in an unbroken carpeting until their individuality was lost in a soft purple haze. In this deliciously perfumed prospect, the grey hoary walls of the Castle, rising above a rocky chasm, stood out stalwart and massive against the dancing sea, the faint coast of Mull, and the radiant blue of the sky.

Mingary Castle, the stronghold of the Mac Iains of Ardnamurchan, is a 13th century building, in shape an irregular hexagon, surrounded on four sides by the sea, and protected on the other two by a deep fosse cut out of the rock, alongside which we stood in the field of hyacinths. Here we were faced by the north wall, in which, beneath a more regular row of openings, are four lancet windows, very irregularly arranged. Of the upper pair, the further is a double lancet, and in the lower set the first is placed between the two upper windows and the second beyond them. All now are very rudely blocked up with stones, and besides them the only others are found in the east wall, which does not face the open sea. All the walls have their angles rounded and all the way round there are embrasures. The apertures which are seen below the battlements are for the most part probably simply gargoyle-less gutters to carry off the water from the walk round the parapet. The upright loopholes on the north

MINGARY CASTLE, ARDNAMURCHAN, FROM NORTH-EAST

walls were probably designed to allow the shooting of assailants in the ditch below, and those above the landward entrance probably took joists carrying a platform to defend the doorway beneath. That above these specific apertures there are larger ones which would open out on to such a platform, strengthens the likelihood of this conjecture.

The tide being low, it was possible to go right round the Castle, and climbing down into the chasm that yawned below, I walked along a huge rampart of rock thrusting far out into the sea. From the vantage ground thus afforded, I remarked what a splendid natural causeway of rock led up to the rude stairway which gave access to the seaward entrance of the Castle. This, in the case of a sea-going race was the principal gateway, and probably the galleys would find shelter in the natural gulley round the corner on the east side. Traversing the causeway, the basaltic formation upon which the Castle was reared is very striking, for its pillars are hoary with lichen and the hollow left by one which has broken away right in the front forms a niche which exactly imitates an empty shrine. The wall in which the seaward port opens is crowned on both sides with angle turrets, the third turret to which Macgibbon and Ross allude and which they depict on the north wall, being conspicuous by its absence, as a photograph conclusively demonstrates. Nor could I see their projection on single corbels, as alleged by the same authority, to allow of the opening thus secured being used for defensive operations. On the contrary, both turrets had every appearance of retaining their original solid bases. On the shore, to the west of the Castle, lies a cannon associated with Colkitto's siege, the only one left there by an erstwhile alien proprietor.

We entered the Castle by the landward port, crossing the ditch by the remains of a stone bridge which had probably superseded an original one of wood. There is a long narrow ingoing from this postern, and here are the remains of the outside stair which led up to the battlements. The under-structure of this, together with two small

garde-robes in the east and west walls respectively, and
what is possibly the remains of a dungeon on the west
side, are apparently the only original interior buildings
left.   Probably all the others, if they were not wholly
demolished, at least suffered very material damage at the
hands of Sir Donald Macdonald of Lochalsh in 1517, and
subsequent sieges may have completed their ruin.   However that may be, the present buildings within the Castle
only date from the 18th century and are probably
due to the Campbells of Lochnell.   They are entirely
uninteresting; very dilapidated; full of rubbish; and rank
with a profuse growth of nettles.   The space enclosed by
the walls is about 65 feet from north to south and 53 feet
from east to west, and the only object of interest within
them is the seaward port, its width on the outside only
2 feet 10 inches.   The ingoing, however, is splayed until it
attains about another foot in width on the inside.   Midway
within the entry was an inner wooden door, for the sliding
bar of which the slot in the wall still remains, as well as
the recess which probably the sentry used to store his
arrows or other missiles.   This water-port, standing high
above the sea, used to be defended on the outside by an
iron yett which has only suffered " removal " within
recent years, apparently at the same hands as those which
" removed " Colkitto's cannon.

Concerning the history of the Castle, Mr. Henderson has
preserved a local tradition which might have reference to
some previous Norse castle, the forerunner of the present
building.   According to this tradition, between the
flight of Evan and the arrival of Iain Sprangach, the
fortress of Mingary was held by some Macdougals of
Lorne.   Iain Sprangach and his force landed at Ormsaig,
and sending out a party to reconnoitre, met in Mingary
park a company of Macdougals out for the same purpose.
In the fight that ensued, the Mac Iains killed all the
Macdougals save one only, and he, to save his life, agreed
to accompany the Mac Iains to the Castle.   Thus, under

cover of night, the Mac Iains stealthily advanced to the postern, where the solitary Macdougal demanded admittance. The sentry, recognising the voice of a comrade, opened the gate, and so the Mac Iains were enabled to rush in and seize the stronghold.

After the Crown's forfeiture of the Lordship of the Isles, James IV., in pursuit of his policy of crushing the powerful Clan Donald, visited Mingary Castle and held Court there, first on October 25th, 1493, and again on May 18th, 1495, when he received the submission of several island chiefs. This act entailed not only the transference of allegiance from the Lord of the Isles to the Scottish King, but in the case of chieftains of Clan Donald also involved a renegade attitude. Though several of its chiefs thus yielded an obedience which involved disloyalty to him who had the highest claim on their attachment, the Lord of the Isles, whether *de facto* or *de jure,* only one of them permanently associated himself with Lowland interests. This was John Mac Iain, chief of Ardnamurchan, a very astute man who, by yielding willingly what was practically forced from all the other chiefs, advanced himself and his interests greatly. Faithfully serving a Lowland monarch who was seeking to gain ascendancy in Gaeldom over its ancient king *de jure,* John Mac Iain, as the representative of an alien power, became detestable in the eyes of the other chiefs, more especially as his gain involved their loss. Sir Donald of Lochalsh's ravaging of the Castle in 1517, due to the hatred Mac Iain's unscrupulous loyalty inspired amongst the clans, has been already mentioned. The next incident in its history, therefore, is its siege, in the absence of the Chief Mac Iain, in 1588 by Lachlan Maclean of Duart, who brought a hundred Spaniards from a ship of the Armada to help him in the attack. But after three days' leaguer, Maclean and his mercenaries were repulsed with great slaughter, and the name of the " Bay of the Spaniards," on the west of Mingary Castle still commemorates the event.

When Sir Donald Campbell of Ardnamurchan was in possession of the fortress, Colkitto, on his way from Ireland to join Montrose, captured a vessel containing, amongst other persons, three Covenanting ministers. Purposing to exchange them for his father, a captive in Argyll's hands, Colkitto took the ministers and their companions prisoners, and landing in Ardnamurchan, compelled the surrender of Mingary Castle by piling against the walls and setting fire to combustibles obtained by destroying the adjacent buildings. Then depositing his prisoners in the stronghold under charge of a garrison of his own men, Colkitto himself continued his voyage to join Montrose. Hearing what had taken place, Argyll, anxious to release the ministers from their durance, laid siege to Mingary Castle, but only succeeded in imposing suffering upon those he sought to succour. For in the course of the siege which ensued, both food and water ran short, until the besieged were reduced to a little barley meal and such water as could be collected on the battlements, for the castle has no well. After seven weeks' leaguer, Clanranald appeared, fell upon the invaders, and very speedily sent them flying to their galleys, when the Macdonald chief revictualled the castle and renewed its defences. All the prisoners except the ministers had been liberated, and of these, two succumbed to the severity of the winter, while the third was released, after ten months' imprisonment, in exchange for a Royalist.

————

PART IV

KILMORY OF ARDNAMURCHAN

As far as Camphouse or Cairn, the road to Kilmory was the same as that we had taken on our tramp by the back of Ben Hiant to Camus nan Geall. In comparison with the wonderful road over to Ardnamurchan Point, it is in itself monotonous, but on the climb up we found interest in ranging with our eyes the side of Ben Hiant for a sight of the deer, and nearer at hand, in admiring the fine, shaggy, light or dark coloured Highland cattle which grazed by the road-side. Not until we had begun to descend and had continued for some considerable distance on the downward path, did we find any ascent in the quality of the scenery, but the sight of an old, familiar, and dearly-loved friend in the Island of Eigg evoked, as it always must evoke, admiration and affection. Seen from this unfamiliar point of view, its configuration, of course, presented different features, but it was still in every respect the same stately serene isle of our earliest memories.

At the bottom of the hill, the road to Kilmory turns off on the right, and when we had crossed the bridge over the river our eyes were caught by quantities of the striking water avens in full bloom, its drooping bell-flowers of a curious rusty red. In a few minutes we were at the deserted clachan of Branault, where I noticed in front of the empty cottages some cairns, and wondered if these had been erected as a sign of mourning and in remembrance of the days that are past, when Gaels lived in their own Highlands and no one sought to evict them. In the evening, as the shadows deepen, these deserted buildings, seen on the far side of the gate which crosses the road here, make a most beautiful picture against the stately aloofness of Ben Hiant—one we were loath to leave as we turned back by them to take a track on the left through the gate for the monolith called Clach Chatain.

This monolith, beautifully situated in a hollow of the moorland, is a tall tapering stone standing out against the long, low length of Eigg and the peaks of Rum rising behind. A woman living near by told me that when she was a girl she often clambered on to the top of a second standing stone, but of this one I could find no trace. It is strange to come across an unhewn standing stone associated with a saint, for Cathan or Catan was a bishop, probably an Irishman who seems to have spent the greater part of his life in Bute, where he tutored his nephew, S. Blane. This is practically all that is known of the saint (after whom Ardchattan was called) except that at Stornoway there was a cell which was said to have been the residence of S. Cathan, and to have contained his relics. He died in 710; his festival is observed on May 17th; and from him the confederacy of clans known as Clan Chatan takes its name. But that none of the clans comprised in this confederacy were native of Ardnamurchan, I would have been disposed to associate this standing stone, though a relic of prehistoric times, with Clan Chatan rather than with the ecclesiastic, since I cannot recall any other instance of an unhewn, uninscribed monolith being associated with a saint. Where stones of pagan erection have been taken over to serve Christian purposes, such transference is always made plain by the inscribing of some Christian symbol, generally the cross, to consecrate and hallow the stone, as I think has probably happened in the case of the sculptured monolith at Cladh Chiarain.

When we cut across the fields to rejoin the Kilmory road, I noticed down in the hollow on the left by the roadside a well, suggestive, from its proximity to Clach Chatain, of some holy well.

It is a clearly ascertained fact that in the Celtic Church it was usual to dedicate churches either to their founder or to some other Celtic saint associated with the country, S. Martin being the only exception that occurs to me, though his association with S. Ninian may be held to place him in the category of Celtic saints. Dedications, latterly so common, to Our Lord and to Our Lady, as Kilchrist and Kilmory (where the traditional pronunciation does not indicate S. Maelrubha), all appear to be of mediæval origin. In the Irish Church, dedications to any other than Celtic saints are quite unknown before the twelfth century. I conjecture, therefore, that the earlier dedication here was to S. Cathan (who, assuming he went to Stornoway, may well have broken his voyage here), and that when, in the Middle Ages, the church was re-dedicated to the Mother of God, the old dedication became transferred to the standing stone.

This surmise finds support in similar instances of what took place elsewhere, as there is documentary evidence to prove. Thus, a charter of David I. mentions the re-consecration of the monastery church of Deer, originally possessing a dual dedication to S. Columba and S. Drostan, under the style of the church of S. Peter. Similarly, the ancient church of Rosemarkie, founded in the sixth century by S. Moluoc of Lismore, and in consequence called after him, also re-appears as the church of S. Peter. The church of Stirling, dedicated to S. Modan, was, in the Middle Ages, re-dedicated to the Holy Rood, and is now known as the High Church, an interesting illustration of the three revolutions through which the ecclesiastical life of Scotland passed.

It may be fittingly observed here that while Roman custom required, and still requires, every church to be a shrine erected on the relic of some saint, and while, as has been seen in the chapter on Iona, the Celtic Church, too, had its *marta* or relics, these were exceptional. It was the peculiar and beautiful custom of the Celtic Church for any holy man or woman desirous of founding a church to go to the chosen spot and there to continue in prayer and fasting for forty days and forty nights. Sundays, however, in consonance with Catholic custom, were exempt from fasting, and therefore the fast was exclusive of them. This act of devotion consecrated the place, and the church erected there bore the founder's name. Sometimes, however, if the keeper of this season of consecration were a religious attached to the monastery of some famous foundation, the church thus sanctified by prayer and fasting would be dedicated to the founder of the monastery, *e.g.*, let us say, to S. Columba, rather than to his unknown, or less well known, disciple.

In such fashion S. Cathan, if indeed he broke his journey to Stornoway at **Ardnamurchan**, may well have consecrated a church bearing his name.   While one must regretfully acknowledge the declension in the Celtic Church, and in consequence welcome the revival of religion which came, through S. Margaret, from England, one cannot but deplore the wholesale contemptuousness of Saxon ecclesiastics for all things distinctively Celtic, causing them to be swept aside, the good with the bad, without discrimination.   Better had it been for the Church in Scotland had the reforming English clerics remembered the wise words of the Pope, S. Gregory the Great, in answer to S. Augustine's question regarding different customs obtaining in different (national) Churches where the Faith is identical:

> "Choose . . . from every Church those things that are pious, religious, and upright; and when you have, as it were, made them up into one body, let the minds of the English [for which let us here substitute " Scots "] be accustomed thereto."

But to the Saxon ecclesiastic, as still to many a Saxon layman, all things Celtic were barbarous, and thus he even attempted to oust the Celtic saints in his wholesale revolution, succeeding, indeed, to the extent of supplanting S. Columba by S. Andrew as the patron saint of Scotland.

Now to resume the road.   When you reach the point where, at the ending of the wall, the clachan of Kilmory lies spread before you, it presents a very attractive, old-world picture, the cottages neatly thatched in straw, nestled in a hollow, and, across the sea, the islands once again. But before turning down to the shore, there is the old burial-ground, enclosed in the fields lying low on the right, to be visited, and a search to be made amongst the stones, as far as the lengthy overgrowing grass will allow.   By far the greater number of the headstones are unhewn, uninscribed pieces of stone, many of them chosen probably

AT KILMORY OF ARDNAMURCHAN, RUM AND EIGG IN DISTANCE

because of their curious natural form.   I did discover, crookedly stuck in the ground, at the top of one grave the broken head of a solid wheel cross, but it was not in any way remarkable, and there was no trace of any sculpturing upon it.   Then I disinterred a long stone, which I thought at first might prove to be the shaft of this cross head, but examination shewed it was certainly not that, for it looked more like a companion to the monolith at Clach Chatain.   Indeed, had it been longer, I should have been disposed to identify it with the second standing stone missing from its original situation.   I could not identify the two recumbent gravestones that are said to be in this graveyard, one having the rough figure of a sword and the other a " horse-shoe design " over it, for of the two slabs I did lay bare, both were so badly weathered and so overgrown with moss that evidences of sculpturing at all were only discernible on one.   The "rectangular block of stone, 2 feet long, having a bowl-shaped depression," I also failed to find.   This stone is presumably identified with a font, since it is called locally *an Tobar Baistidh,* but the description does not read like one.   There did not appear to be any trace whatever of a building which would indicate the site of the old church, but the grass may have obscured its foundations.

It is only a few yards from the burial-ground, across the fields and the burn, to the clachan of Kilmory, where the majority of cottages snuggle closely together on the opposite side of the road.   I greatly regret that I did not find out until I had left Ardnamurchan that, less than a mile beyond Kilmory, on the Swordle-Chorrach shore, is *Uamha Thuill,* a " cave of the hole," associated with S. Columba.   It is said that, finding it in the occupancy of a company of robbers, the saint, converting them, baptised them all from a natural basin which was filled by water dropping from the roof.   In later times healing powers were attributed to the waters thus consecrated, and the cave was resorted to by sick people, who left offerings, after the ordinary use and wont, beside the basin. I also heard, after I had left, from Mr. Henderson of an ancient grave, called *Cladh Aindreis,* or the " grave of Andrew," near the estuary of the Ockle Burn, on the farm of Swordle. Had we only known of the cave and the grave, we would have taken the road to the right, but instead we turned to the left, finding more picturesque cottages dotted about the landscape, many of them by the side of a little stream.

This short walk down to the sea is in the early summer one of the loveliest I know, for not only is the general outlook glorious, but the luxurious growth of wild flowers in the fields through which you pass is astonishing. I have never seen elsewhere such a varied growth of milk-wort, nor anywhere else seen this usually insignificant little plant attain to such a size. Both in a reddish and a bluish purple, in pink, in royal blue, and in royal blue tipped with white, it grew to the size of large sprays of heather, which, indeed, the reddish purple variety closely resembled. Beside the milkwort shot up the straight purple spikes of the early orchid; in long sequences hung the purple bells of the stately *lus nam ban sith,* the "plant of the little people " or folk's glove, while marvellous masses of bird's-foot trefoil made pools of deep orange, lightened by patches of paler gold. In contrast to the more assertive beauty of these flowers, there was hidden amongst them the shy and modest little heart's-ease, the herb Trinity, with its triple coloration of purple, yellow, and white. But above all the flowers of the field rioted the wild rose, generally of the most intense pink, but here and there with flowers subtly shaded into white.

It was through this Garden of Eden that we gained the wonderful bay where Nature, with cunning hand, had sculptured the rocks around into fantastic shapes—pillars and arches of the greatest interest. We were greatly interested, too, in observing on a pool left behind by the sea a shelduck and a sheldrake afloat. These handsome birds, so called from their "shelled" or variegated plumage, are the most striking of all British ducks, for not only are they very large, but boldly marked in feathers of white, greenish-black, chestnut, and steel blue.

But apart altogether from the approach to it, the rocks framing it, and the birds whose playground it is, the bay is a place of sheerest beauty in itself, its pure white sand picturesquely strewn with seaweed-covered rocks and boulders. In the sunlight, truly

> " The rocks of gold are carven,
>   And the white beach shines below,
> Where the far-borne sapphire of the sea
>   Breaks into sighing snow."

Beyond the sea, of course, are the beloved and eternally beautiful islands, shimmering in pale purple, and in the sea, cooling themselves, were handsome Highland cattle.

Such is the final picture I leave with the reader, whom I would have realize something of the treasure and delights of Ardnamurchan. Here associations of the holy men of old time are enshrined in scenes of beauty which surely reflect, in so far as earth can reflect them, the loveliness of those heavenly places whither Columba, Ciaran, Cathan, and Finan [11] have attained.

> " O happie harbour of the saints,
>   O sweet and pleasant soyle,
> In thee noe sorrow may be founde,
>   Noe griefe, noe care, noe toyle."

[11] There is, on the hill separating Ockle from Gortenfern, a ridge called " S. Finan's Seat," where a view of Eilean Finan is obtainable. This gives confirmation to the tradition that S. Finan was in Ardnamurchan proper before he settled on Eilean Finan.

CHAPTER IX

PLACES OF UNIQUE INTEREST OUT OF THE BEATEN TRACK

PART I

A PILGRIMAGE TO THE " HOLY ROCK "

OBAN, the " little bay," is for me a magnetic spot whither I have always been willingly drawn by the attraction of reunion with friends prior to embarking upon some merry holiday or congenial expeditions in their company. Or when I have gone to Oban alone, with no such alliance in prospect, the alluring town has always been the starting-point of mild adventurings. Thus, in fair weather or foul, Oban always retains affection because of its happy associations, which no mere accident of weather can ever efface.

I had had for many years a supreme longing to gain that one of the Garvelloch Isles, na h-Eileacha Naomha,[1] which is generally identified with the Hinba of S. Columba's day. Studying one day its situation in the Firth of Lorne from the map, I judged it would be most easily reached from Cullipool on the island of Luing; and I then and there determined that at the first opportunity I would walk from Oban to Cullipool, there to discover someone who would sail me over to my island of desire. Since there appeared to be no inn anywhere on Luing

---

[1] Professor Watson informs me that in Gaelic speech this is the invariable form of the name of vhat the natives always term the " Holy Isle."

when the desired opportunity was within sight of realization, I wrote to the Post Office at Cullipool to ascertain where accommodation might be had. A discouraging reply in no wise hindered my determination to devote a week-end to the expedition, and, consequently, on a certain Friday in June I set forth from Oban on my pilgrimage to the " Holy Isle." In view, however, of the unknown quantities of Cullipool, it seemed wise to take some provisions with me; and, since it might be desirable to put up for the night short of my destination, though only eighteen miles from Oban, I thought I would do well —in one sense—to carry all my traps for the trip on my person. This, consequently, I did, with the single exception of a box of photographic plates which I posted to Cullipool Post Office.

When I was loaded up, I felt more like a pantechnicon than anything else, and, smothered in packages, I must have looked more like an undersized camel. On my back, a knapsack carried a half-plate camera and three slides, kettle, cup, milk, spirit stove, and methylated spirits; in a mackintosh roll I carried the minimum of toilet requirements; a bulging string bag of provisions safeguarded against starvation, and these, together with an oilskin and camera stand were distributed about my person. Thus equipped, I had only reached Kilbride,[2] about $3\frac{1}{2}$ miles on my journey, when it began to rain, and soon poured with a vigour and sturdy determination I have never seen excelled, so much so that my whole impression of that tramp is of water. Of the scenery there was nothing whatever to be seen, for the rain wiped out everything within a few yards, whilst it was obviously out of the question

---

[2] There is here, in the shamefully neglected ancient churchyard, the three fragments of a cross which, erected in 1516, used to dominate the landscape. Knowing there was a crucifixion presenting some curious features to be found on the cross, I once walked out from Oban to see it, but was greatly disappointed. The fragments now prone in the neglected graveyard have been so defaced by the tread of irreverent feet that it is very difficult to make out any of the sculpturing with any distinctness.

to hunt for any of the many prehistoric remains with which I knew the road to abound. Consequently, when at the end of 12 miles, sodden if not squelching, I reached the inn, *Tigh an Truish* at Clachan, I at once made up my mind to halt there for the night.

Clachan is a picturesque little " village " where a peculiarly graceful bridge spans with a single arch the Atlantic, otherwise that part of it called the Clachan Sound, which like a very narrow stream separates the mainland from the island of Seil, through which I tramped next day, still damp, on my way to Cullipool. It was by no means an interesting walk scenically, and when, at the cross roads, I met a post cart, I gladly seized this chance of a lift to the ferry at Cuan. Cuan Sound, between Seil and Luing, is not a very wide channel, but it has strong currents, and the crossing in the ferry was a strenuous affair. The mails were landed to be taken on to Cullipool by a second dog-cart, and of this, too, I availed myself, and, arriving at the Post Office, I asked for suggestions as to where I might be bestowed until the object of my pilgrimage was accomplished. I was referred to a fisherman near by, and to him I went. Yes, he thought they could put me up, and, after consultation with his wife, I was allocated the newly-painted parlour and a comfortable bedroom. But what elated me was the discovery that my host—lobster catcher, Northern Lights' man, postman to the adjacent islands, and Wee Free Elder, indeed a host in himself—would himself take me over to Hinba on Monday.

I had always understood that landing on na h-Eileacha Naomha was not always possible by reason of contrary tides and strong currents, but Lachie, my landlord, thought that by starting at 4 A.M. on Monday everything would be propitious. With the exception of the atmosphere, it was, but unfortunately a thick mist obliterated all the distances. Na h-Eileacha Naomha, it seemed, was part of the lobster-fishing ground, and my landing there was to be fitted in with lifting and baiting the lobster pots which were sunk about the various islands. With Lachie came Hughie, his young son, to assist in proceedings, and as at the outset there was not much wind, we had to resort to " wooden topsails," *i.e.,* oars, for nearly the whole of the eight miles across. The rocky islets amongst which we passed are not nesting-places, so we saw comparatively few birds. Besides the graceful terns and familiar oyster-catchers (which Lachie, with more descriptive truth, if less poetic feeling, called " limpet pickers "), I noted divers, scarts (or cormorants), the eider or S. Cuthbert's duck, and some herons.

When we were passing the isle of Lunga, Lachie asked me if I had ever heard the tale of the mysterious drum of Lunga. He said the sound of the drum was constantly heard, but its player was never seen. Many years ago, however, a great big man, who had got rather " excited," *i.e.,* drunk, after a feast, declared that if it were the devil himself out of hell, he would discover the player. This he set out to do, and when he returned to his companions and they asked him what he had seen, he replied, " What I have seen I will tell no one," but he *did* say that when-ever he got to the place where he thought the drum was sounding, he immediately heard it in some other quarter. Lachie declared that his brother, who is younger than he, had heard the drum, but that he himself had never heard it.

I give this and subsequent stories not because of their intrinsic interest, but because they so well illustrate the type of story that is so characteristic of the Highlands—tales which translated into English seem to lose the point which presumably the Gaelic conveys.

There are four of the Garvelloch Islands, or Isles of the Sea, as they are alternatively called—a green rocky chain with a character of their own that none of their neighbours can claim. The first island of the group is Dun Chonail, the " fort of Conall," the king of Dalriada who gifted Iona to S. Columba. It is made up of three separate rocky heights, so precipitous as to be almost inaccessible; and landing is a matter of extreme difficulty even in fine weather. Lachie said that he had seen the remains of the fort on the top of the island, and that the builder, Conall, had two brothers who lived in different castles on Seil. Conall, on waking in the morning, was wont to take his snuff mull from under his pillow, and when he had taken a pinch therefrom, passed it on to one brother on Seil, who transmitted it to the other, to be returned finally to its owner!

The second and biggest island, from which the group takes its name of Garvelloch, is *Garbheileach,* or the "rough island," on which is a burial ground called *Cladh dhubhan,* the grave-stones of which are of the roughest description, and unsculptured. While *dhubhan* is a fish-hook, yet, in view of the fact that there was more than one prince and certainly one king called Duban, this grave-yard is more probably named after one of these. Of this, the biggest island of the group, Lachie told me another whimsical story, this time of the *bodach glas,* or the grey old man, apparently a smuggler who was murdered on the next island, A' Chuili, or Cuil-i-Breannan, and buried beneath its rocks. The solitary family who live on Garbh-eileach claim often to have heard the whistle of the *bodach glas,* and then " they are as sure as though they had received a telegram that a boat would be calling for them," said Lachie.

One day Lachie and Hughie had gone over to the island to deliver letters and to look after the cattle, as the family were away on Mull. Lachie went up to the house with the letters, and Hughie went to look after the cattle, amongst which was a " bad," *i.e.,* wild, bull. When the father had reached the farm-house, he heard a shrill whistle, and, thinking it was Hughie wanting help against the bull, Lachie turned and ran down to the shore, only to meet Hughie rushing up. He, too, had heard the whistle, and thought it was his father wanting *him!* They both solemnly declared that no one was on the island, and that there was no sort of boat, bird, or beast that could have been responsible for the whistle they heard. So they were satisfied that it was the *bodach glas,* but, as nothing happened in consequence, I could see no point in his whistling.

A' Chuilidh, or Cuilidh Bhrianain, the " retired place of 'S. Brendan," the famous voyager and contemporary of S. Columba, is the little island between Garbheileach and na h-Eileacha Naomha. Though it is said there are now no remains to be seen upon it, this rocky retreat was obviously originally the site of a cell or chapel used by S. Brendan.

Na h-Eileacha Naomha, the " holy rocks," is, by a combined process of elimination and cumulative evidence, identified by the greatest authorities of the past with the Hinba or Himba of S. Adamnan's *Life of S. Columba.* Those who deny their identity on various grounds, have not, in my estimation, succeeded in making out a convincing case for any other islands they think might claim to be Hinba. But it is only fair to state that a gentleman of such status as Professor Watson considers that Hinba is not na h-Eileacha Naomha, and I only regret that lack of space forbids me to set forth in detail the arguments *pro* and *con.*

It was not until 1824, when Dr. MacCulloch voyaged amongst the Western Islands, that Hinba was practically re-discovered, if one is right in identifying it with " Ilachanu," as it was then called, or the *Helant Leneow,* as Fordun phonetically renders the name. Of course, it is not a conclusive argument to urge that the group of very ancient monastic remains still found on na h-Eileacha Naomba certainly identify that island with Hinba. For even if they be the most ancient ecclesiastical remains extant in Britain, of course others more ancient may have disappeared, yet most of the probabilities seem to point, the archæological evidence overwhelmingly so, to na h-Eileacha Naomha as ancient Hinba against all other competitors of which I have heard.

An early *Life of S. Brendan* records his foundation of a monastery on the "island of Aileach"—clearly na h-Eileacha Naomha—an event which is placed somewhere about 542 A.D.—some twenty years before S. Columba landed on Iona. He, however, is said by Adamnan to have "sent over Ernan a priest, an old man, his uncle, to the presidency of that monastery which he had founded in Hinba island many years before." Thus it has been conjectured that S. Columba refounded S. Brendan's original monastery—a proceeding which neither implied nor necessitated the erection of any new buildings, but might infer no more than a taking over to order a community on different lines, as frequently happened elsewhere.

The morning continued grey and calm, with a thin mist falling for some time. At last we got alongside Hinba. It is frequently impossible to land there, but by great good fortune, the tide happened to be favourable, and it was possible to jump ashore. Precisely at 7 A.M. we put in at the bay just below the famous double-beehive cell, and it required considerable care and dexterity to land safely on the very rough rocks and slippery weed. Lachie took me up to the double-beehive cell, shewed me where the church lay, and the place where Eithne, the mother of Columba, is said to be buried, and then left me.

For the infinitesimal space of one-and-a-half hours, while the mist steadily fell, I was alone on this wonderful islet, $1\frac{1}{4}$ miles long and only $\frac{1}{4}$ mile broad at its widest part, and all the time I was conscious of a most strange but lively sense, quite outside any of my own generating or creating, that I was in actuality transported back to the very days of S. Columba. Yet it was the sensing of an absence, not of a presence—as though someone had just newly carried off the entire community, leaving behind their cells, their church, their other buildings all entire, and, most vivid sense of all, palpitating with monastic life. It seemed as though, while I was wrapped about in this atmosphere and in the realization of active work but temporarily suspended, awaiting a material return which could never be made, the buildings fell into decay, but still retained their atmosphere of being but recently inhabited. I think this extremely realistic experience, which it is almost impossible to convey to another, was due to the fact that the buildings actually belong to S. Columba's day, and have not suffered any alien violation which would destroy the atmosphere they are capable of generating. Thus, upon those whose realization of the welcome companionship of S. Columba is vivid, such buildings are capable of exercising a psychic influence due to some subtle emanation from stones saturated with the life of the past. Indeed I am not alone in having a capacity for thus hearing the stones cry out of the wall,[3] and for being insensibly gathered into that atmosphere of the past which enfolds them and which constitutes something so tangible, and so forceful that it wipes out the present and carries one back into its own past.

It was only 8.30 A.M. when, in the exigences of his calling, to which my pilgrimage was perforce subsidiary, Lachie led my reluctant footsteps down the hillock to the boat which was anchored below in *am Port,* as the natives call that just below S. Columba's Well. On this occasion, photography under the curious gaze of thirteen Highland cattle occupied most of my utterly inadequate time, and there was no opportunity to make that complete survey of the antiquities which was required.

I have found it impossible to reconcile with one another the few recent accounts which have been published of the ancient remains in the island. In some of these articles, indeed, there is not even consistency of nomenclature throughout. In most there is a more or less confused

3 Habakkuk, ii., 11.

description and the vaguest indication of the nature of the various ruins and enclosures mentioned, and their situations are so ambiguously stated, where stated at all, that you are left to conjecture precisely to what building reference is being made. More especially where masses of stone, architectural remains, are so numerous, identification from such "descriptions" is obviously impossible.

In all these circumstances, it was inevitable that I should make up my mind, before even leaving the island, to pay a return visit, which, however, only materialized after an interval of seven years. During this time Lachie had died, but, since Hughie was "carrying on" in his father's place, I was happily able to arrange with him to take a friend and myself across to na h-Eileacha Naomha in his motor-boat—if possible over night, as we were both eager to sleep on the island. As our designs necessitated the cartage of so many traps, instead of walking this time to Cullipool, we took four public conveyances over the four stages of our journey. Our second conveyance, a motor mail, refusing the hills, we had to get out and push: in the fourth, a mail gig, the horse initially refused us, and again we had to get out. But after the animal had satisfied himself by shewing us how well he could shy, we clambered up into the dog-cart again, and reached Cullipool without further incident, there to receive the heartiest of welcomes from Hughie's mother and sister. The former, abeam with kindliness, contentment, and hospitality, could not understand our preference for sleeping out of doors, on an uninhabited island moreover, when we could have a good bed indoors at Cullipool. Nothing would induce *her* to sleep on the Holy Isle: were *we* not afraid the "brounies" would get us? It was, however, a toss up if a landing *could* be effected that evening on na h-Eileacha Naomha, for, though the weather was gloriously settled, the wind was very high and the sea was in consequence very rough, with the currents running strong. However, at last Hughie decided to risk it, and we set out at 7.35 P.M. (summer time) to make the attempt, the parting admonition from the shore being " See and not let the brounies get ye ! " We had borrowed a couple of blankets wrapped up in a coverlet, and, beside these and our oilskins, we had a goodly bag of provisions, our tea traps, a large can of milk, sketching and photographic paraphernalia respectively, not to mention our toilet requirements and extra clothing to wear at night. Of these seven bundles, two were not only extremely weighty but clumsy as well. Precisely at 8.15 P.M., after an expeditious switchbacking over the sea, we managed to run into Geodha Iain, the " port of John," a little north of the centre of the east coast of na h-Eileacha Naomha. Here, at the base of some steep and slippery black rocks, Hughie and the old man, his assistant, landed us and our belongings and left us, telling us that they might be expected back next day between 3 and 4 P.M. unless, indeed, the tide was too strong to allow of them coming for us at all. But we had no idea of anticipating misfortunes, and with no thoughts except of great elation and content at thus compassing our hearts' desire, we waved our farewells and, in transport of delight, began the transport of our baggage.

It certainly was an undertaking demanding great care initially—especially over the milk-can—for such foothold as the climb up the rocks afforded was very precarious, and, had we slipped, we should have been precipitated into the sea. However, we triumphantly negotiated this initial difficulty, and when at last we had collected on one spot our seven articles of baggage, we began to move them inland by stages and in instalments. The trouble here was that, owing to the nature of the ground, we often mislaid some piece of our baggage, and had to go off and hunt for it. Our course, viewed from an inland starting-point on an eminence, seemed quite clear, but the hollows into which we descended were broken up by rising ground and rocks, which very often effectually obscured our " dumps." Of course, we should have used our compasses, and so saved ourselves time, temper, and tiredness. It took us nearly an hour-and-a-half thus to transport all our traps to the hollow in which the church is situated. And there, after a welcome meal and a wash in the sea, we spread our oilskins, crowded on extra clothing, extemporized a pillow a-piece, and, wrapping ourselves up in our blankets, laid us down for the night. I was of opinion, which my friend did not share, that our bed lacked no comfort, and we passed a peaceful and unadventurous night, since neither the visit from a passing toad nor a few half-hearted midges could be considered as constituting either disturbance or adventure. The novelty of our situation was such that I got up once or twice during the night to look around, but neither then nor at any other time did I have a return of my previous psychic experience.

My friend's impression of the island, however, as she gave it me, is worth recording, because the novelty of the whole experience to her made it very vivid, for not only was it her first visit to the island, but her first night out in the open. Beyond the charm of freshness which pervaded everything, she found great fascination in the quietness that gradually fastened upon the island until, one after another, the voices of the birds were hushed, the calm sea made never a murmur, no wind gave a sigh, and even a solitary gull ceased its lament, until everything was held in an absolute stillness, the apotheosis of peace. So wrapt was she in the glamour of the island that she lay awake throughout the night, watching the pale grey of the dusk pass into the deeper grey of night, then slowly lifting till the western sky became tinged with pink, and again the voices of the birds broke the spell, heralding the dawn.

We both rose at 4 A.M. (summer time) for our first breakfast, to be in readiness for the sunrise. As we sat at our meal, we were very interested to notice that in a hole in the remains of the vallum exactly opposite us, a pair of wheatears had their nest. These birds of the " white arse " or rump, were very busy supplying their nestlings with a sufficient breakfast, and it was curious to watch their characteristic bobbing and bowing motions as they alighted after a short, swift flight for insects. These the young came out of the nest to receive from the bill of father or mother, not distinguished birds, but quite distinctive in their habits.

While there was nothing of surpassing splendour in the returning glories of the day, as they were unfolded before us, yet from our different vantage points the outlook over the sea eastwards was sufficiently lovely. As the sun gradually raised himself to his high throne in the heavens, the sea was slowly stained, and the islands and the mainland beyond were gilded with brightly-burnished gold, the distant hills each paling behind the other till the farthest was scarcely visible. When the day was full-fledged, we descended to the shore, and, as we made our way over the rough pebbles of a very uneven beach, we were received by the incessant piercing piping of two oyster-catchers whirling overhead, evidently in great alarm. The cause we soon discovered at our feet in the presence of several baby oyster-catchers, fascinating fluffy little balls crouching down amongst the stones, from which they were almost indistinguishable. We were so close to one that, stooping very quietly and slowly, we were able to stroke it before we moved away to ease the anxious parents, who steadily maintained all the while their shrill shrieking.

I shall describe the buildings in the order in which I first saw them, starting from the bay where I was originally landed by Lachie.

The double-beehive cell, locally called " the ovens," is, of course, like all the others on the island, a dry-stone building. It is situated on a slope close to the shore, and is built on the ground plan of the figure 8, the landward, upper, or northern cell being internally 14 feet in diameter, the lower one 13 feet. At the point where the walls are contiguous, the intersecting passage which originally connected the two cells is now broken down, and the one entrance to both is through the larger and lower cell on the south-west side. The upper cell has only a square opening, too low for a door, on the level of the ground of the outer wall on the same side, and this opening possibly served as a drain. The lower cell has suffered badly from its exposure to the full stress of winds from the sea, and its roofing has entirely disappeared. The northernmost part of the upper cell has its walls still standing to a height of 6 feet or more, and, while you can still see that the roof has been dome-shaped, it has now almost entirely disappeared. I have seen it conjectured that one of the two was a dwelling, the other an oratory. The ruins of a third beehive cell, which I was not able to discover here, are said to be visible still.

Could it have been in either of these buildings that S. Columba lodged when he visited Hinba? There is the beautiful incident of the appearing to him one night of an angel of the Lord having in his hand " a book of glass [4] of the Ordination of Kings." Columba read therein what the angel commanded, but, refusing to ordain Aidan king as directed in the book, because he loved better Eogan, Aidan's brother, the angel smote the Abbat on his side with a scourge. Three nights in succession did the angel appear to Columba with the book of glass to urge its commands upon him, until at last Columba left for Iona to ordain Aidan king, as related in a previous chapter.

Adamnan also speaks of " a house " on Hinba in which Columba on another occasion was " locked " during the three days and nights he spent there in an ecstasy of spiritual illumination, neither eating nor drinking nor allowing any to approach him. Adamnan states that this house was filled with " celestial brightness " and that " from this same house rays in intense brilliancy were seen

---

[4] Probably having a glass cover.

OF APPROXIMATE
MONASTERY BUILDINGS ON
NA H·EILEACHA NAOMHA

by Isabel Bonus

2. Underground Cell

4. Beehive Cells

6. "S Columba's Pulpit"

8. Abbat's House ?

10. Indeterminate remains of building

12. Claodh Eithne

at night bursting from the chinks of the doors and the keyholes," and that " certain hymns which had not been heard before were heard being sung by " Columba.

Fergno, an Irish saint, who was vouchsafed a vision of the passing of S. Columba, retired to Hinba, spending twelve years as an anchorite on Muirbulcmar, meaning, apparently, a " great sea inlet " somewhere on Hinba—a description which certainly can be relatively applied to the situation of the beehive cells.

Just below the cells, amongst a bed of iris, is a rough, curiously-shaped natural pillar of stone rising several feet high, and this is known as S. Columba's *crannag,* or pulpit. The curved upright has, set aslant upon it, a block of stone very suggestive of a canopy, and beneath it a man could certainly stand. But the whole configuration is due to weathering, and beneath it lies a mass of stone whose position is attributable to the same agency.

Passing inland over a stretch of smooth greensward, only varied by bracken, I climbed to the left a little green hillock with constantly recurring out-crops of stone, and here I came across the ruins of an indeterminate building. This, measuring roughly 16 feet by 28 feet externally, and in a very ruinous state, is very loosely compacted of lichen-covered stones: it has rounded corners, and the centre of each side has a break in the wall opposite the other which may indicate doorways, but there are no traces of windows. Presumably because the building occupies a position overlooking the vallum enclosing the church, similar to the situation of S. Columba's cell with regard to the monastery of Iona, this building is sometimes called the " Abbat's house." Of course it may be, for the surmise is a logical one, but, if so, the construction does not compare with that of the church, and the fact seems to suggest a different date, but where all the buildings, of whatever age, are of the most primitive style of architecture, it is impossible even to hazard the exact age of any.

Continuing straight up the hillock and then descending,

I came upon a small building, north-west from the beehive cells, of very rude and higgledy-piggledy masonry, approximately 14 feet by 8 feet internally, and this is generally called " the kiln," but more rarely the chapel, though it is not correctly orientated. It has a semi-circular end at the " east," and the remains of a gable on the " west " wall, and close to this end, two doors are opposite each other in the " north " and " south " walls. About two-thirds of the interior at the rounded end consists of a raised stone platform, 3 feet 3 inches high, in the centre of which is a funnel-shaped pit with which a channel, piercing the basement of the platform, communicates from the front. If this be indeed a kiln for drying corn (and similar constructions have been used within living memory), this passage would supply the necessary draught. On the 6-inch Ordnance Survey map, close to the kiln, it is noted, " Human remains found here in 1859," but this is the only reference I have ever seen to such a discovery, concerning which I can obtain no particulars.

Going on southward over the ridge, when I reached the edge on its further side, I saw in the hollow below me the tiny rectangular church, the tops of the walls (which are entire, and 3 feet thick) overgrown with a thick tangle of heather and ferns. Looking down upon the wonderful little building, perhaps the oldest church in Great Britain, I noted the solitary little deeply-splayed, square-headed window above the site of the altar. Although both are alike drystone buildings, there is a great contrast between the clumsy masonry of the kiln and the wonderful precision of the church's architecture. Wide, flat, undressed stones, obviously the same as the rocks around, are laid in skilfully compacted courses marvellously free from chinks, and exteriorly the walls, some 8 feet high, are now thickly covered with grey lichen. On my second visit I found that some barbarian had actually lit a fire under the east window, not only burning off the lichen right up the wall, but badly scorching the stones. The church is duly

THE CHURCH ON NA H-EILEACHA NAOMHA FROM THE EAST

orientated, and measures 21 feet 7 inches by 11 feet 6 inches internally, having its door with inclined jambs at the west end. After walking round the beautiful little building, I passed inside—to have my sense of decency again outraged by finding there quantities of rubbish and traces of recent fires. Had I only had the time, I would have cleared out the church, chiefly as an act of reparation to the memory of S. Columba, and, having reported the dangers to which the present building is at present exposed, I hope soon to hear it has been duly scheduled. As it was, I could only strive to banish the feeling of desecration as I stood before the little window (also deeply splayed within), to the right of which is a projecting slab of slate, 5 feet from the ground and 11 inches deep, all that remains of what probably constituted the *mensa* of the altar.

Here, probably, S. Columba himself had often stood to celebrate the Holy Mysteries. Adamnan relates how "four holy founders of monasteries," SS. Comgall, Cainnech, Brendan, and Cormac, "coming over from Ireland to visit S. Columba, found him in Hinba." They, anxious that he should celebrate the Eucharist for them, gained his consent, whereupon Columba entered "the church together with them according to the custom on the Lord's Day, after the reading of the Gospel." After the Divine Liturgy was ended, S. Brendan told Comgall and Cainnech that he had seen "a certain blazing and most luminous globe of fire burning over S. Columba's head and rising up like a pillar as he stood before the altar consecrating the Holy Oblation until the same most holy ministrations were completed."

It is in consequence of this vision that S. Columba is represented in art with a globe of light, a comet with rays, or a pillar of fire as his emblem.

The church, together with a mound of stones on the north, which may represent the remains of a cell, and on the south-west an underground structure about to be

36

described, were enclosed by a roughly hexagonal vallum, following the lines of the natural configuration of the hollow. Traces of the walls supplementing the enclosure, naturally afforded by rising ground and rocks, may still be seen. Only a little distance from the church is the curious and interesting underground cell, known to the natives as *Am Priosan,* a name which probably faithfully perpetuates the penitential cell of the monastery. It is entered by a slanting aperture just where the walls join the roof, which is formed of a few big slabs laid across the walls on the ground level. I slid backwards through the fern-grown opening into the cell until, at a depth of just over 4 feet, I found I had reached the bottom. Then, lighting the candle with which one pocket is usually provided, I found myself in a cell of an irregular oval shape, measuring about 5 feet 4 inches by 4 feet 5 inches, regularly built of large stones, with a few stones and earth on the floor. Facing the door in the opposite wall, 1 foot from the roof, is a recess, 2 feet deep, 1 foot 1 inch high, and 1 foot 10 inches broad. It is traditionally said that " prisoners " were confined here by *a' ghlas laimh* (the hand lock). There used to be a large stone at the bottom of the cell with a V-shaped depression in which the prisoner placed his clasped hands. Then " a wedge-shaped stone was securely fastened down over the palms of the hands so tightly that it was impossible to extricate them."

It might have been in this underground cell that a certain Neman, son of Cathir, was performing his penance when S. Columba once visited Hinba. In accordance with Celtic custom on the coming of a visitor, fasts were relaxed, and better food allowed in honour of the occasion. But when Columba enjoined this mitigation of penance, Neman refused it, whereupon the Abbat exposed him as a mock penitent.

But a little to the south of the church are very inferior buildings in four compartments, now, if not originally, used as sheep fanks. One compartment, in which the natural rock at one end has been used in the structure of the wall there, looks older than the others, obviously late, rude additions, in connection with which the term "architecture" could never be employed. But the older-looking compartment has both a stone lintel over the low doorway and a cupboard recess in one wall, so that conceivably, it may at one time have served as a house. Lachie told me that his grandfather had been born on the island—where he could not say—but this seems the most likely place.

The enclosure adjoining the sheep fanks is considered to represent the monastery garden, since it is said there are still to be found there several varieties of flowers much esteemed of old for their medical properties. I, however, failed to find any trace either of herbs or any sort of flowers here.

To the east of the church, and between the sheep fanks and monastery garden, is a semi-circular structure round the remains of a wall with gable-like termination. The foundations of a second building extend northward from the gable-end, and these are generally referred to as the " domestic buildings of the monastery," which, being outside the vallum, they were not likely to be. A " guest house " is a more probable conjecture.

An extensive ancient graveyard, surrounded by a greatly dilapidated stone wall, adjoins the monastery garden, but the growth of vegetation makes it difficult to carry out anything like a thorough search. Besides several natural uninscribed slabs erected as gravestones and still standing, I found one with a plain square cross incised, the fellow to a second now in the Antiquarian Museum in Edinburgh. In addition to these headstones, there are, opposite a standing stone in the corner gap of the wall leading down to " the port," the foundations of a small square structure, and, in the opposite corner, the remains of a similar one rising some 18 inches above ground. These I imagined to be the " vaults " to which Lachie had referred as being found here. I also came across a raised bank and traces of four circular cells in the centre of the graveyard which, like the monastic buildings, would well repay judicious investigation with the spade.

Apparently, even so recently as the beginning of the nineteenth century, this graveyard used to be rich in carved stones, for MacCulloch speaks of numbers, but nearly all appear to have been stolen. MacCulloch mentions, too, a *clach na brath* here as well as upon Iona, but of this nothing is now known. One inscribed stone of slate, shewing a design of foliage, much weathered, now lies in two pieces on the south side of the church near the west end. A font, too, has apparently been discovered within recent years on the island, but I infer that its finder has not yet relinquished it.

An easy ascent by way of a grassy slope takes you up to the brow of the ridge, where a circle of rough, unhewn stones represents Cladh Eithne. Here is one headstone deeply incised with a cross, whose almost equal arms terminate in what is best described as full-stops. A plain stone on the left inclines towards it, and, due south, a little over 9 feet, practically the diameter of the ground, is a thin slab of slate. In this tiny graveyard, constant tradition avers, lies the body of the mother of S. Columba, hence the name of the " burial place of Eithne," and *Geodha Eithne,* or the " port of Eithne " below, suggests the place where her remains were landed.

From Cladh Eithne the outlook is most romantic, even when the mist veils the more distant views. On the left is the highest point of the island, Dun Bhreannan, the " hill of Brendan "; beyond, further north, is Carn-na-Manaich, the " cairn of the monks "; looking over to the east, the sea is broken by rugged crags; while immediately below are the green uplands and hollows of the island, miniature hills and valleys, where nestle the main grouping of the monastic settlement.

At the head of *am Port* there issues from beneath a rock, precisely as in the case of its fellow in Ardnamurchan,[5] S. Columba's Well. The spring runs into an artificial basin overgrown with water-cress, which also grows in a thick bed below it. Striking inland to the left and above S. Columba's Well is a large oval heap of stones, most suggestive of a burial cairn, and, adjacent, there is a small rectangular flat structure, almost $6\frac{1}{2}$ feet by 10 feet, regarding which I have no conjecture to make. On the right, immediately at the head of *am Port,* I seemed to detect amongst the growth of iris, bracken, and nettles, traces of artificial walling, supplementing a natural disposition of rocks, enclosing a large rectangular space. A depression forms a natural passage-way leading from *am Port* to the church, and, some yards up, there is an abutting fragment of wall, and, above it, the suggestion of a fort. On the opposite side of the passage way are two short lengths of parallel walls enclosing but a few feet. All or most of these various remains round about and up from S. Columba's Well are rather suggestive of early, possibly prehistoric, structures, mainly fortifications guarding *am Port,* but probably only excavation could certainly determine their nature and age.

Probably no place in Scotland has a richer field than this small island to offer to the ecclesiological excavator, and in my fervent and aspiring estimation a more enviable undertaking could not become the privilege of any individual.

PART II

AT THE HEART OF THE MALCOLM COUNTRY

AFTER my initial landing on na h-Eileacha Naomha, my next objective was the ancient capital of the Dalriadan, kings, and, with the discomforts of my recent herculean

[5] See p. 419.

tramp still vividly in mind, I succumbed to the temptation to sail to Crinan, walking thence rather than all the way by the devious route from Luing. It was, however, when the memories of the pantechnicon tramp had faded that, by a roundabout road my friend and I gained the same goal, when Hughie, taking us off na h-Eileacha Naomha at 3.30 P.M. on the day after he had left us there, landed us about 5.30 P.M. at Daill in Craignish. Thence, on a very hot evening, thick with midges, we, overloaded beasts of burden, had a twelve-mile trudge, mostly uphill and presenting much sustained climbing, to Kilmartin. As we did not reach here till 10.15 P.M., and had put in a strenuous day of 18 hours, we felt we had really earned a night's rest on this if on no other occasion.

But the time before, I had taken the then available and easy way of boarding the *Chevalier* at Blackmill Bay in Luing, and sailing through the Sound of Scarba. So long as the rocky Isles of the Sea were in view, they, and especially na h-Eileacha Naomha, chained my eyes. When they were lost to view, I concentrated attention on the famous whirlpool of Corrievreckan, *Coire-bhreacain,* that is to say, "Breacan's whirlpool," between the deer forest of Scarba and the island of Jura. But I was very disappointed in identifying it with a positively peaceful channel of water, innocent of anything approaching the roar which is said to carry twenty miles, and giving no indication whatever of the devastating properties which have made it a passage of dread—after a westerly gale and with a flood tide—both conditions absent whenever I have seen it. It is said that S. Columba once saved from shipwreck the boat in which he was sailing through Corrievreckan, stilling the waters by casting upon them some clay which he had carried away from the grave of S. Kiaran.[6]

According to one account, this " Cauldron of Brechan " takes its name from the loss there of fifty *curachs,* and

[6] See p. 415.

with them the grandson of Niall of the Nine Hostages, who flourished in Ireland *c.* 450. But more romantic than the gulf's association with this Irish chieftain is the legend which has for its hero a Scandinavian prince. This youth fell in love with the daughter of an island chief, who, disapproving of the proposed union, said he would only yield his daughter to her suitor if Brecan succeeded in anchoring his vessel for three days and three nights in the whirlpool. Before he undertook the enterprise, Brecan returned to Lochlann, his native land, to consult a wizard in the matter, and was counselled to procure three cables, one of hemp, one of wool, and one woven of maiden's hair. This last was willingly provided for him by the young women of the country, and with the three cables in his possession, Brecan set sail for Jura, and anchored his ship in the whirlpool. The hempen cable broke on the first day, the woollen on the second, but that of hair lasted until the close of the third day when it, too, gave way, owing to the hair of some frail woman having been incorporated in it. The ship was consequently wrecked, and all on board drowned, the unfortunate royal lover's body being dragged ashore by his faithful dog, ultimately finding burial beneath a cairn of stones.

Another legend, which has formed the subject of a poem, associated Corrievreckan with one M'Phail, probably intended for a M'Phee, of Colonsay. He was passing through the gulf on his way home from the wars to claim his lady-love on Colonsay, when a mermaid rose to the surface. Dragging M'Phee out of the boat, she dived down with him to her home beneath the sea.

> " Like music from the greenwood tree.
> Again she raised the melting lay,
> ' Fair warrior, wilt thou dwell with me,
> And leave the maid on Colonsay?' "

For many years M'Phee did live with her, longing all the while, however, for his true love. One day, after expressing his ardent desire to see his old home once more, the mermaid swam with him on her back, and, as they were passing Colonsay, M'Phee jumped off on to the rocks, and so escaped his enchantress.

The danger of Corrievreckan is due not only to the force of the Atlantic tidal wave which rushes, sometimes at the rate of 15 knots an hour, through the passage, but to a great pyramidal rock, called by the natives *Cailleach,* the " hag," sunken only about 12 fathoms below the surface of the water. A little beyond this whirlpool, on the left is another similarly dangerous spot, the *Dorus Mor,* or " great gate " between Craignish Point and Gartbreisha, where the tides race through at the rate of about 8 miles an hour.

There was mist about the great mass of Mull, which we had left behind, and in front rose the peaks of Jura, misty, too, and cloud-wrapped. To me there is a fascina-tion which almost amounts to mesmerism in watching the mist which swathes the hills slowly unwind itself and lift, leaving patches here and there to hint at the mystery of the mountains which is never fully unveiled. The Paps of Jura, rising in majestic grandeur above the mist, held my. eyes until Crinan was reached and we landed.

Taking the road that, passing in front of the hotel, ascends to a parting of the ways, you descend on your left a short distance until you come, also on your left, to the old burial-ground of Kilmahumaig, probably that of " my Charmaig," the conjectured saint to whom the church on Eilean Mor is dedicated, thought to be S. Abban. The graveyard is, as usual, entirely abandoned to a rank over-growth in which nettles predominate, and my search for old stones only resulted in fresh stings. In a field opposite is a green mound about 30 feet high, crowned with a rudely formed chair of stone. This hill, *Dun Domhnaill,* some 120 yards in circumference, was one of the many through-out the territory of his jurisdiction on which the Macdonald,

Lord of the Isles, sat to dispense justice, surrounded by his court as already described.

The retinue of a Highland chief formed a most imposing array in the number and variety of the officers constituting his personal and household attendants. Besides the officials I have previously mentioned as holding hereditary office in Clan Donald, other officers, common to most clans and generally hereditary, were those of the harper, standard-bearer, and cup-bearer. In the households of the great chiefs there were two seneschals, well versed in the genealogies and nice points of clan precedences; gentlemen of the household and a quartermaster; a domestic usher and a forester. In constant personal attendance on the chief were his henchman and armour-bearer, while a body-guard, composed of the clan's most valiant youth, skilled alike in arms and seamanship, was in wider waiting. The chief had his special confidant or privy counsellor, a jester, a running footman, and a baggage man, whilst on specific occasions *an gille cas-fhliuch,* the servant who, when the chief travelled afoot, carried him across fords, and *an gille-comh-sreang,* the servant who led his horse by dangerous precipices, exercised each their offices. Both the harper and the piper had a special attendant who carried for them their respective instruments; and the Lord of the Isles was singular in having *Fear sguabaidh,* a man charged with the curious office of " sweeping the dew " away before his sovereign!

There is a tradition of *Dun Domhnaill,* the sequel of which has a quaint interest in the wording of a charter. On one occasion a clansman who had been condemned to death managed to escape from his keepers, and fled up the hillside. The then Lord of the Isles, furiously angry at such a happening in his presence, ordered a pursuit, and one of his followers, remarkable for fleetness of foot, succeeded after a strenuous struggle in capturing the condemned man. He was brought back before his judge, and executed then and there, while as a reward to his captor, the Lord of the Isles granted to him the adjacent lands of Kilmahumaig in the following curious terms:

> " I, Donald of Clan Donald, sitting in Dundonald, give a right from to-day till to-morrow to you, little Mackay of Kilmahumaig, up to God's heaven and down to hell, as long as wind blows and water flows. This I do in presence of my wife Catriona and little Effie, my nurse."

This Donald was apparently the Grumach, whose first wife was Catherine˙ (Catriona), a daughter of the Chief of Clanranald.

From Bellanoch you obtain a fine view across the flat region of *an Mhòine Mhór* (the great moss) to Poltalloch, fortunately still the seat of the small but ancient clan of Malcolm, whose country is entered at Crinan. Sprung apparently from the sept of the Macleods of Raasay, *MacGhille Chaluim*—" son of the servant of Columba," was the original form of the synonymous Malcolm—the " shaveling (monk) of Columba "—a rendering which was only permanently adopted as the name of the clan in 1779. Throughout their long history, the record of the clan has been, as it continues to be, one of honourable and distinguished service of Church, King, and Country, splendidly exemplifying in deed the motto of their chief, who has consistently proved that he " aims at lofty things."

A more interesting country than this in which the Malcolms still happily hold sway is not to be found in the whole of Scotland, for it embraces the ancient capital of Dalriada and the treasures of prehistoric and other remains that are found in lavish abundance round about it.

It is extraordinary that, with so much of this wealth of the past lying literally at the feet of the Briton, it is so generally ignored by him, the archæologically disposed flying to Egypt for antiquities. Indeed there is no subject which the ordinary man and woman more persistently shun than archæology, under the delusion that it is not only very abstruse, but the apotheosis of dullness, dryness, and every unattractive attribute. But once let them approach archæology without prejudice and intelligently, making a start, if possible, by accompanying some one capable of introducing them in vivid fashion to some relics of our country's past life, and, as I have triumphantly proved by such an experiment, a new world of living interest is opened up to those capable of being interested in anything outside mere frivolities.

To go over all the archæological wealth in which the Malcolm country abounds—cup-and-ring markings on rocks and monoliths, standing stones, and stone circles, chambered cairns, vitrified and ordinary hill-forts, inscribed gravestones, ruined churches and castles—would involve writing a lengthy treatise. So my main aim being to kindle interest in a neglected subject capable of exercising great fascination, I shall strive to attain my object by introducing a specimen of each type which has not heretofore been dealt with in these pages. Then awakened interest will be quickened by independent expeditions in search of further treasure.

Crossing the foot of Loch Crinan by Island Add Bridge, it is a dull straight road cutting through *an Mhòine Mhór* that takes you up past Poltalloch itself to Nether Largie. Here, on a farm, is a fine collection of antiquities, which include a group of standing stones associated with a chambered burial cairn. So extensive are the sepulchral relics here on the low-lying ground to the south of Kilmartin, that it must have constituted one of the largest and most important prehistoric cemeteries in Scotland—a district comparable in importance to Stonehenge and Avebury in England.

Standing stones are one of the many forms taken by prehistoric burial-places, which, however, is only one of the commemorative purposes they served. They often marked the site of a battlefield or a boundary line, and whilst the primary object of the stones was in most cases to mark burials of the late Stone or Bronze Age, stone circles at least often served secondarily as places where religious rites were observed, probably in connection with sun-worship. Standing stones, as in this instance, and stone circles alike, are often associated with chambered cairns, which were probably the prehistoric equivalent to the modern family vault, for they often contain the osseous remains of several generations. Those later burials made, of course, subsequent to the construction of the cairn for the first burials, are termed " secondary " burials.

The standing stones of Nether Largie consist primarily of five large monoliths, all of the native slate, averaging a height of between 8 feet and 9 feet, one in the centre, and two set in pairs on either side, at not quite equal distances, being 117 feet and 120 feet respectively apart from it, and from 10 feet to 11 feet apart from each other. Round the centre monolith are set four small stones averaging 2 feet high, and at 23 feet to the south-west from them is a rough semicircle of three slightly bigger stones. Both the centre stone and the south stone on the west side have cup-marks—those strange features which, together with rings and concentric circles, are so abundantly displayed on rocks and stones in this district.

To the north-east of the Largie standing stones lies the large sepulchral chamber that, together with two smaller cists, was laid bare when the stones of the superimposed cairn were removed by the ignorant as convenient material for walls. It is deplorable, too, that at the present time the large chamber should be used as a receptacle for barbed wire, since its presence not only makes examination impossible for all but the most determined and persistent, but its insertion and removal are bound in time to leave their effect upon the structure in some measure of destruction.

It was usual in the Bronze Age to burn the dead, and

CENTRAL CHAMBER OF BURIAL CAIRN, NETHER LARGIE

where this has been done, bones, thus rendered indestructible, are always found, often in an urn of a broad shape, generally ornamented, and often with some object of bronze incinerated with the bones. These burial urns were either placed mouth downwards over the ashes, or the mouth of the urn in which ashes had been deposited was covered with a small stone slab. Unburnt bodies of secondary burials are frequently found together with burnt remains, and generally they had as accompaniments weapons and a food or drinking vessel. These features are of the greatest interest as pointing to a belief in a survival of life beyond the grave—a life for which the living would make provision for their departed both as regards food and arms. A chamber lined with stones or slabs, and often, as in the case of the Largie central burial-place, divided into compartments, was then ready to receive the cists, or stone coffins, in which were placed the urns or unburnt body, often in a crouching position, with knees drawn up almost to the chin. The chamber would be roofed in with flags and then completely covered out of sight, and topped by an enormous cairn, the size of the cairn indicating the importance of the persons buried beneath. Leading into the burial chamber through the cairn generally ran a passage, usually constructed of flags set on edge. But this feature is absent in the Largie Cairn, which was a very large one, in diameter 134 feet, and the central chamber, which I shall describe as at once the largest, the most interesting, and " one of the most instructive places of sepulture " in Great Britain, is entered by a rude low portal opening on the north-east. This chamber is 19 feet long, averages $3\frac{3}{4}$ feet across and about $9\frac{1}{2}$ feet high. It is constructed for the most part of great slabs of unworked schist, and is divided into four compartments by three flags which, like another solitary one stretching from side to side above them, were evidently primarily intended to prevent the walls from collapsing. When this chamber was explored, several burials of different types and of different periods were distinguished in the different compartments; and I will merely summarize the general result. Remains and indications of both burnt and unburnt bodies were found, representing respectively primary and secondary burials. Burnt bones were found under carefully-laid little pavements of small pebbles and in burial urns, one of a novel and peculiar type: unburnt bones and fragments of pottery in cists, and also with one of these secondary burials, an urn of the drinking type pattern. Besides the very usual find of small articles of flint, there were quantities of broken quartz pebbles and a cow's tooth, which, from their frequent association with such burials, are considered to have been placed with intention, as having some symbolic or religious significance. It has been conjectured that, since these white quartz stones, not easy to find, are so frequently met with in these burials, they, as pretty things, were possibly sought after to serve as the prehistoric equivalent of the floral remembrances of later ages.

The smaller chamber, to the north of the larger and on the other side of the cart track which runs past it, consists of a cist covered by a huge slab, which might easily be overlooked as being merely a flat stone, so close does it rest to the ground.

From Nether Largie onwards to Kilmartin, through the fields, are to be seen the remains of cairn after cairn; and, taking this route, the churchyard of Kilmartin is soon gained after a final clamber up a slippery steep. Passing through the gateway, now spanned by a War Memorial Arch, of which the less said the better, there is on the left of the pathway one of the earliest Christian monuments in Argyllshire—a pillar cross, probably of twelfth century date. It consists of a rude slab of greenish slate on which the figure of a cross with abnormally short arms was sculptured, and ornamented both back and front variously with key and spiral patterns. But of far greater intrinsic interest was the unexpected discovery of the broken shaft

UNIQUE CROSS SHAFT AT KILMARTIN

37

of a cross on the right of the pathway, bearing upon it an exquisite figure of the Crucified. There is a tender grace and a simple dignity in this devotional representation of Christ upon the cross which makes the strongest appeal; it is so different from the usual earlier conceptions of the Crucifixion which often impress one not merely as crude but actually grotesque, despite the reverent intention obviously animating their sculptors.

There are only two known representations of the Redeemer in relief on the cross previous to the ninth century; and in the earliest types Christ appears as the King reigning from the tree, His head, held erect, regally crowned, His body vested in an albe, both arms and legs stretched out straight, His feet separate. In Celtic representations, too, the arms at right angles to the body, the head with hair short and neither crown nor halo, and the face beardless, are generally characteristics of work of tenth century date.

On the Kilmartin shaft, the Redeemer is represented without crown or halo, short-haired and beardless, and the remains of the cable moulding, which originally outlined the wheel of a cross, now suggest a vesica surrounding, however, only the upper half of the body. The legs hang down straight, and apparently the arms, too, were stretched out straight, but the feet are crossed, the one late feature in the representation, though its advance in conception contradicts an early origin. Below the feet is what looks in the photograph like a representation of intertwining serpents, elsewhere a favourite symbol of our Lord's victory over the evil one, but rarely found on West Highland stones. But on the stone itself, the weathered sculpturing, in so far as it can be made out, is more like a folaginous design. On the other side of this wonderful cross shaft there are faintly discernible traces of the figure of our Lord, fully draped, His hands raised in blessing, while the position of the feet suggest a seated figure. The head is missing. Probably the representation was one of Christ enthroned in glory, less likely of the Ascension or Resurrection.

I have only seen one allusion to this cross, which ought to receive more recognition for its unique features. Apparently it was originally erected by the roadside about a quarter of a mile from the churchyard. Thence it was removed by the village smith, who, after West Highland use and wont, appropriated it to his own use, and by whose descendants, in consequence, it is, or was, claimed.

There is also in the churchyard, left carelessly lying about, another fragment of a crucifix that at once struck me as being very familiar from a drawing of the original, certainly not at Kilmartin, but I thought somewhere either in Knapdale or Kintyre. I find that the illustration in point is of a fragment at Saddell Abbey in Kintyre, and, though I have only my memory of the Kilmartin stone to compare with it, it seems so much a facsimile that I wonder if Saddell can have been robbed to enrich Kilmartin. The fragment I saw is so weathered that the figure has lost most of its relief and all detail, and I observed no trace of the square of basket work shewn in the illustration, made nearly fifty years ago.

While the majority of the sculptured stones, of the ordinary West Highland type but much weathered, have been gathered together in one quarter of the churchyard and left unenclosed, others have been subjected to an incredible act of vandalism. Within some high and imposing railings have been literally fitted some seven or eight of the finest stones of the Malcolm chiefs that the churchyard contained. Apparently the railings were considered the most important feature, and their dimensions must have been decided upon arbitrarily at first, for when the stones selected for the honour of enclosure therein proved to be too long, they were cut down, and, to complete the indignity, " Poltalloch " was cut into them in enormous letters, without any regard for the original carving beneath. This unique outrage was perpetrated about the beginning of the last century, and the factor responsible for it was—one Campbell of Prospect. Comment is entirely superfluous.

The capital of ancient Dalriada, the hill fort of Dunadd, is about four miles south of Kilmartin, and rises, a craggy precipitous rock, in one aspect shaped like a camel's back, a conspicuous landmark in the surrounding plain of the Great Moss. It is mentioned by its alternative name of Dun Monaidh, or the Fort of Monadh, in the Tale of Deirdre, and it also appears as the residence of King Eochaidh Buidhe (Egbert the yellow-haired), who died 693, while Malcolm MacKenneth, who reigned from 1005 to 1034 A.D., was called *Ri Monaidh,* or the King of Monadh.

The kingdom of Dalriada was founded in 498 by Scots from the north of Ireland, Fergus Mor MacErca and his brothers Lorn and Angus, all sons of the High King of Ireland, sailing up the River Add, according to the Irish Annalists, and landing at the fort of Dunadd. It is these three princes who were said to have been buried in Reilig Odhran on Iona before the coming of S. Columba. Fergus, a man of commanding presence, was elected *Ard-righ,* with his seat at Dunadd, which thus became the capital of Scottish Dalriada, whilst under him ruled his brothers as sub-kings, one of whom gave his name permanently to that district of Argyllshire in which he held sway—the land of Lorne. The kingdom of Dalriada passing under the rule of the Britons, Dunadd evidently lost its status as an independent capital about 640, but when Briton and Scots alike became subject to the Angles, rebellion broke out. Fearchar Fada, King of Scots, united with Bredei, King of the Picts, to besiege Dunadd in 683, but they failed to capture it. Later, regaining its position as capital of the Scots, Dunadd was again besieged and taken in 736 by Angus MacFergus, King of the Picts.

Tradition and folklore have also their tales to tell of Dunadd. The rock is reputed a home of the fairies, and whilst one more generally associates the little folk with gentler surroundings and stretches of smooth greensward, whereon they may disport themselves in the moonlight, the fort is not without some suggestions of fairy hills. Ossian, too, is said to have lived at Dunadd, and one day, charged by a stag he was hunting on Lochfyneside, he turned and fled homewards. In two bounds he regained Dunadd, not, however, without falling on his knee, and being obliged to stretch out his hands to save himself from falling backward. His " left " footmark and the impress of his knee are the ingenious explanations of the symbols to which I shall allude later as being found on the rock of Dunadd, but the imprint of his fingers is yet to seek.

Tradition associates S. Columba with Dunadd, and if two of the relics found within during the excavations do not bear witness to a visit of S. Columba himself, they certainly testify to the penetration of Christianity.

You obtain the best idea of the clever adaptation of the natural defensive advantages offered by Dunadd by a reference to its plan. In this, the thick black outlines indicate the walls of drystone masonry with which the prehistoric builders contrived to supplement the defences already afforded by nature. The rock is naturally divided into a lower part on the plateau and an upper one on the ridge, the upper completely dominating the lower.

You climb up the hill, and enter the fort by a natural gap, probably originally roofed over, through which there is a steep ascent opening upon a wonderful natural amphitheatre, strewn with ice-borne blocks of stone. Turning round at this point, the outlook over the country is very striking. The high rocky chasm in the foreground affords a bold relief to the wide and far-flung distance, and indeed, as you walk round the top of Dunadd, you cannot fail to be impressed with the marvellous extent of country commanded by its ancient capital.

Facing about and entering on the plateau, you are standing within a large area in which would be situated

PLAN OF FORT OF DUNADD, BY THOS. ROSS, ARCHITECT

(By kind permission of the Society of Antiquaries of Scotland)

the wooden turf-roofed buildings which, though naturally there is no trace of any left, probably accommodated the inhabitants of the capital. That Dunadd was not only a fortress, but a permanent settlement, is to be inferred from the large number of quern stones found in the excavations, and to a lesser extent by the clay crucibles, fragments of pottery, small jet and vitreous ornaments, bone and iron implements, including combs. It is difficult to believe that the roughly-calculated 200 square feet of habitable space would accommodate so large a population as 700, but such is an estimate which has been made—not, however, by me!

Probably the wooden houses of the inhabitants would be dotted about amongst the forts of the plateau as shewn on the plan, which indicates several features deserving of attention. What is marked, as it is generally called, a " well," popularly said to rise and fall with the ebb and flow of the tide, is merely a water cistern dug out of the rock to a depth of 6 feet, and covered now by two heavy slabs. It is 4 feet in diameter, and is surrounded by a curious pavement of thin flat stones set on edge and radiating outwards. The last time I was at Dunadd, however, it was to discover that this paving had been entirely obscured by cementing down the slabs over it with a lavish supply of mortar—surely a more drastic action than was called for to prevent sheep falling down the well.

You can quite well see that the nature of the ground suggested the three forts of the plateau, all more or less capable of separate defence. The walls built at right angles, shown in the plan between the walls of forts E and F, are, like other inferior masonry nearer the entrance, remains of structures built after the original walls. Just on the left, as you pass into fort D by the gap in the wall, is its supposed door slab, 4 feet by 3½ feet, and further along on the left you come to the postern. This was probably closed by the stone slab, 5 feet by 4 feet, which was found lying in the gap of the postern, because on the inside of the wall there is on the ground a second slab set on edge, and between this and the wall the door slab could easily be slid into position.

Just by the postern is an original stone structure of the fort, called on the plan a " cell," but, since it is 24 feet long and 4 feet wide until, at its termination against the rock, it gains a width of 6 feet, it is much more suggestive of a passage. For what it was intended, I have seen no conjecture, nor have I one to make, but it was just outside the cell that one of the evidences of the penetration of Christianity into Dunadd during its occupation was found. This was a disc of slate on which was graven in lettering like Irish miniscules *In* (n) *omine,* and its companion witness was a quern having a cross potent incised at its circumference.

You gain the forts on the ridge by a stairway rudely cut in the rock just beside the cell, but regarding their structure, the plan will give the layman all the information wanted. These forts may be said to represent the keep of later ages—the last outwork of defence—and again the discoveries made by the spade show specimens of the weapons with which the garrison was armed. Very strangely, there did not come to light a single arrow-head, and only a solitary sword. Possibly stones were the only projectiles used, but if the relics in which forts A and B abounded afford a witness to the complete armoury of the fort, it must have been restricted to spears, several socketed spear-heads of iron having been found.

But, beyond the tiered structure of the fortress, the features of most unique interest in Dunadd are the remarkable symbols found on the surface of the living rock just outside the south-east corner of the middle fort of the ridge. Cut in the foremost patch, like the others behind, practically flush with the surrounding earth, is the impression of a right foot, seemingly shod with a *cuaran,* a shoe of hide. It is 11 inches long, nearly 4½ inches broad at its broadest part and 3½ inches across the heel. Behind this footmark is the figure of a boar incised in the

THE NATURAL ENTRANCE TO DUNADD, LOOKING OUT

rock and represented as advancing towards the footmark. Only two other possible representations of a boar are known in Scotland, and this, a very spirited one, still shews clearly, originally with the exception of the back. But on my recent visit I was horrified to discover that some barbarian had actually not only scratched over the outline, but with rude and unskilled hand had attempted to supply the missing part of the back. Thus Colonel Malcolm has been obliged to secure the boar against further injury by padlocking a hinged slab of concrete over it.

On the third rock surface, and in a line with both the other symbols, is cut out a basin 10 inches in diameter and 4 inches deep. These rock basins are of quite common occurrence in the Highlands, where they have generally been made for use as a mortar, with a stone for pestle, for separating the husk from the barley. Other similar rocky hollows, found in conjunction with standing stones and others in churchyards, suggest some religious or ceremonial use. Probably the story of Ossian's leap was invented by the ingenious mind of the Celt to explain the foot and " knee " marks, but the real explanation almost certainly is that they indicate the place of the inauguration of the ancient kings of Dalriada. One tradition states indeed that the footmark is the original impression of the foot of the first king, Fergus Mor Mac Erca, who died 501 A.D.

A stone was the permanent feature of first importance in all Celtic inaugurations, a relic that survives in the stone of Scone still used for the coronation of our British sovereigns in Westminster Abbey. In these stones a footmark was generally cut, as in the case of the stone on the isle of Finlaggan in Islay, where took place the solemn ceremony of the installation of the Lords of the Isles. On this great occasion the Bishops of Argyll and the Isles and seven priests were sometimes present, but a bishop at least was indispensable. Then in the presence of all the principal chiefs, the Lord of the Isles, in token that he would walk in the footsteps of his forefathers, set his foot in the footmark carved in the stone of inauguration. He was clothed in white, typifying his innocence and integrity of heart, and received into his hand a white rod as a symbol of unimpeachable rule. Then his forefathers' sword was given him as a symbol of his duty to protect his people, and the bishop and priests blessed the new ruler and anointed him. During this ceremony, the hereditary bard MacVurich, a venerable man wearing a red mantle, recited from memory the long line of the chief's ancestors, to proclaim his right to possession by descent, and the celebration of the Eucharist consummated the inauguration.

In this Christian solemnity was most certainly incorporated the essential features of the prehistoric ceremony, thus preserving an all-important continuity with the past. Here on Dunadd the placing of the foot in the footmark would obviously convey to all beholders the taking possession of the country upon which the ruler, thus standing, looked out both far and wide, truly a royal prospect. Behind him the figure of a boar, adopted as its device by the 20th Roman Legion, would, as with it, typify the courage which should distinguish those having dominion. It is scarcely probable that any ceremony of anointing found place in any prehistoric inauguration, and thus, unless the bowl was cut later for domestic purposes having, therefore, no association with the other symbols, it might have been used for some ceremonial purification in connection with the inauguration. During the probable period of the fort's occupancy, it could hardly have been used as a baptismal font, since in those days the river below would probably have been the scene of the administration of the Sacrament of Initiation.

I left Dunadd intending to proceed to Tayvallich, and, in order to see a very fine cup-and-ring-marked rock *en route,* I went round by Cairnbaan to Bellanoch. A short distance beyond the house that used to be the Inn, and on the same side of the canal, a track winds up the hill to an abandoned slate quarry. Taking this path, you follow it as far as the eminence on the right, on which are situated some ruined cottages, and climbing the hill and passing in front of and round the buildings, you gain the open moorland below. The situation of the stone is neither easy to describe nor to find, and can, therefore, only be roughly indicated by saying that you bear round to the left and, keeping below a ridge of rocks, you may—or may not—come across it. It is a large, gently-sloping slab of living rock absolutely flush with the ground, and the sculpturings, occupying a space of 9 feet by $5\frac{1}{2}$ feet, comprise 16 simple and 21 ringed cups, the former being from 2 inches to 4 inches in diameter, and the latter, with from 1 to 4 concentric circles, varying from 5 inches to 14 inches. The general disposition presents a curious appearance, of cups and ringed-cups linked up—most commonly in groups of three, by channelings taking an erratic course. The appearance of the whole is very suggestive of the plan of a maze, or of a series of fortifications, perhaps a prehistoric map or chart.

The meaning of the cup-and-ring markings has so far baffled the archæologist, though there have not been wanting many and various conjectures as to their origin. They are found on works of nature, such as rock surfaces and boulders; on sepulchral remains, monoliths, cromlechs, cairns, covers of cists and urns; on brochs and forts, underground houses and lake dwellings, and even in churchyards. So remote is the origin of these strange sculpturings, generally sprinkled quite promiscuously broadcast over stone surfaces, that not even the Highlander, seldom lacking in explanations, has any tradition whatever concerning them.

Recently, however, Mr. Ludovic M'L. Mann, F.S.A., Scot., to whom Scottish archæology already owes so much, has been engaged on an exhaustive study of these stones with a view to elucidating, if possible, their mystery.

Thus, those interested in the question are eagerly anticipating Mr. Mann's promised publication of a monograph
on the subject on which he is at present engaged. He
intends to demonstrate by the application of certain mathe-
matical and astronomical principles that these stones were
intended to serve, amongst other things, as luni-solar
calendars, and were associated with the astrological conceptions of late Neolithic and Bronze Age man.

———

PART III

FURTHER AFIELD IN THE MALCOLM COUNTRY TO THE END AT CULLODEN

IT was on my first tramp from Bellanoch to Tayvallich,
a distance of six-and-a-quarter miles, that I took " Green
Maria " for her first run. " Green Maria " was my own
invention and construction throughout, a wooden box, $25\frac{1}{2}$
inches by $11\frac{1}{2}$ inches by $12\frac{1}{2}$ inches, divided longitudinally
to within $2\frac{3}{4}$ inches from the top, into two compartments,
and again across the end into two smaller; its lid, hinged
to both sides of the box, opening down the middle, the
whole covered with canvas painted green to render it
invisible in a cache. Leather handles screwed to both
ends gave it the appearance, when not on wheels, of an
ordinary piece of luggage. Inside, one side of the larger
division took my half-plate camera, six slides, two lenses,
etc., the other, night and toilet requirements and a change
of blouse, boots, and skirt. Of the little compartments,
one was designed for my kettle and picnicking traps and
provisions for the way; the other for a box of photographic plates, map, writing-paper, etc. On top of everything reposed my oilskin, camera-stand, four small
rubber-rimmed wheels, axles, bolts, nuts, split-pins, and

PORTRAIT OF "GREEN MARIA," WITH AUTHOR

a spanner. The axles were very easily bolted on when I wanted " Green Maria " to run behind me, and still easier was it to affix the wheels, which simply slipped on till they met the stop of the axle, being kept on with split pins inserted through holes bored to receive them. Then I only had to slip a strap through one handle, and " Green Maria " followed after me—exactly like Mary's little lamb. I found this method of conveying my various loads on my tramps much more satisfactory and far less burdensome than hanging myself round with them, nor have I as yet found any drawback to the contrivance.

Bellanoch is a picturesque little hamlet, where in the peaceful pool of the flower-fringed loch ducks swim contentedly, a sailing boat lies at anchor, and on the shore a mother-hen with her family scratch amongst the stones— the whole a restful, homely scene. You climb up the road to Tayvallich through scenery in no wise remarkable, but after nearly two miles, moorland and hills rise on either side to offer you their companionship.

Just half a mile beyond the fork in the road where the turning to the right leads to Tayvallich, you reach a sharp bend. Here on the left hand, just past a wooden gate, close to the roadside, but within a wall, you see a monolith, and, when you climb over, another at the opposite end, and between them, some lumpish-looking blocks of stone shewing through a tangle of bracken. This site is well worth examination as exhibiting something unusual if not unique [7] in Scotland—the remains of a stone circle of a very regular oval in shape, measuring 65 feet by 42 feet. Each end of the long axis is marked by another unique feature, the only standing stones in the circle, and between these on the north-east side is a row of thirteen recumbent stones, set fairly close to each other. Though the south-east side is quite clearly defined, there is on it only one stone to be seen, the others most probably having been

[7] Its follow I think I discovered in Glenbeg. See p. 216.

removed for some utilitarian purpose, as so often, alas,. happens wherever antiquities are concerned. The erect stone at one end is a strangely shaped three-sided block, two of its corners rising like horns from the top.

Turning back to the wooden gate and passing through it, you enter upon a scene remarkable in many features. You follow a road, now clothed with the loveliest short green turf, constructed on a shelf raised 90 feet above the exquisite little Loch Coille a' Bharra—" the grove-topped lake." After some 500 yards, you come across a scene of infinite pathos, the deserted ruinous little cottages of a secluded hamlet situated in the most perfect of surroundings. This is Kilmory Oib, but its desertion is not due to any such shameful cause as that which accounts for the abandonment of the " Back Settlement " on Loch Linnhe. Colonel E. D. Malcolm, C.B., of Poltalloch, told me that it was during the great famine that passed over the West Highlands that the inhabitants of Kilmory Oib sought a new home beyond the seas. They strikingly testified the nature of their feelings to their old chief by taking the horses out of his carriage and themselves drawing it to his hotel when he visited them in Australia.

A rough track succeeds to the smooth lawn-like road, and on the right—reeds, bracken, and small boulders scattered in the foreground, here and there a solitary tree in the distance—are nestling in the lee of the hill the tumbled remains of a few cottages, deep in bracken. So very rude is their masonry, that they might have been built in very early ages, and indeed the original settlement must have been very old, for, situated in ground that must always have been, as now, marshy, stands an ancient cross slab at the head of a well, to which stepping-stones lead up. All about and in the well itself, which is square and carefully built, is an abundant crop of water-cress, and partly covering the well is a huge and heavy slab, beyond which rises the cross slab set in a growth of reeds.

This slab is not only a very early one, but is almost

CROSS SLAB AT KILMORY OIB

unique in its sculpturings on both sides—now so worn with age and weathering that the designs are difficult to trace clearly. On the well side of the shaft, a rude cross is incised in outline. It has the unusual features of a head longer than the arms and an expanded top; three slanting strokes suggestive of oghams pendent from the top outline of the right arm: at the bottom of the cross three horizontal strokes cutting across the right hand side outline almost over to that on the left, and both outlines of the cross terminating outwardly in two short lines at right angles, as if to represent a base. The reverse of this slab is more worn, and, if you can make it out, it is equally unique in its form and sculpturings. It appears to be an example of a patriarchal cross, *i.e.,* one with two sets of arms separated from each other, in this case by a pair of bosses, and here both arms have expanding ends like the cross head in the obverse. Two birds, now very indistinct, are represented at the top, smaller than those in the angles below the second arm, where two birds of the size of a thrush are suggested. The well was evidently a holy well, doubly hallowed by this pillar cross erected above it—a stone which should be compared with that I discovered in Ardnamurchan.[8]

Regaining the track and pursuing it, you come to a second cluster of ruins, most picturesque in their setting of ferns and bracken against trees, and these are obviously more modern cottages, for the masonry is much better, and they are not in quite so ruinous a state as the others. The beautiful little Loch Coille a' Bharra only becomes visible when you reach the edge of the shelf and look over, and then you have a view across its serenely still waters over to its tree-fringed cliffy banks that suggests a landscape in fairyland.

I would have liked to pursue the way through by the track to Oibmore where there are more interesting

[8] Described on p. 415.

inscribed stones of great age, but there was, unfortunately, no time to spare, so I retraced my steps, and, retrieving " Green Maria " from her hiding-place in a bed of bracken by the gate of entry, I regained the road by the stone oval " circle."

The next mile of the road, still gently ascending, passes through the wildest, and, therefore, to my mind, the finest part of the way, and before you take the bend of the road, your eyes will probably be attracted by the very obtrusive debris at the bottom of the great ridge that rises on the left. Looking upward at this point, nothing in particular is visible at the summit, but when you have swung round the ridge, it is possible to catch a suggestion of piled stones on the top—the site of one of the best preserved forts in Argyllshire. As it has also been excavated, it is thus one of the best to convey some idea of the general construction of these mysterious buildings, about the full use and exact purpose of which, as well as of their inhabitants, so little is known.

You can climb up Druim an Duin—the ridge of the fort— by an easy slope on the east, and at once you realize what a site of strategic importance and natural strength it occupies on the west of the long knife-edged ridge that is protected on the west by a rocky precipice. While to the north, the view is cut off by near hills, to the south you look down *Caol Scotnish,* and beyond to Loch Sween— a far-stretching picture of beautifully-wooded, land-locked water, and of hills rising in tiers everywhere.

Like most of the sites of these hill forts, the summit seems to have been naturally level, and here an oval space, measuring 48 feet long by 25 feet at the north end and 33 feet wide at the south end, has been enclosed, excepting possibly where guarded by the precipice, by cyclopean walls, generally 14 feet thick, and which still average 7 feet high. Two entrances, at the north and south ends respectively, though they are not in a line with each other, seem to constitute a weakness in the defence, but probably

SOUTH ENTRANCE TO FORT ON DRUIM AN DUN, SHEWING DOORWAY INTO GUARD CHAMBER

the builders foresaw some necessity for providing an entrance at either end—a feature not general in these forts.

It is not necessary for my purpose to describe the fort in detail, and for this reason I will not particularize the points of the north entrance, but will concentrate on the much more interesting south entrance as including features common to both, and having, in addition, a guard-chamber unpossessed by the other. The south doorway has a double interest, for it reproduces almost exactly the characteristics of the entrance to a broch. Thus, approaching from outside, you notice the division into an outer and an inner part, the first straight and extending for five feet with a width of four feet, ending at the checks, still projecting, for the door. An idea of what this was like may be obtained just outside the north entrance, where lies a big slab which probably closed the opening into the fort at this end. Behind the checks, you can see the rectangular opening of the bar-hole, and beyond this is the inner entry, which widens out to 5 feet 9 inches and is slightly curved on the east side. It is in the middle of this side, too, that the guard chamber is built in the thickness of the wall, entered through a doorway, 4 feet high and 2 feet 9 inches wide, and still roofed. The low entry leads into a passage, 4 feet long, by which the guard-chamber is reached. This cell measures 12 feet long on one side and 10 feet on the other; nearest the passage, the width is 7 feet, while it narrows into 3 feet at the other end, which is rounded. The shape of the cell itself is like a horse's hoof viewed in profile, and it was probably no more than 5 feet high, judging from one of the roofing slabs still in position over the passage. The lighting of these intramural chambers must have been wholly artificial, since their construction in the thickness of the walls obviously precludes any possibility of a window. Probably such lamps as those hollowed out of stone which have been found in excavations would be used. They are akin to the cruisie: a twist of moss would serve as wick, which would be fed by animal oil in the open body of the lamp.

Dunadd is quite unusual amongst the forts in possessing a well, and it is one of the many puzzles of these forts how the inhabitants obtained their water. As in the case of Druim an Duin, it must have involved considerable toil in carrying up the hill supplies from the nearest source in times of peace—in presence of the enemy quite impossible, one imagines. Thus it has been conjectured that a supply must have been kept stored in the fort in skins, scarcely in jars, since so few remains of pottery have been found in excavations. Here the one interesting relic revealed by the spade was a portion of a stone cup, the handle complete, and a prehistoric attempt at riveting being shown on one side of the broken edge. It is the same type of cup that has been found in the brochs.

It is another moot question whether these forts generally were usually inhabited or only resorted to when the necessity to take defence against an enemy arose. Shelter would be needed if the forts were in permanent use, and shelter could only have been afforded to a few by a solitary guard chamber, unless, indeed, it was usual to augment its accommodation by huts of turf and wood built within the area, as probably was done at Dunadd.

As I sat on Druim an Duin one day, watching the rain fall with steady persistency into the loch, across the water floated the plaintive wail of the pipes in a lament, and I knew it for MacCrimmon's " *O cha tu, cha tu thilleas,*" composed in prophetic significance by the famous hereditary piper of the Macleod, who, before he left Skye to follow the Prince, received a warning that he would " never return." Nor did he. This intensified the mournful spirit in which I was enwrapped, and helped to make an atmosphere all too suitable for the recollection that next day I should be leaving the beloved Western Highlands for another period of exile—I knew not how long. From this unwelcome reflection, my thoughts passed on

by a natural transition to that fatal field which fastened
the yoke of the foreigner with all its attendant miseries
upon the Highlands, harrying the homes of the Highlanders, and often ousting them, indirectly but certainly,
in favour of aliens having no interests other than their
own. Because, therefore, the " day of Culloden " so
entirely epitomises the Highland character, nothing can
more fittingly close this book of my wanderings than a
picture of that most pathetic of all the battlefields of Great
Britain, and none the less aptly because Culloden is
geographically outside my limits. For, historically, it
brings before you, one after the other, representatives of
the clans of which these pages have spoken, and thus, in
a double sense, if not in the primary one, Culloden may be
rightfully included in a book of the Western Highlands.

I can never forget the day when, being left to myself,
I stood on the saddest spot in all Scotland, where had been
fought, two hundred years before, the last battle on British
soil, April 16, 1746.

> " The moorland. wide and waste and brown,
> Heaves far and near and up and down;
> Few trenches green the desert crown,
>   And these are the graves of Culloden."

The heath and ling at my feet glowed in the wonted purple
of autumn. But in the springtide of that fatal " year of
Charles " it had been dyed in another purple—sinister, yet
brighter by far than that the moor has ever known before
or since. And still down through the years comes the
call of that blood to the clansmen whose ancestors were
numbered among those sleeping beneath the sod of Drummossie Muir " who fought and died for Charlie." As I
stood there, in profoundest community of feeling, my own
blood from a freshly-wounded hand fell where the blood
of kinsmen crying out to me already had fallen. At once,
in the company of the encompassing spirits of the slain
Highlanders, I seemed to see the five thousand clansmen,
famished and weary, face to face with the eight thousand

of the well-fed and well-rested forces of the Elector of Hanover. While I waited with them, halted in the path of wind and hailstorm, the vision of great leaders of old passed before my eyes ; the pale form of the Great Marquis and of his brilliant lieutenant, Left-handed Coll, and the wraith of *Iain Dubh nan Cath,* " dark John of the battle," the gallant Dundee. Even so they might have appeared to the devoted Jacobites, beckoning them on to fight, even as they themselves had fought in the past, for the native House of Stewart.

As through the lashing of the hailstones the enemy advanced, upon the Highlanders fastened the *crith ghaisge,* " tremblings of valour," before they were seized with the *mire chatha,* the terrible " frenzy of battle " that takes possession of the Gael. Mingled with the howling of the icy blast was the hum of the great pipes of war: bonnets were waved, broadswords brandished, and loud above all others rang out the battle-cry of the Camerons, with its invitation, so welcome to all the clans: " Sons of the hound, come hither and get flesh ! " And, like hounds at leash, the Highlanders, baying, strained forward in response—the advanced lines to break tether at last in face of intolerable fire from the Southron artillery, against which but six poor pieces, ill-served, took no effect.

> " In vain the wild onslaught, in vain
> Claymores cleft English skulls in twain,
> The cannon fire poured in like rain,
> Mowing down the clans on Culloden."

The Macdonalds, still awaiting the command to charge, in savage impotence hacked with their impatient swords at the heather at their feet, and, *mo thruaighe,* the heather was white that they destroyed !

Omen of ill, indeed, for the tide of battle flowed with the foreigner. In the teeth of the biting wind and hail, foot to foot and hand to hand, the clansmen fought as only clansmen can—with valour more akin to gods than men.

There smote the stalwart chief of MacBean, felling with his broadsword thirteen of the enemy before he himself fell, his head fearfully wounded, a thigh broken.

> " With thy back to the wall and thy breast to the targe,
> Fair flashed thy claymore in the face of their charge,
> The blood of their boldest that barren turf stain,
> But alas, thine is reddest there. Gillies MacBean."

Most foolishly deprived of their hereditary place of honour on the right of the Highland army, the Macdonalds, smarting under the undeserved blow dealt to their pride, angrily took up the position allotted to them on the left. It is grievous to recall that Sir Walter Scott is responsible for the libel that attaches to their conduct on this occasion —that the clan deserted the chief who led them—the gallant Alexander Macdonald of Keppoch. In actual fact, the Macdonalds not only charged with their chief, but the company led by his brother even outran the line, whilst the Keppoch clan were the last of any to lay down their arms. Not once but twice did Keppoch himself fall, on the second occasion fatally pierced by a bullet. The spot is still shewn where Keppoch fell.

But for all the prodigies of valour performed by the Highlanders with inferior numbers, useless artillery, the snow, and the smoke of the enemy's guns blowing in their faces and the fumes choking them, in a brief half - hour it was for them a lost battle. In stricken heaps upon the blood-soaked moorland lay the bodies of the clansmen piled one above the other, so close had been the fighting. There crawled the yellow-haired chief of Clan Chattan, Macgillivray of Dunmaglas, mortally hit, trying to drag after him towards a tiny stream a wounded lad, moaning for water. But even as he gained the brink of the fountain, the yellow head of the gallant chief dropped in death where now the forget-me-not meetly blossoms by this " Well of the Dead." . . . Then the Hanoverian soldiers gleefully, acting under the orders of that hound of hell, *Am Feoladair* (The Butcher), coursed the stricken field to slay the wounded as they lay . . . In the distance, near the still standing farmhouse of Leannach, was a hut where thirty-two wounded Highlanders sought shelter, and this the ruthless soldiery set on fire, the ascending smoke of its burning crying aloud to heaven for vengeance.

As for Charles himself, would he had fallen with his clansmen, dying as he had lived—a chief amongst heroes! The determination of those surrounding him, however, prevented him from leading his men on foot to the charge, as he wished to do, and he was fain to content himself with the part of a spectator of the fight. Careless of the risk he ran, the Prince sat unmoved on his horse, which was struck by a splinter from the storm of shot which hurtled around his head. A cannon-ball decapitated one of the grooms standing by the Prince, who was spattered all over by the mud it threw up. Charles behaved throughout the battle with coolness and courage in the passive and uncongenial part that was forced upon him; and it was only by hands being forcibly laid upon the bridle of his horse that he, when desirous of rallying his men in person, was led away off the field.

To-day a huge cairn commemorates the spot about which the battle raged the thickest, and the graves of the fallen are marked by simple rough headstones inscribed with the names of the clans. It is a sight upon which no Jacobite clansman can look unmoved, and for the heroic fallen the prayer ascends: " *When thou rewardest the Saints, remember, O Lord, we beseech Thee for good, those who have sacrificed themselves for us, and, in that day, shew them mercy.*"

There is an infinite pathos in the long green trenches marking where Stewarts of Appin, Macgillivrays, Frasers, Camerons, Macintoshes, Macleans, and other loyal Highlanders lie buried side by side on the lonely, silent heath of Drummossie; and once in the shelter of the pine trees, which now no longer grow behind the " Well of the Dead," are the nameless graves of the Macdonalds. As though to atone for the shameful misrepresentation they have suffered, the wind that once sighed ceaselessly amongst the tree-tops above them now sweeps across the open moor, ever singing their coronach—*A' Cheapach 'na fhàsach,* " Keppoch in his Desolation," the lament of the Macdonalds of that ilk.

*   *   *   *   *   *

With the death of Cardinal Henry Benedict, Duke of York, the direct line of the Stewarts came to an end. But the House of Windsor can trace its descent from the Royal House of Stewart, and did our present King and Queen but graciously favour the Western Highlands with a visit, they would find themselves acclaimed by the Gael as rightfully succeeding in every sense, to the devotion yielded in the past to Prince Charlie. Our very dear King and Queen, as their country's most precious possession, are enthroned in the hearts of the Highlander as truest father and mother, the personal possession of every one, worthy of all the love that loyal subjects bear towards them, an example in all things, and an inspiration at all times.

*   *   *   *   *   *

Farewell, beloved Western Highlands and Islands, you who have so often said to me in your kindly mother-way, as my lagging footsteps left your sacred soil, " Would it not be the beautiful thing, now, if you were coming instead of going?" Yea, " beautiful " indeed, although every Highland heart passing into exile bears with it treasures of home. And, when it finds voice, that heart exclaims:

> "Go back, O breath of the hills! Would that we went together!
> Tell how their lost child fares!
> Whisper amongst the bracken and say to the broom and the heather,
> That still my heart is theirs!"

MEANINGS OF PLACE-NAMES

MEANINGS OF PLACE-NAMES[1]

WHERE DISCOVERABLE, AND WHERE THEY HAVE NOT BEEN GIVEN IN THE TEXT

SOME GENERAL PRELIMINARY OBSERVATIONS.

THE place-names of Scotland in many instances disclose how the Gael has accepted his country as being his second self, and therefore has discovered in its various distinctive features, likenesses to himself. Thus there recur over and over again amongst the place-names *ceann,* a head; *claigionn,* a skull; *mala,* a brow; *aodann,* a face; *suil,* an eye; *beul,* a mouth; *teanga,* the tongue; *sròn,* the nose; *cluas,* an ear; *guala,* the shoulder; *slinnean,* shoulder-blade; *uileann,* the elbow; *glac,* the hollow of the hand; *druim,* back, backbone; *cliabh,* the thorax; *uchd,* the breast, etc., etc.

It is also interesting to note the nice distinctions conveyed by the different names given to mountains. Whilst *beinn* signifies a mountain that rises into a distinct peak, a *sgorr* or *sgurr* a height as distinct as a *beinn,* but rough and scarred; *mam* or *cìoch,* a peak suggesting a breast; *maol,* a bald peak; *monadh* implies an expanse of mountain devoid of any definite head; and a *meall* denotes a lumpish hill of the nature of a mound.

I cannot, I do not, lay any claim to that linguistic equipment which alone can qualify one to determine, or even pronounce upon the correct meaning of place-names—

----

[1] A few clan names have been included under M.

where any meaning is discoverable. Where I have not been able to ascertain these meanings locally (and Mr. Angus Hendersons are not found in every locality), I have sought it from experts. To the kindness of Mr. J. B. Johnston, author of the *Place-Names of Scotland,* I am greatly obliged, for he has answered many queries. But I am most of all indebted to Professor Watson, of the Celtic Chair in Edinburgh University, the acknowledged ultimate authority on the subject, showing the greatest kindness and generosity to an entire stranger. Professor Watson has revised this list of place meanings, transforming a glossary of questionable value into one stamped with unquestionable authority. On my own initiative, I wish to make it perfectly clear that with this glossary, Professor Watson's responsibility begins and ends. If incorrect Gaelic spellings or meanings be found in the text of the book, they must be attributed to me solely, for Professor Watson has never seen the MS.

With the rare exception of a river, place-names will be found under the same style as they appear in the foregoing pages: *e.g.,* Loch Snizort, under L, Glen Salachan under G, Castle Tioram under C, etc., etc.

Achindarroch: field of the oak.

Achnahannait: the field of the mother church, *i.e.,* that where the patron saint was educated or where his relics were kept.

Allt-a-Choire Riabhaich: a stream of the brindled corry.

Aoineadh Mor: great steep.

Arasaig: water's mouth bay.

Ardintoul: height of the barn.

Ardnamurchan: heights of ? sea hazel.

Ardshiel: probably cape of streamlets, see below, Loch Linnhe.

Ardslignish: height of shells.

Argyll: coast-land of the Gael.

Arnisdale: Dale of Arni.

Ballachulish: village on the straits.

Balvraid: homestead of the upper part.

Bealach Maim: pass of large round hill.

Beinn a' Chapuill: mare's peak.

Beinn nan Cailleach: hags' peak.

Beinn nan Sealg: hill of hunts.

Belnahua: cave mouth.

Ben na Greine: peak of the sun.

Ben Hiant: charmed or blessed peak.

Ben Sgrial: scree hill.

Ben Vair: hill of the monster, *or* thunderbolt.

Bernera: Björn's Isle.

Blar dubh: black moor.

Borrodale: fort-dale.

Branault: head of streams.

Brecklet: speckled slope.

Caigionn: a path.

Callart: hazel point or height.

Caol Scotnish: strait of Scotti's cape?

Caradale Burn: copse water dale.

Carnach: place of cairns or stone-heaps.

Carn Liath: grey cairn.

Castle Maol: castle of the mull or blunt promontory.

Castle Tioram: dry castle, *i.e.*, left dry at low tide.

Ceann na Creige: head of the rock.

Clachaig: stony place.

Clach Ghlas: grey stone.

Cladh an Dìseirt: burial ground of the hermitage.

Cnoc nam Bristeadh Clach: hill of the stony eruptions?

Coire Chatachan: corry of wild cat-place.

Coolin: holly? in reference to holly-edge-like contour of
the hills.

Corran: a symmetrical tapering point or cape.

Corrary: an odd shieling, *i.e.*, in an out of the way place,
isolated.

Corrie na Creiche: hollow of the spoil.

Crinan: barren, withered place?

Cuagach: a kink, or curved place.

Cuan: narrow bay.

Cuil Bay: nook bay.

Cullipool: homestead of ? ?

Culloden: nook of the puddle.

Dalnatraid: field by the shore.

Dalriada: portion of Riada, an Irish chief.

Dorlin: an isthmus.

Dornie: place of rounded pebbles.

Druim an Aoinidh: ridge of the cliff.

Duisdale Beg: little black dwelling.

Dunadd: fort of the River Add.

Dun nan Manach: fort of the monks.

Dunscaith: Sgàthach's Fort, traditionally associated with the Amazon who trained Cuchullin.

Dun Skudiburg: jutting out fort.

Dun Telve: ⎫
Dun Troddan: ⎭ forts named after two brothers, sons of a lady who lived in the broch of Caisteal Grùgaig, Totaig.

Dunvegan: Began's fort.

Duror: rocky water.

Eas nan Con: waterfall of the hounds.

Edinbane: white slope or face of hill.

Eilean nan Gobhar: island of goats.

Eilean Port nam Murrach: island of the port of seamen.

Eilean Shona: look-out-island.

Ellanreoch: brindled isle.

Fasnacloiche: station of the stone.

Girgadale: field of gravel.

Glaisbheinn: (Glasven) green mount.

Glenelg: glen of Elg, a bardic name for Ireland, from old Gaelic for " noble."

Glen Salachan: willow-place glen.

Gruline: gravel, pebbles.

Harta Corrie: stag's water corrie.
Hinnisdale: Tindr's dale ? ?

Inshaig: little haugh or waterside meadow.
Inverlochy: confluence of black goddess.
Invernahyle: adze confluence ?
Isle Ornsay: ebb tide island.

Jura: deer island.

Kentallen: head of the little inlet or arm of sea.
Kilvaxter: the baker's church.
Kintail: head of salt water.
Knapdale: knobdale, dale with hillocks.
Knock Ullinish: round hill of the owl's cape, or ulli's (owl-like man) cape.

Lag-na-ha: hollow of the kiln.
Làrach: site, stance.
Leiter More: great half land, or side of a hill.
Liveras: muddy place.
Loch an Athain: loch of the little ford.
Loch Caroy: loch of the red pass (path).
Loch Coille a' Bharra: loch of the wood of the summit.
Loch Leven: elm loch.
Loch Linnhe: a tautology of English invention. The part below the corran of Ardgour is *an Linne Sheileach,* hence, probably, Ardshiel, *q.v.* A local man explained the name as derived from the quantity of fresh water pouring into it. See below, *Loch Shiel,* for the same idea. The part inside the corran is *an Linne Dhubh,* the black pool.
Lochan Mor: great little loch.
Loch nam Madadh: loch of the dogs.
Loch nan Cilltean: loch of the churches.
Loch nan Eala: loch of the swans.
Loch an Nighean Dughaill: Dugald's daughter's loch.

Loch Shiel: loch of the brackish water ? (a free rendering) see above Loch Linnhe.

Loch Slapin: loch of the lump fish.

Loch Snizort: S——'s fiord, probably from some Norseman.

Mac an Leigh: physician's son.

Mac Crimmon: famed protector's son (?).

Mac Vurich: son of Muredach, *i.e.,* mariner.

Mam Ratagan: breast shaped hill of the little fort.

Marsco: sea-mew's copse.

Mingary: great garth.

Moidart: muddy fiord.

Morar: big water.

Morvern: sea gap.

Muck: isle of the pigs.

Nether Largie: lower plain.

Oibmore: great bay.

Onich: place of foam, *i.e.,* sea foam.

Ord: literally " hammer," applied to rounded, hammer-shaped eminences.

Ormsaig: Orm's bay.

Peindun: penny-land of the fort
Peinmore: big penny-land
} a relic of the Norse custom of measuring land by rental.

Port na Cairidh: port of the wall thrown across the mouth of a stream for the purpose of catching fish.

Raasay: Roe's island.

Reilig Odhran: burial-place of Oran.

Rhu Bornaskitaig: promontory of the top of the *skiotāg,* a word of unknown meaning.

Roshven: horse hill.

Rudh na lice: point of the flagstone.

Sandaig: sandy bay.

Scallisaig: bay of Sgalli, a nickname, " bald head "?

Scalpay: shallop isle.

Scarba: cormorant's (scart's) island.

Sgurr Dearg: red peak.

Sgurr na Banadich: small-pox peak, so called from its pitting or markings.

Sgurr nan Uamh: peak of the caves.

Sgurr Ouran: Oran's peak.

Shiel Bridge: Bridge over River Shiel.

Skeabost: S——'s (?) homestead.

Sligachan: shell place.

Sloc: a pit or deep hole.

Soay: sheep island.

Strath: a wide, clear valley.

Staffa: staff island, from its columnar formation.

Struan: little stream.

Suardalan:
Suardail: } grassy field.
Swordle:

Tarskavaig: cod bay.

Tayfuirst: i.e., Tigh a' Phuirt: ferry house.

Tayvallich: house on pass.

Tobar Lon nan Gruagach: well of the marsh of the *gruagachs*.

Tokavaig: hawk bay.

Tolain: the hill.

Torran: little hill.

Totaig: roofless dwelling.

INDEX

INDEX

NOTE.—The simplest and most obvious method of indexing has been adopted. Names of old Highland chiefs, etc., will be found under the first of their names or style, exactly as given in the book, and usually in their English rendering unless the Gaelic is more familiar, as, *e.g.*, *Ailean nan Sop*. Thus Prince Charlie comes under *Prince*, Black Donald of Clanranald under *Black*. Sir Donald of Lochalsh under *Sir*. The only exception is military titles: *e.g.*, Captain Roy Macdonald will be found under *Roy*, Lt.-Col. Hill under *Hill*, etc., etc. Modern people appear under their surnames, thus *Chinnery-Haldane*, Bp., *Scott*, Sir Walter. Whenever possible, subjects have been classified, to avoid cross-indexing as much as possible. Thus, all lochs will be found under *Lochs*, and every saint appears under *Saints*—thus the Blessed Virgin Mary, *S. Mary*; Queen Margaret of Scotland. *S. Margaret*; Adamnan, *S. Adamnan*; etc., etc. Under *Stones* will be found *Cup and ring marked, Sculptured, Standing*, etc.; and all *Castles, Caves, Cairns, Crosses, Coats-of-Arms, Wells*, etc., etc., are given under their respective headings. For the benefit of English readers let it be stated that the different religious systems will be found under *Episcopacy. Roman Catholic*, and *Presbyterianism* respectively.

"Abbat's" or S. Columba's House, Iona, 362.
—— House," na h - Eileacha Naomha, 449.
Achara, Duror, 318, 319.
Acharn, Duror, 321, 328.
Achatreachatain, Glencoe, 296, 306.
—— Lairds of. 294, 296, 305.
Achnacon, Appin, 310.
—— Glencoe, 294, 303.
Acunn and Readh, legend of, 188, 204.
Aidan, King, 354, 448.
—— Bishop, 360.
"Aileach," island of, 442.
Ailean nan Sop, 372.
Aird Ferry, 196, 198.
Aketon, the (or gambeson), 368, 369, 410.
Alasdair MacAonghas, bard of Glencoe and Jacobite, 305.

Alasdair MacMhaighstir Alasdair, 72, 73, 423.
—— poems quoted, 50, 52, 74, 168, 186, 422-23.
Alastair Crotach, 152, 203, 255.
Alexander I., 384.
Alexander Macdonald of Glencoe, *see* MacIain, chief of.
Alexander Macdonald of Keppoch at Culloden, 483.
Alexander Stewart, 1st of Invernahyle, *An Teochail,* 316.
Allan Breac Stewart, 328, 330, 333.
Allan Dearg, chief of Clanranald, 35.
Allan MacRuari of Clanranald, 38-39.
Allan MacIain of Clanranald, 240.
"Allan of the Foray" (Allan Breac Cameron), 76, 239, 285.

Allan Og, murder of, 70.
Allt-a-Choire Riabhaich, 145-46.
Altar vessels, historic, 276.
Amie MacRuari, 34-35.
Am Piobair Mor of Eigg, 234, 241.
Am Port, na h-Eileacha Naomha, 443, 455.
Am Priosan, na h - Eileacha Naomha, 452.
An Duine Mor, apparition of, 281.
An Mhoine Mor, Crinan, 460, 461.
Angus John Mac Mudzartsone, 256.
Angus Mor, Lord of the Isles, 398.
Angus Oig, Lord of the Isles, 21, 370.
Animals associated with saints, 416.
Annait, meaning of, 119.
Antlers, cast, 41.
"Anvil of the Mist," Glencoe, 306-7.
Aodh Mor Maccuinn, the Solomon of Skye, 136.
Aoineadh Mor, Eigg, 232.
Aonghas Mac Alastair Ruaidh, 296 footnote.
Appin, banner, 322-23.
—— district of, 309.
—— ecclesiastical affairs in, 310, 312, 313.
—— murder, 274, 328-33.
—— to Duror, 317-18.
Archery, Highland, 84, 85, 98, 195 footnote.
Archibald Dubh, 107-8.
Architecture, Highland, 77-79, 82.
Archæology, fascination of, 460-461.
Arco Brann Mhor, the Norse robber, 172.
Ardelve, 193.
Ardnamurchan, 309, 395-97.
—— birds of, 404, 405, 434, 435.
—— Episcopacy in, 411-13.
—— flowers of, 399, 413, 429, 434.
—— gate hinges of, 404-5.
—— history of, 397-99.
—— parochial divisions of, 408-409.
—— road to Point of, 403-6.
—— sea-shells of, 407.

Ardsheal, Appin, 326.
—— *see* Charles Stewart.
Argyll, 3rd Earl of, 398, 399.
—— 4th Earl of, 33-34.
—— 3rd Duke of, 330-31.
—— "gley-eyed" Marquis, 263-265.
Arisaig (Arasaig), 63, 409.
—— Rhue of, 62, 63.
—— road to, from Kinlochailort, 40-42, 61.
Armadale, Skye, 100, 101, 104.
—— across Sleat from, 105-10.
—— to Broadford, 110-14.
Armour of effigies, 368-69, 410.
Arnisdale, road to, 218.
Art, Celtic schools of, 75, 367.
Ashaig, Skye, 113.
Austin Canonesses, 383.

"Bad Step," Skye, 144.
Baghans at Glenelg, 212, 213.
Ballachulish, North, 269.
—— South, 275, 278.
—— Ferry, 273.
—— House, 292, 334, 335.
Balmacara, 193.
Banner, Appin, the, 322-23.
—— *Bratach Bhan*, the, 24, 25.
—— Fairy, the, 158, 159.
Barker, Sergeant, Hanoverian, at Massacre of Glencoe, 291.
"Bay of the Spaniards," the, 427.
Bean nighe, the, 227.
Bean tuiridh, the, 237.
Beehive cells on na h-Eileacha Naomha, 447-8.
Beinn na h-Urchrach, 414.
Bellanoch, Crinan, 475.
Belted plaid, the, 25.
Ben Hiant, 395, 400, 413 414, 429.
Ben nan Cailleach, Broadford, legend of, 116.
Ben Vair, 321, 322.
—— dragon of, 333-4.
Bernera Barracks, Glenelg, 203.
"Betty Burke," 179-183.
Bishop Hugh Macdonald, 26, 87.
Black Donald of Clanranald, tales of, 36-7.
"Black Raven," tale of the, 196-7.
Blar a' Bhuailte, last stand of Norsemen in Skye, 171.
Blaven, Skye, 118, 120, 143.

Bloody Hand. tale of the, 115, 174.
—— Pool, tale of the, 307.
—— Stone, battle at the, 147.
Borrodale House. Arisaig, 43-45, 54, 55.
Brahan Seer's prophecies, 159-60, 193, 211.
Branault, Ardnamurchan, 429.
Brecklet. Ballachulish, 278, 297-298.
Broadford. Skye. 113. 114, 116.
—— to Sligachan road, 127-28.
Brochs in general, 199-200.
Bronze Age burials, 402, 462-3, 464.
Bruce, the, 21, 223.
Buarblaig, Ardnamurchan, 417-418.
Burial customs, 284, 285, 462-3, 464.
—— islands. 29, 282-6.
"Butcher, The," 278, 484.

Cailleach, the, of Corrievreckan, 458.
Cairn at Culloden, 484.
—— Glenure's. 329-30.
Cairns, chambered, 114, 172, 401-403. 414, 462-4.
—— resting, 41, 42, 226, 317.
Caisteal Dubh nan Cliar, Ardnamurchan, 399, 400.
Caisteal Grùgag, Totaig, 200-1.
Caisteal Uisdein, Skye, 169.
Cameron Clan, the, 25, 26, 263, 265, 268, 484.
Campbell of Airds, 314.
—— of Ardkinglass, 319.
—— of Breadalbane, 288, 290.
—— of Glenfalloch, 305.
—— of Glenlyon, 292, 293.
—— of Glenure, 328-30.
Campbells, the, 156, 263, 273, 306, 398, 399.
Campbells at Castle Tirrim, 33-4.
—— at Glencoe, 293-4, 302, 306.
—— at Inverlochy, 264-65, 266.
—— at Mingary Castle, 426, 428.
Campbells, atrocities of, 268, 269, 288-90, 293-95, 330-32.
—— burial-places of some, 273, 306, 418.
—— in Appin murder trial, 330.
—— Macdonald animosity to, 155-6, 187-88, 282, 284, 288.

Campbells, murder of chiefs at Dunvegan, 157.
—— of Lochnell, Jacobites, 418-419.
—— origin of name, 33.
—— proverbs concerning, 156, 288 footnote, 293.
—— popular estimate of, 30, 31.
—— tombstones of some, 370, 419.
Camus Cuil an-t-Saimh, Iona, 347.
Camus nan Geall, Ardnamurchan, 414-20.
Camusunary, Skye, 143.
Canoes, ancient, 170-71.
Caoineag, the, 296-7.
Caolas-ic-Pharuig, Ballachulish, 273.
Carmichaels, the, 322, 323.
Carnach, Glencoe, 298, 301, 305.
Carn cuil-ri-Eirinn, Iona, 344-345.
Carn Liath, Skye, 172.
Cas chrom, the, 136.
Castle, Armadale, 101.
Castle Camus (or Knock), 109-110.
—— Chonil (or Dun Grugaig), 217.
—— "Clanranald's," 43, 61.
—— Dunringil, 120.
—— Dunscaith, 107-9.
—— Duntulm, 154, 174, 175, 177.
—— Dunvegan, 151-161.
—— Eilean Donnan, 193-98.
—— "Hugh's," 169.
—— Inverlochy, 262, 267-8.
—— Island, Eigg, 224.
—— "Macleod's," 203.
—— Maol (or Dunakyne), 188-9.
—— Mingary, 395, 424-28.
—— Stalcaire, 313-17.
—— Tirrim (Tioram), 32, 34-38.
Cave, see also Uamh.
—— Ardsheal's, Duror, 322, 324-325.
—— Boat, Staffa, 388.
—— Clamshell, or Scallop, Staffa, 389.
—— Clanranald's, Eigg, 233.
—— Fingal's, Staffa, 388, 390.
—— Goat, Staffa, 391.
—— in Sgurr nan Uamh, 147.
—— lost, of Iona, 344.
—— Macdonald's, Eigg (Uamh Fhraing), 253, 254, 257.

Cave, Mackinnon's, Elgol, 125.
—— Mackinnon's, Staffa, 391, 394.
—— Macleod's, Eigg, 234.
—— Macleod's, Loch nan Uamh, 58.
—— of Devotion, Eigg, 257.
—— Ossian's, Glencoe, 306.
—— Prince Charlie's at Elgol, 125.
—— Prince Charlie's at Loch nan Uamh, 55-58.
—— Prince Charlie's at Morar, 89.
—— S. Columba's, Ardnamurchan, 433.
—— Spouting, Iona, 347.
Celtic art, 367.
Celtic Church buildings, 171, 351.
—— Church discipline, 352.
—— Church dress, 350.
—— Church ecclesiastical order, 352, 353.
—— Church fare, 352.
—— Church life, 351.
—— Church monastery on Iona, 351, 352.
—— Church monastery on na h-Eileacha Naomha, 447-54.
—— Church monastery on Skye, 171.
—— Church peculiarities, 350, 352, 353.
—— Church, Saxon contempt for, 431, 432.
—— Church, services of worship of. 352, 353.
—— Church, work of, 353.
—— tonsure, 350.
Charles I., King, 363.
Charles Stewart, 5th of Ardsheal, 322-26.
Chinnery-Haldane, Bp., 271, 272.
"Christ Child's Lullaby," the, 257-8.
Cill Chainnich, Iona, 378, 383.
Cill Chaluimchille, Duror, 318.
Clach a' Charra, Onich, 269-70.
—— Chatain, Ardnamurchan, 429-30.
—— Eanruig. Glencoe, 301-2.
—— Ghlas, Skye, 118, 143.
—— na h'Annait, Skye, 119.
—— Pharuig, Ballachulish, 273-274.
—— Ruric, Ardsheal, 326.
Clachan, Lorne, 438.

Clachan Brath, 376, 454.
Cladh Aindreis, Ardnamurchan, 434.
—— an Diseart, Iona, 356, 357.
—— Chiarain, Ardnamurchan, 415, 419.
—— Eithne, na h-Eileacha Naomha, 454.
Clan, chief of, 18-19, 179.
—— chief, retinue of, 459.
—— confederacies, 19, 99.
—— constitution of, 18, 19.
—— dispositions in battle, 265.
—— distinctions and equipment, 19.
—— functionaries, 298-99.
—— septs, 298-300.
Clans, broken, 19, 300.
Clansmen's dress and equipment, 25, 26.
Clanranald, the, 18, 21, 428.
—— at Castle Tirrim, 33, 34, 35, 36, 37, 38, 39.
—— country, 18, 23, 39, 40, 223.
—— Dawn Prayer of, 31-2.
—— Gaelic sayings re, 39.
—— greatness of, 22, 224.
—— origin of war-cry, 21.
—— seats of, 29, 61.
Claymore, the true, 86.
Cleadale, Eigg, 244, 246.
Cnap Chaolais Mhic Pharuig, 274, 332, 333.
Cnoc Angel, Iona, 347, 348.
—— na Piobaireach, Eigg. 245.
—— nam Bradhan, Iona, 351.
—— Roill, Skye, a hill of justice, 177, 179.
Coat-of-arms, indeterminate on Iona, 379.
—— Macdonald, 102.
—— Macdonald of Clanranald, 37, 81, 102.
—— Macdonald of Glencoe, 301.
—— Macdonald of Glengarry, 104.
—— Macdonald of Morar, 80-82.
—— Macdonald of Sleat, 104.
—— Mackinnon, 118.
—— Maclaine of Lochbuie, 370, 371, 372, 373.
—— Macquarrie. 370.
—— Stewart, 283, 308, 309.
Coire Chatachan, Skye, 116.
—— -mhuilinn, Ardnamurchan, 397, 413, 422, 423.

"Coire Salchan," Appin, 317, 318.
Coliu Campbell, Sheriff Clerk of Argyll, 290.
Colkilto, Old. 224.
—— Young. 74. 425. 426. 428, 482
Colman Ela, Bishop. 418.
Conall. King of Dalriada, 350, 354, 439.
Coolin, The, 105, 133, 144, 218, 233, 259.
Coronation Stone. 354.
Corrie na Creiche, Skye, 140, 145.
Corrievreckan, Whirlpool of, 456-458.
Crannogs, 61, 62, 250, 404.
Crest, legend of origin of Macdonald, 115.
—— legend of origin of Mackinnon, 125.
—— legend of origin of Macleod, 202.
Crest of Macdonald of Glencoe, 301.
—— of Macdonell of Glengarry, 196.
Crinan, 458.
Crofter fare in olden days, 93.
—— problems, 130, 131.
Crois Moraig, Eigg, 251.
Croon. Death, the, 237-8.
—— Death, of S. Donnan, 236.
—— Wizard's, the, 248.
Cross, cenotaph, to Fr. Mackonochie, 271.
—— Glencoe, memorial of massacre, 301.
—— Iona, fragments of, 370.
—— Iona, Mackinnon's, 378.
—— Iona, Maclean's, 339, 382-3.
—— Iona, S. John's, 357, 375, 380.
—— Iona, S. Martin's, 380.
—— Iona, S. Matthew's, 380.
—— Kilmartin, 464.
—— replica of Oronsay, 271.
—— slab discovered in Arduamurchan, 415.
—— slab, Kilmory Oib, 477.
Crucifix, Kilmartin, 465-6.
Crucifixion, Celtic representations of, 437, 465.
Cuagach, Eigg, 227.
Cuan Sound, 438.
Cuchullainn, legends of, 105, 108-109.

Cuil Bay, Loch Linnhe, 326, 327.
Cuil - i - Breannan, Garvellochs, 440, 441.
Culdees, the, 349.
Cullipool, Luing, 438, 444.
Culloden, 59, 276, 278, 309, 318, 322, 323, 343, 481-82.
—— battle of, 482-84.
—— graves of clansmen at, 484-485.
—— memorial at Achnacon, Appin, 311.

Dalriada, capital of, 467, 468-71.
—— kingdom of, 364, 467.
Dalrymple, Master of Stair, 289, 290.
—— letters of, 290, 291.
Daoine uaisle, 19.
Dedications, Celtic and mediæval, 173, footnote; 430, 431.
"Devil's Staircase," Glencoe, 294, 307.
Diormit, servant of S. Columba, 354, 355, 375.
Domestic life in the Highlands, 95-97.
Donald Balloch of the Isles, 262.
—— Breac Macleod, 156, 167.
—— Cameron, the "Gentle Lochiel," 54.
—— Campbell of Barbreck, 399, 428.
—— Galldach, 107-8.
—— Gorm, 110, 129, 154, 155, 176, 177.
—— Gormeson, 154 footnote.
—— Grumach, 108, 129, 189, 195-6.
—— Livingstone, 323.
—— Macleod of Guattergill, 54-55.
—— of Harlaw, 240, 374.
"Donald of the Hammer," 316-7.
Donald, Roy Macdonald, Capt., Jacobite, 184, 185.
Dornie, Ross-shire, 193, 198.
Dorus Mor, Sound of Jura, 458.
Dr. Samuel Johnson, 116, 152, 137, 160, 338, 377.
Drumhain, the Coolin, 145, 146.
Drum nan Cleoc, Skye, 129.
Dun Dhomhnuill, Crinan, a hill of justice, 458, 459-60.
Dun Grugaig, Glenelg, 217-8.
—— Telve, Glenelg, 214-15.
—— Troddan, Glenelg, 216-17.

Dunblane, Jacobite tombstone at, 305 footnote.
Duncanson, Major, 292, 293.
—— letter of, 292.
Duncan MacIntyre quoted, 124.
—— Stewart, 7th of Appin, 314.
Dun I, Iona, 348, 355, footnote.
Dunskudiburg, Skye, 170, 181.
Dunvegan Cup, 160.
—— to Portree, coach ride from, 162-66.
Duror, Appin, 318-21.
Dyes, native, 91, 92.

Earth house, Struan, 148.
—— houses in general, 148, 149.
Effigies, ecclesiastical, 83, 84, 370, 371, 378, 379, 383, 384.
—— warriors', 368-9, 370, 371-73, 379, 380, 466.
Eigg, Island of, 222-25.
—— birds of, 231, 234, 235.
—— cliffs of, 230, 233, 234, 244.
—— flowers of, 230, 242, 243, 247, 253.
—— geology of, 229, 230, 233, 234, 250, 251.
—— massacres of, 232, 250, 254-256.
—— poets of, 228.
—— rùns, etc., of, 228, 236-37, 247, 248, 258.
—— sail to, from Arisaig, 65-68.
—— Sgurr of, 222, 224, 226.
—— women of, 226-28, 242.
—— views of, 62, 87, 218, 222, 405, 407, 429, 432.
Eilean Chaluim Chille, Arduamurchan, 407.
—— Choinnich, Loch Leven, 274-75.
—— Finan, Loch Shiel, 29, 409, 435.
—— Munde, Loch Leven, 281-86, 296.
Elgol, Skye, 120-25.
"English" Church in Scotland, 276.
Episcopacy of Celtic Church, 352-53.
—— in Highlands, native not exotic, 117-18, 221, 275-78, 309-310, 312, 313.
—— in Highlands, forcible suppression of, 219-21, 411-12.
—— in Highlands, proscription and persecution of, 271-72, 276-78.

Episcopalian native priests, famous, 117-18, 220, 276-78, 287, 309 footnote, 411-12.
Episcopalians, devoutness of, Highland, 271, 275, 287.
Eun Ban nan Corp, 245.
Evan Cléirich, tale of, 397, 413, 414.
Evictions in Duror, 327.
—— in Glenmore, Glenelg, 210-211.
Evil Eye, the, 90, 135.
Evan MacLachlan quoted, 87.
Ewan Mor MacColl, the Ballachulish seer, 280.
"Ewan of the Little Head," tale of, 373-74.

Fairy at Dunvegan, tale of, 161-162.
—— Banner, Dunvegan, 158-60.
—— Bridge, Dunvegan, 152, 158.
—— hills or sithean, 117.
—— hill at Broadford, 116.
—— Hill, Great, at Iona, 347, 386.
—— hill at Struan, Skye, 149.
—— hill at the Braes, Skye, 136.
—— lore of Highlands, surmised origin of, 205-6.
—— Tower, Dunvegan, 152, 157.
"Fairies' foot-prints," Glenelg, 204-5.
Fairies in Harta Corrie, 147.
—— seen on the Isle of Muck, 260-61.
Féinne, the, 206, 231, 306.
Fergno, the anchorite, 449.
Fergus Mor MacErca and his brothers, 364, 467, 471.
Ferguson, Capt., Hanoverian Hun, 55, 58.
Fiery Cross, the, 25, 150.
Fingal, 206, 210, 388, 390, 401, 402
Flora Macdonald, career of, 101, 167.
—— death and burial of, 167, 173, 174, 185.
—— relics of, 161.
—— with Prince Charlie, 179-85, 190.
"Foreigners," footnote, 37.
Fort of Druim an Duin, Crinan, 478-9.
—— of Dun Add, Crinan, 467, 468-71.
—— of Dun Choinail, 439-40.

Fort of Dun Grugaig. Glenelg, 217-18.
—— vitrified, of Rudh Ard Ghamshgail. Arisaig, 47-8.
Forts, hill, purpose of, 480.
Fort William, 226, 268, 289 footnote, 295, 307, 329, 332.
—— to Ballachulish, 269, 270.

Gaelic, the language of Eden, 51.
—— the language of Scotland, 51.
—— poets, 72.
Galleys on the sculptured stones, 308 footnote, 367, 368, 409, 410.
Garaidh Eachainn Oig, Iona, 343.
Garbh Chriochan, the, 40.
Garbheileach, one of the Garvellochs, 440-1.
Garmisdale, Eigg, 252, 253.
Garvelloch Isles, Firth of Lorne, 439-41.
Gate hinges, ingenious, 404-5.
"Giant's footmark," Eigg, 243.
"Giant's grave," Eigg, 252.
Giants' graves, Glenelg, 203-4.
Gipsies, 126-7.
Girgadale, Ardnamurchan, 405, 406.
Glaistig, the, 110.
—— tales of, 321-2, 385.
Gleann Leac nan Muidhe, Glencoe, 303-4, 321.
"Glen, The," of Arisaig, 61-2.
Glenbeg, Glenelg, 213.
Glencoe, 286, 300-7.
—— bards of, 295, 296, 305.
—— curse of, 298.
—— massacre of, 288-98, 300-4.
—— massacre of, warnings given of, 296-98.
—— how snatched from the Macdonalds, 307.
Glen Duror, Appin, 321, 322, 325.
Glenelg, 202-4, 220.
—— brochs of, 214-17.
Glenfinnan, 23-8.
Glenmore, Glenelg, 207-13.
Glen Sligachan, 141-2.
Goir a' Bhlair, site of Norse battle, Skye, 126.
Graves of clansmen at Culloden, 484-5.
Graveyards, see also Cladh, and under Iona, burial-grounds of.
—— Appin, 310, 312.

Graveyards, Camus nan Geall, Ardnamurchan, 415, 419.
—— Eilean Munde, Loch Leven, 282-4.
—— Keil, Duror, 318.
—— Kilbride, Oban, 437 footnote.
—— Kilchoan, Ardnamurchan, 409-11.
—— Kilchrist, Skye, 117, 118.
—— Kilmahumaig, Crinan, 458.
—— Kilmartin, 464-6.
—— Kilmory of Ardnamurchan, 432-3.
—— Kilmory of Arisaig, 71-2.
—— Kilmuir, Skye, 173.
—— na h-Eileacha Naomha, 453-454.
—— S. Bride's, Ballachulish, 271
"Green Colin," tale of, 316-7.
"Green Maria," 474-5.
Greideal Fhinn, denuded cairn, Ardnamurchan, 401-3.
Grugach, the, 110, 321, 322.
—— Stones, 136, 321.
Gruline, Eigg, 251, 252.

Hamilton, Lt.-Col., Hanoverian, 291, 292, 295.
Harta Corrie, Skye, 146, 147.
Heather liquor, tale of secret of, 250-1.
Hebrides, the, 99.
Hendersons, the, 298, 299, 399.
Highland burial customs, 284, 285.
—— characteristics, 64, 89.
—— cottages, typical, 89, 90, 92, 114, 198, 269, 432.
—— fidelity, instances of, 59, 325-6.
—— nomenclature, 131, 299-300.
—— oath, 122 footnote.
—— transport, 96, 162-6, 191-2, 211, 225-6.
Highlander's English, 64-5, 67, 97, 115, 116, 188, 189-90, 246.
Highlanders in battle, 265, 482.
"Highlandman's Prayer," the, 140.
Hill, Colonel, Hanoverian, 289, 290, 291, 292, 294.
Hill of Hanging, 36.
—— Judgment, 178, 485-9.
—— Punishment, 179.
Hinba, of Adamnan's Life of S. Columba, 441-42.

"Hollow of the Holy Feasts,"
272, 275, 278, 322.
Hugh Macdonald of Armadale,
168, 179.
Hugh MacGhilleasbuig, tale of,
169, 175-6.
Hunting scenes on stones, 85,
410.

Iain Breac, 152.
Iain Dubh Macleod, tales of, 156,
157, 167, 169, 258.
Iain Garbh, proverb due to, 175.
Iain Lom, the Bard of Keppoch,
his name, career, etc., 263, 266.
—— poems quoted, 104, 266.
Iain Muidearteach, chief of
Clanranald, 33-4, 239.
Iain Sprangach, progenitor of
the MacIains of Ardnamur-
chan, 398, 426.
Iain the Fairhaired, 156, 167,
169.
Inauguration ceremony of the
Lords of the Isles on Eigg, 240
—— on Dunadd, 471-2.
—— ceremony, or hallowing, on
Iona, 354.
Innsegall, the, 99, 224, 240.
Inshaig, Duror, 320.
Inveraray, 290, 330-2.
Invercoe, 287, 300, 303, 305.
Inveriggan, tale of, 293, 302, 303.
Inverlochy, 267.
—— first battle of, 262-3.
—— second battle of, 263-6, 272.
Iomair nam fear mora, Glenelg,
203, 204.
Iomaire nan Righ, Iona, 365, 371,
372.
Iona, the island of, 336-40, 341-
342, 385.
—— Abbey Church of, 337, 339,
375-80.
—— "Black Stones" of, 382.
—— burial grounds of, 356, 364-
366, 371-4, 382, 383.
—— crosses, *see* under Crosses.
—— flowers of, 342.
—— gravestones from, 75, 409.
—— history of, 360-3.
—— monastery, the first, 350-2.
—— monastery, the second, 361,
362.
—— monastery, the third and
last, the present ruins, 280-2.
—— name of, 336, 344.
—— nunnery of, 383-4.

Jacobites, barbaric treatment of,
261.
Jacobite badge, 19.
—— relics, 161.
—— songs, 50-53. 60, 72-4, 186.
Jacobites, voluntary self-assess-
ment of, 325-6.
James IV at Mingary Castle. 427
—— V. in the Islands, 139, 152,
157.
"James' daughter," tale of, 36.
"James of the Glen," the Appin
victim, 328-33.
John MacFingon, Abbat of Iona,
378.
—— MacIain of Ardnamurchan,
379, 427.
"John MacInnes' Loch," Glen-
elg, tale of its waterhorse, 209.
John of Isla, first Lord of the
Isles, 34, 35.
Jura, island of, 458.

Keil, Duror, 318.
—— general significance of
name, 318.
Keitil Flatnefr, 402.
Kelpie, the, 111.
Kentallen, 329, 330.
Kidnapped, R. L. Stevenson's,
321, 328.
Kilbride, Oban, 437 footnote.
—— Skye, 118.
—— Bay, Skye, 170, 180.
Kilchoan, Ardnamurchan. 395,
399, 400, 408.
—— ancient churchyard and
stones of, 409-11.
—— Episcopal incumbents of,
411-12.
Kilchrist, Skye, 113, 117, 118,
377.
Kildonan, Eigg, 224.
Kilmaree, Skye. 120.
Kilmahumaig, Crinan, 458.
Kilmartin, sculptured stones of,
464-6.
Kilmory of Ardnamurchan. 430-
431.
—— Ardnamurchan, Bay of,
434-5.
—— Ardnamurchan, old burial-
ground of, 432-3.
—— of Arisaig, 71, 75-86.
—— of Arisaig, sculptured stones
of. 80-6.
—— Oib, 476-7.
—— Oib, cross slab at, 477.

Kilmuir, Skye, burial-place of Flora Macdonald, 173.
King Haco. 188.
King of the birds, tale of, 243.
Kingsburgh House, Skye, 167, 182-3.
"Kiln" at na h-Eileacha Naomha. 450.
Kilt, 20, 25.
—— representation on gravestones, 34, 369.
—— its prohibition, 93.
Kyle Akin, Skye, 188-89.
—— of Lochalsh, 191-2.
—— Rhea, 203, 206.

La Doutelle, the ship that brought Prince Charlie, 53.
Lachlan Maclean of Duart, assault on Mingary Castle by, 427.
"Lady Ardsheal," the, 323-4, 326.
Lady Margaret Macdonald, 168, 180.
Lag-na-ha, Ben Vair, 322-4, 325.
Laig Bay and House, Eigg, 227-232. 243, 259.
—— drive over to, 226-8.
Larach Tigh Mhic Dhomnhuill, Loch Alsh, 196.
Léine chroich, the "yellow shirt" of the Highlands, 369, 397.
Leiter More, scene of Appin murder, 329-30.
L'Heureux, the ship that bore Prince Charlie away, 59.
Lindsay, Lt., Hun at Glencoe, 293, 294.
Livingstone, commander of the forces in Scotland, 289, 290.
Lochaber, district of, 262 footnote.
Loch Ailort, 40-1.
—— Ainort, Skye, 129.
—— Alsh, 193, 197, 201.
Lochalsh, district of, 193, 219-220.
Loch Brittle, Skye, 139-40.
—— Caroy, Skye, 150.
—— Cill Chroisd, Skye, 117, 118.
—— Coille a' Bharra, 476, 477.
—— Columcille, Portree, 139.
—— Columcille, Monkstadt, Skye, 170-71.
—— Coruisk, 144-5.

Loch Duich. 193, 198, 201.
—— "John MacInnes'," Glenelg, 209.
—— Leven, 275, 335.
—— Linnhe, 269, 272, 273, 326, 329, 335.
—— Long, Ross-shire, 193.
—— Moidart, 32-3, 34.
—— Morar, 87-8.
—— nam Ban Mora, Eigg, 250.
—— nam Beinn Tighe, Eigg, 247-8.
—— nam Madadh, Skye, 128.
—— nan Cilltean, Arisaig, 70-1.
—— nan Dubrachan, Skye, 111-112.
—— nan Uamh, 42, 45-6, 50, 53, 55, 59-60.
—— Nighean Dughaill, Eigg, 249-50.
—— Scavaig, Skye, 121, 144.
—— Shiel, 24, 29, 31.
—— Slapin, Skye, 120.
—— Sligachan, Skye, 135-6.
—— Staonaig, Iona, 346.
—— Triochatan, Glencoe, 305-6.
Lordship of Lorne, 309.
—— the Isles, 18, 366.
Lota Corrie, Skye, 147.
Lowland versus Highland, 51.
Low side windows, 79-80.
Luib, Skye, 128-9.
Luideag, a hopgoblin, 112-13.
Luing, Isle of, 436.
Luireach, 368-9.
Lundie, Ensign John, Hun, 293.
Lunga, Isle of, tale of, 439.

Macallister, Donald, boatman of Arisaig, 63-70.
——Clan, 63 footnote, 100.
MacArthurs, the, 173, 299.
Macbean chief at Culloden, 483.
MacColls, the, 311-12.
Macdonald, Donald, late of Tormore, 131-2.
—— of Kingsburgh, 130, 180-4.
—— of Kingsburgh, his wife and daughter, 182-3.
—— Rev. Dugald, Rector of Ballachulish, 273, 275.
Macdonalds, the, see also the Clanranalds, and below Macdonalds of Keppoch, Macdonalds of Sleat, Macdonells of Glengarry, and MacIains of Ardnamurchan and of Glencoe.

Macdonalds, animosity towards Campbells, fundamental and hereditary, of the, 155-6.
—— chiefship of, 22.
—— fame of, 18 footnote.
—— functionaries of, 299.
—— greatness of, 366.
—— hereditary right in battle of, 21, 483.
—— meaning of name, 18.
—— motto of, 18.
—— pipers of, 173, 299.
—— proverbs concerning, 104, 154 footnote.
—— septs of, 299-300.
—— tombs, of, Iona, 370-2.
Macdonalds of Keppoch at Culloden, libelled, 483.
—— celebrated Bard of, Iain Lom, 263.
—— lament of, 485.
Macdonalds of Sleat (*Clann Uisdean*), 99, 100, 101, 102, 107.
—— chief of, 102.
—— dispute concerning chiefship of, 102-3.
—— fights with Macleods, 140-1, 147.
—— peerage, 102 footnote, 103.
—— seats, successive, of, 101, 107, 109, 151, 170.
—— septs of, 299.
—— "touching" for *glacach*, 103-4.
Macdonells of Glengarry, a tale of the, 196-7.
Macdougals, tale of, at Mingary Castle, 426-7.
MacEacherns, the, 45.
Macgillivray of Dunmaglas, death of, at Culloden, 483.
Machar, the, Iona, 346-7, 354.
Mac Iain Ghiòrr, the Ardnamurchan freebooter, 405-6, 409.
Mac Iains of Ardnamurchan, 309, 379, 398-9, 426-7.
—— (Macdonalds) the, of Glencoe, *Clann Iain Abrach*, 27, 289-94, 298, 301.
—— Alexander, massacred chief of, 285, 289-90.
—— Alexander, his sons, 293, 294, 307.
—— badge, crest, motto, etc. of, 301, 366.
—— bards of, 296, 305.
—— burial isle of, 281-83.

Macintyre, legend concerning name, 407-8.
Mackenzie, John, of Sligachan, 132, 133, 147.
Mackenzies of Kintail, 192, 194, 196-7.
Mackenzie's "shirt-of-mail," 195.
Mackinnons, the, 99-100, 117-8, 299.
—— and Prince Charlie, 88, 121-123.
—— burial-place of, 117-18.
—— castles of, and house of chief, 120, 124, 188.
—— origin of crest, 125.
—— tombs on Iona, 378.
Mackonochie, Fr., tragedy of, 270, 271.
Macleans, the, at Culloden, 484.
—— meaning of name and spellings, 38, 343.
—— pipers of, 320.
—— tombs of, Iona, 372, 373, 379.
—— of Duart, incidents concerning, 38-9, 256, 343.
"Maclean's Nose," Ardnamurchan, climb over, 421.
Macleod, Dr. Norman. 159-60.
Macleods, the, 99, 100, 150.
—— at Dunvegan, 151, 153-155.
—— country of, 99, 148, 202.
—— crest, legendary origin of, 202.
—— fights with Macdonalds, 140-1, 147.
—— gathering ground of, 150.
—— massacre of Macdonalds by, 254-6.
—— name, meaning of. 150.
—— pipers of, 150, 151.
—— proverbs concerning, 162.
—— tartan of, 151.
—— tombs of, Iona, 372, 380.
—— the "wicked chief" of, 130.
"Macleod's Maidens," 150, 159.
—— Tables," 150.
Macquarries, their tombs on Iona, 370.
MacQueen, true origin of Skye name, 136.
Macraes, the, 195.
Macrimmons, the, 150, 151, 162.
"Macrimmon's Lament," 480.
Macsween, the Celtic champion of Skye, 136, 172.

Maighstir Alasdair, the famous, 73, 411-12.
Malcolm Macleod, 3rd chief, 202.
—— Macleod, Capt., 121-3.
Malcolms, the, 460.
—— country of the, archæological wealth of, 460-1.
Mallaig, 98.
Mam Ratagan Pass, 207-8.
Marsco, Skye, 141, 142.
Marta, meaning of, 340.
Martyr's Bay, Iona, 340-1, 361.
Massacre of Eigg, 254-6.
—— of Glencoe, 288-95.
—— of Glencoe, local tales of, 295-8, 301-3.
—— of Glencoe, memorial cross of, 301.
Matheson, the Clan, 195.
Moidart, tale of, 32.
Monkstadt, Skye, 170, 180.
Montrose, the great Marquis, 263, 264, 265.
—— his letter to Charles I., 266.
Morar, 87.
—— its people, 89, 91, 93-4, 97-8
Motto of Clanranald, 21.
—— Glencoe, 301.
—— Macdonalds, 18.
—— Malcolms, 460.
—— Stewarts of Appin, 309.
M'Queen, the Skye Solomon, 136.
M'Robs, the, of Glen Duror, 325-326.
Muchdragan Mac Righ Lochlunn, 397, 413, 414.
Muck, Isle of, tale of " little folk " seen on, 260-1.
—— views of, 405-407.
Muirbolc Paradise, the, of Adamnan, 417-18.
Muirbulcmar, on *Hinba,* 449.
Mull, the Island of, 421, 458.

Na h-Eileacha Naomha, one of the Garvellochs, 442, 443-4, 445-6, 447, 449, 454.
—— " Abbat's House," 449.
—— church of, 450-1.
—— double beehive cell on, 447-449.
—— graveyard of, 453-4.
—— *Hinba,* reasons for identification with, 441-2.
—— indeterminate buildings on, 452-3.
—— " Kiln " on, 450.

Na h-Eileacha Naomha, monastic enclosures on, 451-2.
—— night on, 446.
—— prehistoric remains on, suggestions of, 455.
—— psychic influence on, 442-3.
—— sunrise on, 447.
—— underground cell on, 452.
Neil Mac Eachainn, 168, 179, 180, 181, 184, 185.
Nether Largie, chambered cairn and standing stones at, 461, 462-4.
Night out on Eigg, 259-60.
—— out on na h-Eileacha Naomha, 446.
—— out on Staffa, 392-3.
Norse and Celtic ethnological distinctions, 100-1.
—— battles and invasions, 126, 171, 326.
—— idol, 272.
—— measurement of land, 244.

Oan, Superior of Eigg, 239.
Oban, 436.
Onich, 269.
Ord, Skye, 109.
Ormsaig, Beg and Mor, Ardnamurchan, 399-401.
Ossian, 306, 468, 471.
—— quoted, Preface, 108-9, 231-232, 275, 304.
Oyster-catchers, baby, 447.

Peat industry, 94-5, 241-2.
Peindun House, Skye, where Flora Macdonald died, 167.
Penny lands, explanation of, 244.
" Pibroch of Donald Dhu," the, 263.
" Pilgrim's Run " of Eigg, 258-9.
Piper Macdonald, tale of, 187-8.
Poltalloch, Crinan, 460.
Ponies, Skye, 137-8, 142.
—— Eigg, 241-2.
Port a' Churaich, Iona, 342, 343.
—— *a' Churaich,* Iona, road to and from, 341-2, 346.
—— *Laraichean,* Iona, 344.
—— *na Cairidh.* Ardnamurchan, 406-7.
—— *na Crois,* Appin, 309, 313.
Portree, 139, 185.
—— road to, from Sligachan, 137-9.

Portree, sail from, to Kyle of Lochalsh, 187-8.
Presbyterianism, alien nature of, in Highlands, 28, 221, 276, 310, 411.
—— Erastian origin and character of, 219-21, 276, 412.
—— forcible imposition of, 219-221, 234, 411-12.
Prince Charlie and Flora Macdonald, 179-85.
—— and the Gaelic, 43-4, 181 footnote.
—— as "Betty Burke," 179-183.
—— as "Lewie Caw," 121-3.
—— at Borrodale, 43, 54-5.
—— at Culloden, 484.
—— at Elgol, 121-3.
—— at Glenfinnan, 25, 27.
—— at Kingsburgh House, 182-183.
—— at Mallaig, 98.
—— Morar, 88-9.
—— Portree, 184-5.
—— attachment of Highlanders to his memory, 116.
—— costumes of, at Loch nan Uamh, 53, 58-9.
—— departure to France, 59.
—— in Glen Sligachan, 141.
—— journey to Elgol, 121.
—— landing of, at Loch nan Uamh, 54-5.
—— lock of hair of, 161, 183.
—— on board La Doutelle, 53.
—— relics of, 161.
—— reward offered for head of, 59.
—— tramping through Strath Mor, 121, 128-9.
—— voyage of, from Elgol to Mallaig, 123.
—— voyage of, from Loch nan Uamh to Benbecula, 54-5.
—— voyage of, from Uist to Skye, 180.
Prince Charlie's Beach, Loch nan Uamh, 45.
—— Cave, Elgol, 125.
—— Caves, Loch nan Uamh, 55-58.
—— Monument, Glenfinnan, 24.
—— Point, Skye, 170.
Prioress Anna, stone of, Iona, 383-4.
Psychic experience on na h-Eileacha Naomha, 442-3.

Quartz pebbles in prehistoric graves, 464.

Ranald Herrach, conduct of, at Dunscaith, 108.
Raonull Mac Ailein Oig, famous composer of pipe music, 37, 80, 240.
—— na Sgeithe, Bard of Glencoe, 296.
Red Coolin, the, 116, 129.
Reginald, Lord of the Isles 372, 383, 384.
Reilig Odhran, Iona, 364-6, 371-374.
"Religion of the Yellow Stick," the, 234.
Restoration, false, 194, 337-9, 374, 376-7.
—— true, 214.
—— Ruskin on, 337-8.
Rev. Paul MacColl, celebrated priest of Appin, 277-8.
Rhu Bornaskitaig, Skye, 174.
Ridge of the Chiefs, Iona, 372-3.
—— of the Kings, Iona, 365-6, 371-2.
River Duror, Appin, 320, 321.
—— Hinnisdale, Skye, 167, 182.
—— Sligachan, Skye, 134.
—— Snizort, 165-6.
Robin, legend in verse of the, 358-9.
Roman Catholic Church in the Highlands, 28, 40, 71, 87-8, 219, 226, 234, 246, 413.
Ronald Gallda, tale of, 37-8.
Ronald Macdonald, the younger, of Kinlochmoidart, on La Doutelle, 53-4.
Rory Mor, the famous Macleod chief, 140, 152, 153, 154.
—— relics of, 161.
Rory Mor's drinking horn, 160, 202.
—— "Nurse," 152.
—— sister, 154.
Rudh Ard Ghamshgail, vitrified fort of, at Arisaig, 46-8.
Rudha Bhad Bheithe and Rudha Cuilcheanna on Loch Linnhe, 272.
Rum, Isle of, 62, 87, 218, 226, 229, 231, 242, 248, 256, 259, 405, 407, 429.
Rùn of Hospitality, Eigg, 228.

S. Adamnan, 360.
S. Adamnan's Church, Duror, 322.
—— *Life of S. Columba*, 349-50.
—— *Life of S. Columba* quoted, 166, 262 footnote, 317, 336, 347, 348, 355, 356, 364, 407. 417-8, 419, 442, 448-9, 451, 452.
S. Brendan, 441, 442.
S. Aidan, Bishop, 360.
S. Blathmac, 361, 375.
S. Bride's Church, North Ballachulish, 270-1.
S. Cainnech, 383, 451.
S. Cathan, 429-30, 432.
S. Columba, 32, 347. 348.
—— burial-place and translations of, 356, 357, 364.
—— cell of, on Iona. 351.
—— death and burial of, 355-6.
—— dedications to, 318.
—— fare of, 352.
—— hallows Aidan king, 354.
—— horse of, 354.
—— in Ardnamurchan, 407, 417, 418, 419.
—— in art, 451.
—— in Dunadd, 468.
—— in Skye, 165-6.
—— landing on Iona, 342-3.
—— last days of, 354-5.
—— legends of, 353, 358, 359.
—— lineal spiritual successors of, 276, 359, 411.
—— *marta* of, 356, 377.
—— *minna* of, 357, 375.
—— on *Hinba,* 448-9, 451, 452.
—— personal appearance of, 349-50.
—— poem by, quoted, 345.
—— proverbs concerning, 357.
—— visions of angels of, 347-8, 448-9.
S. Columba's bird, 357.
—— Church, Portree, 139, 185.
—— Day, 357.
—— flower, 357-8.
—— pillow, Iona, 378.
—— pulpit, na h-Eileacha Naomba, 449.
—— tomb, 357, 361-2, 375.
S. Comgall, 451.
S. Congan, 202, 409.
S. Donnan, 194, 235-6.
—— Church of, on Eigg, 239-40.
—— death croon of, 236.
—— relics of, 239.

S. Finan. 29-30, 435 footnote.
S. Finan's bell, 30.
S. John's Church, Ballachulish, 275, 277.
S. Kiaran, 415-7.
S. Maelrubha. 71, 113.
S. Maelrubha's bell, 113.
—— Day, 113.
—— Ferry, 113.
S. Margaret, Queen of Scotland, 362, 366, 432.
S. Mary the Virgin, dedications to, 71, 173 footnote, 374, 383, 430-1.
S. Oran, 364.
S. Oran's Chapel, Iona, 366-70.
S. Oswald, King, 360.
S. Ronan's Chapel, Iona, 384.
Scallisaig, Glenelg, 210-11.
—— story of shepherd of, 211-2.
Sconser, Skye, 129-30.
Score Bay, Skye, 174, 177.
Scots tongue, the true, 51.
Scott, Capt., Hanoverian, 323, 324, 333, 334, 355.
Scott, Sir Walter, 157, 161.
Scottish Automobile Club, 300.
Seals, tradition concerning, 345.
Second sight, 279.
—— stories of, 280-1, 286-7, 305-306.
Seonaid Nic Aonghais, tale of, 333.
Seonaid Vic Alastair Macdonald, tales of, 305, 334-5.
"Serpent mounds," concerning, 212.
Sgurr nan Gillean, Skye, 133.
—— of Eigg, 222, 224, 226, 250.
—— Sgaileach, Eigg, 233-34.
—— Uamh, Skye, 147.
Shearwater, the, 234-5.
Sheep, rescue from drowning of, 68-9.
"Signal Rock," Glencoe, 303.
"Singing Sands," Eigg, 232.
Sir Alexander Macdonald of Sleat, 130, 168, 203.
—— Alexander Macdonald of Sleat, epitaph on, 203.
—— Donald Campbell of Ardnamurchan, *see* Campbell of Barbreck.
—— Donald [Macdonald] of Lochalsh, 108, 398, 426, 427.
—— Donald of the War, 178.
—— James Macdonald, 224.

5

WESTERN HIGHLANDS AND ISLANDS

Sir Lachlan Mor Mackinnon, 118.
Simon Fraser of Lovat, hiding and capture of, 87, 88.
Sithean, see fairy hills.
Skeabost, Skye, 165.
Skye, Isle of, 99.
—— its clan divisions, 99-100.
—— views of, 62, 67, 68, 87, 98.
Skye Jacobites, 130, 150.
Sleat, Skye, 101.
Sligachan, Skye, 131-5.
—— to Camsunary, 142-4.
—— to Dunvegan, 148-50.
—— to Portree, 137-9.
Slinneineach, method of divination, 296.
Somerled, founder of Clan Donald, 101, 102, 397, 407, 408.
Spinning, 91-2.
Staffa, Isle of, 388-93.
Stags and their antlers, 41.
Stone circles or ' ovals,'" 216, 475-6.
—— cupped at Glenelg, 204-5.
—— cup and ring-marked, at Cairnbaan, 472-3.
Stones, cup and ring-marked, concerning, 473-4.
—— sculptured, age of, 75-6, 367
—— sculptured, art of, 367.
—— sculptured, at Appin, 310.
—— sculptured, at Arisaig, 82-6.
—— sculptured, at Camus nan Geall, 415, 419.
—— sculptured, at Kilchoan, 409, 410.
—— sculptured, at Kilmartin, 466.
—— sculptured, fragments of, at Kilchrist, 118.
—— sculptured, source of, 75, 367.
—— sculptured, symbolical interpretation of representations on, 85, 368.
—— sculptured, symbols on, and their meaning, 367-8, 470-2.
—— standing, 461-2.
—— standing, of Nether Largie, 462.
Stewarts of Appin, the, 27, 308-312, 314, 315.
—— cadet families of, 308.
—— followers of, 312.
—— " March of," quoted, 308.
—— septs of, 311-13, 325.
Strath, Skye, 116-19.

" Street of the Dead," Iona, 339, 341, 348, 382.
Struan, Skye, 148, 149.
" Study," the, Glencoe, 306.
" Sugar Brook," the, of *Mac Mhaighstir Alasdair,* 422, 423.
Sunrises, 259 447.
Sunsets at Arisaig, 67-8.
—— on Eigg, 231.
—— on Lochs Linnhe and Leven, 335.
Superstitions, 90, 111, 112.
Swords, " cold iron," 98.
Swords on stones, 86.

" Tailor's Hole," Iona, 386.
Tarskavaig, Skye, 106.
Tartan as *camouflage,* 20.
—— Clanranald, 21.
—— Glencoe, 301.
—— Glengarry, 21.
—— Mackenzie, 151.
—— Macleod, 151.
—— of the Isles, the red, 20, 178, 184.
—— origin of, 20.
—— weaving of, 21.
Tartans, diversity of, in each clan, 20-1.
Teampull, meaning of, 366.
—— *Odhran,* Iona, 366, 370.
Telegraphic circular tours, 100.
Tir fo Thuinne, 245.
Tir nam Bèo. 245.
The Braes, Skye. 136.
Tobar, see also *Wells.*
Tobar a' Phrionnsa, Skye, 182.
—— *an Tuirc.* Eigg, 230.
—— *Chaluim Chille,* Eigg, 244.
—— *lon nan Grugach,* Eigg, 244.
—— *Maolruaidh,* Skye, 113.
—— *na Gaoith Tuaith,* Iona, 386.
—— *na h'Annait.* Skye, 119.
—— *na h-Aois,* Iona, 385.
—— *nan Bean Naomha,* Eigg, 252.
—— *nan Ceann.* Eigg, 241.
—— *nan Eun,* Eigg, 231.
Torran, Skye, 119.
Totaig, Loch Duich, 199, 201.
—— Broch of, 200, 201, 213.
Traigh 'bhan nam Manach, Iona, 348, 361.
Treasure of the Prince, the lost, 71.
—— of Sgurr Uamh, the lost, 147.

Uamh, see also Cave.
Uamh Chloinn Diridh, Eigg, 234.
—— *Fraing,* Eigg, 253-4, 257, 433.
—— *Thuill,* Ardnamurchan, 433.
Uig, Skye, 169.
—— drive to, from Portree, 166.
"Use," West Highland ecclesiastical, 84.

Vestments and accessories, Eucharistic, and ecclesiastical generally, 83-4, 371, 378.
Victoria, Queen, as a Jacobite, 23.
Viking antiquities, 241, 272.
Vitrifaction, experiments in, 47-49.

War Cry of Camerons, 265, 482.
—— Clanranalds, 21.
—— Macdonalds, 301.
Waterhorse or bull, 111, 306.
—— of John MacInnes' Loch, Glenelg, 209.
—— of Loch Nighean Dughaill, Eigg, 249.
—— of Loch nan Dubhrachan, Skye, 112.

Well, *see* also *Tobar.*
Well at Tolain, Eigg, 232, 244.
—— "Five Pennies," Eigg, 244, 245.
—— of Donald Grumach, Skye, 129.
—— of S. Katharine, Eigg, 252-253.
Wheatears, 446-7.
William Macleod, 9th chief, 156, 157, 167.
—— of Orange, 262, 288, 289.
—— of Orange, his order for Massacre of Glencoe, 291.
Windsor, House of, in succession of Stewarts, 485.
Witchcraft, modern charge of, 169.
Witch and Lochiel, tale of, 273-274.
"Wives of the Glen" pipe march, 297.
"Wizard's Croon," the, 248.
Women's ancient dress and distinctions, 95.
Wren, legend of, 243.

Yarn, its dyeing, spinning, and winding, 91-2.

WS - #0052 - 151121 - C0 - 229/152/35 - PB - 9780282581602 - Gloss Lamination